THE CRUSADER
of the
20TH CENTURY:
Plinio Corrêa de Oliveira

THE CRUSADER
of the
20TH CENTURY:
Plinio Corrêa de Oliveira

Roberto de Mattei

First published in English in 1998

Gracewing
Fowler Wright Books
2 Southern Avenue
Leominster
Herefordshire HR6 0QF

ISBN 0 85244 473 7

Typesetting by
Action Typesetting Ltd, Gloucester, GL1 1SP

Printed by Cromwell Press
Trowbridge, Wiltshire, BA14 0XB

Contents

List of Abbreviations

AAS
: *Acta Apostolicae Sedis*, Vatican Press, Vatican City-Rome, 1909ss.

BSS
: *Bibliotheca Sanctorum*, Istituto Giovanni XXIII, Rome 1961–1970, 10 vols.

CATHOLICISME
: *Catholicisme hier, aujourd'hui, demain*, edited by G. Jacquemet, Letouzey et Ané, Paris 1947 sgg.

DB
: *Dictionnaire de la Bible*, edited by F. Vigouroux, Letouzey et Ané, Paris 1895–1912, 10 vols.

DDC
: *Dictionnaire de Droit canonique*, Letouzey et Ané, Paris 1935–1965, 7 vols.

DHBB
: *Dicionário Histórico-Biográfico Brasileiro 1930–1983*, edited by the Fundação Getúlio Vargas, Forense-Unitersitária-Finep, Rio de Janeiro 1984, 4 vols.

DM
: *Dizionario di Teologia Morale*, directed by cardinals Francesco Roberti e Pietro Palazzini, Studium, Rome 1961

DENZ-H
: Heinrich Denzinger, *Enchiridion Symbolorum*, edited by Peter Hunermann, EDB, Bologna 1995

DHGE
: *Dictionnaire d'Histoire et de Géographie Ecclésiastiques*, Letouzey et Ané, Paris 1912 sgg.

DIP
: *Dizionario degli Istituti di Perfezione*, directed by Guerriero Pelliccia and Giancarlo Rocca, Edizioni Paoline, Rome 1974 sgg.

DR
: Pius XII, *Discorsi e Radiomessaggi*, Tipografia Vaticana, Vatican City 1959, 21 vols.

DSp
: *Dictionnaire de Spiritualité*, Beauchesne, Paris 1937–1994, 16 vols.

DTC
: *Dictionnaire de Théologie Catholique*, Letouzey et Ané, Paris 1928–1972, 33 vols.

EB	*Encyclopaedia Britannica*, H. Hemingway Benton Publisher, Chicago 1975, 30 vols.
EC	*Enciclopedia Cattolica*, Sansoni, Florence 1949–1954, 12 vols.
ER	*Enciclopedia delle Religioni*, Vallecchi, Florence 1970–1976, 6 vols.
GAF	*Grande Antologia Filosofica*, edited by Umberto Antonio Padovani, Marzorati, Milan 1954
GER	*Gran Enciclopedia Rialp*, Ediciones Rialp, Madrid 1971–1976, 24 vols.
HKG	*Handbuch der Kirchengeschichte*, Herder, Freiburg im Bresgau 1965–1973, 9 vols.; It. tr. *Storia della Chiesa*, Jaca Book, Milan 1975–1980, 13 vols.
IP	*Insegnamenti Pontifici*, edited by the monks of Solesmes, It. tr. Paoline, Alba, 1957–1965, 14 vols.
LTK	*Lexikon für Theologie und Kirche*, Verlag Herder, Freiburg 1957–1965, 10 vols.
NDB	*Neue Deutsche Biographie*, Duncker & Humblat, Berlin 1953 sgg.
PG	*Patrologiae Cursus Completus, Series Graeca*, edited by Jaques-Paul Migne, Migne, Paris 1857–1866, 164 vols.
PL	*Patrologiae Cursus Completus, Series Latina*, edited by Jaques-Paul Migne, Migne, Paris 1844–1864, 226 vols.
TRE	*Theologische Realenzyklopädie*, de Gruyter, Berlin-New York 1977 ss.

Preface

of

His Eminence Alfons Maria Cardinal Stickler[*]

In history's frequent periods of crises and confusion, biographies of significant men can often better reveal or indicate the right path to follow than abstract volumes of morality and philosophy.

Indeed, individuals must concretely put principles into practice. However, inasmuch as tempestuous times are more hostile to the historical realization of these principles, it is all the more necessary to recognize those who place these principles at the centre of their own lives.

This is what happened in our century with Plinio Corrêa de Oliveira, the great Brazilian thinker and man of action who died in São Paulo, Brazil, on 3 October 1995, and about whom Prof Roberto de Mattei has written, within this year, the first European biography.

With the integrity of his life as an authentic Catholic, Plinio Corrêa de Oliveira offers us a confirmation of the church's continuing fecundity. The difficulties of these times for true Catholics are, in fact, occasions to influence history by affirming perennial Christian principles. Such was the case with the eminent Brazilian thinker, who demonstrated it by boldly maintaining, in an age of totalitarianism of every stripe and colour, his unshakeable faith in the fundamental teachings and institutions of the Church. Besides his fidelity to the Papacy, a characteristic trait of his spirituality that I am pleased to remember is his conspicuous devotion to Mary Help of Christians, Our Lady of the Rosary and the Victory of Lepanto, whom he vener-

---

[*] Cardinal Alfons Maria Stickler, a Salesian, was born in Neuenkirchen (Austria) in 1910. His special vocation to the study of legal sciences led him to teach in the Pontifical Salesian University, of which he was initially Dean of the Faculty of Canon Law and subsequently Rector from 1958 to 1966. Having placed his marked academic talents at the service of the Holy See, he first directed the Pontifical Institute of Higher Latin Sciences, and was then nominated Prefect of the Vatican Library. In 1983 Pope John Paul II raised him to the episcopate and then, creating him cardinal with the diaconal title of San Giorgio in Velabro, he made him Librarian and Archivist of the Holy Roman Church. He is the author of important theological and canonical studies which have been translated into numerous languages (Editor's note).

ated in the Salesian church of the Sacred Heart of Jesus in São Paulo. I still remember with pleasure having presided the ceremony in Rome of the launching of Plinio Corrêa de Oliveira's masterful work, *Nobility and Analogous Traditional Elites in the allocutions of Pius XII*, a book that constitutes, in my opinion, along with *Revolution and Counter-Revolution*, one of the highest achievements of this Brazilian thinker's genius.

In short, I congratulate the author of this work, Professor Roberto de Mattei, with whom I share sentiments of friendship and consonance of ideals, for the fine way in which he has succeeded in recalling the character and accomplishments of Plinio Corrêa de Oliveira, of whom he is a worthy disciple in Europe.

All founders and others who have stood out in the history of the Church have had to suffer calumny and misunderstanding. It should come as no surprise, then, that Plinio Corrêa de Oliveira was, and will continue to be, the target of a campaign of denigration, skilfully orchestrated by those who oppose his ideal of re-Christianizing society. In our century, such defamatory campaigns have also attacked other Catholic associations, demonizing them as "cults". It is interesting to note that these campaigns are much more aggressive when they are directed against associations that express a greater fidelity to the Catholic Church. This reveals that the true object of these accusations and falsehoods is the Church and that they are made to deny the Church's role as the "teacher of truth", recently affirmed by the Holy Father John Paul II in *Veritatis Splendor*. It is disturbing that these campaigns of denigration promoted by the enemies of the Church are often aided by Catholics who pretend to be orthodox.

I hope that this biography of Plinio Corrêa de Oliveira can help to dissipate the criticism and misunderstanding and create an ideal point of reference for all those who generously wish to dedicate their energies to the service of the Church and Christian civilization.

These efforts, which are at the service of the Church, require not only doctrinal rectitude, but also the personal practice of an authentic interior life accompanied with a spirit of penance and sacrifice proportional to the gravity of our times.

Plinio Corrêa de Oliveira offers us, through his life and work, a clear example.

I assure my prayers and blessing for all those who imitate and propagate this authentically Catholic spirit and vision of the world.

Alfons Maria Cardinal Stickler
Rome, 2 July 1996
Feast of the Visitation

Introduction

*"Whether we like it or not,
we are all writing
our biography.
And on the day of judgement
the book will be opened and read."*

The pages which follow are written to bring the European reader closer to the figure of an eminent thinker and man of action, who is destined to be remembered as a great protagonist of the century that is drawing to a close: Plinio Corrêa de Oliveira.[1]

Notwithstanding his writings, translated into numerous languages and his work, spread throughout twenty-six countries on five continents, there is hardly any mention of Plinio Corrêa de Oliveira in the great encyclopaedias or in scholastic texts; nor is he spoken of by the mass media or intellectuals. This is the greatest proof of how foreign he was to the cultural fashions of the time and also the reason that drives me to write these pages for publication.

I do not claim to produce a complete biography of Plinio Corrêa de Oliveira, which would have to be a monumental work in order to be

---

[1] This study has been carried out in an objective and scientific spirit, through a scrupulous control of the documents. The main sources consulted for studying the work of Plinio Corrêa de Oliveira, apart from the nineteen books that he published, are the more than 2,500 articles and essays that appeared in the weekly *O Legionário* (1927–47), in the monthly *Catolicismo* (1951–95) and in the daily *Folha de São Paulo* (1968–93). An initial overview of his main activities may be found in the books *Tradition, Family, Property: Half a Century of Epic Anticommunism* (The Foundation for a Christian Civilization, Inc., Mount Kisco, New York 1981), *Um Homem, uma Obra, uma Gesta. Homenagem das TFPs a Plinio Corrêa de Oliveira* (Edições Brasil de Amanhã, São Paulo s.d.) and in the work of João S. Clá Dias, *Dona Lucilia* (Artpress, São Paulo 1995), dedicated to Lucilia Ribeiro dos Santos, mother of our subject. Special mention should also be made, due to the depth of its research, of the doctorate thesis of Lizanias de Souza Lima, *Plinio Corrêa de Oliveira, Um cruzado do século XX*, (Faculdade de Filosofia, Letras e Ciências Humanas, São Paulo 1984).

Naturally, great importance must be attributed to the accessible unpublished writings: among these is a *Philosophical Self-portrait* published in *Catolicismo*, no. 550 (October 1996); also important are the numerous testimonies of all those who had the chance and the privilege to be personally acquainted with Plinio Corrêa de Oliveira.

comprehensive, nor do I claim to expound the collection of his doctrinal *corpus* which is still being published. Further, I do not claim to produce the history, likewise vast and still in full activity, of the Societies for the Defence of Tradition, Family and Property, inspired by him and spread today throughout the world. For all this there is neither the time nor the strength.

More simply I propose to offer the reader an introduction to the thoughts and work of Plinio Corrêa de Oliveira, an introduction that will make it possible to formulate a judgement of this great personage, loved and opposed with the same passion, but mostly unknown or deliberately ignored. This then is an initial proposal to become more acquainted with him, while leaving it to others to develop all the aspects of his personality so versatile and rich in unexpected depth.

"Whether we like it or not" Plinio Corrêa de Oliveira wrote "we are all writing our biography. And on the day of judgement the book will be opened and read."[2]

Every man must try to give a meaning to the book of his life, of which God is the first true author. Our existence will have a meaning in time only to the extent that it corresponds to the mysterious plan outlined for us from eternity. The usefulness of biographical books is to be found in their helping us in this difficult journey through the living examples of those who preceded us. *"Verba movent, exempla trahunt"*:[3] the models of those men who wrote their biographies in the "lived Christianity" of their existence can also contribute to direct our lives and our future. I hope that this may be the main fruit of my work that I have dedicated to Plinio Corrêa de Oliveira.

I also wish to sincerely thank all those who contributed to the publishing of this book. Among these, for their valued help and suggestions given generously, I especially thank Armando Alexandre dos Santos, Julio Loredo, José Messias Lins Brandão, Juan Miguel Montes, Stefano Nitoglia, Francisco Javier Tost Torres, José Antonio Ureta and Guido Vignelli. For the English edition, special thanks to Barbara Donovan for her translation, Mario Navarro da Costa and Philip Moran for their review, as well as the Tradition, Family, Property Bureau for the UK without whose support this edition would not have been possible.

I consider it a gift of Providence that I had the chance to personally meet Plinio Corrêa de Oliveira a number of times, between 1976 and 1995. Without this direct acquaintance, this book would not have been possible.

Roberto de Mattei

---

[2] Plinio Corrêa de Oliveira, "Seriedade", in Catolicismo, no. 485 (May 1991).
[3] Adolfo Tanquerey, *Compendio di Teologia Ascetica e Mistica*, It. tr., Desclée, Rome 1928, p. 27.

Chapter I

"When still very young ..."

"When still very young
I marvelled at the ruins of Christendom,
gave them my heart,
turned my back on all I could expect,
and made of that past full of blessings
my future."

1. The last rays of the "sweetness of living"

Talleyrand's phrase, according to which those who had not lived prior to 1789 had not experienced the sweetness of living, can be applied, with a certain analogy to the *Belle Epoque*, the period that preceded the First World War.[1]

This famous phrase is difficult for twentieth-century man to understand, both in its meaning and its importance. In fact our century has gone by under the sign of the "bitterness of living" whose most obvious expressions today are to be found in the new social illness of "depression" and in the terrible spread of suicides, even among the very young. For modern man, immersed in hedonism and incapable of feeling authentic spiritual joys, the expression "sweetness of living" has a purely material significance and cannot but be reduced to the bitter satisfaction that is born from consumerism and the enjoyment of purely sensual goods.

"Sweetness of living", in Talleyrand's meaning, has a deeper and more spiritual significance. It can be interpreted as an atmosphere that hovered throughout society, since the remote times of the Middle Ages. The origins of this sweetness of living date back to Medieval Christian civilization and they are connected with the Christian

---

[1] Talleyrand's famous phrase is referred to by, among others, the French historian Guizot in his *Memoires*. François Guizot, *Mémoires pour servir à l'histoire de mon temps*, (8 vols., Paris, M. Lévy, 1859–72), I, p. 6. Already at the end of the seventeenth century as Paul Hazard recalls, "France is par excellence the home of polished manners, good breeding, intellectual refinement, of the art of living, of courtesy, culture and all the social graces." P. Hazard, *The European Mind, 1680–1715*, (Harmondsworth, Penguin, 1973), p. 78.

conception of existence, that inseparably links the happiness of man to the glory of God.

Catholic doctrine and everyday experience teach us how dramatic human life is. And yet effort, suffering, sacrifice, struggle can give us an interior joy that manages to fill with sweetness the vale of tears that is our existence. Outside the Cross no real happiness or sweetness is possible, only the search for blind pleasure exists, which, because it is disordered, necessarily leads to bitterness and despair.

> "One can say the same thing about joy what St Bernard said of glory, that it is like a shadow: if we run after it, it flees from us; if we flee from it, it runs after us. There is no true joy but in Our Lord Jesus Christ, that is, in the shadow of the Cross. The more a man is mortified, the happier he is. The more he seeks after pleasures, the sadder he is.
>
> "This is why, in the centuries during which Christian civilization reached its apex, man was happy: one only need recall the Middle Ages. And as man becomes less and less Catholic, the sadder he becomes.
>
> "This change has become increasingly accentuated from generation to generation. The man of the nineteenth century, for example, no longer enjoyed the delightful *'douceur de vivre'* as did the man of the eighteenth century. Nonetheless, how much more peace and interior well-being did he have than man today!"[2]

"Sweetness of living" was not an unrestrained enjoyment or modern "easiness", but a reflection of Divine Love in modern society, a ray of divine light that illuminated and filled with spiritual joy a society that was still devoted to God, at least in its exterior structure. This "sweetness of living", that Talleyrand considered had already faded away with the French Revolution, continued to hover over Europe up to the eve of the First World War.

The *Belle Epoque* meant optimism and euphoric confidence in the myths of Reason and Progress, symbolized by the choreography of the Excelsior Ballet.[3] But the *Belle Epoque* was also the aristocratic and orderly style of life, that even at the dawn of the twentieth century reflected the way of living of the *Ancien Régime*.

The *Belle Epoque* was the dream of the "construction" of modern

---

[2] P. Corrêa de Oliveira, "Ambientes, Costumes, Civilizações", Catolicismo, no. 29, May 1953.
[3] *Excelsior* is the name of the naïve allegorical opera by Luigi Menzotti (1835–1905), with music by Romualdo Marenco (1841–1907), which thrilled not only Italian audiences for over twenty years after its first performance in Milan in 1881. In it, the cutting of the isthmus of Suez, the tunnel of the Cenisio, and the Peace of the Nations were celebrated, among the pirouettes of the dancers, as the ascension and apotheosis of Progress.

civilization that began the century; but it also was that lingering patri-
archal society whose last rays were to be found in the
Austro-Hungarian monarch, heir to the Crown of the Holy Roman
Empire. At the dawn of the century, Positivistic Europe lived alongside a Catholic and Monarchical one, in a continent that still had four
empires and fifteen great monarchies.[4]

The luminous intensity of the Impressionists' paintings and the
psychological novels of Paul Bourget reflected the atmosphere of
those years. The principal tool of this cosmopolitan society was
conversation, an art that required grace, amiability, diplomacy and in
which "authentic *savoir-vivre*" was identified.[5]

Paris, the *Ville-Lumière*, is the symbol of this era, the acknowledged capital of an ideal world that extends its frontiers well beyond
France and even Europe. Wherever the influence of European civilization reaches, it is to France that recognition is given for the
primacy of its language, its culture and its fashion.

Among the "French islands" in the world, one, at the beginning of
the century, shone more brightly than the others: São Paulo, Brazil,
one of the cities that best knew how to integrate the values of its traditions with those of French culture. The best that was produced by the
Belle Epoque, the good taste, the refined manners, the elegance that
had nothing in common with dandyism, flourished then, under the
tropics, in the other hemisphere. Against a backdrop of horizons illuminated by the Southern Cross, the last sparks of the *Ancien Régime*
shone in hearts that preserved with simplicity, the mother of all the
other virtues, a loyalty full of *saudade* (nostalgia) towards that
Christian civilization that had enlightened their country and the world.

The word *saudade* expresses something more than "nostalgia". It is
at once the memory and the desire of an absent good. It is a sentiment
that is incommunicable and veiled with the typical melancholy of the
contemplative and intuitive soul of the Portuguese and Brazilian
people.[6] The Paulista (inhabitant of the State of São Paulo) had
saudade of a Christian and European Brazil, just at the time when the

---

[4] Cf. Roberto de Mattei, *1900–2000. Due sogni si succedono: la costruzione, la distruzione*,
(Rome, Edizioni Fiducia, 1990), pp. 11–15.

[5] Duke de Lévis-Mirepoix, Count Félix de Vogué, *La politesse. Son rôle, ses usages*, (Paris,
Les Editions de France, 1937), p. 1. Cf. also Verena von der Heyden-Rynsch, *Europäische
Salons*, (München, Artemis & Winkler Verlag, 1992), p. 227, and more in general, Camille
Pernot, *La politesse et sa philosophie*, Paris, PUF, 1996.

[6] Cf. the entry *Saudade*, in *Grande Enciclopédia Portuguesa e Brasileira*, (Lisbôa-Rio de
Janeiro, Editorial Enciclopédia, 1945), vol. 28, pp. 809–10. The Portuguese philologist Carolina
Michaelis de Vasconcelos (1851–1925) underlined the complete harmony existing between the
Portuguese term *saudade* and the German *Sehnsucht. A Saudade portuguesa*, Porto, Renascença
portuguesa, 1922.

United States began to exercise the enticing call of "modernity". *Saudade* of old ways, loyalty to distant principles, of which Europe seemed to offer a last, faded reflection.

2. Brazil: a vocation for greatness

Visiting Brazil in the 1930s, Stefan Zweig was amazed by this land that he foresaw would "play one of the most important roles in the future development of our world".[7]

What first impresses one about Brazil is the enormous size of its surfaces and its horizons. This country, with its 8,511,965 square kilometres, covers over half of the total area of South America. The great mountains that descend precipitously to the sea, the forests of lush vegetation, the tumultuous Amazon river, which with its basin of over five million square kilometres is the most extensive fluvial system in the world, give the image of a country where everything is present in superabundance: nature, light, colours, so much so as to make one think, according to the image of Rocha Pita, of a real "terrestrial paradise".

"In no other region is the sky as serene, nor the dawn more beautiful; in no other hemisphere are the sun's rays more golden, nor the moonlight reflections more brilliant; the stars are the most gentle and are always happy; the horizons, whether at sunrise or at sunset, are always clear; the waters, whether from springs in the countryside or from the aqueducts of the towns, are the most pure; in short, Brazil is terrestrial paradise rediscovered".[8]

The vast Brazilian continent appears perpetually clothed in light

"like a sparkling diamond in the shadows of the Infinite. (...) Its refulgence opens up, within the silence of space, an inextinguishable, tawny, ardent, mild or pallid clarity. Everything is always light. Dazzling luminous waves come down from the sun that maintain the profound calm on the earth. Light invades everything, it absorbs everything".[9]

---

[7] Stefan Zweig, *Brazil. Land of the future*, (London, Cassell, 1942), p. 2; Cf. also Ernani Silva Bruno, *Historia e Tradições da Cidade de São Paulo*, 3 vols., Rio de Janeiro, Livraria José Olympio Editora, 1954; Affonso A. de Freitas, *Tradições e reminiscências paulistanas*, 3rd edn., Governo do Estado de São Paulo, São Paulo 1978; Luiz Gonzaga Cabral S.J., *Influência dos Jesuitas na colonização do Brasil*, in *Jesuitas no Brasil*, (São Paulo, Companhia Melhoramentos de S. Paulo, 1925), vol. III.

[8] Sebastião da Rocha Pita (1660–1738), *História da América Portuguesa*, in E. Werneck, *Antologia Brasileira*, (Rio de Janeiro, Livreria Francisco Alves, 1939), p. 210.

[9] José Pereira da Graça Aranha (1868–1931), *A esthetica da vida*, (Rio de Janeiro–Paris, Livraria Garnier, 1921), p. 101.

This light, that spreads an inextinguishable radiance and seems to preserve the earth in an atmosphere of intent calm, covers the great spaces with a mysterious spiritual dimension. It almost seems that the luminous extension of the horizons prepares the soul for a generous and great vocation.

Brazil's date of birth was 22 April 1500, when on the horizon of the new land there appeared the white sails of the Portuguese fleet, commanded by Pedro Alvares Cabral. The first gesture of the *descobridores* (discoverers) was to erect a Cross on the beach and to celebrate on the new land the unbloody sacrifice of Calvary. From then on Brazil became the *"Terra da Santa Cruz"*.[10] The constellation of the Southern Cross seemed to seal this scene in the skies, a scene that will remain impressed for all eternity in the Brazilian soul. "The Southern Cross, heraldic emblem of the fatherland, with its sweet nocturnal light, eternally recalls the continuity of the alliance. It speaks of an immortal hope to the Christian nation that grows on the land of the holy Cross."[11] Ever since, an Italian diplomat remarked, "the original perfume of Christianity spread to every corner of the Brazilian land, as if it had been sprinkled once for all time".[12]

The Cross, recalls Father Leite, "was a symbol and a promise. But not yet a seed. This was to come, prolifically and abundantly, almost a half century later, in 1549, with the establishment of a General Government and the arrival of the Jesuits".[13] In that year, six missionaries of the Society just founded by St Ignatius followed the governor Tomé de Souza, an envoy sent by John III of Portugal to evangelize

---

[10] "Brazil was born Christian. Its first historian, who was also one of its discoverers, called it the Island of the True Cross." Padre Serafim Leite S.J, *Páginas de História do Brasil*, (São Paulo, Companhia Editora Nacional, 1937), p. 11. The chronicler of the expedition, Pedro Vaz de Caminha, wrote to the king: "We cannot tell if there is gold, silver, metals or iron; we have seen none of them. But the land itself is rich (...) However the best fruit that can be drawn from it, in our opinion, is to bring to its inhabitants the salvation of their souls." in Roger Bastide, *Brasil terra de Contrastes*, It. tr., *Il Brasile*, (Milan, Garzanti, 1964), p. 13; text of the letter of Pedro Vaz e Caminho in Jaime Cortesão, *A expedição de Pedro Alvares Cabral*, (Lisbôa, Livrarias Ailland e Bertrand, 1922), pp. 233–56.

[11] Yves de la Brière, *Le règne de Dieu sous la Croix du Sud*, (Bruges-Paris, Desclée de Brouwer & C., 1929), p. 20.

[12] Roberto Cantalupo, *Brasile euro-americano*, (Milan, Istituto per gli Studi di Politica Internazionale, 1941), p. 89.

[13] S. Leite S.J., *Páginas de História do Brasil*, pp. 12–13. "Without ignoring the part others had to play, one can, without fear, make this exact statement: the history of the Jesuits in Brazil in the sixteenth century is the history of the formation of Brazil itself as regards its catechetical, moral, spiritual, educational formation and, in great part, its colonial formation as well. The contribution of other religious factors does not significantly modify these results" (p. 14).

the new land.[14] They, Stefan Zweig observed, brought with them the most precious thing necessary for the existence of a people and a country: an idea, and precisely "the idea of Brazil".[15]

The Jesuits infused a soul into what up to then had been a land rich in potential, but shapeless. "The land is our task"[16] declared Father Manuel da Nóbrega[17] who, with Father José de Anchieta,[18] may be considered the founder of Brazil. From the *Descobrimento* (Discovery) to our times, the missionaries carried out a "task, unparalleled in history",[19] of Christianizing and, at the same time, of civilizing the lands of Brazil. The Jesuits catechized the natives, gathering them into special villages (*Aldeias*), they opened the first schools, they built colleges, churches, roads and cities.[20] When the Huguenots tried to take over the new land, Fathers Nobrega and Anchieta were the overseers (*orientadores*) of the military operations against the French Protestants who had disembarked in the Bay of Guanabara.[21] In the centre of the arching coastline of the splendid bay they had conquered,[22] a small city was founded that was destined to become the capital: Rio de Janeiro. Here all the natural beauties of Brazil seemed to

[14] The *Regimento* of 17 December 1548 in which the King John III of Portugal outlined to his governor Tomé de Souza the rules of government which he should adhere to in Brazil, stated: "The main reason that drove me to send people to populate the aforesaid lands of Brazil was that the people of that country should convert to our holy Catholic faith". *Regimento de Tomé de Souza*, Biblioteca Nacional de Lisbôa, Arquivo da Marinha, liv. 1 de ofícios, de 1597 a 1602. Cf. also Padre Armando Cardoso S.J., "O ano de 1549 na historia do Brasil e da Companhia de Jesus", Verbum, no. 6, 1949, pp. 368–92.

[15] S. Zweig, *Brazil*, p. 38. Cf. Carlos Sodré Lanna, "Gênese da civilização cristã no Brasil", Catolicismo, no. 519, March 1994, pp. 23–4; Idem, "A epopéia missionária na formação da Cristandade luso-brasileira", Catolicismo, no. 533, May 1995, pp. 22–3.

[16] In Antonio de Queiroz Filho, *A vida heróica de José de Anchieta*, (São Paulo, Edições Loyola, 1988), p. 43.

[17] Father Manuel da Nóbrega was born in Entre-Douro-e-Minho in Portugal on 18 October 1517 and died in Rio de Janeiro on 18 October 1570. Doctor in Canon Law and Philosophy in Coimbra, in 1544 he entered the Society of Jesus and in 1549 he was sent by St Ignatius to Brazil, where he was the first superior of the Jesuit mission and then Provincial. His mission developed for over twenty years, up to his death.

[18] Born on 19 March 1534 in La Laguna (Canaries), Blessed José de Anchieta died in Reritiba (now Anchieta) on 9 June 1597. In 1551 he entered the Society of Jesus and two years later embarked for Brazil with a group of missionaries who followed the Portuguese governor Duarte da Costa. Ordained to the priesthood in 1566, he participated in the Foundation of São Paulo (1554) and of Rio de Janeiro (1565) and in 1578 became Provincial of Brazil, while carrying out a tireless apostolate that earned him the title of *"Apóstolo do novo Mundo"*. He was beatified by John Paul II in 1980. Cf. Alvares do Amaral, *O Padre José Anchieta e a fundação de São Paulo*, São Paulo, Conselho Estadual de Cultura, 1971.

[19] Serafim Leite S.J., *História da Companhia de Jesus no Brasil*, (Lisboa, Livraria Portugal, 1938), vol. I.

[20] Alongside the Jesuits, the Benedictines (from 1582), the Carmelites (from 1584), the Capuchins (from 1612) and other religious orders carried out their apostolate. The Jesuits, expelled in 1760 by the Marquis of Pombal, returned to Brazil in 1842. On the 40 Jesuit martyrs of 1570, cf. Mauricio Gomes dos Santos S.J., *Beatos Inacio de Azevedo e 39 companheiros martires*, Didaskalia, no. 8, 1978, pp. 89–155; pp. 331–66 (translation of the study made for the historical office of the Congregation of Saints).

flow together in an unrepeatable synthesis: mountains, hills, forests, islands, inlets.[23] In the beginning, the capital of the Portuguese colony was Salvador da Bahia, one of the "genetic cells"[24] of Brazil, together with São Paulo, Rio, Pernambuco and Maranhão.

The immense territory was divided into twelve hereditary *Capitanias*, from which evolved the various States that would make up the Brazilian Confederation.[25] The beneficiaries, provided with ample concessions, were chosen by the king of Portugal from among "the best people. Former navigators, veterans, personages of the court."[26] Brazil continued to be an integral part of the kingdom of Portugal even during the period between 1580 and 1640, when the Portuguese crown was personally united with that of Spain. In the struggle against the Dutch, who managed to get a foothold in Bahia (1624–5), and for a longer period in Recife (1630–54), the Brazilian national conscience began to be formed.[27] When Recife, the last

---

[21] Giuseppe Adorno was counsellor to Fathers Nobrega and Anchieta. He was an Italian aristocrat of the family of the Genoese Doges, who had put his fortune and his life at the service of the new Lusitanian country, after having been forced to abandon his city. As well as the Adorno family, the Acciaiuoli (Accioly), Doria, Fregoso, Cavalcanti (Cavalcanti d'Albuquerque) families all transferred to Brazil in the sixteenth century.

[22] Carlos Sodré Lanna, "A expulsão dos franceses do Rio de Janeiro", Catolicismo, no. 509, May 1993, pp. 22–4.

[23] "Rio de Janeiro, from the point of view of its panorama, can be considered a synthesis of Brazil. It is the heart of Brazil that continues to beat there, in spite of the fact that the capital has officially been transferred to Brasília. There is a mysterious synthesis of the country there, an invitation to a future laden with mysterious promises." P. Corrêa de Oliveira, "Meditando sobre as grandezas do Brasil", Catolicismo, no. 454, October 1988.

[24] "The noted historian of Brazil, Sr. João Ribeiro, calls, with energetic exactness, the following places of its territory as genetic cells of the fabric of Brazil: Bahia, Pernambuco, S. Paulo, Rio and Maranhão. Now, of these five genetic cells, two (...) were the exclusive result of the Jesuits: S. Paulo, which they founded with their own hands, and Rio de Janeiro, which they were able to found against all odds. The other three: Bahia, Pernambuco e Maranhão developed as they did because of the Jesuits" L. G. Cabral S.J., *Jesuitas no Brasil (século XVI)*, (São Paulo, Companhia Melhoramentos de São Paulo, 1925), p. 266.

[25] Homero Barradas, "As capitanias hereditárias. Primeiro ensaio de um Brasil orgânico", Catolicismo, no. 131, November 1961.

[26] Pedro Calmon, *História do Brasil*, (Rio de Janeiro, Livraria José Olympio Editora, 1959), vol. I, p. 170.

[27] Cf. Lucio Mendes, "Calvinistas holandeses invadem cristandade luso-americana", Catolicismo, no. 427, July 1986, pp. 2–3; ID., "Martírio e heroismo na resistência ao herege invasor", Catolicismo, no. 429, September 1986, pp. 10–12; Diego Lopes Santiago, *Historia da Guerra de Pernambuco*, Fundação do Patrimonio Histórico e Artístico de Pernambuco, Recife 1984. There were many Italian officers, especially Neapolitans, who came to Brazil during this period (cf. Gino Doria, *I soldati napoletani nelle guerre del Brasile contro gli olandesi (1625–1641)*, Riccardo Ricciardi Editore, Naples, 1932). When in 1624, the Dutch West Indian Company had occupied Bahia, Philip IV sent a fleet, which included a Neapolitan *tercio*, guided by Carlo Andrea Caracciolo, Marquis of Torrecuso. Another Neapolitan commander, the Count of Bagnoli Gian Vincenzo Sanfelice, in 1638 successfully defended Bahia from the Dutch Calvinists, who aspired to form a Protestant State in South America. Between Brazil and the Kingdom of Naples there was always a fruitful exchange (cf. for example: Paolo Scarano, *Rapporti politici, economici e sociali tra il Regno delle Due Sicilie e il Brasile (1815–1860)*, Società Napoletana di Storia Patria, Naples 1958).

Dutch outpost, surrendered to the Brazilian army, a united people already existed. "The Dutch wars had the advantage of consolidating into one type, unknown up to then, all the different elements of the colonization."[28]

The first Brazilian aristocratic type was that of the sugar mill lords (*senhores de engenho*). Sugar cane was the most typical Brazilian crop in the feudal picture of the *Capitania*, throughout the whole colonial period.[29]

The sugarcane plantations and the mills, the small refineries where the slaves worked, built near water courses, constituted the beginning of the Brazilian farming civilization. The Great House (*Casa-grande*), the manor of the sugar mill lords, looked like a military fortress.[30] The sugar mill lords formed the great strength that opposed the invasions of the Dutch, the French and the English, enemies of the Faith and of the King.[31]

The sugarcane cycle was the main agricultural and industrial activity during the first two centuries of national life. In the eighteenth century, after the unexpected discovery of gold in the state of Minas Gerais, this metal took first place in the economic production of the country.

The protagonists of the cycle of gold and of precious stones were the *bandeirantes* (armed explorers),[32] direct heirs of the *descobridores* for their courage and spirit of adventure. On horseback, with the flag up front, like riders of fortune, they followed the course of the rivers,

---

[28] P. Calmon, *Storia della Civiltà brasiliana*, It. tr. (Rio de Janeiro, Industria Tipografica Italiana, 1939), p. 52.

[29] Sugarcane, an ideal product for a country beginning its development, was cultivated up to the end of the sixteenth century in the north and in the south of Brazil. The centre of cultivation was the state of Pernambuco, whose port of Recife became in the seventeenth century the greatest emporium of coffee in the world (P. Calmon, *Storia della Civiltà brasiliana*, p. 85). Cf also P. Corrêa de Oliveira, "Genesis, Development, and Twilight of the "Nobility of the Land" in Colonial, Imperial, and Republican Brazil", appendix to the American edition of *Nobility and Analogous Traditional Elites in the Allocutions of Pius XII*, (York, Hamilton Press, 1993), pp. 331–79.

[30] Gilberto Freyre, *Casa-Grande & Senzala*, 5th edn., (São Paulo, Editora José Olympio, 1946), vol. I, p. 24.

[31] The conquest of lands has after all a warrior characteristic "Every ploughed estate, every 'peopled' sesmaria, every fence built, every sugar factory 'constructed', has a difficult military operation as a necessary premise. From north to south, the establishment of new farms and pastures is made with the sword in hand". Francisco José Oliveira Vianna, *O Povo Brasileiro e a sua Evolução*, (Rio de Janeiro, Ministério da Agricultura, Indústria e Comércio, 1922), p. 19.

[32] On the *Bandeirantes*, cf. the imposing *História Geral das Bandeiras Paulistas*, 11 vols., São Paulo, 1924–50, by Affonso de Taunay, summarized in *História das Bandeiras Paulistas*, Edicões Melhoramentos, 2 vols., São Paulo 1951; cf. also J. Cortesão, *Raposo Tavares e a formação territorial do Brasil*, Ministério da Educação e Cultura, Rio de Janeiro 1958; Ricardo Roman Blanco, *Las "bandeiras"*, Brasilia, Universidade de Brasilia, 1966.

scaled mountains, ventured inland in search of gold and precious stones.

After the socio-economic cycle of sugar and that of gold, the mid-eighteenth century saw the beginning of the third great civilization, that of coffee, which up until 1930 was the main source of wealth for the Brazilian economy.

During the nineteenth century, Brazil gained its independence, but in a different way from the other Latin-American nations: not through armed struggle, but through the establishment of an empire with the son of the King of Portugal, Dom Pedro I of Braganza (1798-1834) on its throne.

In São Paulo, on 7 September 1822, Dom Pedro I proclaimed the independence of Brazil. Two years later he issued its first constitution. He was succeeded by his son, Dom Pedro II,[33] a philanthropic sovereign, whose long and peaceful reign ended immediately after the abolition of slavery with the Republican Revolution.[34] The Empire lost the support of the landed aristocracy, who had considered the liberation of the slaves as erroneous and premature. After a bloodless coup, the Republic was proclaimed in Rio on 15 November 1889.

"The Brazilians" the historian Guglielmo Ferrero wrote "saw the

---

[33] Dom Pedro II (1825-91) married in 1843 Princess Teresa Cristina, sister of Ferdinand II, king of the Two Sicilies. Her eldest daughter Isabella (1846-1921) married Prince Gaston of Orléans, Count d'Eu, of whom she had three sons: Pedro de Alcântara, Luiz and Antônio. The first having renounced, in 1908, for himself and for his descendants, the right of succession, his brother Prince Luiz of Orleans-Braganza (1878-1920) became heir to the throne. He married Princess Maria Pia of Bourbon-Sicily (cf. Armando Alexandre dos Santos, *A Legitimidade Monárquica no Brasil*, São Paulo, Artpress, 1988). On Dom Pedro II, cf. Heitor Lyra, *Historia de Dom Pedro II: 1825-1891*, Editora Nacional, São Paulo 1940. "Dom Pedro was a magnanimous, generous and just sovereign, a model of patriotism and culture, of zeal and integrity, of tolerance and simplicity. He was wise and a philanthropist. A Member of the Institute of France and of the main foreign scientific and literary societies, he was a protector of the arts, sciences and literature. He gave monetary aid for the education of many distinguished Brazilians; this great patron never closed his purse to them." S. Rangel de Castro, *Quelques aspects de la civilisation brésilienne*, (Paris s.d., Les Presses Universitaires de France), pp. 29-30. Cf. also Leopoldo Bibiano Xavier, "Dom Pedro e a gratidão nacional", Catolicismo, no. 491, December 1991.

[34] A first law of 1871, the so-called "law of the free womb", granted freedom to children born of a slave mother starting at 21 years of age. In 1885 the "law of the sixty-year-olds" was approved; this emancipated slaves over 65 years of age. On 13 May 1888, under the conservative ministry of João Alfredo Corrêa de Oliveira, the Princess Isabella, Countess d'Eu and Imperial Regent during the absence of her father travelling in Europe, ratified the law that definitively abolished slavery. At that time Brazil had a population of 14 million inhabitants with a little over 700,000 slaves. The phenomenon of slavery was actually fading out spontaneously. On the act of abolition of slavery cf. P. Corrêa de Oliveira, "A margem do 13 de maio", O Legionário, no. 296, 15 May 1938. Cf. also Robert Conrad, *Os últimos anos da escravatura no Brasil, 1850-1888*, 2nd edn., Rio de Janeiro, Civilização Brasileira, 1978; Emilia Viotti da Costa, *A abolição*, São Paulo, Global, 1982.

monarchy fall gently, without any bloodshed, just like lovely summer days end, calm and luminous."[35]

In 1891 the Empire of Brazil became the Republic of the United States of Brazil. Its new flag bore the positivistic motto "Order and Progress".[36] "Brazil was then at the beginning of a time when it would excel in making 'Progress' a god, and 'Science' a goddess for its intellectual elites."[37] The Republic was composed of a federation of independent states, each with its own parliament and its own government. The Church was separated from the State, civil marriage was decreed and the political economy was altered. The first ten years of the century in Brazil were characterized by a climate of euphoria and optimism, due to the hopes aroused by the institutional change and by the economic and social progress of the country.[38] It was the "golden period" of the First Republic.[39]

3. São Paulo: a European island in the American continent

São Paulo was the vital centre of Brazilian economic, political, and social life at the beginning of the century. Spread over a plain eight hundred metres above sea level, the city had grown from about fifty thousand inhabitants in 1880 to over three hundred and fifty thousand in 1910.[40] A wide, slow-moving river, the Tietê, flows along one side of it and a mountain range, the Serra da Cantareira, nourishes it with its waters. The houses are all one storey high, built very close together. However, the streets have already been widened into tree-lined avenues and the colonial houses are being replaced by villas, modern constructions and wide avenues. It seems like a European city in the tropics, destined for a great future.

In a letter from São Paulo, dated July 1911, a writer who uses the

---

[35] In S. Rangel de Castro, *Quelques aspects de la civilisation brésilienne*, p. 29.

[36] Guglielmo Ferrero tells of having visited in Rio de Janeiro, on Benjamin Constant Street, a "temple of mankind" where one discusses "pleasantly about many things with the high priest, Mr Teixeira Mendes". G. Ferrero, *Fra i due mondi*, (Milan, Fratelli Treves Editori, 1913), p. 187.

[37] G. Freyre, *Ordem e Progresso*, 3rd edn., 2 vols., (Rio de Janeiro, Livraria José Olympio Editora, 1974), vol. I, p. 515, and more in general, Ronald M. Schneider, *"Order and Progress." A Political History of Brazil*, Boulder (Colorado), Westview Press, 1991.

[38] The successive Heads of State were: Prudente de Morais (1894–8), Campos Sales (1898–1902), Rodrigues Alves (1902–06), Afonso Pena (1906–09), Nilo Peçanha (1909–10), Hermes da Fonseca (1910–14), while Brazilian foreign policy was continuously directed during this period by the Baron of Rio Branco (1845–1912).

[39] "It was 'the golden period' of the First Republic, if we are to give names to different epochs as did the historians of old ...." Plinio Doyle, *Brasil 1900–1910*, (Rio de Janeiro, Biblioteca Nacional, 1980), vol. I, p. 14. At the turn of the century, Brazil had 17,318,556 inhabitants, over 60 percent of whom lived in the rural areas.

[40] Ibid, p. 180.

pseudonym "italicus" describes it as a city that lives in the preceding era as it prepares for its full prosperity.[41]

"São Paulo grew in twenty years with North American rapidity. It was a city that was famous almost exclusively for its Law University. The students were its whole life and everything had the slightly solemn and slightly calm rhythm of a provincial town. (...)
Now it is a city that is trembling and resounding with work. Big businesses and great industries have been established in just a few months; the banks are doing tremendous business; journalism, which has been transformed in five years, competes with that of Europe."[42]

A fever of work and initiative devours the city, while the movement of electric trams, inaugurated in 1901, by 1910 reaches the unbelievable number of thirty million passengers. "The city bustles with feverish movement. The immense populace undulates like a river. And, sullying one's view of the blue sky, are the towering chimneys spewing smoke."[43]

The reasons for this extraordinary growth are, as Stefan Zweig remarks, the same geopolitical and climatic causes that had led Nobrega, four hundred years earlier, to choose this place as the one most suited for a rapid expansion throughout Brazil.[44] From as early as the seventeenth century, the Paulistas demonstrated more energy and ability than other Brazilians. "Real bearers of the national energy, the Paulistas conquered and discovered the country, *semper novarum rerum cupidi* (always desirous of new things); and this desire for risk, progress and expansion was carried over, in subsequent centuries, to commerce and industry."[45]

São Paulo, the city of the *fazendeiros* (farmers), "people who were prouder of the farm than the city; and when they thought of a city, it was one in Europe, strictly speaking in Paris",[46] has the look and soul of a great city, where European cultures and ways of life come together. The underlying note is still that of Portuguese goodness and

---

[41] Italicus, *"Dove vive un milione di Italiani. Lo stato di São Paulo in Brasile"*, L'Illustrazione italiana, no. 34, 20 August 1911, pp. 177–200. The magazine dedicates a large article to the State of São Paulo, a third of its population being Italian. The Italians in 1911 were about one million, six hundred thousand of whom worked in the *fazendas* or other farming enterprises, one hundred and thirty thousand lived in the capital, the others lived in the hinterland towns of the State (p. 181).
[42] Ibid.
[43] Batista Cepelos, *O fundador de S. Paulo*, in E. Werneck, *Antologia Brasileira*, p. 326.
[44] S. Zweig, *Brazil*, pp. 212–13.
[45] Ibid, p. 213.
[46] E. Silva Bruno, *História e Tradições da Cidade de São Paulo*, vol. III, p. 1315.

universality. This allows the fusion and amalgamation of so many different elements. If it is mostly Italian emigrants,[47] who are at the head of the economic growth, French is the culture, courtesy and social life.[48] Along 15 de Novembro Street, the most elegant street of the so-called Triangle, we find shops with unmistakable names: *Au Printemps, Au Louvre, Au Palais Royal.* The bookshop, *Garraux,* one of the meeting points of elegant São Paulo, does not only import books from Europe, but also French champagne, wine from the Rhine Valley, Swiss chocolate, while the most aristocratic area of the city is called *Champs Elysées.*[49]

Georges Clemenceau notes this aspect of his journey in Latin America in 1911:

"The city of São Paulo is so curiously French in some of its aspects that not once during a whole week did I have the sensation of being in a foreign country (...) São Paulo society (...) has a dual tendency: While it resolutely orients itself by the French spirit, it develops in parallel all the aspects of Brazilian individuality that determine its character. Be sure that the Paulista is Paulista to the depth of his soul, whether he is in Brazil, France, or anywhere else. This said, tell me if there ever was a Frenchman with more courteous manners, more agreeable conversation, and more aristo-cratic delicacy of spirit in the figure of a businessman who is prudent yet audacious, and who knows how to value coffee."[50]

Vendean in origin and character, but a Protestant and a republican, Clemenceau saw the paradoxes of his soul and the contradictions of

---

[47] This mass immigration coincided with the end of slavery. The vast majority of the Italian immigrants who arrived in Brazil settled in São Paulo. Almost all the workers of the develop-ing Paulista industry crowded above all into the area of the Brás, whose main street was Caetano Pinto. In 1881 the twenty-seven-year-old Francesco Matarazzo, accompanied by his wife Filomena and two children, arrived in Brazil. In 1910, he owned the largest industrial group of South America, the Indústrias Reunidas F. Matarazzo. Cf. Vincenzo Grossi, *Storia della colo-nizzazione europea nel Brasile e della emigrazione italiana nello Stato di São Paulo,* Milan, Società Editrice Dante Alighieri, 1914; Angelo Trento, *Là dov'è la raccolta del caffé. L'emigrazione italiana in Brasile, 1875-1940,* Padua, Antenore, 1984; *A presença italiana no Brasil,* edited by Rovílio Costa and Luis Alberto de Boni, It. edn. edited by A. Trento, Turin, Fondazione Giovanni Agnelli, 1991.

[48] Count of Gobineau relates a conversation with the Emperor who asked him: "So what do you think of the Brazilians?" He replied: "Well, a Brazilian is a man who passionately desires to live in Paris" (Letter to Mme de Gobineau of 7 June 1869, in Georges Raeders, *Le comte de Gobineau au Brésil,* (Paris, Nouvelles Editions Latines, 1934), p. 53. "It seems that there are almost no Brazilians who do not speak French" observes in amazement Ina von Binzer, the German governess of the Prado family. *Os Meus Romanos. Alegrias e Tristezas de uma educadora alemã no Brasil,* (São Paulo, Editora Paz e Terra, 1991), p. 18.

[49] Cf. Paulo Cursino de Moura, *São Paulo de outrora,* (Belo Horizonte, Editora Itatiaia Limitada, 1980), p. 19.

the *Belle Epoque* reflected in Brazil: the aristocratic spirit and naïve positivism, trust in the "immortal principles" of the French Revolution and nostalgia for the civilization and manners of the *Ancien Régime*.

> "In that ambience – comprised of splendour and ceremony, tonified by the noble and joyful French note – the age-old aroma of Christian morality remained alive as something of primary importance in social life. This was a legacy left us by Portugal, a country with which Brazil had formed a united kingdom, not long since. Thus, marked by such characteristics, the aristocracy of São Paulo harmonized some of its typically fundamental elements: Faith, social life and selection."[51]

The 1900s began in São Paulo with a social event that sealed the alliance between the two dynasties that symbolized the economic and social elite of the city at the end of the century: the marriage of the beautiful Eglantina, daughter of Count Antônio Alvares Penteado with the young Antônio Prado Jr, son of Councillor Antônio Prado, mayor in the ten golden years of São Paulo, between 1898 and 1908.

Less worldly and much more private was another marriage that took place a few years later. This marriage united two of the old families of Brazil: that of João Paulo Corrêa de Oliveira and Lucilia Ribeiro dos Santos, and took place on 15 July 1906 in the chapel of the Episcopal Seminary of São Paulo by Mgr Francisco de Paula Rodrigues.[52]

---

[50] Georges Clemenceau, *Notes de Voyage dans l'Amérique du Sud*, (Paris, Utz, 1991 (1911), pp. 231–2. In a volume by Baron d'Anthouard that appeared in that same 1911, under the title *Le progrès brésilien. La participation de la France* (Paris, Plon-Nourrit, 1911), the author observes that "Brazil (...) adheres with its innermost being to the movement of ideas in France" (ibid, p. 41). "The Brazilian feels an unequalled powerful attraction to French culture, he follows our intellectual movement with the liveliest sympathy; he reads and knows all our authors; he is also sensitive to our artistic production. Finally, France is the country of all his dreams, the country of wellbeing and pleasure, of elegance and luxury, of novelties and great discoveries, of the wise, of artists, of philosophers" (ibid, p. 375).

[51] J. S. Clá Dias, *Dona Lucilia*, vol. I, p. 85. The Ribeiro dos Santos are remembered among the families that were noticed at the parties of the Paulista aristocracy. "At these ceremonies, the ambience is one of family intimacy even though richly ornamented uniforms, grand crosses, diamonds and jewels are paraded." Wanderley Pinho, *Salões e Damas do Segundo Reinado*, 4th edn., (São Paulo, Livraria Martins, 1942), p. 112.

[52] J. S. Clá Dias, *Dona Lucilia*, vol. III, pp. 209–10. Among those present at the marriage were Count Antônio Alvares Penteado with his wife Anna Paulina Lacerda; Manoel Antonio Duarte de Azevedo (1831–1912), President of the Senate and of the Instituto Histórico e Geográfico de São Paulo; the historian Affonso d'Escragnolle Taunay (1875–1958), future President of the Instituto Histórico e Geográfico and historian of the *Bandeiras*. Mgr Francisco da Paula Rodrigues born on 3 July 1847 and who died on 21 June 1915 was one of the outstanding figures of Paulista religious life between the two centuries. Canon of the Cathedral of São Paulo (1874), archdeacon (1878), he was then Vicar-General of the diocese, which he governed *ad interim* after the death of Bishop José de Camargo Barros (1906).

The family was soon blessed with two children, Rosée and Plinio, whom the mother offered to God before they were born.[53]

4. The Blessing of the crib

Plinio Corrêa de Oliveira was born on 13 December 1908, a Sunday, while the bells of the church of St Cecilia seemed to be celebrating the event with their festive chimes. He was baptized in that same church on 7 June 1909.[54] His parents, João Paulo Corrêa de Oliveira and Lucilia Ribeiro dos Santos, belonged to old families of the rural aristocracy that had been spontaneously formed in Brazil as early as the sixteenth century and which, because of its social status and refinement of manner, can be compared to the European nobility of that period.

The Corrêa de Oliveiras descended from the sugar mill lords, first colonizers of Brazil, the "well-born, the nobles of their time".[55] João Alfredo Corrêa de Oliveira,[56] brother of Plinio's grandfather, Leodegario, had sketched an unforgettable profile of those "strong generations who loved the land, where they saw shining the gold of their freedom and independence, and from which they harvested wealth and virtue. (...) For these generations the land they inherited was a *fideicommissum* of their families and a coat of arms they treasured more than their lives, to the same extent as honour."[57] João Alfredo, born on 12 December 1835, gifted with extraordinary intelligence, was professor of Law in the University of Recife, and had a brilliant political career: he was congressman for a number of legislatures, minister of the Empire at only 35 years of age in the Rio Branco conservative Cabinet, then Senator for life of the Empire,

---

[53] J. S. Clá Dias, *Dona Lucilia*, vol. II, p. 67. Plinio's sister, Rosenda Corrêa de Oliveira, called Rosée, born on 6 July 1907 and who died in 1993, married a farmer from Minas, Antônio Castro Magalhães.

[54] The church of St Cecilia was built in 1884. In 1895 The Rt Rev Joaquim Arcoverde, then bishop of São Paulo, created the parish of St Cecilia, nominating as parish priest Father Duarte Leopoldo e Silva, his future successor to the government of the diocese. In 1901 he was succeeded by Father Benedito de Souza.

[55] Fernando de Azevedo, *Canaviais e Engenhos na vida politica do Brasil*, in *Obras Completas*, 2nd edn., (São Paulo s.d., Edições Melhoramentos), vol. XI, p. 107.

[56] P. Corrêa de Oliveira, "João Alfredo Corrêa de Oliveira", Diário de São Paulo, 21 December 1936, now in J. S. Clá Dias, *Dona Lucilia*, vol. III, pp. 215–16. In this article the young nephew describes with great psychological penetration the intellectual evolution of his great uncle from positions of strict liberalism to a sincere and practising Catholicism.

[57] João Alfredo Corrêa de Oliveira, *O Barão de Goiana e sua Época Genealógica*, in *Minha Meninice & outros ensaios*, (Recife, Editora Massangana, 1988), p. 56.

Councillor of the Council of State and finally President of the Council of Ministers. In this role, on 13 May 1888, he had Princess Isabella, the Imperial Regent, sign the famous *Golden Law* that abolished slavery in Brazil. After the proclamation of the Republic, he was an important member of the Brazilian Monarchical Directory and President of the Banco do Brasil. He died at 87 years of age in Rio de Janeiro on 6 March 1919.

Plinio's maternal family, the Ribeiro dos Santos, belonged to the traditional class of the "Four-Hundred-Year Paulistas",[58] founders of the city of São Paulo, and descended from those *bandeirantes* who had fought against the Dutch heretics. An important figure among his maternal ancestors was his great-grandfather, Gabriel José Rodrigues dos Santos, professor at the Law School and congressman in the imperial Parliament. He was considered one of the most brilliant orators and experts in public law of his time.[59] His daughter, Dona Gabriela Ribeiro dos Santos, Lucilia's mother, frequented the famous salon of Dona Veridiana, one of the most influential women in Paulista society.[60] At the beginning of the century, the *chácara* of Dona Veridiana, a small palace in Renaissance style in the Higienópolis area, was the centre of social and intellectual life of São Paulo, together with "Vila Penteado", the small *Art Nouveau* palace that Count Antônio Alvares Penteado had had built in the same area by the architect Carlos Ekman.

---

[58] The Four-hundred-year Paulistas "are something more than the noble, than the 'real gentleman', than the aristocratic, they are the authors of the almanac of the Brazilian Gotha. They are the holders and dispensers of Brazilianess. For them the world was born four hundred years ago when the first Portuguese and their families, from whom they descend, disembarked in Brazil. The Four-hundred-year Paulista is amiable, kind and proud. He has a marked sense of caste and is inaccessible: those who constitute 70 percent of the political ruling class of the country, defend themselves from society by every means", Corrado Pizzinelli, *Il Brasile nasce oggi*, (Milan, Eli, 1955), p. 284.

[59] On Gabriel José Rodrigues dos Santos (1816–58), cf. J. S. Clá Dias, *Dona Lucilia*, vol. I, p. 45, vol. II, pp. 19–26. The most complete work on this personage is by Paulo do Valle, *Biographia do Dr. Gabriel José Rodrigues dos Santos*, published with his *Discursos Parlamentares* collected by A. J. Ribas, Rio de Janeiro, Tip. Paula Brito, 1863.

[60] Veridiana Valeria Prado (1825–1910), daughter of Antônio, Baron of Iguape, married Martinho da Silva Prado (1811–91) and had four children, destined to carry out an influential role in Brazilian life: Antônio (1840–1929), Martinico (1843–1906), Caio (1853–89) and Eduardo (1860–1901). A true "matriarch" of the family, she died in 1910 at 85 years of age. Cf. Darrell E. Levi, *A Família Prado*, (São Paulo, Cultura 70, 1977), p. 63; English orig.: *The Prados of São Paulo: An Elite Brazilian Family in a changing society, 1840–1930*. The Prado, with the Penteado, "symbolized the economic and industrial life in São Paulo during the First Republic" (ibid, p. 104).

5. From the hearts of the mothers to the hearts of the children: Dona Lucilia Ribeiro dos Santos

Lucilia Ribeiro dos Santos,[61] Plinio's mother, was born on 22 April 1876 in Pirassununga, in the State of São Paulo, the second of five children. Her childhood was spent in quiet and aristocratic surroundings illuminated by her parents: Antônio (1848–1909), one of the best lawyers in São Paulo at the time, and Gabriela (1852–1934). In 1893 the family moved to São Paulo to a house in the exclusive neighbourhood of Campos Eliseos. Here, at the age of thirty, Lucilia met and married the lawyer João Paulo Corrêa de Oliveira,[62] who had moved to São Paulo from the Northeast of Brazil, perhaps at the suggestion of his uncle, the Councillor João Alfredo.

While Dona Lucilia awaited Plinio's birth, her physician told her the delivery would be risky and that it was probable that either she or the child would die. He asked if she would not prefer therefore to abort, thus avoiding risking her life. Dona Lucilia answered in a calm but firm manner: "Doctor, this is not a question one asks a mother! It should not even have crossed your mind."[63] This act of heroism shows the virtue of a lifetime.

Canon Trochu writes: "Virtue easily passes from the hearts of mothers to the hearts of their children."[64] "Educated by a courageous and strong Christian mother – Father Lacordaire wrote about his mother – religion passed from her heart into mine, like milk that is virginal and devoid of bitterness."[65] In the same way Plinio Corrêa de Oliveira recalled that he owed Dona Lucilia the spiritual stamp that marked his life from his infancy:

"My mother taught me to love Our Lord Jesus Christ, she taught

---

[61] On this extraordinary figure we refer to the biography by J. S. Clá Dias, *Dona Lucilia*, with a preface by Father Antonio Royo Marín O.P. "This is" as the latter writes "an authentic and most complete Life of Dona Lucilia, that can stand up to the best 'Lives of the Saints' published to date around the world" (ibid, p. 11).

[62] João Paulo Corrêa de Oliveira, born in 1887, died in São Paulo on 27 January 1961. Just as Dona Lucilia had had her model in her father, Antônio Ribeiro dos Santos, the life of Plinio Corrêa de Oliveira was enlightened especially by that of his mother rather than by the figure of his father, although being linked to the latter by a long affectionate life together.

[63] J. S. Clá Dias, *Dona Lucilia*, vol. I, p. 123.

[64] Canon François Trochu, *Le Curé d'Ars*, (Lyon-Paris, Librairie Catholique Emmanuel Vitte, 1935), p. 13. From St Augustine to St Bernard, to St Louis of France, up to St John Bosco and to St Thérèse of Lisieux, the number of saints that have recognized their own virtue in that of their mothers is great indeed. At the origins of holiness there often is, as Mgr Delassus observes, a virtuous mother. Cf. Mgr Henri Delassus, *Le problème de l'heure présente*, 2 vols., (Lille, Desclée de Brouwer, 1904), vol. II, pp. 575–6.

[65] P. Baron, *La jeunesse de Lacordaire*, (Paris, Cerf, 1961), p. 39. Cf. also Geneviève Gabbois, *Vous êtes presque la seule consolation de l'Eglise*, in Jean Delumeau (edited by), *La religion de ma mère. Le rôle des femmes dans la transmission de la foi*, (Paris, Cerf, 1992), pp. 314–15.

me to love the Holy Catholic Church."[66] "I received from her something to be taken in a profoundly serious way, the Roman Catholic and Apostolic Faith, devotion to the Sacred Heart of Jesus and to Our Lady."[67]

At a time when Leo XIII had exhorted people to place in the Heart of Jesus "all hope, and from it salvation is to be confidently besought",[68] the devotion that characterized the life of Dona Lucilia was that to the Sacred Heart, the devotion *par excellence* of modern times.[69] There was a church dedicated to the Sacred Heart not far from the home of the Ribeiro dos Santos.[70] The young mother used to go there every day bringing Plinio and Rosée with her. It was here, while observing his mother in prayer amidst the supernatural atmosphere characteristic of

---

[66] P. Corrêa de Oliveira, "Un uomo, un'ideale, un'epopea", Tradizione, Famiglia, Proprietà, no. 3, 1995, p. 2.

[67] J. S. Clá Dias, *Dona Lucilia*, vol. III, p. 85. "There was a trait of my mother that I liked very much: At all times she was the lady of the house, through and through! In relation to her children, she maintained a maternal superiority that made me feel how wrong I would be if I transgressed her authority. And also how such an attitude on my part would sadden her because it was both bad manners and a bad deed. She was the lady of the house, because she made sure order was maintained in all aspects of life. Her authority was mild. Sometimes mother would punish us a bit. But even when punishing, or reprimanding, her gentleness was so apparent that it comforted the person. The procedure with Rosée was analogous, although more delicate, since she was a girl. The reprimand, nonetheless, did not exclude benevolence. And mother was always ready to hear the justification her children wished to give her. Thus, goodness was the essence of her dominion. In other words, it was a superiority exercised for love of the hierarchical order of things, but impartial and affectionate in relation to the person to whom she applied it." Ibid, vol. II, pp. 16–17.

[68] Leo XIII, Encyclical *Annum Sacrum* of 25 May 1899, in IP, *Le Fonti della Vita Spirituale*, (1964), vol. I, p. 198. The consecration of mankind to the Sacred Heart, announced by Leo XIII in his Encyclical, took place on 11 June 1890.

[69] The devotion to the Sacred Heart was illustrated by three magisterial Pontifical documents: the Encyclicals *Annum Sacrum* (1889) by Leo XIII; *Miserentissimus Redemptor* (1928) by Pius XI; *Haurietis Aquas* (1956) by Pius XII. Its great apostle in the nineteenth century was the French Jesuit Henri Ramière (1821–84), who directed the development throughout the world of the "Apostolate of Prayer" association. In Brazil, the great propagator of devotion to the Sacred Heart was Father Bartolomeo Taddei born in San Giovanni Valle Roveto, Italy, on 7 November 1837. Ordained to the priesthood on 19 April 1862, he entered the noviciate of the Society of Jesus on 13 November of the same year and was sent to the new São Luiz Gonzaga School in Itú in Brazil. Here he founded the "Apostolate of Prayer" and began to spread the devotion to the Sacred Heart, the focus of his life. At the time of his death, 3 June 1913, the number of centres of the "Apostolate of Prayer" he had promoted throughout Brazil numbered 1,390 with about 40,000 zealots and 2,708,000 associates. Cf. Luigi Roumanie S.S., *Il P. Bartolemo Taddei della compagnia di Gesù apostolo del S. Cuore in Brasile*, Rome, Messaggero del Sacro Cuore, 1924; Aristide Grève S.J., *Padre Bartolomeu Taddei*, Petropolis, Editora Vozes, 1938. On the devotion to the Sacred Heart cf. the classic work by Auguste Hamon, *Histoire de la dévotion au Sacré-Coeur*, 5 vols., Paris, Beauchesne, 1923–45, and among recent works Francesca Marietti, *Il Cuore di Gesù. Culto, devozione, spiritualità*, Milan, Editrice Ancora, 1991.

[70] The Church of the Sacred Heart that stood in the area of Campos Eliseos had been built between 1881 and 1885, and entrusted to the Salesians. Father Gaetano Falcone was for many years the esteemed Rector of the Shrine. In this Church, where at the end of the right nave stood a lovely statue dedicated to Our Lady Help of Christians, the devotion of young Plinio for Our Lady "Auxilium Christianorum" of Lepanto and for the Most Holy Rosary grew.

the churches of old, that the vision of the Church which d[
him, was formed in Plinio's spirit. He would recall: "I p[
her way of being came from her devotion to the Sacred H[
through Our Lady."[71] Dona Lucilia always remained f[
devotion of her youth. In the last years of her life, when[
had the strength to go to church, she used to spend [
prayer, until late at night, before an alabaster statue of the[
enthroned in the main hall of her apartment.[72]

The dominant note of Dona Lucilia's soul was that of piety and mercy. Her soul was marked by an immense capacity for affection, goodness and a maternal love that was projected beyond the two children she had received from Providence. Plinio used to say:

> "She possessed tenderness to a great degree: she was most affectionate as a daughter, most affectionate as a sister, most affectionate as a wife, most affectionate as a mother, as a grandmother and even as a great-grandmother. But, I have the impression that there is something in her that gives the tonic note of all these affections: it is because she is, above all, a mother! She possessed an overflowing love not only for the two children she had, but also for the children she did not have. One would say she was made to have millions of children, and her heart beat with the desire to know them."[73]

Those who never knew Dona Lucilia can perceive her moral physiognomy through the image passed on in some expressive photographs and through the testimonies of those who remember her in her old age.[74] She represented the model of a perfect lady who would have charmed a St Francis de Sales in his search for Philothea.[75]

We can imagine that Dona Lucilia educated Plinio with the words that St Francis Xavier addressed to his brother, accompanying him one evening to a party: "*Soyons distingués ad majorem Dei gloriam.*"

The perfection of good manners is the fruit of an ascesis that can

---

[71] J. S. Clá Dias, *Dona Lucilia*, vol. I, p. 214.

[72] Ibid, vol. III, pp. 91–2. Dona Lucilia usually implored divine protection through the recital of Psalm 90 and of an "irresistible novena" to the Sacred Heart of Jesus. Ibid, pp. 90–1.

[73] Ibid, vol. III, p. 155.

[74] Among her qualities was the constant polarization between good and evil, as her nephew Adolpho Lindenberg recalls: "She upheld this polarization to a high degree: an action is very good, another is very bad. The fundamental horror she always had of sin was noteworthy. To me, as a child or young man, what stood out in her more than this or that virtue was: the notion that one must become enthused and make sacrifices for the good and the notion that evil is horrible and must be hated and despised". J. S. Clá Dias, *Dona Lucilia*, vol. II, p. 173.

[75] The saint from Savoy teaches in his famous work how a soul can live in the world without absorbing the spirit of the world: "God — he affirms — commands Christians, the living plants of his Church, to bring forth the fruits of devotion, each according to his position and vocation". St Francis de Sales, *Introduction to the Devout Life*, (New York, Harper & Row, 1966), pp. 36–7

only be achieved by an education distilled over centuries and by a virtuous effort, such as is often found in contemplative convents, where a princely education is given to the young novices. After all, man is made up of body and soul. The life of his soul is destined to be noticeably manifested through that of his body, charity to be expressed in external acts of courtesy. Courtesy is a social rite nourished by Christian charity, directed to the glory of God. "Courtesy is to charity as the liturgy is to prayer: the rite that expresses it, the action that embodies it, the pedagogy that encourages it. Courtesy is the liturgy of brotherly charity."[76]

Lucilia Ribeiro dos Santos embodied the best spirit of the old Paulista aristocracy. In the old-fashioned kindness of his mother, an expression of her supernatural charity, the young Plinio saw a Christian love taken to extreme consequences and a similar radical repulsion for the modern and revolutionary world that was being established. From then on, the aristocratic attitude and pleasantness of manner was a constant in his life. Plinio Corrêa de Oliveira, who in his ways reminded one of Cardinal Merry del Val, the great Secretary of State of St Pius X famous for his humility of soul and the perfection of his good manners, was magnificently capable of being in society. His behaviour was exemplary, his conversation inexhaustible and fascinating.

Providence arranged that this maternal stamp would be nourished and renewed by a daily life together that lasted until 1968, when Dona Lucilia died at the age of ninety-two.

6. The first glance towards Europe

Trips to Europe were privileged moments in the cultural formation of the Brazilian elites at the beginning of the century. For Plinio and his family the occasion presented itself when Dona Lucilia had to undergo an operation in the old continent for a serious illness troubling her. Suffering from gallstones, she learned that a famous German physician, Professor August Bier,[77] personal doctor to the Kaiser, operated on this illness with a new technique he had developed.

---

[76] Roger Dupuis S.J., Paul Celier, *Courtoisie chrétienne et dignité humaine*, (Paris, Mame, 1955), p. 182.

[77] Professor of Surgery in Kiel, Greifswald, Bonn and Berlin, August Bier (1861-1949) is famous in the history of medicine for having introduced the use of a special therapeutic technique (biertherapy), especially recommended for acute and chronic inflammatory processes. Cf. Martin Müller, *sub voce*, in NDB, vol. II (1955), pp. 230-1. Dona Lucilia kept up a friendly correspondence with him until his death in 1949. J. Clá Dias, *Dona Lucilia*, vol. II, pp. 31-2.

In June 1912 Lucilia Corrêa de Oliveira embarked at the port of Santos, accompanied not only by her husband João Paulo and her children Plinio and Rosée, but also by her mother Gabriela, her brothers and sisters, her in-laws, her nephews and nieces. This family group did nothing but visit the main European cities for ten months.

In early July, the young mother was operated on in Berlin by Professor Bier. She then spent her convalescence at the thermal baths of Binz, on the island of Rügen, before going on to Wiesbaden and Cologne. The summer of 1912 was spent in that flourishing pre-war Germany to which the prince of Bülow in his *Memoirs* applies the verse of Schiller: "Joy reigned in the halls of Troy/ before the tall rock fell."[78]

It was a summer of cold and bad weather, and it snowed in Paris. The "question of the East", with the war going on in the Balkans, was constantly front-page news. At the beginning of September, while the Kaiser was on an official visit to Switzerland, a great Eucharistic Congress was held in Vienna, in the presence of the Emperor Franz Josef and of the whole Court. Europe, dominated by the figures of the two important emperors, Franz Josef and Wilhelm II, was linked by a strong network of dynastic bonds. In December 1912 in Munich, generations of princes and sovereigns gathered for the death of the ninety-two-year-old Regent Luitpold of Bavaria, known as the "patriarch of the reigning monarchs", and then in Berlin on 24 May 1913 for the magnificent wedding of Princess Victoria Louise of Hohenzollern, daughter of the Emperor Wilhelm II, with Ernest August of Hanover, Duke of Brunswick.

Dona Lucilia and her family spent that winter in Paris, where they remained until the end of March 1913, staying in the Hotel Royal in Avenue Friedland. From there they went to Genoa intending to continue on to Rome, to pay homage to Pope Pius X, but the news of an epidemic in the Eternal City changed their programme. They began their return journey, disembarking in the port of Santos on 17 April 1913.

The journey through Europe was a memorable one for young Plinio, who was then four years of age. The cathedral of Cologne, with its towering spires and which for seven centuries has guarded the relics of the Wise Kings, was his first encounter with the wonders of Gothic art. The course of the Rhine speckled with castles, the snow-covered Alps, the splendours of Notre Dame and Versailles, the Ligurian coastline, a spectacular balcony overlooking the sweetness of

---

[78] Prince Bernhard von Bülow, *Memorie*, vol. III: It. tr., *Guerra mondiale e catastrofe*, (Milan, A. Mondadori, 1931), p. 121 (these are the first two verses of the *Cassandra* by Schiller).

the Mediterranean, left a profound impression on his soul. For each monument of Christian civilization he visited with his family on that occasion, he could have said, *mutatis mutandi*, what he wrote after visiting the Cathedral of Cologne. It states:

"Something mysterious asks my whole soul to be in conformity with the marvels of the Catholic Church! It is a school of thought, will and sensibility. A way of being is derived from there and for which I feel I was born. It is something greater than I and that came much before me. When I was nothing, it was centuries-old. It comes from the Catholic mentality of men who came before me and who also had, deep in their souls, this same desire for the unimaginable. And they even conceived what I did not conceive and did what I did not. But, it is such a lofty desire, so universal, corresponding so well with the profound yearnings of so many men, that the monument remained for ever: the Cathedral of Cologne!"[79]

Forty years would pass before Plinio would return to Europe, but the roots of the old continent were by now planted in his heart. In the meantime the First World War drew near.

7. The decline of the *Belle Epoque*

In January 1919, the Peace Conference[80] took place in the Hall of Mirrors at Versailles. It marked the end of a war without precedents in history, both because of its human cost of over eight million dead as well as the extent of its political and social repercussions.

Germany was humiliated both materially and morally, but the great loser of the war was the Austro-Hungarian Empire.[81]

The objective of a limited circle of politicians, associated with Freemasonry, to bringing about its destruction was to "*republicanize Europe*"[82] thus completing the French Revolution. Having begun as a

---

[79] P. Corrêa de Oliveira, "O inimaginável e o sonhado", Catolicismo, no. 543, March 1996, p. 28.

[80] On Versailles: Pierre Renouvin, *Le traité de Versailles*, Paris, Flammarion, 1969; Michel Launay, *Versailles, une paix bâclée*, Bruxelles, Complexe, 1981; Pierre Milza, *De Versailles à Berlin 1919–45*, Paris, Armand Colin, 1996.

[81] "Germany is humiliated and diminished, but still survives. The Austrian-Hungarian Empire is torn apart and the only thing left is German Austria, which only survives with difficulty" (P. Corrêa de Oliveira, "A conjuração dos Cesares e do Synhedrio", O Legionário, no. 288, 20 March 1938).

[82] François Fejtö, *Requiem pour un empire défunt*, (Paris, Lieu Commun, 1988), p. 308, 311. "The great goal presented by the political and intellectual elite to the soldiers in the trenches was to eradicate the last vestiges of clericalism and monarchism from Europe" (p. 310). On the role of Freemasonry, cf. ibid, pp. 337–49.

classic war, the First World War finished, according to the Hungarian historian François Fejtö, as an ideological war whose aim was to dismember Austria-Hungary.[83]

The Treaties of 1919–20, which imposed or promoted the transformation of the monarchical regimes of Germany and of Austria into Parliamentary Republics, were "more of a European Revolution than a European peace".[84] The European political map, outlined by the Congress of Vienna, was redrawn according to the new criterion of the "self-determination of peoples", affirmed by the American President Wilson. Upon the ruins of the Austrian Empire, while Germany began to develop into the only great power of Central Europe, new "multinational" states were born such as the Republic of Czechoslovakia and the Kingdom of the Serbs, Croats, and Slovenes, later Yugoslavia.

Plinio Corrêa de Oliveira realized how the end of the Hapsburgs would have marked the end of the old European civilization. For him, Austria of the Hapsburgs meant the medieval idea of the Holy Roman Empire, the programme of the "Reconquest" against the Moors and of the Counter-Reformation, the opposition to the world born of the French Revolution.

"Catholicism, Leo XIII said with his sovereign and decisive authority, cannot be identified with any form of government, and can exist and flourish whether in a monarchy, aristocracy, democracy, or even in a mixed form containing elements of all three. The destiny of Catholicism was not connected to the European monarchies. Nevertheless, it is undeniable that these monarchies, at least in their fundamental aspects, were structured according to Catholic doctrine. Liberalism wanted to abolish them and to substitute them with another order of things. It transformed aristocratic monarchies

---

[83] Cf. F. Fejtö, *Requiem pour un empire défunt*, p. 306–13. On the First World War: Leo Valiani, *La dissoluzione dell'Austria-Ungheria*, Milan, Il Saggiatore, 1985; Gian Enrico Rusconi, *Il rischio 1914. Come si decide la guerra*, Bologna, Il Mulino, 1987; P. Renouvin, *La prima guerra mondiale*, Rome, Lucarini, 1989. The year that "the war finds its permanent ideological set-up", according to Furet, is 1917. François Furet, *Le passé d'une illusion,* (Paris, Robert Laffont, 1995), p. 73. The Revolution of February, that leads to the abdication of czar Nicholas II, and then that of October, which sees the coming of Lenin, cancel centuries of Czarist Empire and clears the way for a new Russia that cuts the ties with its past. In the month of April, President Wilson drags America into the war proclaiming the democratic crusade against autocratism. On 8 January 1918, the same Wilson publishes the "fourteen points" that, among other things, announces the foundation of a "Society of Nations" to guarantee world peace.

[84] François Furet, *Le passé d'une illusion*, p. 74. On the end of the Hapsburg Empire, cf. Zybnek A. B. Zeman, *The Break-up of the Habsburg Empire 1914-1918*, London-New York, Oxford University Press, 1961; Edward Crankshaw, *The Fall of the House of Habsburg*, London, Cardinal, 1974; Adam Wandruszka, *Das Haus Habsburg*, Herder, Wien 1989 (1978).

of Catholic inspiration into bourgeois and liberal republics with an anti-Catholic spirit and mentality."[85]

Although we are not surprised by Plinio Corrêa de Oliveira's French cultural roots, linked to the intellectual and social life of São Paulo of that time, what is surprising is a real passion he showed even then for the Austria of the Hapsburgs. This time the young Brazilian's love for the Austrian Empire was rooted in the supernatural. Austria, heir to the Carolingian Holy Roman Empire, was in his eyes the historical manifestation *par excellence* of Christian civilization. Between the sixteenth and eighteenth centuries, in face of the rampant Protestantism of Northern Europe and the secular and pre-Enlightenment culture being formed, the Hapsburg Empire represented the symbol of loyalty to the Church. In an age when the value of dynasties prevailed over that of States, the name of the Hapsburgs symbolized that of the Catholic Counter-Reformation. The Iberian conquistadors making inroads into the interior of Latin America and the warriors defending the frontiers of the Christian Empire on the battlements of Budapest and Vienna were fighting under the same flag. It was in the Austrian capital, in 1815, that the Congress was held that should have ratified the restoration of order in a Europe disrupted by the French Revolution and Napoleon. Until its fall in 1918, the Hapsburg Empire was the principal target for the anti-Christian hatred of secret societies and revolutionary forces. Plinio Corrêa de Oliveira always defended its irreplaceable historical role, writing just after the Second World War:

"Vienna should be the capital of either a great German Empire, or of an Austrian-Hungarian monarchy. Anything else will be an irreparable misfortune for Catholic influence in the Danube basin."[86]

8. The rise of the American myth

Historians have stressed the serious, geopolitical consequences of the breaking-up of the Austro-Hungarian Empire. However it has still

---

[85] P. Corrêa de Oliveira, "Terceiro acto", O Legionário, no. 421, 6 October 1940.
[86] P. Corrêa de Oliveira, "7 dias em revista", O Legionário, no. 570, 11 July 1943. "In this sense, it is especially necessary to have strength and prudence. Strength to destroy within Germany and without everything that should be destroyed. Prudence so as not to destroy what should not be destroyed, in order not to exacerbate what should continue to live. The errors of Versailles should not be repeated. Never, never more within the Germanic world should there be a central axis consisting of Prussia and Berlin. The right thing to do is to transfer the axis to Vienna. Herein lies, more than in any other measures, the key to most of the problem" (P. Corrêa de Oliveira, "7 dias em revista", O Legionário, no. 632, 17 September 1944).

not been revealed what the consequences were in the realm of mentalities and customs. It was like a breath of life that suddenly diminished in Europe. The atmosphere of stability and security, as Stefan Zweig[87] recalls, that had been the basic characteristic of the *Belle Epoque*, quickly disappeared. A wind of uncertainty and anxiety assailed the old continent. Up to 1914 Europe had had undisputed superiority. After the war it "doubts itself, the legitimacy of its dominion, the superiority of its civilization and its future".[88] Works with titles that would once have been inconceivable, such as *The Decline of Europe* by the geographer Albert Demangeon and *The Decline of the West* by the German writer Oswald Spengler, become veritable best-sellers.

The "American myth" begins to establish itself in the world.[89] "While Europe seemed to sink into chaos, the zenith of 'wilsonian' splendour dawned over America. The United States had attained its apogee."[90] America represented a new way of life that had its shining and artificial model in Hollywood, the Californian city, home of the new cinema empire. In the Twenties, *"les années folles"* or "Roaring Twenties", Europe underwent social transformations which profoundly altered the habits and customs of its inhabitants. Americanization was imposed above all by the cinema[91] which became

---

[87] "When I attempt to find a simple formula for the period in which I grew up, prior to the First World War, I hope that I convey its fullness by calling it the Golden Age of Security. (...) No one thought of wars, of revolutions, of revolts. Everything radical, all violence seemed impossible in an age of reason." S. Zweig, *The world of yesterday*, (London, Cassell, 1987), pp. 13–14.

[88] René Rémond, *Introduction à l'histoire de notre temps*, (Paris, Editions du Seuil, 1974), vol. III: *Le XX siècle de 1914 à nos jours*, p. 52. Cf. also Carlo Curcio, *Europa, storia di un'idea*, 2 vols., (Florence, Vallecchi, 1958), vol. II, pp. 789–880; Jean Guiffan, *Histoire de l'Europe au XX siècle, 1918–1945*, Brussels, Editions Complexe, 1995.

[89] Cf. Appendix I of the second part of P. Corrêa de Oliveira, *Nobility and Analogous Traditional Elites in the Allocutions of Pius XII, The United States: An Aristocratic Nation Within a Democratic State*, pp. 135–330. Cf. also A. Frederick Mark, *Manifest Destiny and Mission in American History*, New York, Alfred A. Knopf, 1963; Ernest Lee Tuveson, *Redeemer Nation: The Idea of America's Millennial Role*, Chicago, University of Chicago Press, 1968. In the second half of the twentieth century, while the Revolution advanced, the United States exercised a role similar to that of Europe in the previous century. Plinio Corrêa de Oliveira, one of his disciples recalls, "compared this role to that of Austria in the nineteenth century". Just as the Hapsburg empire represented the principal target of international liberalism of the time, the American empire ended up by being the "black beast" of the international progressivism, who saw it as a symbol of conservatism and anti-communism. In this new contest, he "began to support the anticommunist attitudes of the United States, as well as the pressure that certain groups, from within the country, exerted by urging the Government to maintain a firm policy against Sino-Soviet expansionism. In no way did this attitude imply an acceptance of the American way of life or of the liberalizing influence of Americanism. It was merely an objective recognition that, for the present, the United States was a power without which one cannot even think of stopping the political and military advance of international communism." (Julio Loredo, Letter to the author).

[90] P. Corrêa de Oliveira, "A dynamite de Christo", O Legionário, no. 321, 5 November 1938.

[91] In the twenties its heroes were Charlie Chaplin, Buster Keaton, Douglas Fairbanks, Rodolfo Valentino, Gloria Swanson, Mary Pickford.

the most popular pastime after the sports of the masses, such as football and boxing spread by the press and by the radio.

The new style of life, the antithesis of the spirit of the *Belle Epoque*, did not only affect the upper classes, but also extended to the middle classes and to a large degree to the working classes. Its symbol was the emancipation of women, who in many countries, such as France and Italy, still did not vote. It offered a "modern" and aggressive image of themselves that was very different from the traditional female model. It was a new type of woman who cut her hair "*à la garçonne*", who shortened her skirts and sleeves, who drove and went to the beach, while the male type was a practical and dynamic man, who pursued success in the wake of the American self-made man. The myth of money relentlessly forced itself into society together with an unbridled search for pleasure. Life underwent a strong process of democratization in every aspect: social relationships, fashion, language.

Even in Brazil, in the Twenties, a change in taste began to be felt. Plinio Corrêa de Oliveira was to recall:

"This decade was for us a 'life of idleness', of fabulous expenditures, of high coffee bean prices, of constant trips to Europe, of orgies and of the carefree life. (...) The mental stagnation of the Brazilian was total. The famous jazz band, the shimmy, cinema, and sports monopolized every spirit."[92]

He was to define "Americanism" as

"a subconscious state of spirit, at times becoming conscious, that makes the life of pleasure the supreme value of man and attempts to see the universe and organize existence in an inherently delightful way".[93]

In the centre of São Paulo, the upper halls of the Mappin stores displayed English furniture, more modern and "hygienic" than its French counterpart. Football begins to find favour among the young people, while a new hedonistic view of life finds its symbol in Rio, the city of beaches and of the Carnival. The Week of Modern Art that was held in São Paulo in 1922, under the patronage of the Paulista social elite,[94] already foreshadows the revolution in architecture whose symbol will be Oscar Niemeyer, the Communist architect who

---

[92] P. Corrêa de Oliveira, *A dynamite de Christo*.
[93] P. Corrêa de Oliveira, "O coração do sabio está onde há tristeza", Catolicismo, no. 85, January 1958, p. 2.
[94] José de Azeredo Santos, "Semana de arte moderna: precursora dos 'hippies'", Catolicismo, no. 256, April 1972, p. 7.

was to design Brasília. That same year sees the construction in São Paulo of the "Martinelli skyscraper", the tallest in South America; the Russian architect Gregori Warchavchik begins that "international style" which would upset the typical characteristics of the Brazilian urban centres,[95] while Le Corbusier became the model of Latin America's new architects. The radical transformation of the city, in less than twenty years, reflected the similarly profound transformation in customs and ideas.[96] The Corrêa de Oliveira family, however, in which, under the influence of his mother, the young Plinio was being formed, was a little patch of the *Ancien Régime* that survived and opposed the floodtide of modernity.

9. A militant conception of spiritual life

In February 1919, at ten years of age, Plinio Corrêa de Oliveira began his studies in the São Luiz School of the Society of Jesus, where the traditional ruling class of São Paulo was educated.[97] Between his maternal education and the school's, there was, as there should be, continuity and development. In the teaching of the Jesuits, he again found the love for method, already instilled in him by his German governess Mathilde Heldmann,[98] and above all that militant conception of spiritual life to which his soul so deeply aspired.[99]

The school was for him his first clash with the world and his first battlefield. There the young Plinio found the "two cities" of St Augustine mixed like the grain and darnel, the wheat and straw, of

---

[95] In 1925 Warchavchik published in the *Correio da Manhã* of Rio the article "Acerca da Arquitetura moderna" in which he presented Le Corbusier to the Brazilian public. It was he who built the first "modernist house" of Brazil, on Santa Cruz Street in São Paulo.

[96] The town planning of São Paulo altered under the mayorship of Fabio Prado (1935-8), but especially when the urbanist Francisco Prestes Maia (1896-1965) was elected mayor of São Paulo from 1938 to 1945, and again from 1961 to 1965. His urbanist philosophy is expounded in works such as *São Paulo, metrópole do século XX* (1942) and *O plano urbanístico da cidade de São Paulo* (1945).

[97] The São Luiz School was founded in 1867 in Itú and transferred to São Paulo to an imposing building at no. 2324 of Avenida Paulista. Rector of the School was then Father João Baptista du Dréneuf (1872-1948) cf. A. Grève S.J., "Fundação do Colégio São Luiz. Seu centénario, 1867-1967", in A.S.I.A., no. 26, 1967, pp. 41-59. Among his professors young Plinio had Father Castro e Costa, who followed his battle in defence of Catholic Action and whom he met again in Rome in the 1950s (cf. J. S. Clá Dias, *Dona Lucilia*, vol. II, p. 259).

[98] Mathilde Heldmann was a native of Regensburg, and had been governess in some European aristocratic houses. "One of the greatest favours mother did for us was to hire the Fräulein" Plinio Corrêa de Oliveira was later to recall. (J. S. Clá Dias, *Dona Lucilia*, vol. I, p. 203).

[99] On the "militant" conception of Christian spirituality, cf. Pierre Bourguignon, Francis Wenner, *Combat spirituel*, in DSp, vol. II,1 (1937), coll. 1135-42; Umile Bonzi da Genova, *Combattimento spirituale*, in EC, vol. IV (1950), coll. 37-40; Johann Auer, *Militia Christi*, in DSp, vol. X (1980), coll. 1210-33.

which the Gospel speaks[100] and he realized how the life of man on earth is a hard struggle, in which "the only one to be crowned will be he who has fought".[101] *"Vita militia est."*[102] That the spiritual life of the Christian is a battle is one of the concepts that is most insistently confirmed by the New Testament, especially in St Paul's Epistles. "Christians are born for combat"[103] affirms Leo XIII. "The whole essence of a Christian life is to reject the corruption of the world and to oppose constantly any indulgence in it."[104]

From St Ignatius, Plinio learnt that "every man's soul is a field of battle, upon which good and evil fight".[105] As a result of Original Sin, we all have disordered tendencies that drive us to sin; the devil tries to encourage them and divine grace helps us to conquer them, transforming them into occasions for sanctification. "Man's free will is the decisive factor of the forces that lead him to the good or to the evil."[106] Plinio appears to us as one of the Paulista children of his generation, whom Father Burnichon, in his visit to the School of São Luiz in 1910, describes as

"serious, grave, reflective. Their faces rarely shine, a smile seems to be unfamiliar to them; on the other hand, they assure me, they are able to stay still for five whole hours listening to academic speeches; this happens from time to time. In short, because of the climate, the race does mature early and this has its advantages and disadvantages, but on the other hand, has a natural calm that does not exclude vivid impressions and violent explosions."[107]

In São Luiz, the young Plinio sensed the radical contrast between his family life and that of his companions at school who were already imbued with malice and immorality. As so often happens in schools, the young people who assert themselves over the others were the most worldly-wise: purity was despised and ridiculed, vulgarity and obscenity were considered signs of distinction and success. He reacted with all his strength to this situation. He realized that what was happening was not by chance, but the result of a mentality that was

---

[100] Matt. 13:24-7.
[101] 2 Tim. 11:5.
[102] Job 7:1.
[103] LEO XIII, Encyclical *Sapientiae Christianae* of 10 January 1890, in IP, vol. III, *La pace interna delle nazioni*, (1959), p. 192.
[104] LEO XIII, Encyclical *Exeunte iam anno* of 25 December 1888, in IP, *Le fonti della vita spirituale*, vol. II, pp. 345, 358 (pp. 337-59).
[105] P. Corrêa de Oliveira, "Lutar varonilmente e lutar até o fim", Catolicismo, no. 67, July 1956, p. 2.
[106] Ibid.
[107] Joseph Burnichon, *Le Brésil d'aujourd'hui*, (Paris, Perrin, 1910), p. 242.

the opposite to that of his family. If he were to accept this mentality, this would have led him to lose, together with his purity, the ideals that sprung from his heart. He understood that the foundation of everything he loved was his religion, and he chose to fight to the death in defence of that conception of life in which he had been formed. A conviction was thus born in him that, over the years, found ever increasing rational foundations:

> "It was a counter-revolutionary conception of religion as a persecuted force that teaches us the eternal truths, that saves our soul, that leads us to Heaven, and marks our life with a style that is the only style that makes life worth living. Hence, the idea that, when I reached manhood, I must undertake a fight to overthrow this order of things that I held to be revolutionary and bad, in order to establish a Catholic order of things."[108]

Plinio precociously finished his secondary studies in 1925, at the age of 17. Later, when recalling the interior anxiety and isolation of those years, he would pause on that acute crisis of adolescence that was one of the most important phenomena of the history of mankind in the nineteenth century and one of the causes of its deep incoherence.

> "The attitude of the nineteenth century in face of Religion and Morality was an essentially contradictory one. (...) Religion and Morality were not considered necessary and obligatory for every human being, throughout one's whole life. On the contrary, for each sex, every age, each social class, there was a religious situation and moral conduct opposed to that which the nineteenth century prescribed for a different sex, age and social class. The nineteenth century admired the 'faith of the stoker' for its simplicity and purity, but ridiculed the faith of the scientist as being biased. It accepted the faith for infants, but condemned it in the youth and in adult men. At most, it tolerated it in old age. It demanded purity of the woman and demanded impurity of men. It demanded discipline for the manual worker, but applauded the revolutionary spirit of the philosopher."[109]

On this occasion, addressing his colleagues from a younger generation, Plinio made a vibrant call to the fight and to heroism.

> "For us life is not a party, but a fight. Our destinies should be that

---

[108] P. Corrêa de Oliveira, *Memórias*, unpublished.
[109] P. Corrêa de Oliveira, Speech on the closing of the year 1936 to the Archdiocesan College of São Paulo, Echos, no. 29, 1937, pp. 88–92.

of heroes and not sybarites. This truth was the subject of meditation a thousand times over and that I repeat to you today (...). Place Christ in the centre of your life. Let all your ideals converge upon Him. In face of the great fight, the most noble vocation of your generation, repeat the famous phrase of the Saviour: *'Domine, non recuso laborem'.*"[110]

In 1926, Plinio Corrêa de Oliveira, following the family tradition, enrolled in the Law School of the University of São Paulo. A young man of contemplative spirit and a great reader, he continued to cultivate his philosophical, moral and spiritual culture next to that of law. Among the works that deeply affected his formation during these years were the *Treatise on Natural Law* by Father Luigi Taparelli d'Azeglio[111] and *The Soul of the Apostolate*[112] by Dom Jean-Baptiste Chautard. The latter work, that remained one of his favourite books, was a precious antidote to the "heresy of action"[113] that was beginning to characterize the era and to which Dom Chautard contrasts the interior life defined by him as

"the state of activity of a soul which reacts against its natural inclinations in order to regulate them, and which endeavours to acquire

---

[110] Ibid.

[111] On the Jesuit Father Luigi Taparelli d'Azeglio (1793–1862) author of the famous *Saggio teoretico di diritto naturale*, Rome, La Civiltà Cattolica, 1949, 2 vols. (1840–43), in which the relations between law, morals and politics are carefully analyzed in the light of Catholic doctrine, cf. Robert Jacquin, *Taparelli*, Lethielleux, Paris 1943 and the entry of Pietro Pirri, S.J., in EC, vol. XI (1953), coll. 1741–5.

[112] Dom Jean-Baptiste Chautard, *The Soul of the Apostolate*, Burns & Oates, London 1957. "It is not possible to read these admirable pages, whose unction sometimes reminds one of the *Imitation of Christ*, without feeling the treasures of charm his great soul embodied" (P. Corrêa de Oliveira, "Almas delicadas sem fraqueza e fortes sem brutalidade", Catolicismo, no. 52, April 1955). Dom Jean-Baptiste Chautard was born in Briançon on 12 March 1858. He was a Cistercian religious of strict observance. In 1897, he was elected abbot of the Trappist monastery of Chambaraud (Grenoble) and in 1899 of that of Sept-Fons (Moulins). During his long government he was forced to look after temporal problems regarding his order which he had to defend against the anti-religious policies of his time. The perfect model of that union of contemplative and active life laid down in the *The Soul of the Apostolate*, he managed to assert his authority, through his personality, over the minister Clemenceau, convincing him to mitigate his position against the contemplative orders. He died in Sept-Fons on 29 September 1935.

[113] The "heresy of action", understood as a vision of the activist and naturalist world that denies the decisive role of grace in the life of man, had been one of the characteristics of the "Catholic Americanism" at the end of the 1800s, and that had been condemned by Leo XIII in the Letter *Testem Benevolentiae* of 22 January 1899 in *Acta Leonis XIII*, vol. XI, Rome, 1900, pp. 5–20. Cf. Emanuele Chiettini, *Americanismo*, in EC, vol. I (1950), coll. 1054–6; G. Pierrefeu, *Américanisme*, in DSp, vol. I (1937), coll. 475–88; H. Delassus, *L'américanisme et la conjuration antichétienne*, Lille, Desclée de Brouwer, 1899; Thomas McAvoy, *The Americanist Heresy in Roman Catholicism 1895–1900*, University of Notre Dame Press, Notre Dame (Indiana) 1963; Robert Cross, *The emergence of Liberal Catholicism in America*, Harvard, Harvard University Press, 1967; Ornella Confessore, *L'americanismo cattolico in Italia*, Rome, Studium, 1984.

the habit of judging and acting in everything according to the light of the Gospel and the example of Our Lord".[114]

Plinio Corrêa de Oliveira loved and profoundly lived this spirit from the years of his adolescence. Even while dedicating himself at a very young age to public action and apostolate, he never forgot to develop his interior life through an assiduous and constant exercise of the faculties of the soul.

Against the confused backdrop of the Twenties that witnessed the birth and spread of Communism and Fascism and the establishment of an American way of life that was antithetical to the traditional way, the ideal of the restoration of Christian civilization, indicated by St Pius X, seemed distant. In the heart of the young Brazilian student, however, the awareness of a vocation had been formed during all those years.[115] It was linked in a mysterious and providential way to the unfulfilled mission of the great Pope who, from his first encyclical *E supremi Apostolatus* of 4 October 1903, had chosen the motto *Instaurare omnia in Christo* (Eph.1:10) as the programme of his Pontificate and as the goal for the newly begun twentieth century.

With St Pius X, Plinio wanted to restore in Christ "not only what properly pertains to the divine mission of the Church, namely, leading souls to God, but also what (...) flows from that divine mission, namely, Christian civilization in each and every one of the elements composing it".[116]

Plinio Corrêa de Oliveira himself would one day define his vocation with these words:

"When still very young I marvelled at the ruins of Christendom, gave them my heart, turned my back on all I could expect, and made of that past full of blessings, my Future."[117]

---

[114] J.-B. Chautard, *The Soul of the Apostolate*, p. 8.

[115] *"Illos quos Deus ad aliquid eligit, ita praeparat et disponit ut id ad quod eliguntur, inveniantur idonei"* [God so prepares and endows those, whom He chooses for some particular office, that they are rendered capable of fulfilling it] (St Thomas Aquinas, *Summa Theologica*, III, 27, 4c). The vocation is the special form in which God wants his elect to develop. Elect, that is, chosen and, therefore, prepared and willing to be up to the purpose to which God had destined them from eternity.

[116] St Pius X, Encyclical *Il fermo proposito* of 11 June 1905, in IP, vol. IV, *Il laicato*, 1958, p. 216.

[117] These words of Plinio Corrêa de Oliveira appear, written in his hand, as the epigraph of the book *Tradition, Family, Property: Half a Century of Epic Anticommunism*.

Chapter II

"The *Legionário* was born to fight ... "

"What was Legionário's *ideal from the beginning?*
... We had no doubts. It was Catholicism,
the plenitude of all true and noble ideals."

1. The importance of the Catholic Church in the life of Brazil

The religious climate in the Brazil of the Twenties was still imbued with the profound and beneficial action of the pontificate of St Pius X.[1] The struggle against modernism promoted by this Pope had brought, at least on the surface, internal peace to the Catholic Church, which appeared as a great force united around the Pope and his bishops. On 11 December 1905, St Pius X nominated the first Latin American cardinal in the person of the Brazilian Archbishop Joaquim Arcoverde de Albuquerque Cavalcanti.[2] Cardinal Arcoverde, who since 1897 had been the bishop of Rio de Janeiro, strove to instil new energy into the Catholicism of his country. However after 1921 his health suffered a noticeable decline and he was assisted more and

---

[1] Under St Pius X, religious life in Brazil received a great boost. During his pontificate, he increased the archdioceses from two to seven, four *nullius* prelacies and three apostolic prefectures. cf. Manoel Alvarenga, *O Episcopado Brasileiro*, (São Paulo, A. Campos, 1915), pp. 11, 94–5.

[2] Joaquim Arcoverde de Albuquerque Cavalcanti was born on 17 January 1850 in Pernambuco and was ordained to the priesthood on 4 April 1874. In 1890 he was appointed Bishop of Goiás and was consecrated in Rome. He was bishop of São Paulo from 1894 to 1897, succeeding Bishop Lino Deodato de Carvalho, and then became archbishop of Rio de Janeiro until his death on 18 April 1930. "This prince of the Church, the first Brazilian and Latin-American cardinal, besides having native blood (Arcoverde) and the Portuguese blood of the Albuquerques, also had Italian blood, indeed very Italian blood, in the cultural sense of the word, of the Cavalcantis of the sixteenth century." G. Freyre, *Casa-Grande & Senzala. Formação da Família Brasileira sob o Regime de Economia Patriarcal*, Rio de Janeiro, Livraria José Olympio, 1958; It. tr. *Padroni e schiavi. La formazione della famiglia brasiliana in regime di economia patriarcale*, (Turin, Giulio Einaudi, 1965), p. XIII.

more by his auxiliary Sebastião Leme da Silveira Cintra[3] who, at his death in 1930, succeeded him, thus becoming one of the youngest cardinals of the Sacred College.

Brazil at the beginning of the Twenties witnessed a reactionary movement to the prevailing positivism. It was spectacularly demonstrated in the conversion to Catholicism of Jackson de Figuereido.[4] A young intellectual, he founded, in 1921 in Rio de Janeiro, with the support of the auxiliary Bishop Leme, the magazine *A Ordem* and in 1922 the Dom Vital Centre. The very choice of the name of Bishop Vital Maria Gonçalves de Oliveira (Dom Vital)[5], the great "Brazilian Athanasius",[6] bore witness to Jackson's position, who openly defined himself as a reactionary and ultramontane. The characteristic trait of his apostolate was, as Plinio Corrêa de Oliveira himself noted, "his absolutely clear notion that the great religious problem of Brazil was essentially the fight against the general indifferentism".[7] He was to recall:

"Brazil never crossed a more asphyxiating phase, from a spiritual, moral and intellectual viewpoint, than the long years of stagnation that preceded Jackson's apostolate .... It was in this panorama that Jackson appeared. And he appeared with the providential mission of dynamiting the grey and shapeless quarry of the unconcern of the environment. He planted the seeds of concern and struggle, in

[3] Sebastião Leme da Silveira Cintra was born in Espírito Santo do Pinhal, in the state of São Paulo, on 20 January 1882. Having completed his studies in Rome in the Pio Latin-American College and the Gregorian University, he was ordained to the priesthood in the Eternal City on 28 October 1904. He was then transferred to São Paulo as an assistant in the parish of St Cecilia, and appointed director of the *Boletim Eclesiástico*. He was also a leading figure in the Confederação Católica, a body destined to co-ordinate all the associations of Catholic action within the diocese. On 4 January 1911 he was consecrated bishop of Ortósia, in the same chapel of the Latin-American College where he had been ordained a priest, and was appointed to the diocese of Rio de Janeiro, as auxiliary bishop to Cardinal Arcoverde, at the suggestion of the latter. In April 1916, he was appointed to the diocese of Olinda (which two years later became the archdiocese of Olinda and Recife). In 1921, because of the serious condition of Cardinal Arcoverde's health, he was nominated coadjutor archbishop of Rio de Janeiro, with the right to succession. On the death of Cardinal Arcoverde, in April 1930, he was raised in his turn to archbishop of the Diocese and then a cardinal. He died on 17 October 1942 in Rio de Janeiro. A not exhaustive biography is that of Irmã Maria Regina do Santo Rosario O.C.D., *O cardinal Leme (1882-1942)*, Rio de Janeiro, Livraria José Olympio, 1962.
[4] On Jackson de Figuereido (1891-1928), cf. Francisco Iglesias, *Estudo sobre o pensamento reacionário: Jackson de Figuereido*, in *Historia e Ideologia*, (São Paulo, Perspectiva, 1981), pp. 108-58; Cléa de Figueiredo Fernandes, *Jackson de Figuereido, uma trajetória apaixonada*, Rio de Janeiro s.d., Editora Forense Universitária (ma 1987-8); Antonio Carlos Villaça, in *O pensamento católico no Brasil,* (Rio de Janeiro, Zahar Editores, 1975) calls him "an agitator of ideas" (p. 11) who "personified, in Brazil, the thinking of Joseph de Maistre" (p. 12). On the tenth anniversary of his death, in number 321 of *O Legionário* (5 November 1938), Plinio Corrêa de Oliveira dedicated an article to Jackson de Figuereido ("A Dynamite de Christo") and an entire page with writings of Father Ascanio Brandão and of Alceu Amoroso Lima. On ultramontane Catholicism in Brazil cf. also Riolando Azzi, *O altar unido ao trono. Um projeto conservador*, São Paulo, Edições Paulinas, 1992; Tiago Adão Lara, *Tradicionalismo católico em Pernambuco*, Recife, Edições Massangana, 1988.

the lethal and shameful placidity of the Brazil of the time .... Jackson, in the amorphism of the society of the day, was a loud and epic defender of the rights of the Church .... Jackson's apostolate echoed throughout Brazil, and from north to south, from the depths of the interior to the Atlantic, souls upon souls, forming legions and multitudes, hurried to gather under the authentically and exclusively Catholic banner this great paladin had raised."[8]

Between 1925 and 1930 the Catholic movement in Brazil included all the various groups and religious associations spread throughout the country and throughout all the social classes. It had an extraordinary impulse, encouraging entire legions of young people to develop an interior life and the apostolate. The backbone of this fruitful Catholic movement in Brazil was the Marian Congregations.[9]

---

[5] Vital Maria Gonçalves de Oliveira was born on 27 November 1844 in Pedras de Fogo (Pernambuco) and studied in the seminaries of Olinda and Saint-Sulpice in Paris. On 16 July 1863 he entered the Capuchin Order with the name of Friar Vital Maria de Pernambuco. On 2 August of the same year he was ordained to the priesthood in Paris, and in the month of November he returned to Brazil, where he taught philosophy in the seminary of São Paulo. At the suggestion of the Emperor Dom Pedro II, on 17 March 1872 he was consecrated bishop of Olinda in the cathedral of São Paulo. Violently attacked by a calumnious campaign promoted by the Masonic Lodges, in 1874 he was arrested and condemned by the government of the viscount of Rio Branco. After the pardon granted to him the following year, he went to Rome to clarify his behaviour to Pius IX, who had heard many slanders. He died in Paris on 4 July 1878 under mysterious circumstances which led one to believe that he had been poisoned. In 1882 his remains were transferred to Brazil and interred in the Basilica of Penha in Recife. The cause for his beatification, begun in 1953, was reopened in 1995 following the *nihil obstat* of the Holy See. Cf. Antonio Manoel dos Reis, *O Bispo de Olinda D. Frei Vital Maria Gonçalves de Oliveira perante a História*, Rio de Janeiro, Typographia da Gazeta de Noticias, 1878; F. Louis de Gonzague O.M.C., *Une page de l'histoire du Brésil, Monseigneur Vital*, Paris, Librairie Saint-François, 1912; Fr. Felix de Olivola, *Um grande brasileiro. D. Frei Vital Maria Gonçalves de Oliveira, Bispo de Olinda*, 3rd edn., Recife, Imprensa Industrial, 1937; Ramos de Oliveira, *O conflito Maçônico-Religioso de 1872*, Petropolis, Editora Vozes, 1952. Between August and September 1944, Plinio Corrêa de Oliveira dedicated a series of five articles in *O Legionário* to Dom Vital. "In the religious life of the Brazilian people, the name of Dom Vital was like a great beam of light. He symbolized intrepid Faith, apostolic courage, unbreakable coherence of life with the doctrine, of action with thought, all at the service of Holy Mother Church." P. Corrêa de Oliveira, "7 dias em revista", O Legionário, no. 587, 7 November 1943.

[6] A. M. dos Reis, *O Bispo de Olinda*, p. IV.

[7] P. Corrêa de Oliveira, "Mais um anniversario", O Legionário, no. 373, 5 November 1939.

[8] P. Corrêa de Oliveira, *A Dynamite de Christo*.

[9] The Marian Congregations were established and promoted by the Society of Jesus, with the aim of forming select Christians, whatever their state and devotion. In the golden book of the Congregations we find saints such as Francis de Sales, Alphonsus de Liguori, Louis Marie Grignion de Montfort, and courageous defenders of Christian civilization such as John of Austria, John Sobieski, Gabriel Garcia Moreno. The first Marian Congregation in Brazil, after the return of the Society of Jesus, was established on 31 May 1870. Between 1870 and 1928 over 250 Congregations were founded. At the end of 1927, in São Paulo, the First Diocesan Federation for co-ordinating and guiding the Marian Congregations was founded. In 1930, Father Irineu Cursino de Moura was placed at its head. Cf. Pedro Américo Maia S.J., *História das Congregações Marianas no Brasil*, São Paulo, Edições Loyola, 1992. Cf. also Clemente Espinosa S.J., *Magisterio Pontificio sobre las Congregaciones Marianas*, 2nd edn., Bilbao, El Mensajero del Corazón de Jesús, 1965.

At the beginning of the 1930s, the "Marian movement" was noticeable for the extent of its influence and the intensity of its enthusiasm. Together with Cardinal Leme, it was particularly encouraged by another great person of the day: Duarte Leopoldo e Silva,[10] Metropolitan Archbishop of São Paulo, a grave and austere figure, who guided the archdiocese for thirty years.

Crossing the city centre in a tram, the young Plinio saw the announcement of a congress of the Catholic Youth to be held in São Paulo from 9 to 16 September 1928. For him this was the discovery of a world whose existence he had never even imagined. The Congress took place in an atmosphere of great enthusiasm in the historic church-monastery of São Bento, in the presence of the new papal nuncio, Archbishop Benedetto Aloisi Masella.[11] Already a Marian Congregation member in São Luiz, Plinio then entered that of the Legion of St Peter, attached to the parish of St Cecilia, where he found the ideal of dedication to which he deeply aspired. The

---

[10] Archbishop Duarte Leopoldo e Silva was born in Taubaté, in the state of São Paulo, on 4 April 1867. Having been ordained to the priesthood in October 1892, in 1894 he became parish priest of the Church of Saint Cecília in São Paulo. He received his Episcopal consecration from St Pius X in Rome in May 1904; he was appointed bishop of Curitiba in October of the same year. In December 1906 he was transferred to the diocese of São Paulo, to replace the bishop, José de Camargo Barros, who had died in a shipwreck. He was then made archbishop, on 7 June 1908, after the establishment of the new archdiocese for São Paulo. For his merits, he received from the Holy See the titles of Roman count, assistant to the papal throne, Domestic Prelate of His Holiness. He governed the archdiocese until the day of his death 13 November 1938. From the very beginning of his episcopate, he wished to represent in a symbol the great mission of the Paulista people entrusted to him: he did this by erecting a new cathedral in São Paulo, that would be "a school of art and a stimulus to the most noble and elevated thoughts, (...) an opulent cathedral that, by bearing witness to the abundance of our material resources, will be a hymn of thanksgiving to God Our Lord". In Arruda Dantas, *Dom Duarte Leopoldo*, (São Paulo, Sociedade Impressora Pannartz, 1974), p. 42. The new cathedral of São Paulo was only inaugurated in 1954. Cf. Sonia Dias, Sérgio Flaksman, *Silva, Duarte Leopoldo e*, in DHBB, vol. IV, pp. 3150–1. Cf. also the volume that contains his writings and his speeches *Pastoraes*, São Paulo, Escolas Profissionaes do Lyceu Salesiano S. Coração de Jesus, 1921, and the biographical essay by Júlio Rodrigues, *D. Duarte Leopoldo e Silva, arcebispo de São Paulo. Homenagem do Cléro e dos Catholicos da Archidiocése, por occasião do Jubileu de sua Sagração Episcopal*, São Paulo, Instituto D. Anna Rosa, 1929. Cf. also P. Corrêa de Oliveira, "Um bispo providencial", O Legionário, no. 323, 20 November 1938; "O grande Dom Duarte", O Legionário, no. 374, 12 November 1939; "Dom Duarte", O Legionário, no. 535, 8 November 1942 and the memoir that he wrote in "Junto à sepultura do nosso grande Cardeal", O Legionário, no. 533, 25 October 1942.

[11] Benedetto Aloisi Masella was born in Pontecorvo on 29 June 1879, of a noble family that had already given one cardinal to the Church. He died in Rome on 1 October 1970. Ordained to the priesthood in 1902, after having studied in the Pontifical Ecclesiastical Academy he was secretary and regent of the Nunciature in Lisbon (1905–08), apostolic nuncio in Chile (1919–26) and Brazil (1927–46) until he was promoted to cardinal. Suburbicarian Bishop of Palestrina, Cardinal in 1946, Prefect of the Holy Congregation of the Sacraments, Dean of the Lateran Basilica, Camerlengo of the Holy Roman Church during the vacant Papal Sees of the pontificates of Pius XII and of John XXIII. He participated actively in the preparation of the Council and was nominated pontifical legate for the crowning of Our Lady of Fatima in 1946.

Congregation, founded on 26 December 1926 by Mgr Marcondes Pedrosa,[12] the parish priest, and placed under the protection of the Annunciation, had a newsletter entitled *O Legionário*. Its Congregation members numbered as many as one hundred.

The beginning of Plinio Corrêa de Oliveira's public activity dates from this period, when, within the Law School of the University of São Paulo, then the centre of secularism and of legal and political positivism, he founded, with a handful of young Marian Congregation members, the University Catholic Action (AUC). On the occasion of the graduation ceremony, he dared to do something that until then had never taken place in a state university in Brazil. He had the Mass, which traditionally concluded the higher course of studies, celebrated, not in the church of St Francis next to the University, but inside the University itself, in the internal courtyard. The celebrant was the Vicar-General of the Diocese, Mgr Gastão Liberal Pinto and the sermon was preached by Father Leonel Franca of the Society of Jesus.[13] When, on 11 December 1930, Plinio Corrêa de Oliveira graduated in Law, his name was already "very well-known and admired among Brazilian Catholic youth".[14] From then he began to be known among his friends as "Doctor Plinio".[15]

2. The historical "turning point" of 1930

The Revolution of the Thirties was for Brazil what the First World

---

[12] Paulo Marcondes Pedrosa was born in São Bento do Sapucái (SP) on 6 November 1881 and died in São Paulo on 29 April 1962. Ordained priest in 1904, he was coadjutor, then parish priest until 1932 of the Church of St Cecilia, monsignor and Papal Chamberlain on 21 April 1920. On 27 April 1932 he entered the Benedictine Order in the monastery of São Bento, of which he was prior.

[13] On Father Leonel Franca S.J. (1893-1948), considered by many to be the "spiritual father" of the Brazilian intelligentsia of this period, cf. Luiz Gonzaga da Silveira d'Elboux S.J., *O Padre Leonel Franca S.J.*, (Rio de Janeiro, Livraria Agir Editora, 1953), p. 173; Heliodoro Pires, "Leonel Franca, apóstolo do Brasil moderno", Revista Eclesiastica Brasileira, 1953, vol. 13, pp. 911-21. Father Franca, whose *Obras completas* are contained in fifteen volumes, is the author of essays such as "A Igreja, a Reforma e a Civilização" (1922) and "A crise do mundo moderno" (1940) which are original reflections on the crisis of our time in the light of Catholic doctrine. He founded and directed for eight years the Catholic University of Rio, the first in Brazil. "Pedagogue, apologist, spiritual director, he dedicated his life to the History of Philosophy and the Philosophy of History." A. C. Villaça, *O pensamento católico no Brasil,* op. cit., p. 124.

[14] O Legionário, no. 70, 14 December 1930.

[15] This title is frequently used in Brazil, just as in other European countries, where the title of "doctor" is given to all those who have received a degree. Plinio Corrêa de Oliveira began his public life immediately after obtaining his degree, before becoming a congressman and a university professor. He, then, began to be known as "Doctor Plinio" which since then became incorporated into his name, as is the custom in Brazil.

War had been for Europe, an historical caesura between two eras. The era of the "Old Republic"[16] (1889–1930) came to an end and that of Getúlio Vargas began.

Up to then power had been in the hands of the axis São Paulo-Minas Gerais, that is, the alliance of the two main producing States of Brazil.[17] This predominance was expressed by the formula of "coffee and milk" (Minas Gerais was also committed to farming), which provided for the rotation of the presidency of the Republic between the political representatives of São Paulo and of Minas. The system did not vary greatly until 1930, when the outgoing president, Washington Luiz, indicated another Paulista member as his successor, Julio Prestes de Albuquerque, instead of the Mineiro candidate. The State of Minas then coalesced with the State of Rio Grande do Sul, rallying around the name of Getúlio Vargas,[18] president of the latter State since January 1928.

The climate of political confrontation was worsened by the collapse of the New York stock exchange and by its repercussions on the Brazilian economy. Wall Street's famous "black Thursday" on 24 October 1929 was the detonator for the world crisis. Its first effect was the collapse of the international prices for Brazil's coffee: the income in foreign currency fell from £67 million sterling in 1929 to £41 million in 1930.[19] The gold reserves, which in September 1929

---

[16] In the *"República Velha"*, cf. José Maria Bello, *História da República: 1889-1954*, 4th edn., São Paulo, Companhia Editora Nacional, 1959. An interesting, but usually underestimated, essay is that by Charles Morazé, *Les trois âges du Brésil*, Paris, A. Colin, 1954. One of the most profound criticisms of the "República Velha" was made by a monarchist, José Maria dos Santos, after the Revolution of the 1930s: *A política geral do Brasil*, São Paulo, J. Magalhães, 1930. Two other studies of a general nature containing important information are those by Sertório de Castro, *A República que a revolução destruiu*, Rio de Janeiro, F. Bastos, 1932; and by Dormund Martins, *Da república à ditadura*, Rio de Janeiro, Typ. São Bento, 1931.

[17] From 1916 on, Rio Grande do Sul also became important. Its economy was not characterized by a single product, like in the case of São Paulo and Minas. The other seventeen States of the Federation were much weaker. Cf. Joseph Love, *Rio Grande do Sul and Brazilian Regionalism 1882-1930*, Stanford, University Press, 1971; ID., *A locomotiva. São Paulo na Federação brasileira 1889-1937*, Rio de Janeiro, Paz e Terra, 1982; John D. Wirth, *O fiel da balança. Minas Gerais na Federação brasileira 1889-1937*, Rio de Janeiro, Paz e Terra, 1982.

[18] Born in 1883 in Rio Grande do Sul, Getúlio Vargas was congressman and federal minister, then president of the State of Rio Grande (1928-30). He came into power in 1930 and exercised it as a dictator until 29 October 1945, when he was removed by a bloodless coup d'état. After the war Vargas continued to be politically active. He was a national senator, in 1946 he founded the Trabalhista Party and in 1950 he was again elected president of the Republic. Having been compromised in scandals in 1954, he committed suicide. His political itinerary which peaked with the creation of the *Estado Novo* (1937–45), shows many analogies to that of Juan Domingo Perón in Argentina (1946–55). On Vargas, cf. among others Thomas E. Skidmore, *Brasil: de Getúlio Vargas a Castelo Branco (1930–1964)*, Rio de Janeiro, Paz e Terra, 1988; Paulo Brandi, Dora Flaksman, entry *Vargas*, in DHBB, vol. IV, pp. 3436-505.

[19] A. Trento, *Le origini dello Stato populista. Società e politica in Brasile 1920-1945*, (Milano, Franco Angeli, 1986), pp. 106-107.

amounted to £31 million sterling, in August 1930 fell to £14 million and by December of that same year practically no longer existed.[20]

In this crisis situation, the presidential elections were won on 1 March 1930 by Júlio Prestes. However, there was a climate of popular unrest in the country and in the month of October it exploded with a military revolt which spread from Porto Alegre, Belo Horizonte and Recife to the whole country. In less than a month the government was forced to give in. President Washington Luiz was sent into exile and, at the beginning of November, Getúlio Vargas was nominated head of the provisional government.

Vargas' rise to power was an authentic break with the past. It marked the fundamental change of the role of the State, which from that time became the regulating agent of the economic activity of the country.[21] The rural aristocracy, which had guided Brazilian society for centuries, lost control over the nation and was replaced by new industrial and financial interests.[22] The establishment of the Republic in 1889 had been a political revolution, but it maintained unchanged the social organization of Brazil. That of 1930 had much deeper consequences.[23]

3. The Catholic Electoral League

After the formation of Vargas' provisional government, the new cardinal of Rio, Sebastião Leme, had begun to promote a movement of lay people in order to give a voice to the Catholics in the organization of the new political regime in Brazil. On 30 May 1931, the image of Our Lady of Aparecida was carried in triumph from her shrine to Rio de Janeiro.[24] The next day, a crowd of about one million people accompanied Our Lady to the *Esplanada do Castelo*, where she was awaited by the head of State, Vargas, and the highest civil

[20] Nelson Werneck Sodré, *História da burguesia brasileira*, (Petrópolis, Vozes, 1983), p. 243.

[21] A. Trento, *Le origini dello Stato populista*, p. 121.

[22] Robert J. Havighurst, J. Roberto Moreira, *Society and Education in Brazil*, (Pittsburgh, University of Pittsburgh Press, 1919), p. 42.

[23] The revolution of the 1930s was prepared by the so-called *"tenentismo"*, the movement of the junior officers of the army (the lieutenants) who between the 1920s and 1934 were protagonists of agitation and revolts, culminating in the episode of rebellion of the *Prestes* column, having received its name from its commander Luís Carlos Prestes. Composed of about a thousand men, by the end of February of 1927 when it retreated to Bolivia, it had travelled over 25,000 km., bringing guerrilla warfare to various states of Brazil.

[24] Gustavo Antonio Solimeo, "1717–1967. Rainha e Padroeira do Brasil", Catolicismo, no. 202, October 1967; Hamilton d'Avila, "Três episodios na história da Padroeira nacional", Catolicismo, no. 418 October 1985, pp. 10–12. Cf. also Júlio Brestoloni C.S.S.R., *A Senhora Conceição Aparecida*, Aparecida-São Paulo, Editora Santuario, 1984.

and military authorities. The image was placed on the altar and Cardinal Leme officially proclaimed her "Patroness of Brazil". "The name of God is crystallized in the soul of the Brazilian people", Cardinal Leme stated. "Either the State ceases to be atheistic and agnostic, and recognizes the God of the people, or the people will not recognize the State."[25]

Meanwhile, on 9 July 1932, a "constitutionalist" revolt developed in São Paulo but, without the support of the other regions, it failed after just a few months;[26] however, the Paulista rebels forced the government to call elections for the following year to vote for a new Constitutional Assembly.

Plinio Corrêa de Oliveira, who had never actively participated in the revolt, did however understand the importance of the calling of the Constitutional Assembly, which offered an occasion to create, not so much a party, but a Catholic movement "above parties".[27]

It was Plinio, too, who in October 1932 suggested to the Archbishop of São Paulo, Duarte Leopoldo e Silva, to do something in Brazil similar to what General de Castelnau[28] had done in France: create a liasing association among the electors in order to direct their vote to candidates who would undertake to respect the Catholic programme. Archbishop Duarte willingly accepted the proposal and invited the young Marian Congregation member to put it in motion starting with a discussion about it with Cardinal Leme. The following month, "Doctor Plinio", as he had already come to be known, went to Rio where he spoke about it with two young militants of the Catholic movement, Heitor da Silva Costa and Alceu Amoroso Lima. They, in turn, approached Cardinal Leme with the proposal. The latter thought the idea to be excellent and invited them to draw up the Statutes of the new association. Thus the Liga Eleitoral

---

[25] "Palavra de S. Eminenza", O Legionário, no. 89, 1 November 1931.

[26] On the Paulista revolution cf. among others: Hélio Silva, *1932: a guerra paulista*, Rio de Janeiro, Civ. Brasileira, 1976; Stanley E. Hilton, *A guerra civil brasileira*, Rio de Janeiro, Nova Fronteira, 1982.

[27] P. Corrêa de Oliveira, "Liga eleitoral católica", O Legionário, no. 111, 15 January 1933. "Either Catholicism is able to win in the ballot boxes and make the country progress resolutely towards religious reform, or extreme socialism will take over Brazil to make it a victim of the numerous Calles and Lenins who fill the backrooms of our politics and who are anxious to 'mexicanize' and 'sovieticize' the Land of the Holy Cross" (ibid).

[28] General Edouard de Curières de Castelnau (1851–1944) was one of the commanders of the French army during the First World War, in which he lost three children. Formerly congress-man of the Aveyron from 1919 to 1924, starting from 1925 he devoted himself to the *Féderation Nationale Catholique*, of which he was president until his death, to promote a civic action "in the interest of the Catholic religion, the family, the society and the national patrimony". He was refused the field marshal's baton because of his convictions as a fervent Catholic. Cf. the recent study Yves Gras, *Castelnau ou l'art de commander, 1851–1944*, Paris, Denoël, 1990.

Católica (LEC),[29] was born with the aim of orienting the Catholic vote in the elections for the National Constitutional Assembly. It would present the candidates of the various parties with a series of requests, defined as "minimum demands", in order to commit them to operate as Catholics in Parliament. Pandiá Calógeras was nominated as president of the LEC, with Alceu Amoroso Lima as his secretary-general.

On 13 November the LEC was also officially established in the city of São Paulo. Dr Estevão Emmerich de Souza Rezende was appointed as the local president and Plinio Corrêa de Oliveira as secretary. Cardinal Leme invited the archbishops, bishops and apostolic administrators of the country to rapidly create local councils. Thus every diocese had its council and in the early months of 1933 the LEC was able to draw up its programme and choose its candidates for Parliament. When, at the end of March, the list that included the Catholic Paulista candidates was compiled, Plinio Corrêa de Oliveira was chosen by Archbishop Duarte as one of the four candidates of the *Chapa única* (Single ticket) of São Paulo.[30]

On 3 May 1933 the elections were held all over the country. To the general surprise, the congressman who received most votes in the whole of Brazil was Plinio Corrêa de Oliveira, a Marian Congregation member who had only recently finished his university studies.[31] It was "A Marian victory", as the *Legionário* entitled its editorial:

> "The central figure of this beautiful page in the history of the Congregations in São Paulo was Plinio Corrêa de Oliveira, the pious son of Mary, the leader of the Catholic Electoral League, the Marian candidate to the Constitutional Assembly."[32]

---

[29] Statute (1932) and programme (1933) of the LEC in Oscar de Figuereido Lustosa O.P., *Igreja e Política no Brasil. Do Partido católico a L.E.C. (1874–1945)*, (São Paulo, Edições Loyola, 1983), pp. 101–26. Cf. also Mônica Kornis, D. Flaksman, *Liga Eleitoral Católica*, in DHBB, vol. III, p. 1820; Raul Silva, *Influência política da Igreja Católica na Assembleía Constituinte de 1933/34. Dissertação de mestrado*, Brasília, Universidade de Brasília, 1978.

[30] The *"Single ticket for a united São Paulo"* was a result of the link-up of all the frontline political or social forces of the Paulista life of the day. Of these forces, two were of a typically party nature: the *Partido Democrático*, that represented above all the urban intelligentsia and some incipient left-wing groups, and the older PRP (*Partido Republicano Paulista*), which was conservative. The currents of social expression were the *Associação Comercial*, the *Federação dos Voluntários*, representing the generation that had risen against Vargas, and the *Liga Eleitoral Católica*.

[31] P. Corrêa de Oliveira received 24,714 votes, 9.5 percent of the total. The number of votes was sufficient to elect two congressmen and was double those received by the lawyer Alcântara Machado, his former professor, who came in second. Among the others elected for the *Liga Eleitoral Católica* were Andrade Furtado for Ceará; Mgr Arruda Câmara and Barreto Campelo for Pernambuco; Lacerda de Almeida for Paraná; Aldroaldo Mesquita da Costa for Rio Grande do Sul.

[32] "Uma vitoria mariana", O Legionário, no. 120, 7 May 1933.

On 15 November 1933 the Third National Constitutional Assembly of Brazil was solemnly installed in the Tiradentes palace of Rio de Janeiro. However, Cardinal Leme's instructions to the LEC deputies were quite precise. No bloc of clearly identifiable Catholic congressmen was to be formed and nobody in the Assembly should take on a prominent role as a Catholic leader. Furthermore no congressman was to openly intervene on the Catholic demands, because too strong of a "face-to-face" confrontation would compromise the aim of the LEC, which was to modify the secularist physiognomy of the Brazilian state. The strategy chosen aimed at obtaining this result by indirect ways, in scattered order. Plinio Corrêa de Oliveira followed these instructions, but the greatest defenders of the LEC proposals were the very exponents of the Paulista bloc.[33]

In the name of the Catholic congressmen of São Paulo, Plinio Corrêa de Oliveira asked the Assembly to pay special homage to the figure of Father Anchieta, the four hundredth anniversary of whose birth fell on 19 March 1934.[34] On the floor he defended the freedom of teaching and the right to vote of the religious, reflecting on the worthy role of the Society of Jesus in Brazil.[35] This was sufficient for him to be attacked during the debate as "sectarian". "I prize my religious beliefs above any possible affection", he responded.

This incisive action of the LEC was not without results. The Assembly not only approved the "minimum demands" of the League – indissolubility of the marriage bond (art. 144), the right to give religious instruction in the schools (art. 153), religious assistance to the armed forces and in the prisons (art. 113 no. 6)[36] – but also numerous other requests such as: to invoke the name of God in the preamble of the Constitution[37]; state assistance to large families (art. 138 § d7); the right of religious to vote (art. 108); Sunday rest (art.

---

[33] Cf. M. Kornis, D. Flaksman, *Liga Eleitoral Católica*.

[34] "If we may have recourse to a profane comparison, in order to give an idea of Anchieta's importance in our History" he wrote at the time "we would say that he was for Brazil what Lycurgus was for Sparta and Romulus for Rome. In other words, he is one of these fabulous heroes to be found at the origins of some great races who raise the first walls, build the first buildings and organize the first institutions". P. Corrêa de Oliveira, "A nota da Semana", O Seculo, 7 September 1932.

[35] Cf. O Legionário, no. 145, 13 May 1934.

[36] In an article of the magazine *A Ordem*, entitled "O sentido da nossa vitória", Alceu Amoroso Lima greeted the 30 May 1934 as "a date of capital importance in the history of Brazilian Catholicism", stating that after the Masonic Constitution of 1824, the Positivist one of 1891 and the Secularist one of 1926, with the fourth Brazilian constitution "the Catholic programme triumphed entirely" (Tristão de Athayde, "O sentido da nossa vitória", A Ordem, no. 52, June 1934, pp. 417, 421–2 (pp. 417–23)).

121 § 1); authorisation for religious cemeteries (art. 113 § 7); military service of ecclesiastics done in the form of spiritual or hospital assistance (art. 163 § 3); the plurality and freedom of workers' unions (art. 120); the law against subversive propaganda (art. 113 § 9). The Constitution of 1934 was the high point of the work carried out by the Catholic movement and the success of the LEC remained unique in the history of the country. As the former Brazilian minister, Paulo Brossard, admitted: "In the history of Brazil, no independent political organisation had more electoral influence than the Catholic Electoral League."[38]

In 1934 the possibility of establishing private universities was introduced in Brazil. In São Paulo, the Free School of Philosophy, Science and Arts of São Bento already existed. It was founded in 1908 by the Benedictines and important personalities such as Professors Alexandre Correia and Leonard van Hacker taught there. It was now recognized by the government. Likewise the government recognized the female School of Philosophy, Science and Art of Sedes Sapientiae Institute run by the Regular Canonesses of St Augustine. Both Schools, destined to be incorporated into the Pontifical Catholic University of São Paulo, invited Plinio Corrêa de Oliveira to hold the Chair of History.[39] Plinio saw this as an excellent chance offered to him by Providence for entering into direct contact with young people. He accepted the post, together with that of Professor of History of Civilization at the University College, attached to the historic Law School. Thus he began his teaching activity which for many years was his main professional occupation, together with that of practising law.

---

[37] The new constitution, that replaced that of 1891 and that of 1926, came into effect on 15 July 1934. cf. Themistocles Brandao Cavalcanti, *Las constituciones de los Estados Unidos del Brasil*, (Madrid, Instituto de estudios politicos, 1958), pp. 379–533. With 168 votes against 37, the congressmen inserted this preamble: "We, the representatives of the Brazilian People, placing our trust in God, gathered in a Constitutional National Assembly to organize a democratic regime that safeguards the unity of the Nation, liberty, justice, and social and economic well-being, decree and promulgate the following Constitution ... " P. Corrêa de Oliveira, "Deus e a Constituição", O Legionário, no. 74, 8 February 1931.

[38] Jornal de Minas, Belo Horizonte, 3 July 1986. On the influence of the LEC, and in particular on the article that placed the State "under the protection of God", cf. also Thales de Azevedo, *A religião civil brasileira. Um instrumento político*, (Petropolis, Editora Vozes, 1981), pp. 79–87.

[39] In 1946 these two institutions merged into the Catholic University of São Paulo of which Archbishop Vasconcellos Motta was grand chancellor and Paulo de Tarso Campos, bishop of Campinas, was rector. The following year saw its canonical establishment with the granting of the title of "Pontifical" cf. AAS, (1947), vol. 39, pp. 134 sgg.

4. Editor of the *Legionário*

The *Legionário*, the official voice of the Marian Congregation of the Parish of St Cecília, directed by Mgr Marcondes Pedrosa, was a monthly paper of four pages when it began publication on 29 May 1927.

The topics the paper dealt with were the defence of traditional and family principles, the safeguarding of the rights of the Church, the formation of new Catholic elites, and the struggle against Communist infiltration. The first article by Plinio Corrêa de Oliveira, regarding the Catholic University, appeared in no. 43 of 22 September 1929; the second, published in November 1929 under the title "The Vatican and the Kremlin",[40] already gives an idea of what will be one of the fundamental themes of his thought: the impossibility of any agreement between the Catholic Church and Communism. In an article entitled "Our Political Demands", in the issue of 8 February 1931, he rallied the Catholics to demand from the new government the defence of the "rights of the Church".

With his concise style, his polemical strength and his love for the truth, the young Marian Congregation member, who had as his examples great Catholic journalists such as Louis Veuillot[41] and, in Brazil, Carlos de Laet,[42] demonstrated that he corresponded perfectly to the journalistic model indicated by Pius XI in the encyclical *Rerum omnium* of 26 January 1933. In it the Pontiff had declared St Francis de Sales as Patron Saint of "all those Catholics who, with the publication of newspapers and of other writings, illustrate, promote and defend Christian doctrine".[43] Addressing Catholic journalists, the Supreme Pontiff added:

---

[40] P. Corrêa de Oliveira, "O Vaticano e o Krêmlin", O Legionário, no. 46, 10 November 1929. Cf. also "A Igreja e o problema religioso na Russia", O Legionário, no. 54, 16 March 1930.

[41] On Louis Veuillot (1813–83), courageous director of the daily *L'Univers* cf. le *Oeuvres Complètes*, 40 vols., Paris, Lethielleux, 1924-40, Cf. also Eugène and François Veuillot, *Veuillot*, 4 vols., Paris, Lethielleux, 1902–13. "He understood – wrote St Pius X to François Veuillot – that the power of society is to be found in the full and complete recognition of the sovereignty of Our Lord Jesus Christ and in the unqualified acceptance of the doctrinal supremacy of the Church" (Letter *C'est avec*, of 22 October 1913, in IP, vol. VI, *La pace interna delle nazioni* (1959), p. 299).

[42] Carlos Maximiano Pimenta de Laet (1847–1927) was a brilliant journalist, professor in the famous Pedro II Secondary School of the Academia Brasileira de Letras. He received the title of count from St Pius X for the services he rendered to the Catholic cause.

[43] AAS, (1923), vol. 5, p. 49.

"First of all they must study with the utmost diligence and should strive, as much as possible, to know Catholic doctrine; they must beware of failing to tell the truth or, under the pretence of avoiding offence to their adversaries, of diminishing or disguising it."[44]

On 6 August 1933, Plinio Corrêa de Oliveira was called to assume the direction of the *Legionário* which, in that same month, became the unofficial organ of the Archdiocese of São Paulo. The publication was not destined to the general public, but to the circles of the Catholic movement in order to guide their thoughts and their actions. It was within these circles, from the North to the South of the country, that the powerful influence of the weekly soon extended.

To those who accused him of not being very "charitable" towards his enemies, Plinio replied that the attitude of the *Legionário* was one of combat yes, but a defensive combat and not an offensive one. "The main goal of *Legionário* is to orient the opinion of those who are already Catholic."[45]

Plinio was the author of the editorials and of the regular feature "À margem dos factos", subsequently called "7 dias em revista" (7 days in review). He gathered around him a team of able collaborators[46] among whom were two young priests destined to become leading figures in the Brazilian clergy: Father Antônio de Castro Mayer,[47] ecclesiastic assistant to the journal, and the Divine Word priest,

---

[44] Ibid.

[45] P. Corrêa de Oliveira, "Offensiva?", O Legionário, no. 181, 29 April 1935. "And if we were permitted to choose a motto for this fight, we would formulate it thus: towards Catholics, charity and unity; towards non-Catholics, charity to obtain unity" (ibid).

[46] Besides Dr Plinio, the editing staff of the *Legionário* included: Fernando Furquim de Almeida, José Carlos Castilho de Andrade, José de Azeredo Santos, Adolpho Lindenberg, José Fernando de Camargo, José Gonzaga de Arruda and Paulo Barros de Ulhôa Cintra. *Tradition, Family, Property: Half a Century of Epic Anticommunism*, pp. 384–5.

[47] Antônio de Castro Mayer was born in Campinas, in the state of São Paulo, on 20 June 1904. He graduated in theology at the Gregorian University of Rome (1924–7) where he was ordained to the priesthood on 30 October 1927. Assistant General of Catholic Action of São Paulo (1940), then vicar-general of the Archdiocese (1942–3), on 23 May 1948 he was consecrated bishop and nominated coadjutor, with the right to succession, of the bishop of Campos. He governed the diocese of Campos as bishop until 1981. Bishop de Castro Mayer publicly broke with Plinio Corrêa de Oliveira and with the TFP in December 1982. The fact soon became public (*Folha da Tarde*, 10 April 1984; *Jornal do Brasil*, 20 August 1984) and is to be linked to the progressive leanings of the former bishop of Campos towards the position of Archbishop Marcel Lefèbvre. A climax was reached with Bishop de Castro Mayer's participation in the Episcopal consecrations in Ecône on 30 June 1988, which led him to incur an excommunication *latae sententiae*. He died in Campos on 25 April 1991.

Father Geraldo de Proença Sigaud.[48] Among the most brilliant lay collaborators, José de Azeredo Santos stood out. He was a young Mineiro Marian Congregation member who had come from Rio to São Paulo to practise engineering.[49] The team, composed of between five and eight members, met regularly to examine, in the light of the doctrine of the Church, articles from newspapers and pieces of news from all over the world. Dr Plinio was to recall: "From the editorial staff of this weekly was gradually formed a group of friends, all members of the Marian congregation like myself. We dedicated ourselves body and soul to Catholic journalism."[50] In 1936 under the direction of the dynamic editor, the newspaper changed from being a fortnightly of two pages to a weekly of eight pages and from a simple parish newsletter it became the most heeded Catholic voice of the country.

The subjects dealt with during 1936 were of the most varied kind. Religious persecution in Germany, the Revolution in Spain, the socialist *"poussée"* in France, the dynastic crisis in England, the

---

[48] Geraldo de Proença Sigaud was born in Belo Horizonte on 26 September 1909. A member of the Divine Word Congregation, he studied theology in Rome (1928–32) where he was ordained to the priesthood on 12 March 1932. On 1 May 1947 he was consecrated diocesan bishop of Jacarezinho (1947-61); he was then Metropolitan archbishop of Diamantina (1961–80). Plinio Corrêa de Oliveira's association with Archbishop Sigaud lasted thirty years and had begun in 1935, on the occasion of a spiritual retreat in the Seminary of the Holy Spirit. "This friendship — wrote Dr Plinio in 1946 – lasted for over ten years during which the two of us found ourselves in every possible situation: of pain and jubilation, of hope and of passing discouragement, of uncertainty and decisiveness. Together we received applause, together we received censures; our hearts beat in unison, in face of every current event; we went through everything that could unite and separate men" (P. Corrêa de Oliveira, "Padre Sigaud", O Legionário, no. 711, 24 March 1946). Their separation, probably dating from the mid 1960s, was officially announced by the same archbishop of Diamantina on 2 October 1970 when, coming out from an audience with the president of the Republic, Emílio Garrastazu Medici, he stated that the TFP had distanced itself from him because of his support for the land reform promoted by the government and for the liturgical reform of Paul VI. The TFP replied immediately with a long press release in which it stressed the contrast between the consistency of its own positions as opposed to the inconsistency of Archbishop Sigaud's, confirming "the total uprightness of its attitudes before civil and ecclesiastical law" ("Archbishop Geraldo Sigaud e a TFP", Catolicismo, no. 239, November 1970). Cf. also P. Corrêa de Oliveira, "Dentro e fora do Brasil ... ", Folha de S. Paulo, 11 October 1970.

[49] "A profound, lively and brilliant journalist, he was, in the full sense of the word, a polemicist. And as such, his name is written in our annals with letters of gold (...). If the History of Brazil is one day written with entire impartiality, his name will rank among the most distinguished." (P. Corrêa de Oliveira, "O 'premio demasiadamente grande' ", Folha de S. Paulo, 17 July 1973). Thus began a long friendship and co-operation that lasted almost forty years, until the day when Plinio Corrêa de Oliveira, kneeling at the foot of the bed of his dying friend, in the Samaritan Hospital of São Paulo, recited in his name the Consecration of St Louis Marie Grignion de Montfort. José de Azeredo Santos is responsible, in Legionário and then in Catolicismo, for discerning articles on Maritainism, on the politics of "outstretched hand", on modern art, and on Gnosis.

[50] P. Corrêa de Oliveira, "Kamikaze", Folha de S. Paulo, 15 February 1969.

presidential elections in the United States, the failure of the League of Nations, the intensifying of Communist propaganda in the world were objects of always profound and clarifying analyses and comments inspired by the doctrine of the Church. "To detoxify readers from the fruits of the neutral press and give them truly Catholic civic news was our constant aim."[51]

In January 1937 the *Legionário* moved from the parish room of St Cecilia towards the centre of the city; it had become the most influential Catholic weekly of Brazil, with a circulation of over 17,000 copies.

5. The European "civil war"

According to the French historian, François Furet, "there is a mystery of evil in the dynamics of the political ideas of the twentieth century".[52]

After the Soviet revolution of 1917, the birth of the Komintern contributed to the world expansion of the new Bolshevik doctrine. The attempts at violent Communist revolution in the world, beginning with the so-called "red biennium" (1919–21), did however provoke a strong anti-Communist reaction. It was on the wave of this reaction that the "Fascist" movements were born and consolidated.

Bolshevism and Fascism thus entered the scene almost at the same time. The dynamic European and world history, between 1917 and 1945, was determined, according to Ernst Nolte, by the great "European civil war" waged between communism and national socialism and therefore, between the Third Reich and the Soviet Union.[53] Furet wrote:

"What renders inevitable a comparative analysis of fascism and communism is not only the fact of their date of birth and appearance being both simultaneous and sudden from an historical point of view, but also their mutual dependence."[54]

This intimate dependent relationship which today is on the way to becoming an acquired historiographic datum, was understood by Plinio Corrêa de Oliveira, who, in absolute loyalty to the Christian

---

[51] P. Corrêa de Oliveira, "Um ano de luta e de vigília", O Legionário, no. 225, 3 January 1937.
[52] F. Furet, *Le passé d'une illusion*, p. 44.
[53] Ernst Nolte, *Der europaeische Bürgerkrieg 1917–1945. Nationalsozialismus und Bolschewismus*, Berlin, Propyläen Verlag, 1987. Cf. also Stuart J. Woolf (edited by), *European Fascism*, London, Weidenfeld and Nicolson, 1968; George L. Mosse, *Masses and Man. Nationalist and Fascist Perceptions of Reality*, New York, Howard Ferty Inc., 1980.
[54] F. Furet, *Le passé d'une illusion*, p. 39.

model of society, refused to take the side of one or other of the contenders who occupied the stage.

He saw a concept in communism that was diametrically opposite to that of Catholicism, but he considered Nazism to be a similarly dangerous false alternative. He wrote:

"It is undeniable that communism is the antithesis of Catholicism. Nazism, in its turn, is another antithesis of Catholic doctrine, and is much closer to communism than either of them is to Catholicism."[55]

The refusal of "middle-class" life in the name of a mystical-heroic conception of existence and the call to the warrior tradition of Germany and of Europe could, and in fact did, constitute an appealing call for many young people who were incapable of discerning the sinister aspect of an ideology saturated with socialism and paganism. Plinio Corrêa de Oliveira understood that the best way of warning the young people of his country against the Nazi pseudo-mysticism, as well as denouncing its errors, was that of proposing an heroic and supernatural vision of Catholicism. It was this flag, opposed to Nazism and Communism, that the *Legionário* raised high in Brazil.

6. The denouncement of National Socialist paganism

On 30 January 1933, Adolf Hitler received from President Hindenburg the mandate of chancellor of the *Reich*.[56] After the elections of 5 March to the *Reichstag*, held in a climate of blatant intimidation, on 23 March "full powers" were granted by law to the National Socialist cabinet. That same spring, the Führer asked that a Concordat be drawn up between the Holy See and the new regime. The agreement was signed in the Vatican on 20 July 1933.[57] However the Holy See stated that the Concordat with the *Reich* should not in

---

[55] P. Corrêa de Oliveira, "À margem da crise", O Legionário, no. 315, 25 September 1938.

[56] After the death of president Hindenburg, on 2 August 1934, the powers of the president of the *Reich* and of the Chancellor were united in the hands of Hitler. Thus began the rapid transformation of the society in the totalitarian sense. On this development, cf. among others: Karl Dietrich Bracher, *Die deutsche Diktatur*, Köln, Kiepenheuer und Witsch, 1380 (1969); Martin Broszat, *Der Staat Hitlers*, München, Deutscher Taschenbuch Verlag, 1981; Hans-Ulrich Thamer, *Il terzo Reich – La Germania dal 1933 al 1945*, It. tr. Il Bologna, Mulino, 1993.

[57] The plenipotentiaries of Pius XI and of Hitler in the negotiations were respectively Cardinal Eugenio Pacelli, Secretary of State, and the Vice-Chancellor of the Reich, Franz von Papen. On the Concordat of 1933 and on the relations between the Holy See and National Socialism, cf. Michele Maccarrone, *Il Nazionalsocialismo e la Santa Sede*, Rome, Studium, 1947; Friedrich Engel-Janosi, *Il Vaticano fra fascismo e nazismo*, Florence, Le Monnier, 1973; Anthony Rhodes, *The Vatican in the Age of Dictators 1922–1945*, London, Hodder and Stoughton, 1973; Robert Graham, *Il Vaticano e il nazismo*, Rome, Cinque Lune, 1975; Giacomo Martina, *Storia della Chiesa*, vol. IV, *L'età contemporanea*, (Brescia, Morcelliana, 1995), pp. 129–218.

any way appear as an approval of the doctrines and tendencies of National Socialism.[58]

As the person in charge of the "surveillance" of the ideological education of the party and of all the aligned associations, Hitler nominated Alfred Rosenberg, the man who was "the quintessence of all the forces present in the NSDAP hostile to the Church and Christianity".[59] The decade that goes from 1935 to the end of the regime was marked by a growing aggravation of the anti-religious struggle, with the progressive suppression of Catholic schools, institutions and press and the systematic denigration of the principles and institutions of the Church.

On 14 March 1937, the Encyclical of Pius XI, *Mit brennender Sorge*, was published. Moved by the desire to see that "faith in God, the first and irreplaceable foundation of every religion", should remain "pure and integral in the German regions", the Pope condemned the errors of National Socialism, stating moreover:

> "Whoever exalts race, or the people, or the State, or a particular form of State, or the depositories of power, or any other fundamental value of the human community – however necessary and honourable be their function in worldly things – whoever raises these notions above their standard value and divinizes them to an idolatrous level, distorts and perverts an order of the world planned and created by God; he is far from the true faith in God and from the concept of life which that faith upholds."[60]

"*Mit brennender Sorge,* for its clarity, its call to the truths of the Christian faith and to their opposition to Nazi neopaganism, for the

---

[58] Cf. l'*Osservatore Romano* of 27 July 1933. "The question may certainly be raised whether the conclusion of the Concordat with the Reich did effectively contribute, as was later stated a number of times, to the Nazi Machtbefestigung (consolidation of power), once it had attained power. It is certain that the Concordat, signed by Pacelli not without anxiety, gave the government of the Church an indisputable legal foundation and at the same time the effective possibility to constantly reproach the German regime, in the subsequent period, with the abuses and violations of peoples' rights." Bukhart Schneider, *Pius XII. Friede, das Werk der Gerechtigkeit*, Göttingen-Zürich-Frankfurt, Münsterschmidt, It. tr. *Pius XII. Pace, opera della giustizia*, (Rome, Edizioni Paoline, 1984), p. 24.

[59] H.-U. Thamer, *Il terzo Reich*, p. 550. With his two pamphlets *To the obscurantists of our time* (1935) and *Protestant pilgrims of Rome* (1937), Rosenberg openly declared the incompatibility between National Socialism and Christianity.

[60] Pius XI, Encyclical *Mit brennender Sorge*, of 14 March 1937, in Igino Giordani, *Le encicliche sociali dei Papi, da Pio IX a Pio XII*, (Rome, Studium, 1944), p. 410, pp. 405-426. The text of the encyclical was secretly sent to hundreds of towns and villages in Germany, where it was printed on the spot and distributed to the various dioceses. On 21 March 1937, in order to give the greatest importance to the event, the German bishops personally read, from the pulpit, the encyclical of Pius XI. On the encyclical cf. Heinz-Albert Raem, *Pius XI. und der Nationalsozialismus. Die Enzyklika "Mit brennender Sorge" vom 14 marz 1937*, Paderborn, Schöningh, 1979.

condemnation of racism and the totalitarian state, caused a violent shock to German and international public opinion. It surprised the Führer and made him explode in abominable anger. But the encyclical had the effect of a threat."[61]

As Pius XII recalled, it

"revealed to the world what National Socialism really was: the proud apostasy from Jesus Christ, the negation of his doctrine and of his redeeming work, the worship of force; idolatry of race and blood, the oppression of human freedom and dignity."[62]

In the resistance to National Socialism in Germany, two prelates especially were noticeable: Konrad von Preysing,[63] bishop of Berlin, and Clemens von Galen,[64] bishop of Münster. Both intervened from their Episcopal seats to defend the Christian idea of the human person and the sovereign rights of God over society and families. During his sermon on 13 July 1941 in the Church of St Lambert in Münster, Bishop von Galen proclaimed:

"I raise my voice and as a German, an honourable citizen, a minister of the Catholic religion, a Catholic bishop, I cry: we demand justice! If this cry goes unheard, it will never be possible to restore the dominion of sovereign justice. Thus our German people and our homeland, in spite of the heroism of our soldiers who achieve glorious victories, will sink because of internal corruption!"[65]

---

[61] Jean Chélini, *L'Eglise sous Pie XII. La tourmente (1939-1945)*, (Paris, Fayard, 1983), p. 87.

[62] Pius XII, Speech of 2 June 1945, in DR, vol VI, p. 70. In this speech Pius XII outlines the situation of this struggle against the Church and of the resistance opposed to it by the Holy See and the German people.

[63] Count Konrad von Preysing, was born in Kronwinckel on 30 August 1880 and died on 21 December 1950 in Berlin. He belonged to a family of the Catholic aristocracy that had always been in the service of the Church. Ordained to the priesthood in 1912, he met the Nuncio Pacelli in Munich. The latter, when he became Secretary of State, had him appointed bishop of Eichstatt in 1932 and then of Berlin on 6 July 1935. From 1933, he appeared as a point of reference for the unbending opponents to National Socialism, in contrast to the "soft" line of Cardinal Adolf Bertram, President of the Episcopal Conference. He was nominated cardinal on 18 February 1946.

[64] Count Clemens August von Galen was born on 16 March 1873 in the castle of Dinkloge, of an old Catholic family of Oldenburg. Ordained to the priesthood in 1904, he was sent to Berlin, and then appointed parish priest of St Lambert in Münster, of which he was appointed Bishop in 1933. From then to 1945, he led a relentless struggle against Nazism, so much so that he won the nickname of the "lion of Münster". Nominated cardinal in the consistory of 18 February 1946, he died immediately after his return from Rome to Münster on 22 March 1946. The diocese of Münster has introduced the cause for his beatification. Cf. *Clemens August Graf von Galen. Un vescovo indesiderabile. Le grandi prediche di sfida al nazismo*, edited by Rosario F. Esposito, Padua, Edizioni Messaggero, 1985; Aa. Vv., *Il leone di Münster e Hitler. Clemens August cardinale von Galen*, edited by Mgr Reinhard Lettmann and Mgr Heinrich Mussinghoff, Roma-Freiburg-Wien, Herder, 1996.

[65] Quoted in *Clemens August Graf von Galen. Un vescovo indesiderabile*, pp. 123-124.

The attitude and tone of these German prelates was admired by Plinio Corrêa de Oliveira who, like them, belonged to the indomitable ranks of the defenders of the faith. Between 1929 and 1947, a total of 2,936 articles against Nazism and Fascism were published in the *Legionário*, of which 447 were by Plinio Corrêa de Oliveira. It is important to emphasise that a large number of these articles appeared not only before the war, but before the encyclical *Mit brennender Sorge*, at a time when there were still many ambiguities about Nazism. Dr Plinio did not see Nazism's anti-religious persecutions as an accidental and extrinsic aspect of the politics of the Third Reich, but rather the logical consequence of a world view antithetical to the Catholic one.

> "The truth is that the anti-religious policy of the Third Reich is one of its essential characteristics, a fundamental aspect of its ideology, indeed, the deeper meaning and the very reason of being of Nazism."[66]

Plinio Corrêa de Oliveira reconstructed what he defined as a "genealogy of monsters", tracing the ideological ancestors of National Socialism from Luther to Hitler.

> "Protestantism produced in Germany an evolving process of philosophical ideas and socio-political facts that, together with liberalism and apparently in conflict with it, begot with an iron-clad logic (that would be correct if its premises were not wrong) Nazism .... Nazism is the result of a profound evolution; its anti-religious policy is integral to its thought, and that thought is so viscerally anti-religious, that I would be less surprised by the conversion of Freemasonry into a pious association than by the transformation of the Nazi Party into a bulwark of Catholic ideals in Eastern Europe."[67]

Plinio Corrêa de Oliveira did not fail to denounce Nazi anti-Semitism,

---

[66] P. Corrêa de Oliveira, "Falsificação", O Legionário, no. 397, 21 April 1940.

[67] P. Corrêa de Oliveira, "Genealogia de monstros", O Legionário, no. 302, 29 June 1938. He adds: "In the overall German panorama, Protestantism inoculated another virus besides liberalism which was that of the theories of strength. These theories (very similar to the democratic idea of the systematic victory of the majorities) are what brought about the whole militaristic and brutal idea of Frederick II's international policy and of many of the Hohenzollern. Afterwards they created the Empire of Bismark, the German passion for militarism, the German philosophical schools of the nineteenth century and, finally, Hitlerism as an arch-type product of Nietzsche's philosophy" (ibid). On the cultural roots of National Socialism, cf. Edmond Vermeil, *Les doctrinaires de la Révolution allemande*, Paris, Nouvelles Editions Latines, 1948; Peter Viereck, *Metapolitics. The roots of the nazi mind*, New York, Capricorn Books, 1961 (1941); G. L. Mosse, *The crisis of German Ideology*, New York, 1964; Nicholas Goodrick-Clarke, *The occult roots of Nazism*, Wellingborough, The Aquarian Press, 1985; Luciano Pellicani, *La società dei giusti. Parabola storica dello gnosticismo rivoluzionario*, (Milan, Etaslibri, 1995), pp. 371–87.

demonstrating its fundamental difference from the cautious measures historically taken by the Church as regards the Jewish people.

"The prudent measures recommended regarding Jews are legitimate and even necessary when the Jew has not converted, or when he converted with the evident intent of 'impressing the bourgeois'. But this caution is directed exclusively at the doctrinal errors of the Jew and not against his race, which is the race in which the Word was made flesh. When he sincerely converts, the Jew is a well-beloved son of the Church."[68]

This being so, the Church established

"with unrelenting energy, that there be no failing in charity toward God's former people. Nazism, on the contrary, treats the Jews with a cruelty that is at the same time brutal and useless."[69] "A new Saint Bernard is needed in Germany to invoke for the people of Israel the mercy that not even its great victim refused to give it."[70]

7. Loyalty to the Church and intellectual independence

On 19 March 1937, three days after *Mit brennender Sorge*, Pius XI also solemnly condemned Communism with the encyclical *Divini Redemptoris*. Next to National Socialism, Communism was the other great enemy constantly denounced by *Legionário*, especially after the civil war in Spain[71] had shown the world its true face, arousing a "flame of hate" and of "ferocious persecution".[72]

"The contention in Spain is whether the world should be ruled by Jesus Christ or by Karl Marx. The whole of Catholic civilization,

---

[68] P. Corrêa de Oliveira, "Uma velha ambição dos Judeus", O Legionário, no. 308, 7 August 1938.

[69] P. Corrêa de Oliveira, "7 dias em revista", O Legionário, no. 232, 21 February 1937.

[70] P. Corrêa de Oliveira, "7 dias em revista", O Legionário, no. 215, 25 October 1936. In other articles he shows how the anti-Semitic persecutions of Hitler contributed indirectly but powerfully to the realization of the Zionist dream. "What those behind Zionism did not obtain, Hitler did with his anti-Semitic campaign which was to populate Tel-Aviv, the new Hebrew city of Palestine that is now improved and very comfortable. Hitler filled the 'national home' of the Jews." ID., "7 dias em revista", O Legionário, no. 599, 30 January 1944.

[71] On the Spanish civil war, cf. Léon de Poncins, *Histoire secrète de la Révolution espagnole*, Paris, G. Beauchesne, 1938; José M. Sanchez, *The Spanish civil war as a Religious tragedy*, Notre Dame (Indiana), University of Notre Dame Press, 1987; Mario Tedeschi (care of), *Chiesa Cattolica e guerra civile in Spagna*, Naples, Guida, 1989; Javier Tusell, Genoveva Garcia Queipo de Llano, *El catolicismo mundial y la guerra de España*, Madrid, BAC, 1992.

[72] Pius XI, Address to Spanish refugees of 14 September 1936, in IP, vol. V (1958), *La pace internazionale*, p. 223.

all the principles of morality, all the traditions, all the institutions the West holds dear, will irremediably disappear if communism wins."[73]

"A day will come when, standing on the ruins of Hitlerism, of communism, of Mexican Obregonism, we will triumphantly ask: 'Calles, Hitler, Lenin, Stalin, Lunatcharski, where are you?' And only the silence of the tombs will answer us."[74]

Plinio Corrêa de Oliveira's criticism of totalitarianism was quite different however from the individualistic and liberal criticism that shared in the same errors it claimed to denounce. Liberalism, in full decline, could never have been an authentic alternative to Nazism or Communism.

"Both the liberal error of giving freedom to evil as to good, and the totalitarian error of oppressing good and evil are grave and have the same root. In the presence of the Truth which is the Church, both the liberal State and the totalitarian State assume the attitude of Pilate, asking *'quid est veritas'* – 'What is truth?' Agnosticism, indifferentism between truth and error, good and evil, is always a source of injustice. Catholics cannot come to terms neither with one nor the other."[75]

"Whoever exaggerates the role of the State will necessarily be a socialist, whatever the masks he tries to cover his face with. And at the bottom of the socialist slope is communism.

"Whoever exaggerates the rights of the individual or of other groups will necessarily be an individualist, and at the bottom of that slope is anarchy.

"We should free ourselves from complete anarchy (nihilism) or from the stable and organized anarchy that is totalitarianism by forming for ourselves a vigorous and firm Catholic conscience, where there is no place for complacency toward errors of any kind."[76]

"Catholics should be anticommunist, anti-Nazi, anti-liberal, anti-socialist, anti-masonic, etc... simply because they are Catholics."[77]

---

[73] P. Corrêa de Oliveira, "Reflexões em torno da Revolução Hespanhola", O Legionário, no. 224, 27 December 1936.

[74] P. Corrêa de Oliveira, "À margem dos factos", O Legionário, no. 187, 22 December 1935.

[75] P. Corrêa de Oliveira, "A liberdade da Igreja no dia de amanhã", O Legionário, no. 549, 14 February 1943.

[76] P. Corrêa de Oliveira, "Comunismo", O Legionário, no. 552, 7 March 1943.

[77] P. Corrêa de Oliveira, "Pela grandeza e libertade da Ação Católica", O Legionário, no. 331, 13 January 1939.

In Brazil, the "integralist" movement, founded by Plinio Salgado, had begun to develop as of 1933.[78] With its "green shirts" it imitated the troops of European Fascism. Basing themselves on the premise that "the human spirit progresses at the rhythm of revolutions", its leader defined its conception as "integral total revolution"[79] and proposed a reorganization of Brazil based on the model of a trade association-corporatist State similar to that of Mussolini.

Integralism, which claimed to be anti-Communist and anti-liberal, had a fundamental agnosticism in common with liberalism.[80] "Integralism, then, is neither Catholic nor anti-Catholic. It is theist, viewing all religions through a supposedly neutral prism."[81] Faced with what even then he defined as the "false right", Plinio Corrêa de Oliveira repeated that the only solution was authentic Catholicism.[82]

He expressed a similarly negative judgement with regard to Fascism which had by then in Brazil, even among the Catholics and the clergy itself, a great number of supporters and sympathisers. Even if, in 1929, Pius XI had signed the Lateran Pacts with Mussolini, in his encyclical *Non abbiamo bisogno,* dated 29 June 1931,[83] the Pope openly criticized the totalitarian tendencies of the regime and declared as unlawful the oath of loyalty to the Duce and to the "Fascist Revolution". The criticisms by Plinio Corrêa de Oliveira of the statist

---

[78] Plinio Salgado (1895–1975), after being fascinated in his youth by historical materialism and by the Bismarck model, in the 1920s he participated in the "aesthetic revolution" of modernism, making a name for himself as a novelist and man of letters with Nationalist leanings. Elected congressman of the State of São Paulo in 1928, in 1930 he supported the candidacy of Julio Prestes against Getúlio Vargas. After having distributed a *Manifesto da Legião Revolucionária* (1931), he founded, at the beginning of 1932, the Sociedade de Estudos Políticos (SEP) and in October of the same year the Brazilian "integralist movement" (AIB) of which he was "national head" until its dissolution, by Vargas, on 2 December 1937. Exiled in Portugal from 1939 to 1945, upon his return to Brazil he entered political life, without ever reaching the important role that he would have desired. Cf. the term *Salgado* by Paulo Brandi, Leda Soares, in DHBB, vol. IV, pp. 3051–61. On integralism cf. also Helgio Trindade, *Integralismo. O fascismo brasileiro na década de 30*, 2nd edn., São Paulo, Difel, 1979; ID., *La tentative fasciste au Brésil dans les années trente*, Paris, Editions de la Maison des Sciences de l'Homme, 1988; ID., term *Integralismo*, in DHBB, vol. II, pp. 1621–8.

[79] H. Trindade, term *Integralismo*, p. 1624.

[80] P. Corrêa de Oliveira, "E porque não o Catolicismo?", O Legionário, no. 189, 19 January 1936; ID., "A margem de uma crítica", O Legionário, no. 153, 2 September 1934. "Different from the liberal State, the integralist State 'affirms the spirit'. Nevertheless, it does not dare to break all at once with the worst of liberal presuppositions that is official agnosticism" (ibid). Cf. also "Três rumos ...", O Legionário, no. 157, 28 October 1934; "Extremismos", O Legionário, no. 160, 9 December 1934.

[81] P. Corrêa de Oliveira, "Na expectativa", O Legionário, no. 206, 23 August 1936.

[82] P. Corrêa de Oliveira, "E porque não o Catolicismo?"

[83] Pius XI, Encyclical *Non abbiamo bisogno* of 29 June 1931 in I. Giordani, *Le encicliche sociali dei Papi*, quote, pp. 353–74. Cf. also Pietro Scoppola, *La Chiesa e il fascismo. Documenti e interpretazioni*, (Bari, Laterza, 1971), pp. 264–70; Gianni Vannoni, *Massoneria, Fascismo e Chiesa cattolica*, Roma-Bari, Laterza, 1979.

doctrine of the Fascist regime were similar to those of the Pope.[84] He however pointed out that "in practice Mussolini departed from it more than once"[85] and that "one of his great merits"[86] was to be found in this detachment, as happened with the signing of the Lateran Pacts.[87]

From as early as 1937, he observed, with increasing anxiety, the progressive radicalization and decline of Fascism towards Nazism,[88] which had been restrained, up to then, in its totalitarian tendency, by the presence of the Monarchy and, above all, by that of the Papacy. Dr Plinio's criticisms caused a certain reaction among the Catholics of Italian descent residing in Brazil, who perceived these articles to be an attack on their country.[89] His response to these objectors was:

> *"Legionário* will always be on the side of the Pope. For this very reason, it will never be against Italy. Because the cause of the authentic Italy, the Italy of Dante, of Saint Francis of Assisi and of Saint Thomas, can never be separated from the cause of the Papacy."[90]

Today it is not easy to understand the importance of the intellectual independence of Plinio Corrêa de Oliveira, in comparison to the conformism of those whom Jean-Louis Loubet del Bayle referred to in one of his books as "the nonconformists of the 30s",[91] at a time

---

[84] P. Corrêa de Oliveira, "Mussolini", O Legionário, no. 241, 25 April 1937; "Mussolini e o nazismo", O Legionário, no. 296, 15 May 1938.

[85] P. Corrêa de Oliveira, "Mussolini". Plinio Corrêa de Oliveira's distinction between the doctrine and practice of Fascism seems to me to have a certain analogy with that of the historian Renzo De Felice between "Fascism as a regime" and "Fascism as a movement". "Fascism as a regime made the concordat with the Church, but fascism as a movement was anticlerical, and put itself against the most profound values of Christianity." (R. De Felice, *Fascism. An informal introduction to its theory and practice*, edited by Michael A. Ledeen, (New Brunswick (N.J.), Transaction, 1976), p. 105. Also be De Felice, cf. the monumental biography of Mussolini, especially the volumes devoted to *Mussolini il Duce* (Turin, Einaudi, 1974–6). And, in English, *Interpretations of fascism*, translated by Brenda Huff Everett, London, Harvard University Press, 1977.

[86] P. Corrêa de Oliveira, "Mussolini".

[87] On the Lateran Pacts cf. P. Corrêa de Oliveira, "Fides Intrepida", O Legionário, no. 50, 12 January 1930; Date a Cesare, no. 52 (9 February 1930); "No X.· anniversario do tratado de Latrão", O Legionário, no. 335, 12 February 1939. "Fascism was a very bad regime. The Lateran Treaty brought about invaluable results for the Church and for Italy" (P. Corrêa de Oliveira, "A Questão romana", O Legionário, no. 603, 27 February 1944).

[88] P. Corrêa de Oliveira, "A Itália em via de ser nazificada?", O Legionário, no. 306, 24 July 1938; "Para onde caminha o fascismo?", O Legionário, no. 308, 7 August 1938; "Ainda o fascismo", no. 330, 8 January 1939.

[89] On 27 January 1939 Count Rodolfo Crespi died in São Paulo. He desired to be buried in a black shirt and he left 500,000 cruzeiros to Mussolini.

[90] P. Corrêa de Oliveira, "O exemplo dos russos brancos", O Legionário, no. 322, 22 January 1939.

[91] Jean-Louis Loubet del Bayle, *Les non-conformistes des années 30*, Paris, Editions du Seuil, 1969. Cf. also R. Rémond, *Les catholiques dans la France des années 30*, Paris, Editions Cana, 1979.

when the European intelligentsia allowed itself to be attracted by the red star of the Kremlin or by the "immense red Fascism" sung by Robert Brasillach.[92] On the left, the glories of Soviet Humanism were celebrated by the French Romain Rolland, Louis Aragon, André Malraux, André Gide, the Germans Heinrich Mann and Bertolt Brecht, the English Aldous Huxley and E. M. Forster.[93] Other famous intellectuals such as Giovanni Gentile, Ezra Pound, Pierre Drieu-La Rochelle, Carl Schmitt, Martin Heidegger took the side of Fascism and Nazism.

8. You chose shame and you will have war

1938 was the crucial year for the European crisis. The 11 March saw the invasion of Austria and its annexation to Germany, an event that went down in history under the name of *Anschluss*. This was the first action of the Second World War.[94]

With the *Anschluss* the Austrian State was practically erased from the European map.[95] With "an indignant soul and a bleeding heart", Plinio Corrêa de Oliveira denounced, in a five-column article on the front page, the "dramatic disappearance of Catholic Austria from the map of Europe".[96]

---

[92] Bernard George, *Brasillach*, (Paris, Editions Universitaires, 1968), pp. 99–100.

[93] Cf. F. Furet, *Le passé d'une illusion*, pp. 189-364.

[94] Cf. Gordon Brook Shepherd, *Anschluss. The rape of Austria*, London, Macmillan & Co., 1963; Andreas Hillgruber, *Die Zerstörung Europas. Beitrage zur Weltkriegsepoche 1914 bis 1945*, Berlin, Propyläen Verlag, 1988, It. tr. *La distruzione dell'Europa*, (Bologna, Il Mulino, 1991), pp. 133-52. Decisive in the *Anschluss* was the role of the ambassador to Vienna, Franz von Papen (1879-1969) who already in 1933 had opened the way to power for Hitler with his pressure on Hindenburg. Papen, who declared himself a Catholic, was defined by Plinio Corrêa de Oliveira as "the greatest traitor of the Church in our days" (P. Corrêa de Oliveira, "7 dias em revista", O Legionário, no. 516, 2 August 1942). An historical confirmation from Richard W. Rolfs, *The sorcerer's apprentice: the life of Franz von Papen*, London-New York, Lanham, 1996.

[95] "Austria, poor Austria eternally mocked – noted Count Friedrich Reck-Mallenczewen on 20 March 1938 in his diary – whose only mistake was undoubtedly that of opposing the dominating spirit of the great Prussia, preserving to the end the memory of the old Roman-German Holy Roman Empire." *Tagesbuch eines Verzweifelten*, Stuttgart, Henry Goverts Verlag, 1966, it. tr. *Il tempo dell'odio e della vergogna*, (Milan, Rusconi, 1970), p. 66.

[96] P. Corrêa de Oliveira, "A conjuração dos Cesares e do synhedrio", O Legionário, no. 288, 20 March 1938. Plinio Corrêa de Oliveira thus expressed his admiration for Zita of Austria (1892-1989), the wife of the last emperor Karl "She knew what to do in favour of the cause of Monarchy in Europe, to which she was dedicated out of pure idealism and not out of vulgar interest, much more than innumerable sovereigns, ex-sovereigns or heir-apparents throughout the whole world. In this century of gross materialism, she is an energetic and idealistic figure who deserves the greatest respect from every observer" (P. Corrêa de Oliveira, "O destino trágico de duas grandes dynastías", O Legionário, no. 247, 6 June 1937). On Zita, cf. now G. B. Shepherd, *The last Empress*, London, Harper Collins Publishers, 1991.

Mussolini, reversing his 1934 stand, when, to avoid the annexation of Austria, he had sent Alpine divisions to the Brenner border, this time approved Hitler's action. In celebration of Italian-German friendship, the Führer made an official visit to Italy from 3 to 9 May 1938. On that occasion, Pius XI retired to Castelgandolfo, out of season, to avoid taking part. He stated, "on the day of the Holy Cross", the triumph "of another cross that is not the Cross of Christ".[97]

In number 289 of the *Legionário* of 27 March 1938, the first page showed a picture of the Colosseum with the news that the great monument would be illuminated in honour of Hitler's visit to Rome. The caption reads:

"The Coliseum's multi-secular witness to the martyrdom of early Christians and to the insatiable cruelty of paganism will be illuminated in honour of today's illustrious persecutor of Christians and the restorer of paganism in Germany. It will be lit up in red!"

On the 12 September 1938, after the annexation of Austria, it was the turn of the Sudetenland. To avoid things coming to a head, the British Prime Minister, Neville Chamberlain, went personally to Berchtesgaden, to come to an agreement with the Führer. Plinio Corrêa de Oliveira had no illusions. He wrote: "War is a matter of days, or of months, but unfortunately it will explode.... As long as Hitler is in power, it will be inevitable".[98]

To avoid a worsening of the situation, Mussolini proposed, *in extremis,* a four-party conference, which was held in Munich on the 29 and 30 September 1938.[99] The Western democracies represented by England's Chamberlain and by France's Daladier, in the vain hope of avoiding war, sought a compromise with Nazi Germany at any cost.[100] Famous are the words with which Churchill, the head of the Conservative internal opposition, apostrophized Chamberlain: "You had to choose between shame and war: you chose shame and you will have war."

---

[97] M. Maccarrone, *Il Nazionalsocialismo e la Santa Sede*, pp. 211–12.

[98] P. Corrêa de Oliveira, "O verdadeiro sentido do vôo de Chamberlain", O Legionário, no. 314, 18 September 1938.

[99] On the conference of Munich and on "appeasement", cf. Martin Gilbert, *The roots of Appeasement*, London, Weidenfeld and Nicolson, 1966; Charles Loch Mowat, *Britain between the wars, 1918–1940*, London, Methuen & Co. Ltd., 1976; Telford Taylor, *Munich, the price of peace*, London, Hodder and Stoughton, 1979; R.A.C. Parker, *Chamberlain and Appeasement*, New York, St. Martin's Press, 1993.

[100] "France and England could not have been more humiliated. They drank the chalice until the last drop. And when they were told that if they drank just a few more drops they would obtain peace, they wept with joy." P. Corrêa de Oliveira, "Os fructos ideológicos da paz", O Legionário, no. 316, 2 October 1938.

In a brilliant article of the 1970s on détente, Plinio Corrêa de Oliveira thus recalls the event:

"Munich was not just a great episode in the history of this century. It is a symbolic event in the history of all time: at any time and in any place there is a diplomatic confrontation between raving warmongers and raving pacifists, advantage will smile on the former and frustration on the latter. And if there is a lucid person, he will blame the Chamberlains and Daladiers of the future with the words of Churchill: 'You had to choose between shame and war: you chose shame and you will have war'."[101]

Less than six months later, on 15 March 1939, violating the agreements made, Hitler invaded Czechoslovakia and incorporated into the Reich the territories of Bohemia and Moravia for which he established a "protectorate". Thus the Czechoslovak Republic, one of the creations of the Peace of Versailles, also disappeared from the map of Europe. The previous month, Pius XI, already seriously ill, died. On 2 March 1939, Cardinal Camillo Caccia Dominioni announced from the central loggia of St Peter's Basilica the election of the new Pope, Cardinal Eugenio Pacelli, with the name of Pius XII.[102]

That year began with a surprising forecast from Plinio Corrêa de Oliveira. It appeared in the first issue of the year of the *Legionário*:

"In fact, while all the battle fields are being marked out, an increasingly clear process is taking place: that of the doctrinal fusion between Nazism and Communism. In our opinion, the year 1939 will see the achievement of this fusion."[103]

Some months later, in August 1939, the announcement of the so-called Ribbentrop-Molotov agreement "had the immediate effect of a real bomb on European public opinion, amazed by this sudden agreement between the two countries that represented the two ideologies that were up to then the most hostile."[104]

---

[101] P. Corrêa de Oliveira, "Churchill, o avestuz e a America do Sul", Folha de S. Paulo, 31 January 1971.

[102] On Pius XII (1876–1958) in relation to the themes we have dealt with, cf. Cardinal Domenico Tardini, *Pio XII*, Vatican City, Tipografia Poliglotta Vaticana, 1960; B. Schneider, *Pio XII. Pace, opera della giustizia.*; A. Rhodes, *The Vatican in the Age of Dictators.*; J. Chélini, *L'Eglise sous Pie XII.*; G. Martina, *Storia della Chiesa*, vol. IV, *L'età contemporanea*, pp. 219-47; Giorgio Angelozzi Gariboldi, *Pio XII, Hitler e Mussolini. Il Vaticano fra le dittature*, Milan, Mursia, 1995. Cardinal Eugenio Pacelli had been Nuncio in Germany (1917–29) and then Secretary of State (1930–9) before ascending to the Papal throne.

[103] P. Corrêa de Oliveira, "Entre o passado e o futuro", O Legionário, no. 329, 4 January 1939. "Nazism — he had insisted on 8 May 1938 — from an international point of view can almost be compared to communism. And even so this 'almost' is a big problem", ID., "Legitima defesa", O Legionário, no. 295, 8 May 1938.

[104] J. Guiffan, *Histoire de l'Europe*, p. 195.

The non-aggression treaty between Russia and Germany marked the most unexpected "reversal of alliances" of our time. The German historian Andreas Hillgruber wrote:

"Nobody who consciously lived that experience can forget what surprise and bewilderment, what a shock was provoked by a brief announcement of the 'German Information Office' in the late evening of 21 August, and confirmed the following day by Tass: 'The government of the Reich and the Soviet government have agreed to draw up a reciprocal pact of non-aggression. The Minister for Foreign Affairs, Ribbentrop, will arrive in Moscow on Wednesday 23 August to conclude the negotiations.'"[105]

9. "The most enigmatic war of this century"

Plinio Corrêa de Oliveira had written as early as 1936: "Shortly, only the blind can contest it, there will be an international deluge: world war is knocking at the doors of Western civilization."[106] At the beginning of 1939, in the *Legionário* he drew a dramatic picture of the international events. "In this angry sea sails the mystical Bark of Saint Peter. Against it, mysterious wave movements are forming. They will quickly degenerate into an immense storm."[107]

On 1 September 1939, after the Polish refusal to give Hitler the Danzig "corridor", the German army invaded Poland. In his "Nota internacional" of 3 September, Plinio Corrêa de Oliveira commented on the event with these words:

"Everything leads to the belief that war was decided on not by a simple non-aggression pact but by a secret accord between Russia and the Reich, from which will probably result the partition of Poland. Thus, the sides seem to be defining themselves as they were always seen by those who knew how to see: the close ideological proximity between Nazism and communism, translated into

---

[105] A. Hillgruber, *La distruzione dell'Europa*, p. 257. The "non-aggression" agreement was valid for a period of ten years and it committed the two contracting parties to refrain from any 'mutual attack'. Attached to this was a secret protocol which left Hitler free to attack Poland, leaving the USSR to control the three Baltic countries, Finland, Poland and Bessarabia. Cf. Walther Hofer, *Die Entfesselung des Zweiten Weltkrieges*, (Frankfurt a. Main, S. Fischer, 1964), pp. 165 sgg.; Gerhard L. Weinberg, *Germany and the Soviet Union, 1939–1941*, Leiden, Brill, 1972; Arturo Peregalli, *Il Patto Hitler-Stalin e la spartizione della Polonia*, Rome, Erre Emme Edizioni, 1989; Juan Gonzalo Larrain Campbell, "1939: o Pacto Ribbentrop-Molotov confirmou as denúncias do *Legionário*", Catolicismo, no. 532, April 1995, pp. 22-4.
[106] P. Corrêa de Oliveira, "Unidade nacional", O Legionário, no. 219, 22 November 1936.
[107] P. Corrêa de Oliveira, "Ainda o fascismo", O Legionário, no. 330, 8 January 1939.

a positive military alliance against civilization and peace. It is war that begins, with all its hideous cortege of death, misery and suffering, to attempt to impose on Europe a lord who is the antithesis of Catholic civilization, and the product of a centuries-long series of errors, the materialization of error against the Truth."[108]

On that same 3 September, Great Britain and France declared war on Germany. The Second World War, which Plinio Corrêa de Oliveira in a five-column article in the *Legionário* defined "The most enigmatic war of our century"[109] had begun. The enigma was contained in the veil of apparent contradictions with which "the dark forces of evil"[110] covered their manoeuvres to destroy what was still left of Christian civilization. Plinio Corrêa de Oliveira's intention continued to be that of revealing with acuity of vision the *mysterium iniquitatis* which was unravelling itself in the history of his time.

The first months of the conflict saw the fulminating advance of Germany which occupied Poland, Denmark, Norway, Holland, Belgium, and France. On 10 June 1940, on the eve of the entrance of the German troops into Paris and of the armistice between Hitler and Pétain,[111] Mussolini entered the war on the side of the Reich. Meanwhile in England, on 10 May 1940 Chamberlain had resigned and had been replaced as Prime Minister by Winston Churchill. The new head of the government promised the British people "blood, toil, tears and sweat" until the final victory, while declaring at Admiralty House:

"I would say to the House, as I said to those who have joined this Government: 'I have nothing to offer but blood, toil, tears and sweat'. (...) You ask, what is our policy? I will say: it is to wage war, by sea, land and air, with all our might and with all the strength that God can give us; to wage war against a monstrous tyranny, never surpassed in the dark, lamentable catalogue of human crime. That is our policy. You ask, what is our aim? I can

---

[108] P. Corrêa de Oliveira, "Nota internacional", O Legionário, no. 364, 3 September 1939; cf. also ID., "Ao celebrarmos o advento da Paz, não nos esqueçamos da lição que encerra esta guerra", O Legionário, no. 666, 13 May 1945.

[109] P. Corrêa de Oliveira, "A guerra mas enigmática de nosso seculo", O Legionário, no. 381, 31 December 1939. On the Second World War, cf. the classic works of Winston S. Churchill, *The Second World War*, 6 vols., London, Cassell, 1948–54, Alan John P. Taylor, *The origins of the Second World War*, London, Hamish Hamilton, 1961.

[110] Pius XII, Address to the Sacred College of 24 December 1946, in IP, *La pace internazionale*, p. 469.

[111] "We do not understand how one can desire the Reign of Christ in France while at the same time supporting, with brotherly solicitude those who insult, vilify and persecute Our Lord Jesus Christ in Germany. One cannot be a friend of St Peter and of Herod at the same time." P. Corrêa de Oliveira, "As máscaras cairam", O Legionário, no. 504, 10 May 1942.

answer in one word: It is victory, victory at all costs, victory in spite of all terror, victory, however long and hard the road may be; for without victory, there is no survival."[112]

Plinio Corrêa de Oliveira always admired the figure of Churchill, a Protestant, but strong in character and steadfast in his ideas, while the common trait of the Catholic politicians of the time seemed to be willingness to "compromise" and to collaborate with the enemy.[113]

At the end of June 1940, Churchill, having rejected all peace proposals, faced the Battle of Britain, launched by the Führer to break the English people. Already in the month of October the obstinacy of the British resistance forced Hitler to renounce his project.[114] The German hope to conclude the *blitzkrieg* disappeared with the same speed with which it had begun. Europe was however under the heel of the Führer who announced the creation of his millenary "new order". The map of Europe in 1941 seemed to confirm his dreams: in the form of annexed, "protected", collaborating or satellite States, the majority of the European nations by now moved in the orbit of the Third Reich.

For the Catholic Church, this was a radically new situation which, as has been observed, had an analogous precedent only during the Napoleonic expansion.[115] There was talk of the possibility of a Nazi invasion of the Vatican and of the deportation of the Pontiff.[116] The "silence" with regard to Nazism of which Pius XII has been accused, was not born however from this fear, but from that of causing by a solemn protest from him even more ruthless reactions against Catholics and the Jews themselves.[117] The Pope invoked his vocation as moral judge derived from his spiritual Magisterium. The Lateran Pacts, which in art. 24 guaranteed the neutrality and inviolability of

---

[112] Quote in M. Gilbert, *Finest hour. Winston S. Churchill, 1939–1941*, (London, Heinemann, 1983), p. 333.

[113] Cf. for example P. Corrêa de Oliveira, "Quisling, Mosley & C.", O Legionário, no. 396, 14 April 1940 where he criticizes the "great international consortium Quisling, Mosley, Degrelle, Seyss-Inquart & Co.".

[114] "During the war — Pius XII stated — the English people put up with more than what was humanly possible." Pius XII, Address to the new Minister of Great Britain on 30 June 1947, in DR, vol. IX, p. 137.

[115] J. Chélini, *L'Eglise sous Pie XII*, pp. 121–2.

[116] Cf. G. Angelozzi Gariboldi, *Pio XII, Hitler e Mussolini*, pp. 193–4. At the time that Italy entered the war, there was talk of a voluntary exile of Pius XII in a neutral country, to safeguard the independence of his mission as head of the Church. The archbishop of New York, The Most Rev Francis Joseph Spellman, had even suggested that the Pope could take refuge in a country of Latin America and, according to Giorgio Angelozzi Gariboldi, "the name of Brazil was mentioned" (ibid, p. 113).

[117] G. Angelozzi Gariboldi, *op. cit.*, pp. 148–149; A. Rhodes, *Il Vaticano e le dittature*, pp. 347–62.

the Vatican City, offered him a freedom of action which none of his immediate predecessors had been able to enjoy.

"Whose side is the Pope on?" Plinio Corrêa de Oliveira replied in the *Legionário* to this question heard so many times. The Pope is the Vicar of Our Lord Jesus Christ, the infallible teacher of Truth, the sovereign of a spiritual and indestructible kingdom: "Supreme hierarch of the whole universe, the Holy Father represents everything that is divine, supernatural, immutable, eternal".[118] The Pope therefore has neither "allies" nor "enemies". The Pope is not on Hitler's side, nor on that of Stalin. "The Pope is on the side of Jesus Christ, on the side of indefectability, of eternity. It is the Pope who will win."[119]

During the war, Plinio Corrêa de Oliveira sorrowfully commented on the bombardments of the Eternal City, the seat of the Vicar of Christ,[120] and he repeatedly expressed his solidarity with the Pope and the Holy See.

"If the Pope suffers, we should suffer with him, we should fight for him, we should pray for him. On the threshold of 1944, let us form the resolution to shine more than ever in filial and enthusiastic devotion to the Supreme Pontiff."[121]

10. The obscure complicity between Nazism and Communism

The day after the Molotov-Ribbentrop pact, which Plinio Corrêa de Oliveira had clearly forecast, he had put forward another disconcerting prediction: "the Russian-German alliance was a clumsy act. It is possible that within a short time Hitler and Stalin will return to being enemies, to impress the bourgeois and to divert public opinion."[122] On 18 May 1941 he renewed his prediction in the *Legionário*:

---

[118] P. Corrêa de Oliveira, "Com quem está o Papa?", O Legionário, no. 589, 21 November 1943. Cf. also ID., "Pastor Angelicus", O Legionário, no. 568, 27 June 1943. "Our position between two opposing fields – states Pius XII in the Christmas Radiomessage of 24 December 1947 – is averse to any consideration of a temporal nature. To be with Christ or against Christ: this is the whole question". Pius XII, in DR, vol. IX, p. 394.

[119] P. Corrêa de Oliveira, "Com quem está o Papa?" Cf. also ID., "7 dias em revista", O Legionário, no. 541, 20 December 1942.

[120] Cf. P. Corrêa de Oliveira, "O bombardamento de Roma", no. 572, 25 July 1943; ID., "7 dias em revista", O Legionário, no. 597, 16 January 1944. On the occasion of Christmas 1944, he published various articles commenting on the Message of Pius XII. P. Corrêa de Oliveira, "A mensagem de Natal", O Legionário, no. 647, 31 December 1944, no. 648, 7 January 1945, no. 649, 14 January 1945, no. 651, 28 January 1945.

[121] P. Corrêa de Oliveira, "7 dias em revista", O Legionário, no. 595, 1 January 1944.

[122] P. Corrêa de Oliveira, "Anti Komitern!", O Legionário, no. 363, 27 August 1939.

"As everyone can see, the Russian-German collaboration is reaching its peak, because of the active intervention of Russia next to Germany in Asian politics. The *Legionário* had already some time ago forecast what is happening now. But just now, when this collaboration seems to have reached its zenith, we dare to add for our readers something that will surely surprise them: at the point at which these relations now stand, it is possible that they may last for a long time just as it is possible that Germany could suddenly attack Russia, without any of this confuting the reality of the Nazi-Communist symbiosis. Whoever lives will see."[123]

A month later, on 22 June, with "Operation Barbarossa", Hitler opened a sudden offensive against Soviet Russia, convinced that he would liquidate it in a few weeks, after which he would throw himself against England with all his forces. Meanwhile the United States was involved in the lightning Japanese attack on Pearl Harbour on 6 December 1941. The conflict thus began to be "world-wide" and in August of 1942 Brazil also joined the war on the side of the allies.[124] Plinio Corrêa de Oliveira expressed the only authentic significance that the intervention of his country could have:

"Brazil will obtain victory if it fights with cross in hand. This is the sign with which we will win. (...) Let us not fight to kill: we fight and kill in order to live. And, in order to live, we must continue a burning struggle against everything in Brazil which could bring about de-christianization.[125] Brazil will only be genuinely Christian, if it be Roman, Catholic, Apostolic. And, therefore, our civilization will only continue to be Christian if Brazil continues within the fold of Holy Mother Church."[126]

In 1942, the Anglo-American landings on the Moroccan and Algerian coast marked an important success for Churchill who had opposed, in spite of Stalin's insistence, opening another front in Europe.[127] The Italo-German forces were forced to surrender in Tunis and the Anglo-Americans prepared for the new landings in Sicily, which resulted in the fall of Fascism on 25 July 1943. Italy, which had become a battle-field after the armistice of 8 September, split in half. A new ground offensive was needed to beat Germany. Not trusting the Russians,

---

[123] P. Corrêa de Oliveira, "7 dias em revista", O Legionário, no. 453, 18 May 1941.
[124] Brazil was the only Latin American country (except for Mexico which, however, only took part in air operations) to take part directly in the war, by sending a contingent to Italy of 20–25,000 men attached to the United States Fifth Army.
[125] P. Corrêa de Oliveira, "Guerra!", O Legionário, no. 520, 30 August 1942.
[126] P. Corrêa de Oliveira, "Civilisação Cristã", O Legionário, no. 546, 24 January 1943.
[127] J. Guiffan, *Histoire de l'Europe*, p. 217.

Churchill's proposals requesting landings in the Balkans were not listened to this time. On 6 June 1944 the allied landings took place on the Normandy coast.

In the progress of the war, Plinio Corrêa de Oliveira saw the confirmation of the old thesis of the *Legionário* on the ambiguous relationship that bound the two enemy-brothers: National Socialist Germany and Communist Russia. In this relationship he saw a link that went far beyond a convergence of political or diplomatic interests, but touched the very core of the great question of the twentieth century: the moral struggle between the Catholic Church and its enemies animated by a mortal hate towards Christian civilization. "We have only one option: Christ the King or the Antichrist. And for us, the Antichrist is nazism as much as it is communism."[128]

When, at the beginning of 1944 in Russia, in the Balkans, in Italy, the German army is forced to retreat and Hitler's defeat seems by now irreversible, Plinio Corrêa de Oliveira emphasizes how, faced with the impossibility of victory, Hitler tried to open the road to the Soviets rather than to the Western allies.

"This paladin of anti-communism prefers Russian expansion to Anglo-American, as an outcome of the war he cannot win. So much so that, in spite of losing immense ground in Russia as well as whole armies, he prefers this to removing immobilized troops in the European zone who await a second onslaught. Each inch Hitler loses in Russia is, in part, due to his maintaining troops in Western Europe that delay the opening of a second front. In other words, faced with two adversaries, it is up to him to choose between the advance of one or the other. He chose the communist advance, and, thus, remains in total control of the Western front where everything is quiet, and defends — inch by inch no doubt — the Eastern front in the measure possible. Let us take this conclusion: Hitler prefers the advance of Russia to the Anglo-American coalition. Defeated, he tries to influence the configuration of tomorrow's world. This is his ultimate crime."[129]

As the war continued, the propaganda of the left tried to emphasize throughout the world the anti-Nazi role of Stalin and of Soviet Russia to show it as the "liberator" of Western Europe. Plinio Corrêa de Oliveira observed that, while the Allies got bogged down in Italy, the USSR spread out over the eastern front, extending its influence over central Europe. The Nazis defended Italy inch by inch, while aban-

---

[128] P. Corrêa de Oliveira, "7 dias em revista", O Legionário, no. 519, 23 August 1942.
[129] P. Corrêa de Oliveira, "O santo do diabo", O Legionário, no. 601, 13 February 1944.

doning entire provinces in central Europe to the Russians. Nazism "is committing the supreme treason of slowly surrendering Europe to the bolcheviks."[130]

While the Red Army advanced towards the Bay of Riga and the confines of East Prussia, in December 1944 Hitler launched the Ardennes offensive against the West.[131] All available reserves were transferred to the Eifel, without worrying about weakening the eastern front. On 12 January 1945, the Soviet war machine routed the German army between the Memel and the Carpathians and in three weeks it spread as far as the Oder.[132]

> "While the nazi debacle continues" observed Dr Plinio "we stress an important aspect of the military operations. The nazis, ever faithful in their sympathy towards communism, defend the Eastern front much less than the Western or Southern front. This has brought about a series of 'triumphs' that augment the Soviets prestige with the bystanders while the brave Anglo-American soldiers advance under veritable machinegun fire in northern France or central Italy."[133]

In February 1945 Stalin, Roosevelt and Churchill met in Yalta. Invaded on two sides, the Third Reich surrendered between 7 and 8 May, while Hitler committed suicide in his bunker in Berlin. After the two American atomic bombs had been dropped on Hiroshima and Nagasaki in August, Japan, having reached the end of its resources, also surrendered.

The Second World War lasted exactly six years, from the German invasion of Poland on 1 September 1939 to the Japanese surrender on 2 September 1945. Like the First World War, the Second too was an ideological and revolutionary war, whose ultimate aim, apart from the opposing fronts, was, as Plinio Corrêa de Oliveira had foreseen, a violent attack on Christian values and institutions. The Brazilian leader insists on 13 May 1945 in the *Legionário*:

> "This war was, moreover, an ideological fight, in which Catholic opinion was pressed between the pincers of a terrible dilemma: either nazism or communism. Our Lady, 'who crushed all the heresies around the world', wished one of the points be broken in the

---

[130] P. Corrêa de Oliveira, "O discurso de Churchill", O Legionário, no. 617, 4 June 1944.

[131] When General Guderian warned Hitler of the threatening Soviet preparations on the Vistula, the Führer resolutely refused the suggestion to suspend the counter-attack. Basil H. Liddell Hart, *Storia militare della seconda guerra mondiale*, it. tr. (Milan, Mondadori, 1996), p. 997.

[132] Ibid, pp. 927–35.

[133] P. Corrêa de Oliveira, "7 dias em revista", O Legionário, no. 625, 30 July 1944.

month of Mary: nazism died. We should now ask her to break the other point by crushing communism."[134]

Plinio Corrêa de Oliveira's anti-Fascism had nothing in common with the progressivist type that was becoming popular in the wake of the Liberation Armies.[135] Faced with the collapse of Nazism, he was already looking towards the next adversary from whom he felt the potential of a serious threat to the West. The fight against communism, which he had begun in the 30s would from that time be the dominant note of his apostolate.

While the Soviet troops were advancing on Berlin, he wrote:

"Once the hateful nazi scourge is overthrown, the objective is to eliminate communism. To this end, everything should be sacrificed, absolutely everything that logically and licitly one can sacrifice."[136]

"The fight against communism" he writes on 10 March 1946 "should be more unyielding, clearer, more tenacious than ever."[137]

"Socialism today" he adds a few months later "just as nazism yesterday, and liberalism even before, has a thousand faces. With one it smiles at the Church and threatens it with another, and argues against her with yet another. Against this new socialism, just as against liberalism of old, the attitude of Catholics the world over, but especially in Europe, can only be one: a resolute, frank, inflexible, and fearless combat. Socialism is not a wild beast that can be tamed or domesticated. It is an apocalyptic monster combining the falsity of the fox with the violence of the tiger. We must not forget this lest events teach us a very painful lesson ...."[138]

With Pius XII, the Brazilian thinker sees the foundation for the reconstruction in the return to the natural and Christian order denied by modern totalitarianism.[139]

However, with the peace treaties, Europe returned to the contradic-

---

[134] P. Corrêa de Oliveira, "Regina Pacis", O Legionário, no. 666, 13 May 1945.

[135] On the continuity between fascism and progressivist antifascism, cf. Augusto Del Noce, *Fascismo e antifascismo. Errori della cultura*, Milan, Leonardo, 1995. "The result of antifascist unity, in the terms in which it is presented today – Del Noce wrote in 1971 – can only be a reversed fascism, a fascism dissociated from the national cause. We would be faced with the completeness of fascism, as a total dissolution" (ibid, p. 98).

[136] P. Corrêa de Oliveira, "A grande missão", O Legionário, no. 652, 4 February 1945.

[137] P. Corrêa de Oliveira, "O discurso do sr. Winston Churchill", O Legionário, no. 709, 10 March 1946.

[138] P. Corrêa de Oliveira, "A falsa alternativa", O Legionário, no. 723, 16 June 1946.

[139] According to Pius XII, real peace is not the result of a pure equilibrium of forces, but, "in its ultimate and deepest meaning, a moral and legal act" (Radiomessage to the Universe of 24 December 1943, in IP, *La pace internazionale*, p. 398) that can only be achieved "from the principles and norms dictated by Christ and implemented with sincere mercy". Encyclical *Summi maeroris*, of 19 July 1950, in IP, *La pace internazionale*, p. 542.

tory equilibrium of Versailles. As Pius XII noted: "Very few were the times in world history that the sword had drawn such a clear dividing line between winners and losers."[140] An iron curtain, according to the expression of Churchill, by now crossed the continent from North to South. The Europe that was being born would take a very different direction from that hoped for by the Pope and the Church of Rome.

11. The disastrous comedy of the UN

In 1945, after the conference of Yalta, approval was given to the statute of the "United Nations", the new international organization that would replace the "League of Nations". From the beginning Plinio Corrêa de Oliveira foresaw that it was destined to fail for the very same reasons for which the League of Nations had failed before it.[141]

> "The United Nations is doomed to failure, because it is secularist. (...) Nothing is accomplished merely with the 'idea of God'. Firstly, because God is not a figment of the imagination, but rather a reality, the absolute Being. Secondly, because from time immemorial the peoples have believed in God, or at least in gods. And wars nonetheless occurred. The solution is to be found in Christianity. And by Christianity we mean Catholicism.
>
> "If the UN were organized under the shadow of the Papacy, under the presidency of the Vicar of Christ, by Christian people, then a universal order would not be a chimera. However, not all the peoples represented in the UN are Christian, not all the Christian peoples are Catholic. Nor are all the Catholic peoples governed by Catholics, nor is it possible for the Vicar of Christ to exercise an efficacious influence in such an ambience.
>
> "In these circumstances, failure is inevitable. The League of Nations is already in the cemetery of History. There is another plot ready beside it: the one for the United Nations."[142]

---

[140] Pius XII, Address to the Sacred College of 24 December 1946, in IP, *La pace internazionale*, p. 463.

[141] On the failure of the UN, especially with regard to its powerlessness to face the crimes of war and modern genocides, cf. Yves Ternon in *L'Etat criminel. Les Génocides au XX siècle* (Paris, Seuil, 1995) which offers a shocking description of the great mass exterminations of our century, from the Jewish genocide to that of Armenia, from that of Cambodia to those of the Soviet Union.

[142] P. Corrêa de Oliveira, "7 dias em revista", O Legionário, no. 762, 16 March 1947. "The UN purely and simply ignored the existence of the Papacy. It, thus, repudiated the only pillar upon which normally can be organized International Law. And it failed just as the League of Nations did and for the same reasons" (ID., "Um ano em revista. A consolidação das institucões democraticas." "A paz no mundo", O Legionário, no. 752, 5 January 1947, On UN cf. also ID., "A comédia da O.N.U.", O Legionário, no. 704, 3 February 1946.

12. Islam to conquer Europe?

A final prediction of Plinio Corrêa de Oliveira is worthy of mention, at an historic moment when the shadow of Islam is threateningly heading towards Europe.[143] The increasingly massive Muslim immigration in this end of century has a simultaneously religious and political value because of the close bond that links these two realities in the religion of Mohammed. This totalitarian prospect is made even more treacherous by the fact that Islam is a religion without dogma or Magisterium, without a Church or a hierarchy, able to adapt in every way to the social situation in which it develops. As early as the 1940s, Plinio Corrêa de Oliveira foresaw in the *Legionário* the possibility of this danger which is appearing today in all its importance.

While the eyes of political observers were concentrated on what was happening in Europe, he turned his eyes towards the East where, with regard to Islam, he glimpsed the beginnings of "the forming of another vast political and ideological oriental anti-Catholic block".[144] "The Muslim danger is immense"[145] he wrote in 1943 and stated the next year: "the Muslim problem will constitute one of the gravest religious questions of our days after the war".[146]

"The Muslim world possesses indispensable natural resources to suppress Europe. It will have at hand the necessary means to upset or paralyze, at any moment, the whole flow of the European economy."[147]

"While a great and glorious Catholic nation such a Italy thus suffers from communist toxins circulating within its organism, the Muslims become increasingly organized. In the last few days, they had the audacity to present the Western world with the idea of a Palestinian government in exile working from Cairo. This is a veritable diplomatic declaration of war against the West."[148]

"The Arab League, an extremely vast confederation of Muslim

---

[143] Cf. Felice Dassetto – Albert Bastenier, *Europa: nuova frontiera dell'Islam?*, Rome, Edizioni Lavoro, 1988. On the ideological nature of Islam, cf. Stefano Nitoglia, *Islam. Anatomia di una setta*, Milan, Effedieffe, 1994.

[144] P. Corrêa de Oliveira, "Neopaganismo", O Legionário, no. 574, 8 August 1943.

[145] P. Corrêa de Oliveira, "A Questão Libanesa", O Legionário, no. 591, 5 December 1943. "Today, with men, weapons and money, anything can be done. The Muslim world has plenty of money and men. It will not be difficult to obtain weapons ... and, in this way, it will become an immense power all over the East. It will be active, warlike, aware of its traditions, an enemy of the West, with just as many weapons, and that within a period of time could no doubt be as influential as the Asian world" (ibid).

[146] P. Corrêa de Oliveira, "7 dias em revista", Legionário, no. 604, 5 March 1944.

[147] P. Corrêa de Oliveira, "7 dias em revista", Legionário, no. 635, 8 October 1944.

[148] P. Corrêa de Oliveira, "7 dias em revista", O Legionário, no. 728, 21 July 1946.

peoples, today encompasses the whole Mohamedan world. It is the exact opposite of what Christendom was in the Middle Ages. The Arab League acts as a vast block in face of the non-Arab nations and foments insurrection throughout the whole of northern Africa."[149]

13. "The *Legionário* was born to fight"

"The *Legionário* was born to fight."[150] From 1933 to 1947, the courageous and often solitary voice of the *Legionário*, directed by Plinio Corrêa de Oliveira, raised high the flag of the Church and of Christian civilization against modern totalitarianism in all its expressions and forms. He thus summarized the position of the magazine:

"Above all, let us always love the Roman Pontiff. Not a single word of the Pope did we leave unpublished, without explanation, or without defence. Not one right of the Holy See was left undefended with the greatest ardour a human creature is capable. In our words, thanks be to God, no concept or nuance ever swerved from the Magisterium of Peter whether in a comma or even a line. In every aspect, we were the men of the Church Hierarchy, whose prerogatives we defended with strenuous ardour against the doctrines purporting to tear the direction of the Catholic laity from the Episcopate and the Clergy. There have been no mistakes, no misunderstandings, nor tempests that were able to put the slightest stain on our standard in this regard. Let us entirely defend the spirit of hierarchy, of spiritual formation, of mortification, and of rupture with the ignominies of the century. Let us fight for the doctrine of the Church against the grim excesses of statist nationalism that dominated Europe; against nazism, fascism and all its various forms; against liberalism, socialism, communism and the famous 'policy of the extended hand'. No one in the world has ever raised itself up against the Church of God without the *Legionário* (...) protesting. Likewise, we never lost sight of the obligation of stimulating in every way devotion to Our Lady and to the Blessed Sacrament. There was never any genuine Catholic initiative that did not receive our enthusiastic support. Never were the doors closed

---

[149] P. Corrêa de Oliveira, "Mahomé renasce", O Legionário, no. 775, 15 June 1947. On the Islamic problem cf. also J. G. Larrain Campbell, "Uma coisa é ter vista, outra é visão", Catolicismo, no. 478, October 1990, pp. 11–12; ID., "Vinte milhões de Maometanos invadem a Europa", Catolicismo, no. 524, August 1994, pp. 20–2.

[150] P. Corrêa de Oliveira, "365 dias em revista", O Legionário, no. 595, 1 January 1944.

on someone having the glory of God as his sole aim without finding friendly and welcoming support. There is a good fight to be fought in this life. We are exhausted and bleed from every part of the body. This was the fight that tired us out and in which we were wounded. In return, we only dare to request as a reward pardon for everything inevitably fallible and human in this work that should be all for God and only for God."[151]

Ten years before the outbreak of the war, in a letter to a friend, Plinio Corrêa de Oliveira had written:

"I increasingly have the impression that we are in the vestibule of an era full of sufferings and struggles. Everywhere, the suffering of the Church becomes more intense and the struggle draws closer. I have the impression that the clouds of the political horizon are becoming denser. It will not be long before a tempest will break, having a world war as a simple preface. But, this war will spread such confusion throughout the world that revolutions will appear everywhere, and the putrefaction of this unfortunate 'Twentieth century' will reach is apogee. Then, will be raised those forces of evil that, as worms, only appear at the moments of final putrefaction. Society's underlying philosophy will then appear and the Church will be persecuted everywhere. But ... *'et ego dico tibi quia tu es Petrus, et super hanc petram aedificabo Ecclesiam meam, et portae inferi non praevalebunt adversus Eam'*. Consequently, we will either have a 'new Middle Ages' or we will have the end of the world."[152]

---

151 P. Corrêa de Oliveira, "17 anos", O Legionário, no. 616, 28 May 1944.
152 Cit. in J. S. Clá Dias, *Dona Lucilla*, vol. II, p. 181.

Chapter III

In Defence of Catholic Action

"This is our objective, our great ideal.
We advance toward the Catholic civilization
that may arise from the ruins of today's world,
as the civilization of the Middle Ages
was born from the ruins of the Roman world"

1. Pius XI and Catholic Action

The origins of Catholic Action date, in broad terms, to the tumultuous years between the French Revolution and the Restoration, when, faced with the increasing number of attacks on the Church and on Christian civilization, the necessity to organize the Catholic laity became ever more urgent. The former Jesuit Nikolaus Albert von Diesbach[1] and his Italian disciple Pio Brunone Lanteri[2] were responsible for the founding of Amicizia Cristiana and then of Amicizia Cattolica which anticipated the great apostolate of the Catholic laity of the nineteenth and twentieth centuries.[3]

Under the pontificate of Pius IX, various lay associations were

---

[1] On Father Nikolaus Albert Joseph von Diesbach (1732–98) and on the *Amicizie*, Cf. Candido Bona I.M.C., *Le "Amicizie", società segrete e rinascita religiosa (1770–1830)*, Turin, Deputazione Subalpina di Storia Patria, 1962; R. de Mattei, *Idealità e dottrine delle "Amicizie"*, Rome, Biblioteca Romana, 1980.

[2] On Pio Brunone Lanteri (1759–1830), declared Venerable in 1967, as well as the works mentioned in the previous note, Cf. R. de Mattei, *Introduzione* a *Direttorio e altri scritti* of Venerable P. B. Lanteri, Siena, Cantagalli, 1975; Paolo Calliari O.M.V., *Servire la Chiesa. Il venerabile Pio Brunone Lanteri (1759–1830)*, Caltanisetta, Lanteriana-Krinon, 1989. Mgr Francesco Olgiati, indicated Pio Brunone Lanteri as being "one of the most eloquent symbols of the apostolate in general and of Catholic Action in particular". Preface to Icilio Felici, *Una bandiera mai ripiegata. Pio Brunone Lanteri, fondatore dei Padri Oblati di Maria Vergine, precursore dell'Azione Cattolica*, (Pinerolo, Tip. Alzani, 1950), p. 6. Prof Fernando Furquim de Almeida dedicated an important series of articles in *Catolicismo* to the *Amicizie* of Diesbach and Lanteri.

[3] For a description of the lay apostolate in the last century, Cf. Silvio Tramontin, *Un secolo di storia della Chiesa. Da Leone XIII al Concilio Vaticano II*, (Rome, Studium, 1980), vol. II, pp. 1–54.

established to hinder the process of the de-christianization of society: the Piusverein in Switzerland, the Katholischenverein in Germany, the Asociación de Laicos in Spain, the Union Catholique in Belgium, the Ligue Catholique pour la Défense de l'Eglise in France, the Catholic Union in England, the Opera dei Congressi in Italy. The great promoter of Catholic Action was, however, St Pius X[4] who, in his encyclical *Il fermo proposito*[5] and in his Apostolic Letter *Notre Charge Apostolique*,[6] clearly indicated its principles and objectives, condemning political and social modernism, represented in France by the Sillon of Marc Sangnier[7] and in Italy by the "Christian Democrats" of Romolo Murri.[8]

After the short pontificate of Benedict XV, on 6 February 1922, Cardinal Achille Ratti, former Prefect of the Vatican Library and only recently archbishop of Milan, was elected Pope, with the name of Pius XI. It was Pius XI who gave Catholic Action its legal physiognomy and its public status in the Church.

From his very first encyclical, *Ubi Arcano Dei*, Pius XI had wanted to encourage the "holy battle" of "that group of movements, organizations, and works which come under the name of Catholic Action".[9] In his encyclical *Quas Primas*[10] of 11 December 1925,

---

[4] Pius XII thus defined him in the Address for his beatification on 3 June 1951, in DR, vol. XIII, p. 134.

[5] St Pius X, Encyclical *Il fermo proposito* of 11 June 1905.

[6] St Pius X, Letter *Notre Charge Apostolique*, of 25 August 1910, in IP, vol. VI, *La pace interna delle nazioni*, pp. 268–98 and Lepanto, nos. 96–7, March-April 1990.

[7] On the Sillon of Marc Sangnier (1873–1950), Cf. the works of the Abbé Emmanuel Barbier, *Les démocrates chrétiens et le modernisme*, (Paris, Lethielleux, 1908), pp. 358–92; ID., *Le devoir politique des catholiques*, Paris, Jouve, 1909.

[8] On Romolo Murri (1870–1944), Cf. Maurilio Guasco, *Romolo Murri. Tra la 'Cultura Sociale' e il 'Domani d'Italia' (1898–1906)*, Rome, Studium, 1988; Benedetto Marcucci, *Romolo Murri. La scelta radicale*, Venice, Marsilio, 1994.

[9] "Tell your faithful children of the laity – the Pope wrote – that when, united with their pastors and their bishops, they participate in the works of the apostolate, both individual and social, the final end of which is to make Jesus Christ better known and better loved, then they are more than ever 'a chosen generation, a kingly priesthood, a holy nation, a purchased people' of whom St Peter spoke in such laudatory terms." Pius XI, Encyclical *Ubi arcano*, of 23 December 1922, in IP, *Il laicato*, (1958), vol. IV, p. 274. Among Pius XI's numerous texts regarding Catholic Action, we recall the letter to Cardinal Bertram, archbishop of Breslaw (1928), that to the Primate of Spain (1929), that to the archbishop of Malines (1929), that to the Mexican episcopate (1937). Of the bibliography see the two documented degree theses by Walter Scheier, *Laientum und Hierarchie, ihre theologischen Beziehungen unter besonderer Berücksichtigung des Lehramtes unter Pius XI. und Pius XII.*, Pontificium Atheneum Internationale Angelicum, Freiburg im Breisgau 1964; Jean-Guy Dubuc, *Les relations entre hiérarchie et laïcat dans l'apostolat chez Pie XI et Pie XII*, Rome, Pontificia Università Gregoriana, 1967.

[10] Pius XI, Encyclical *Quas Primas* of 11 December 1925, in IP, vol. VI, *La pace interna delle nazioni*, pp. 330–51.

Pius XI had developed the scriptural, liturgical and theological foundation of the social Sovereignty of Jesus Christ, stating that "it would be a grave error to say that Christ has no authority whatever in civil affairs"[11] because, as Leo XIII[12] had already stated, "the whole human race is under the authority of Jesus Christ". The Pope also denounced "the plague which now infects society" in "secularism with its errors and impious activities".[13]

His view of history was similar to that of his predecessors:

"This evil spirit has not come into being in one day; it has long lurked beneath the surface. The empire of Christ over all nations was rejected. The right which the Church has from Christ Himself, to teach mankind, to make laws, to govern peoples in all that pertains to their eternal salvation, that right was denied. Then gradually the religion of Christ came to be likened to false religions and to be placed ignominiously on the same level with them. It was then put under the power of the State and tolerated more or less at the whim of princes and rulers. Some men went further, and wished to set up in the place of God's religion a natural religion consisting in some instinctive affection of the heart. There were even some nations who thought they could dispense with God, and that their religion should consist in impiety and the neglect of God".[14]

Pius XI entrusted Catholics with the task of re-christianizing society, by extending and increasing the Kingdom of Christ and to this end he introduced the liturgical feast of Christ the King, to be celebrated every year on the last Sunday of the month of October:

"Nations will be reminded by the annual celebration of this feast that not only private individuals but also rulers and princes are bound to give public honour and obedience to Christ."[15]

---

[11] Ibid, p. 339.
[12] Leo XIII, Encyclical *Annum Sacrum* of 25 May 1899, in IP, vol. I, *Le fonti della vita spirituale*, p. 191.
[13] Pius XI, Encyclical *Quas Primas*, p. 343.
[14] Ibid, pp. 343–4.
[15] Ibid, p. 349.

2. The "new Christianity" of Jacques Maritain

Jacques Maritain's work,[16] *Integral Humanism*,[17] published in 1936, was the manifesto of a new philosophy of history and society that offered the foundation for an evolution of Catholic Action in an opposite direction to the programme prepared by Pius XI in the *Quas Primas*.

Maritain in fact wanted to replace holy Christian civilization with the "concrete historical ideal of a new Christianity",[18] a profane *civitas humana*, taken as "a temporal regime of an age of civilization whose inspiring form would be Christian and would respond to the historical climate of the times into which we are entering".[19] At the root of his philosophy of history that seeks an hypothetical "third way", between the "medieval ideal" and the "liberal" one,[20] is the deterministic thesis of the irreversibility of the modern world and the Marxist postulate of the "historical role of the proletariat."[21]

What *Integral Humanism* really makes its own are the principles of the French Revolution, condemned by the Pontifical Magisterium and destined, starting from this period, to infiltrate to an increasingly greater extent Catholic circles, all to the advantage of socialism and

---

[16] Jacques Maritain was born in Paris in 1882 and died in Toulouse in 1973. A disciple of the philosopher Bergson, he was converted to Catholicism in 1906, together with his wife Raissa, a Jewess of Russian origin. After having been closely involved in Action Française, he broke loose from Maurras, presenting himself as the new *maître à penser* of the Catholic world. Having spent the period of the war in America, he was nominated French Ambassador to the Holy See (1944–8), after which he again returned to America as Professor in the University of Princeton. It was to Maritain that Paul VI delivered the "message to the intellectuals" at the end of Vatican Council II.

[17] Jacques Maritain, *Humanisme intégral. Problèmes temporels et spirituels d'une nouvelle chré-tienté*, Paris, Aubier-Montaigne, 1936, now in Jacques and Raissa Maritain, *Oeuvres complètes*, (Fribourg, Editions Universitaires, 1984), vol. VI, pp. 293–642. The volume derived from a series of conferences held in August 1934 at the university of Santander. Louis Salleron, in the *Revue Hebdomadaire* of 22 August 1936, (then *Humanisme intégral?* "M. Jacques Maritain, marxiste chrétien", L'Ordre Français, no. 176, December 1973, pp. 11–24), since 1936 had been clearly denouncing as "purely Marxist" Maritain's dialectics (ibid., p. 21). Among the numerous articles on Maritain by Plinio Corrêa de Oliveira, cf. "Maritain e o 'dogma' de sua infalibilidade", O Legionário, no. 190, 28 November 1943. For a critical analysis of the thinking of the French philosopher cf. also Julio Meinvielle, *De Lamennais à Maritain*, Buenos Aires, Theoria, 1967 (1945); Leopoldo Palacios, *El mito de la nueva cristiandad*, Madrid, Speiro, 1952; Rafael Gambra, *Maritain y Teilhard de Chardin*, Madrid, Speiro, 1969; and the important articles in *Civiltà Cattolica* by Father Antonio Messineo S.J.: "Evoluzione storica e messaggio cristiano", no. 102, 1951, pp. 253–63; "Laicismo politico e dottrina cattolica", no. 103, 1952, pp. 18–28; "L'uomo e lo stato", no. 105, 1954, pp. 663–9; "Umanesimo integrale", no. 107, 1956, pp. 449–63, translated with the title *O humanismo integral*, in nos. 75, March 1957, 76, April 1957, 77, May 1957 of *Catolicismo*.

[18] J. Maritain, *Humanisme intégral*, pp. 437–526.

[19] Ibid, p. 442.

[20] Ibid, p. 495.

[21] Ibid, pp. 552–4.

"progressivism". The work of the French philosopher, as Antonio Carlos Villaça observes,

> "had enormous repercussion in the Catholic thought in Brazil. It divided the waters. He brought about profound divisions. It raised terrible divergences. From this moment, Brazilian Catholic thought divides in two: the maritainians and the anti-maritainians".[22]

Despite the declared adhesion of Maritain to the principles of Thomism, his philosophy of history and his sociology converge with the Neo-modernism appearing among the young religious of the Jesuit and Dominican Orders. Priests, such as the Dominican Yves Congar, were already at that point convinced that their generation should "recover and transfer into the patrimony of the Church any worthwhile element that could emerge from an approach to modernism".[23]

Catholic Action was, along with the "liturgical movement", the preferred sector for the infiltration of especially political and social modernism[24] that, after a silent incubation period, had reappeared at the beginning of the 1930s.

3. The "liturgical movement"

The "liturgical movement" of the twentieth century appears as a deviation rather than a development of that promoted in the previous century by the abbot of Solesmes, Dom Prosper Guéranger.[25] The

---

[22] A. C. Villaça, *O pensamento católico no Brasil*, p. 14.

[23] Aidan Nichols, *Yves Congar*, London, Cassel Publishers Limited, 1989, It. tr. *Yves Congar*, (Cinisello Balsamo, Edizioni Paoline, 1991), p. 12. The Dominican Yves Congar (1904–95), pupil of Father Marie-Dominique Chenu, was one of the main exponents of the *"Nouvelle Théologie"*. Called the "father and inspirer of Vatican II" (Bruno Forte, "Avvenire", 23 June 1996), he was made a Cardinal purple, in November 1994, by John Paul II. Cf. Marie Dominique Chenu, *Une école de théologie. Le Saulchoir*, Paris, Editions du Cerf, 1985 (1st edn. Tournai 1937).

[24] On Modernism, Cf. Cornelio Fabro, entry *Modernismo*, in EC, vol. VIII (1952), coll. 1187–96; Ramón García de Haro, *Historia teológica del modernismo*, Pamplona, Universidad de Navarra, 1972 and, among the works in favour of the movement: Emile Poulat, *Histoire, dogme et critique dans la crise moderniste*, Paris, Casterman, 1962; Bernard M. G. Reardon, *Roman Catholic Modernism*, London, Stanford University Press, 1970; Thomas Leslie Loome, *Liberal Catholicism, Reform Catholicism, Modernism. A contribution to a New Orientation on Modernist Research*, Mainz, Matthias Grünewald Verlag, 1979; Gabriel Daly, O.S.A., *Transcendence and Immanence. A study in Catholic Modernism and Integralism*, Oxford, Clarendon Press, 1980.

[25] On Dom Prosper Guéranger (1805–75) restorer of monastic life in France Cf. Dom Paul Delatte O.S.B., *Dom Guéranger, Abbé de Solesmes*, 2nd edn., 2 vols., Paris, Plon-Nourrit, 1909. And recently Cuthbert Johnson O.S.B., *Prosper Guéranger (1805–75): a liturgical theologian*, Rome, Pontificio Ateneo S. Anselmo, 1984. Cf. also F. Furquim de Almeida, *D. "Guéranger, um douto na Lei Divina"*, Catolicismo, no. 66, June 1956 and the entries B. Heurtebize, in DTC, vol. VI (1920), coll. 1894–8 and Jacques Hourlier, in DSp, vol. VI (1967), coll. 1097–106

latter had understood the renewal of monastic life to be a return to the traditional Roman liturgy, after the devastation wrought by Protestantism and, within the Catholic Church, by Gallicanism and Jansenism. The "liturgical movement",[26] which started in Belgium [27] and whose principal centre of reference was the German abbey of Maria Laach,[28] was understood rather as an "irruption of laity in the active participation of the life of the Church".[29]

The reformers tended to eliminate the basic difference between the sacramental priesthood of the priests and the common priesthood of the laity, suggesting an egalitarian and democratic view of the Church. They introduced the idea of a "concelebration" of the priest with the people,[30] they upheld there should be active "participation" in the Mass by conversing with the priest, to the exclusion of every other form of legitimate attendance at the Sacrifice, such as meditation, the Rosary or other private prayers. They advocated the reduction of the altar to a table; they considered communion "extra Missam", visits to the Blessed Sacrament, perpetual adoration, as extra-liturgical forms of piety. They showed little consideration for devotions to the Sacred Heart, to Our Lady, to the saints and, more generally speaking, for Ignatian spirituality and for the moral of St Alphonsus de Liguori. To put it briefly, this was a "reinterpretation" of the doctrine and structure of the Church in order to adapt it to the modern spirit.

Father José Ariovaldo da Silva, who wrote a documented history of the liturgical movement in Brazil, fixed the date of its official birth as

---

[26] On the "liturgical movement", Cf. Olivier Rousseau, *Histoire du mouvement liturgique*, Paris, Ed. du Cerf, 1944; Didier Bonneterre, *Le Mouvement liturgique*, Escurolles, Editions Fideliter, 1980; B. Neunheuser, *Movimento liturgico*, in *Nuovo Dizionario di liturgia*, edited by D. Sartore – A.M. Triacca, Rome, Edizioni Paoline, 1984; Various authors, *Liturgia: temi e autori*. *Saggi di studio sul movimento liturgico*, edited by Franco Brovelli, Rome, Edizioni Liturgiche, 1990. Volumes such as *Das christliche Kultmysterium* (1932) by Dom Odo Casel; *Vom Geist der Liturgie* (1918), *Liturgische Bildung* (1923), *Die Sinne und die religiöse Erkenntis* (1950) by Romano Guardini; *Liturgie und Personlichkeit* (1933) by Dietrich von Hildebrand constituted the cornerstones of the movement.

[27] At the congress of Catholic associations inaugurated in Malines in 1909 by Cardinal Mercier, Dom Lambert Beauduin (1873–1960), a Benedictine from Mont César, had been the first to uphold a new horizonalist and "community" view of the liturgy (B. Fischer, "Das 'Mechelner Ereignis' vom 23. 9. 1909", Liturgisches Jahrbuch, 9 (1959), pp. 203–19). He was also one of the first pioneers of the "ecumenical movement".

[28] In the abbey of Maria Laach, the abbot J. Herwegen and his monks K. Mohlberg and O. Casel were gathered with the young Italian-German priest R. Guardini and Professors J. Dölger and Baumstark. They encouraged, in 1918, the beginning of the three series: '*Ecclesia Orans*', '*Liturgiegeschichtliche Quellen*', '*Liturgiegeschichtliche Forschungen*'.

[29] Erwin Iserloh, *Il Movimento liturgico* in HKG, (Milan, 1980), It. tr. vol. X/1, p. 237.

[30] This principle, condemned in the Council of Trent (session 23, chap. 4, in Denz.-H, no. 1767) was again proscribed by Pius XII (Encyclical *Mediator Dei*, in AAS, vol. 39, p. 556).

1933.[31] In that year a Benedictine monk, Dom Martin Michler, who had come from Germany[32] with the task of holding a course in Liturgy at the Instituto Católico de Estudos Superiores, stirred up the enthusiasm of some of his Brazilian students with his lessons.[33] A Centro de Liturgia (Liturgy Centre) was formed within the University Catholic Action (AUC). The works of this Centre were inaugurated with a retreat that the Benedictine priest held for sixteen young people, on a farm in the State of Rio. It was here on 11 July 1933 that the first dialogued and *versus populum* Mass was celebrated in Brazil.[34] After that, Dom Michler began to dialogue the Mass weekly for the university students in the monastery of São Bento in Rio. "The Liturgical Movement in Brazil had begun."[35]

4. Catholic Action at the cross-roads

In a letter of 27 October 1935 addressed to Cardinal Leme and the Brazilian bishops, Pius XI hoped for the establishment of Catholic Action in Brazil as well.[36] The Brazilian Catholic Action was founded that same year with the apostolic aim "to spread and to foster the Catholic principles in the life of the individual, family life and social life".[37] Its function was to co-ordinate all the Catholic associations

---

[31] José Ariovaldo da Silva O.F.M., *O Movimento litúrgico no Brasil*, Editora Vozes, Petrópolis 1983. Cf. also Bishop Clemente Isnard O.S.B., *Reminiscências para a História do Movimento Litúrgico no Brasil*, appendix in B. Botte O.S.B., *O Movimento Litúrgico. Testemunho e recordações*, (São Paulo, Edições Paulinas, 1978), pp. 208–09.

[32] Dom Martin Michler (1901–69), was a Benedictine in Neusheim, in Maria Laach and in S. Anselmo in Rome, being influenced, after Romano Guardini, by Dom Beauduin and Odo Casel. Cf. C. Isnard O.S.B., "O papel de Dom Martinho Michler no Movimento Católico Brasileiro", A Ordem, no. 36, December 1946, pp. 535–45.

[33] Alceu Amoroso Lima, who confirmed that he owed much to the influence of Michler (A. Amoroso Lima, *Memórias improvisadas*, (Petropólis, Ed. Vozes, 1973), p. 205), saw him as "a great light for all" (ID., "Hitler e Guardini", A Ordem, no. 36, December 1946, p. 550). Another Brazilian Catholic intellectual, Gustavo Corção, was also influenced by him. In his autobiographical work *A Discoberta do Outro* (1944), according to Father da Silva "he shows that he is clearly influenced by the ideas of Dom Martinho A. Michler". J. Ariovaldo da Silva O.F.M., *O Movimento litúrgico no Brasil*, p. 48; Cf. also A. C. Villaça, *O pensamento católico no Brasil*, pp. 144–5.

[34] J. A. da Silva O.F.M., *O Movimento litúrgico no Brasil*, pp. 41–2; C. Isnard O.S.B., *O papel*, pp. 535–9, who recalls: "in the main room he prepared an altar for the celebration of the Mass. But, to our great surprise, instead of placing the table against the wall, he placed it in the middle of the room and arranged the chairs in a semicircle around it explaining he would celebrate Mass facing us. It was the first Mass celebrated facing the people in Brazil!" (*Reminiscências*, p. 218). "Dom Martinho did this with the greatest naturality in spite of the fact that he was actually bringing about a revolution in our midst. He broke a taboo and obliged us to follow him in the subsequent steps he wanted us to take" (ibid).

[35] J. A. da Silva, O.F.M., *O Movimento litúrgico no Brasil*, p. 43.

[36] Cf. *A Ordem* XVI (January 1936) pp. 5–11.

[37] Monica Kornis, Dora Flaksman, *Ação católica Brasileira (ACB)*, in DHBB, vol. I, p. 11.

and works already in existence in the country, subordinating them to the same guidelines. According to its statutes, it should be placed under the immediate dependence of the ecclesiastic hierarchy, carrying out its activity outside any party organization. On 4 April 1937 Catholic Action was solemnly installed in the Archdiocese of Rio de Janeiro and Alceu Amoroso Lima, better known under the pseudonym of Tristão de Athayde,[38] was nominated the first national president while the effective direction was entrusted to an Episcopal commission composed of five members. It was based on the Italian model, and it preferred dioceses as relatively autonomous nuclei within the organizations and grouped the members according to age and sex.[39]

At that time in Brazil there was already a powerful organized Catholic movement which had the Marian Congregations as its main support and, within them, Plinio Corrêa de Oliveira as their natural leader. The creation of Catholic Action was not without its problems, as inevitably certain organizational areas overlapped. Beyond the intentions of the Pontiff, there was a tendency to absorb all the pre-existing organizational realities into the new structure. The problems did not arise only from organizational contrasts but from the risk that movements with ancient traditions and undisputed roots, such as the Marian Congregations, might lose their specific identity or have it diminished. Furthermore, in Brazil, as in many other countries where it was established, Catholic Action appeared more permeable to new progressivist influences.

While Catholic Action was being founded, the Marian Congregations achieved their full development in Brazil. On the eve

---

[38] Alceu Amoroso Lima, known under the literary pseudonym of Tristão de Athayde, was born in Rio de Janeiro on 11 December 1893 and died in Petrópolis on 14 August 1983. In his intellectual formation a profound role was played by the Evolutionism of Silvio Romero, the Idealism of Benedetto Croce and the Vitalism of Henri Bergson, whose lessons he attended in 1913 in Paris. In 1928 he converted to Catholicism under the influence of the Catholic leader Jackson de Figuereido and on the death of the latter he succeeded him as director of the Centro Dom Vital and of the magazine *A Ordem*. He thus began a new phase of his life during which he collaborated closely with Cardinal Leme, becoming secretary general of the Liga Eleitoral Católica (1932) and first president of the Brazilian Catholic Action (1935–45). However, under Maritain's influence, he began a revision of his philosophical and political principles that led him to return to the liberal concepts he had before his conversion. In this ideological dimension he promoted the organization of the Partido Democrata Cristão (PDC) whose manifesto he prepared, participating in 1949 in the so-called Montevideo Movement, whose aim was to organize the Christian Democrats throughout Latin America. He greeted Vatican Council II enthusiastically, giving due consideration to the influence of the new tendencies of Catholic Progressivism. For an analysis of the confused and contradictory intellectual itinerary of Amoroso Lima Cf. Cunha Alvarenga (José de Azeredo Santos), "História das variações do sr. Tristão de Athayde", Catolicismo, no. 43, July 1954.

[39] Necessary requisites defined by the Statutes for militants in C.A. were "to lead an exemplary life," "to frequent the sacraments" and adhere to "programmes of the ACB and one's respective organizaton".

of 1938 there were one thousand Marian Congregation groups with 150,000 members of which over 25,000 were in São Paulo.[40] Father Irineu Cursino de Moura proclaimed "the present-day crusade of the army of Mary for the restoration of the religious relics of our glorious past" indicating as leaders and as

"present-day apostles, of the land of the Holy Cross (...) the Tristão de Athaydes, the congressmen Mário Ramos and Plinio Corrêa de Oliveira, and so many others, who, like lions, have fought so that our constitution finally be promulgated in the name of God Almighty".[41]

Tristão de Athayde and Plinio Corrêa de Oliveira appeared as the undisputed Catholic leaders of Brazil in the middle of the 1930s.[42] The former, in Rio, president of the newly-born Catholic Action; the latter, in São Paulo, soul of the Marian Congregations. The lives and apostolate of these two men were, however, destined to go along different paths, until becoming journeys in opposite directions.

Amoroso Lima was responsible for the transfer of the Brazilian Catholic Action to openly Maritainian positions.[43] A former disciple of Bergson, at the Sorbonne, then a convert to Catholicism, Athayde followed an evolution that was typical of the intellectuals of his time, from pro-traditionalism to the progressivism of Maritain and Teilhard de Chardin whose work reconciled him "with the evolutionism that was in the spontaneity of his thought".[44] If, as has been observed, it is true Bishop Vital embodied the denial of eclecticism and of the spirit of indetermination",[45] the eclectic itinerary of Amoroso Lima represented in Brazil the antithesis of the Catholic consistency of

---

[40] P. A. Maia S.J., *História das congregações marianas*, p. 61.

[41] Ibid, p. 93.

[42] During this period, like Plinio Corrêa de Oliveira in São Paulo, "Athayde is called the great leader of Brazilian Catholic thought, the co-ordinator of the spiritual forces of the Nation. He is acclaimed as a man whose quiet, prudent and fruitful activity has resulted in the splendid victory for the Catholic claims of the LEC at the National Constitutional Assembly" (S. Maria Ancilla O'Neil, M.A., *Tristão de Athayde and the catholic social movement in Brazil*, (Washington, The Catholic University of America Press, 1939), p. 118). Plinio's personal acquaintance with Alceu Amoroso Lima dates to 1930, as Amoroso Lima himself recalled in the *Legionário*. Cf. Tristão de Athayde, "Bello exemplo", O Legionário", no. 97, 8 May 1932.

[43] Cf. José Perdomo Garcia, "El Maritenismo en Hispanoamérica", Estudios Americanos (Seville), no. 11 (1951), pp. 567–92. A. Amoroso Lima, "Maritain et l'Amérique Latine", Revue Thomiste, vol. 48 (1948), pp. 12–17; Eduardo Serafin de Oliveira, "A influência de Maritain no Pensamento de Alceu Amoroso Lima", A Ordem, no. 78, (1983). "It is mostly through Amoroso Lima – Villaça notes – that Maritain has been exercising a profound and decisive influence in the cultural renewal of Brazilian Catholicism" (*O pensamento católico no Brasil*, p. 15).

[44] Marieta de Morais Ferreira, Leda Soares, *Lima, Alceu Amoroso*, in DHBB, vol. III, p. 1831.

[45] A. C. Villaça, *O pensamento católico no Brasil*, p. 10.

Bishop Vital,[46] of which Plinio Corrêa de Oliveira appeared as the legitimate heir.

While Rio de Janeiro represented the progressivist pole of the religious life of the country, personified by Amoroso Lima, in São Paulo the traditional pole developed; its "lay leadership" was, as Father da Silva recalls, "in the hands of Plinio Corrêa de Oliveira".[47] The ideology of the Paulista leader, as Father da Silva observes, was well summarized in this phrase: "Do we want a Brazil that is truly Brazilian? Then let us make one that is entirely Catholic. Do we want to kill the very soul of Brazil? Then let us tear out its Faith".[48]

5. The apogee of the *Legionário*

On 3 May 1938 the new printing offices of the *Legionário* were blessed in the presence of Archbishop Duarte Leopoldo e Silva,[49] and of the ecclesiastic, intellectual and social elite of São Paulo. Numerous were the subscribers and admirers of the magazine who, not being able to participate, sent messages of their esteem and encouragement from every part of Brazil. Among these it is worth quoting the full text of the letter of Octaviano Pereira de Albuquerque, Archbishop-bishop of Campos, one of the most illustrious personages of the Brazilian clergy. It offers an eloquent testimony of the esteem and admiration which surrounded the *Legionário* in this period. The letter, dated 18 April 1938, is addressed personally to Plinio Corrêa de Oliveira:

"Constantly favoured by you with a copy of your weekly – *Legionário* – that you kindly send me and the reading of which I

[46] Amoroso Lima then tried to present the founder of the Centro Dom Vital, Jackson de Figueiredo, whom he had succeeded, as an unwitting "revolutionary". "For the younger generations, if we call Jackson a revolutionary, we will be closer to the truth than if we call him a reactionary, which is something he was very proud of" (Tristão de Athayde, "Foi a 25 anos", Diário de Belo Horizonte, 29 November–1 December 1953). In reality, Jackson, as José de Azeredo Santos observes in *Catolicismo*, was "an irksome burden for those who cast down the flag along the way and exchanged Dom Vital and Veuillot for the unfortunate Dom La Cerda and Maritain" (Cunha Alvarenga (José de Azeredo Santos), "Jackson, um fardo incômodo", Catolicismo, no. 37, January 1954, p. 4). Antonio Carlos Villaça who defines Amoroso Lima as "profoundly liberal" notes that "if Jackson deeply marked Alceu's soul, he did not change the liberal tendency which remained intact" (*O pensamento católico no Brasil*, p. 13).

[47] J. A. da Silva, O.F.M., *O Movimento litúrgico no Brasil*, p. 28.

[48] P. Corrêa de Oliveira, "O Concilio", O Legiónario, 2 July 1939, p. 2; J. A. da Silva, O.F.M., *O Movimento litúrgico no Brasil*, p. 28.

[49] "It is with the heart of a Bishop and with all my soul — the archbishop stated — that I come to bless you today, not only for the inauguration of the machines of our Journal, but, moreover, for your dedication and your spirit of Faith" (Cf. "O Legiónario", no. 295, 8 May 1938).

prefer to other papers, I feel impelled to sincerely congratulate you for all the good you do to society. You show, in light of the excellent use of your intellectual activity, to have received an exemplary religious education from a tender age. You have known how to allow yourself to be guided by proven directors who helped you to become director of a Catholic paper filled with useful and substantial matter on every subject related to Religion and to the social issues of the day without bothering with banal and trivial things. Furthermore, I have noticed the gravity with which political issues are dealt: they do not alter your ideals, and you show no acrimony towards the enemy; they avoid useless and, even, counterproductive arguments which create personal animosities. Wishing you a happy Easter, I ask God to continue to personally bless you, may He always give you courage to, *'sans peur et sans reproche'*, fight for the holy cause of our august religion. From your devoted friend and admirer".[50]

Another important and significant visit dates to this same year. In the summer of 1938, the famous Dominican priest, Father Réginald Garrigou-Lagrange,[51] arrived in Brazil to participate in the first week of Thomist studies held in Rio, under the chairmanship of the Nuncio Aloisi Masella. Father Garrigou-Lagrange then went to São Paulo, where he visited the *Legionário* staff.[52] In the issue dated 18 September 1938, a photograph shows Plinio Corrêa de Oliveira next to the French Dominican. The latter replied as follows to a request from the *Legionário* to comment on the phrase "The Church is neither on the right nor on the left":

"I am a man of the right and I do not see why I should hide the fact. I believe that many of those who use the phrase quoted use it for abandoning the right and then sliding towards the left. While trying to avoid an excess, they fall into the opposite, as happened

---

[50] Cit. O Legionário, no. 296, 15 May 1938. A similarly significant special apostolic blessing of Pius XII to the *Legionário*, was transmitted the following year to Dr Plinio by Cardinal Leme who was in Rome for the coronation of the new Pontiff. This is the text of the letter, dated 5 April 1939: "My dear Dr Plinio. From my heart I thank you for the kind telegram you sent me from Bahia. With pleasure I give the special blessing that the Holy Father granted to our intrepid *Legionário* and its well-deserving director, a true man of the Catholic press, of editors, benefactors and readers", O Legionário, no. 346, 30 April 1939.

[51] Father Reginald Garrigou-Lagrange was born in Auch, near Tarbes, in 1877 and died in Rome in 1964. A pupil of the Dominicans Cormier, Gardeil and Arintero, he was one of the greatest theologians of the twentieth century. Cf. the large bibliography in *Angelicum*, no. 42, 1965, pp. 200–72. Cf. also Innocenzo Colosio O.P., "Il P. Maestro Reginald Garrigou-Lagrange. Ricordi personali di un discepolo", Rivista di Ascetica e Mistica, no. 9, 1964, pp. 226–40; Benoît Lavaud, *Garrigou-Lagrange*, in DSp, vol. VI (1967), coll. 128–34.

[52] Cf. O Legionário, no. 309, 14 August 1938 and no. 310, 21 August 1938.

in France in recent years. I also believe that we should not confuse the true right with false rights, which defend a false order, not the true one. But the true right, that defends order founded on justice, seems to be a reflection of what the Scriptures call "the right-hand of God" when they proclaim that Christ is seated at the right-hand of the Father and the elect will be at the right-hand of the Most High".[53]

6. Diocesan President of Catholic Action

A few months later the archbishop of São Paulo died. His successor, Archbishop José Gaspar de Afonseca e Silva,[54] was a very different person. If Archbishop Leopoldo e Silva's character was that of a man who was unflinching, who commanded respect and even fear, Archbishop José Gaspar's nature was pleasant and attractive. It was not always easy to understand his real thoughts and interpret his choices, which were often inspired by a strong sense of politics and diplomacy. His first actions did not fail to arouse surprise. On 11 March 1940 he entrusted Plinio Corrêa de Oliveira with the most prestigious of roles: that of President of the Archdiocesan Council of Catholic Action of São Paulo. During the same period Father de Castro Mayer was nominated Assistant-General of Catholic Action of São Paulo, while Father de Proença Sigaud was appointed Archdiocesan Assistant of the male and female Student Youth. Thus Plinio Corrêa de Oliveira came to assume all the direction of the forces of the Catholic laity of São Paulo, which then included the student organizations, the men and women of Catholic Action and the auxiliary associations such as the Religious Unions, the Third Orders, the Marian Congregations.[55]

---

[53] Cit. O Legionário, no. 313, 11 September 1938.

[54] Archbishop José Gaspar de Afonseca e Silva, second archbishop of São Paulo, was born in Araxá, in the state of Minas, on 6 January 1901. He was ordained to the priesthood on 12 August 1923 by Archbishop Duarte Leopoldo e Silva. After studying in Rome at the Gregorian University he was consecrated a bishop and on 28 April 1935 he received the appointment as auxiliary to the archbishop of São Paulo. On the death of Archbishop Duarte Leopoldo e Silva in August 1939, José Gaspar succeeded him as archbishop of São Paulo. He died in a plane crash on 27 August 1943. Cf. *In memoriam de José Gaspar de Afonseca e Silva*, São Paulo, Editora Ave Maria, 1944; P. Corrêa de Oliveira, "Probreza edificante", O Legionário", no. 578, 5 September 1943.

[55] "Our programme can be summarized in a motto that we accept with enthusiasm, because it is dictated by the very nature of things established by Providence. It is the saying on the Archbishop's coat of arms: 'that all be one'. (...) Union among Catholics is the tranquil juxtaposition of heterogeneous elements. It is the pacific co-ordination of persons united because of a communion of ideas, by a common action. What ideas? What life? What action? Ideas can only be those of the Church. Life, the supernatural life of grace. Action, Catholic action". P. Corrêa de Oliveira, "Ut omnes unum sint", O Legionário, no. 392, 17 March 1940.

This did not necessarily mean the new archbishop and the head of Catholic Action appointed by him held identical viewpoints. Archbishop José Gaspar's strategy consisted in binding men to him, through collaboration rather than confronting them face to face, especially in the case of a strong personality such as that of Plinio Corrêa de Oliveira. The premature death of the archbishop of São Paulo makes it impossible to reveal the true nature of the relationship that existed between the two men.

What is certain is that in the person of Dr Plinio Archbishop José Gaspar had chosen someone who had a deep and sure knowledge of the evils that had begun to infect the great organizations of the lay apostolate. Thanks to the role he now occupied, Plinio Corrêa de Oliveira who, since 1938, had already begun to denounce these evils in the *Legionário*,[56] had the chance to embrace with a wide and serious glance the chequered Catholic reality of the country. The young president governed the association with great energy, repressing the doctrinal errors that arose and trying to modify the new ways of thinking. After three years of activity, the results were already obvious: the Paulista Catholic Action group was going through a period of unprecedented development. The magnificent Eucharistic Congress of 1942 in São Paulo demonstrated to the whole of Latin America the potential of the Brazilian Catholic movement.

On this occasion, in his role of diocesan president of Catholic Action, giving the official speech before a million people, Dr Plinio thus outlined the historical role of his homeland:

> "The providential mission of Brazil consists in growing within its own borders, to unfold here the splendours of a genuinely Roman Catholic and Apostolic civilization, and to lovingly bathe the whole world in this great light which will really be the '*lumen Christi*' that the Church irradiates. Our meek and hospitable nature, the plurality of races living in fraternal harmony, the providential co-operation of the immigrants who blended in so well into national life, and, above all, the rules of the Holy Gospel, will never transform our yearnings for grandeur into a pretext for narrow-minded jacobinisms, for doltish racisms, for criminal imperialisms. If Brazil be great one day, it will be so for the good of the whole world. 'Let those among you who govern, be as those who obey', says the Redeemer. Brazil will not be great through conquest, but through Faith. It will not be rich with money, but rather through

---

[56] P. Corrêa de Oliveira, "Burocracia", O Legionário, no. 310, 21 August 1938; ID., "Sociologite", O Legionário, no. 311, 28 August 1938. The titles of these articles speak for themselves!

its generosity. Really, if we know how to be faithful to the Rome of the Popes, our city could become a new Jerusalem, of perfect beauty, the honour, glory and joy of the whole world."[57]

Plinio Corrêa de Oliveira wished however to see his work through to the end. He therefore decided to write a book in defence of Catholic Action, offering a careful diagnosis of the ills from which it was suffering.

These ills were not unknown to the Apostolic Nuncio in Brazil, Archbishop Benedetto Aloisi Masella, who for some time had been following and appreciating Plinio Corrêa de Oliveira, although he was not acquainted with him personally. He sent him a trustworthy man, the Italian Jesuit Cesare Dainese,[58] then rector of the Colégio Loyola of Belo Horizonte, who smoothed the way for a meeting with the Nuncio. The meeting took place, a short time later, in Rio de Janeiro. The Nuncio was a sixty-year-old man, with a reserved nature and with perfect diplomatic manner. He listened in silence to the description of the President of the Paulista Catholic Action, he tacitly encouraged him and charged Father Dainese to maintain contact with him. Shortly afterwards, Father Antônio de Castro Mayer was promoted to Vicar-General of the Archdiocese of São Paulo. The intervention of the nunciature was clear and acted as an encouragement for Dr Plinio's project. He submersed himself in the study of his documents to finish his work as soon as possible.

Bishop de Castro Mayer remembers witnessing the whole writing of the book and the author's efforts so that it should be perfectly objective.[59] The authorization of the Archbishop of São Paulo was, however, required. Having received the draft of the book, the archbishop was puzzled at the firmness of the positions of the Paulista leader. Faced with the tergiversations of Archbishop José Gaspar, Plinio Corrêa de Oliveira, through the channel of Father Dainese,

---

[57] P. Corrêa de Oliveira, "Saudação às autoridades civis e militares", O Legionário, no. 525, 7 September 1942.

[58] Cesare Dainese, born in Luvigliano (Padua) in 1894, joined the Society of Jesus in Brazil in 1912, beginning his new noviciate in Vila Mariana (State of São Paulo). After studying philosophy in Rome and theology in the Heythrop College in England, he was ordained to the priesthood in 1927 and in 1930 he returned to Brazil, where he held the positions of Rector of the Colégio Anchieta in Nova Friburgo (in 1934–5 and again in 1940–5), of the Colégio Antônio Vieira in Salvador (Bahia) of which he was provincial (1953–7) and of the Colégio Santo Inácio of Rio de Janeiro (1963–4). He died in 1986.

[59] Bishop de Castro Mayer recalls, for example, that the work of Plinio Corrêa de Oliveira was read by the then Prior of the Monastery of St Benedict, Dom Paulo Pedrosa, and by the aforementioned Father Cesare Dainese, director of the National Confederation of Marian Congregations. Bishop Antônio de Castro Mayer, Bishop of Campos, "Vinte anos depois ...", Catolicismo, no. 150, July 1963.

turned to the Nuncio explaining the difficulties that his book was encountering and asking him to write a preface to overcome the impasse. Having carefully read the work and understood its importance, Archbishop Aloisi Masella willingly accepted, while urging the archbishop of São Paulo not to procrastinate over the publication any further. Archbishop José Gaspar then sent the text to Father de Castro Mayer, his vicar, in order that he should finally grant, in his name, the long-awaited imprimatur.

7. In Defence of Catholic Action

Em Defesa da Ação Católica,[60] with the preface by the Nuncio Benedetto Aloisi Masella and with the imprimatur of the archdiocese of São Paulo, was published in June 1943. It was signed by Plinio Corrêa de Oliveira as president of the archdiocesan council of the Catholic Action of São Paulo. The book, divided into five parts, was the first wide-ranging confutation of the progressivist errors spreading within the Catholic Action of Brazil and, by reflection, in the world.

The work was not a treatise destined to offer a general idea of Catholic Action. "It is first of all", wrote the author in the introduction, "a work to say what Catholic Action is not, what it should not be, what it should not do".[61]

1) The first basic problem that the author dealt with was that of the "nature" of Catholic Action. He had written in the *Legionário*, "As regards Catholic Action there is nothing more important than its juridical nature".[62] The new theories attributed to Pius XI the intention of granting the laity enrolled in Catholic Action a new "mandate" within the Church. Plinio Corrêa de Oliveira examined the legal nature of the association in order to demonstrate how the "mandate" granted to Catholic Action by the Pontiff did not alter in any way its juridical essence, which was identical to that of numerous other Catholic groups that came before and after its birth. The appeal of Pius XI to the laity, although grave and solemn, was no different to the invitations addressed to them by the hierarchy throughout history.

In the Church, the Paulista leader points out, the laity have always collaborated with the hierarchy from the earliest times.

---

[60] Cf. P. Corrêa de Oliveira, *Em Defesa de Ação Catolica*, São Paulo, Ave Maria, 1943.
[61] Ibid, p. 14.
[62] P. Corrêa de Oliveira, "Rumos de Ação Católica sob o Pontificado de Pio XII", O Legionário, no. 510, 21 June 1942.

"Which Church historian would dare to state that there was a century, a year, a month, a day when the Church renounced asking and using the co-operation of the laity with the Hierarchy? Without speaking about the Crusades, a typical example of militarized Catholic action, most solemnly summoned by the Popes; without speaking about Chivalry and the Orders of Knighthood, where the Church invested the knights of extensive faculties and apostolic roles; without speaking about the numerous believers who, attracted by the Church towards the apostolic associations founded by it, co-operated with the Hierarchy, let us examine other institutions in which our reasoning is particularly founded. Everyone knows that there are many religious orders and congregations in the Church which only accept people without the priestly charism. First and foremost among these are all the female religious institutes, but there are also some male Congregations, for example that of the Marist Brothers. Secondly, there are many religious who are not priests, but who are admitted as coadjutors in the priestly religious orders. One cannot deny without being reckless, that, generally speaking, the members of these orders or congregations have received a vocation from the Holy Spirit."[63]

2) A second problem, of similar importance, regarded the nature of the relationship between the laity and the ecclesiastic hierarchy. What is the difference between the mandate given by God to the Hierarchy and the activity carried out by the faithful? Can it be said that Catholic Action as such has a mandate? Plinio Corrêa de Oliveira replied in this way:

"1) Yes, if by mandate we mean a duty of apostolate imposed by the Hierarchy.
"2) No, if by mandate we mean that Catholic Action is in some way an element that integrates the Hierarchy and, thus, is part of the mandate which is direct and immediately imposed by Our Lord on the Hierarchy."[64]

If by "mandate" is meant every order legitimately imposed by an authority on a subordinate, then both the Hierarchy and the laity receive it. However, this does not exclude the existence of a fundamental difference of powers granted in one or the other case on the two different subjects. "The Hierarchy received the task to govern from Our Lord. The laity receive from the Hierarchy not functions of

---

[63] P. Corrêa de Oliveira, *Em Defesa de Ação Catolica*, pp. 41–2.
[64] Ibid, p. 49.

government but tasks that are essentially belonging to the subjects".[65]

It is at this point that Dr Plinio deals with the delicate problem of the "participation of the laity in the apostolate of the hierarchy", according to the famous definition of Pius XI. In fact he warns seriously of how the new concept of participation and of mandate implies a new "theology of the laity", that aims at upsetting in the egalitarian sense the actual government structure of the Church.

In this regard Plinio Corrêa de Oliveira has no doubts: "participation", in the sense given to it by the Pope and, before that by the Magisterium of the Church, is equal to "co-operation". The "mandate" of Catholic Action does not come directly from God to the faithful, but passes through the Hierarchy. It is the latter that must direct the action of the faithful and therefore also Catholic Action.

> "The mission of the faithful consists in fact in exercising, within the mission of the Hierarchy, the role of instrumental collaborators. In other words, the faithful must participate in the hierarchical apostolate as instrumental collaborators.[66]
>
> "By affirming that Catholic Action is a participation in the hierarchical apostolate, Pius XI wishes to say that it is purely and simply a collaboration, an essentially instrumental activity, whose nature does not at all differ, essentially, from the apostolic task exercised by organizations outside the sphere of Catholic Action and this is an organization-subordinate, as any and every organization of the faithful."[67]

3) The third point dealt with, above all in the remaining part of the book, considered the deviations of Catholic Action with respect to the liturgy, to spirituality and the methods of apostolate and action.

Without entering into the problem of the "dialogued Mass", which lay outside the subject of his book, Plinio Corrêa de Oliveira mentioned the doctrines that distorted the traditional teaching of the Church.

From the point of view of interior life, the Liturgicism that was spreading seemed to involve a "new ascesis", linked to a specific "grace of state", belonging to Catholic Action. According to the new theory, the liturgy would have exercised a mechanical or magic action over the faithful, that would render superfluous every effort at co-operation between man and God.[68] The most common devotional

---

[65] Ibid, p. 52.
[66] Ibid, pp. 63–4.
[67] Ibid, p. 64.
[68] Ibid, p. 94.

practices[69] and every effort of will, from the examination of one's conscience to the practice of the spiritual exercises of St Ignatius, were systematically discouraged, because they were considered to be useless and outdated. The origin of these errors, according to Dr Plinio, was to be found in the spirit of independence and the search for pleasure that would free man from the burden of sacrifices imposed by the work of sanctification. "Having eliminated the spiritual struggle, the life of the Christian appears to them as an uninterrupted series of spiritual pleasures and consolations."[70] Plinio Corrêa de Oliveira recalls the phrase of Leo XIII according to which "the perfection of Christian virtue lies in that disposition of soul which dares all that is arduous or difficult"[71] and the words of Pius XI in the letter *Magna Equidem* of 2 August 1924:

> "The unrestrained desire for pleasure, by weakening the strength of the soul and corrupting morals, gradually destroys the conscience of duty. In fact today there is an increasing number of people who, attracted by the pleasures of the world, abhor nothing more strongly, nor avoid anything with greater attention, than the sufferings that arise or the voluntary afflictions of the body or soul and they normally behave, according to the words of the Apostle, as enemies of the Cross of Christ. Now nobody can obtain the eternal beatitude if he does not renounce himself, if he does not pick up his cross and follow Jesus Christ."[72]

Together with the spirit of prayer, Plinio Corrêa de Oliveira further observes, the apostolic spirit is also required. But this starts with our neighbour and extends, in concentric circles, to those who are furthest away.

> "We do not hesitate to affirm that first of all one must desire the sanctification and the perseverance of those that are good; in the second place, the sanctification of Catholics that are far from religious practice; finally, and in the last place, the conversion of those that are not Catholics."[73]

---

[69] "These devotions – Cardinal Palazzini observes – offer precious advantages (indulgences, etc.) and special graces of a spiritual and even material nature. All produce moral and social effects of the greatest interest. It is in the practice of these devotions, so stupidly despised or neglected by short-sighted or blind spirits, that great and small, young and old, learned and ignorant, have learnt and continue to learn to raise their souls above the vulgarity and baseness of this world" (Pietro Palazzini, term *Devozione*, in EC, (1950), vol. IV, col. 1514).

[70] P. Corrêa de Oliveira, *Em Defesa de Ação Catolica*, p. 97.

[71] Leo XIII, Enc. *Auspicato concessum* of 17 September 1882.

[72] Cit. in P. Corrêa de Oliveira, *Em Defesa de Ação Catolica*, pp. 102–93.

[73] Ibid, pp. 184–5.

The Paulista leader also stressed the importance of the "methods" of apostolate. At a time when the politics of the "outstretched hand" had begun to permeate Catholic circles, he confirmed the heroic and supernatural character of the Catholic apostolate.

"It is necessary to clarify that, if an apostolic language imbued with love and gentleness, on the one hand, and one that instils fear and vibrates with holy energy, on the other hand, are equally just and should both be used in any epoch, it is certain that in certain epochs it is better to emphasize more the austere aspect and the gentle in others. However, this concern would never lead us to the extreme – which would be imbalanced – to only speak of one and to abandon the other. Which is the case today? The ears of contemporary man today are evidently fed up with the exaggerated sweetness, with the accommodating sentimentalism, with the frivolous spirit of prior generations. The great movements of the masses, today, have not been obtained through the mirage of easily obtained ideals. On the contrary, it is in the name of the most radical principles, appealing to the most absolute dedication, pointing out the hardest and steepest paths of heroism, that the principal political leaders have generated enthusiasm in the masses to the point of delirium. The grandeur of our day is precisely in the thirst for the absolute and heroism. Why not satiate this praiseworthy craving with the fearless preaching of the absolute Truth and of the supernaturally heroic morality which is that of Our Lord Jesus Christ?"[74]

With the term of "white heresy", he then indicated a sentimental attitude that was demonstrated above all in a certain type of mawkish piety and masked as "charity" towards one's neighbour.

"Say the truth with charity, make charity a means to arrive at the truth, and do not use charity for any kind of diminution or deformation of reality, nor for obtaining applause, nor for avoiding criticism, nor for vainly attempting to satisfy everyone. Otherwise, through charity you will not arrive at the truth but at error."[75]

"Another error consists in hiding or systematically belittling what is evil in heresies, to convince the heretic that the distance that separates him from the Church is small. In the meanwhile, in this way one ends up hiding the malice of the heresy from the faithful and the barriers that separate them from apostasy are opened! This

---

[74] Ibid, p. 238.
[75] Ibid, p. 230.

is exactly what will happen with wide-scale or exclusive use of this method."[76]

"Try to find common ground? There is a risk of getting bogged down in ambiguity, of favouring those we want to fish from murky waters. Let us not make the strategic retreat, the invariable use of ambiguous terms, and the constant habit of hiding our Faith, a rule of conduct that, in final analysis, brings the triumph of human respect."[77]

At the end of the long list of points concerning deviations in the doctrines and mentalities of the circles of Catholic Action, Plinio Corrêa de Oliveira concluded:

"All these are linked, closely or remotely, to the following principles: a denial of the effects of original sin; the consequent idea of grace as an exclusive factor of spiritual life; and a tendency to disregard authority, in the hope that order will result from free, vital and spontaneous combination of intelligences and wills. The doctrine of the mandate, supported moreover by European authors, many of whom merit consideration for various reasons, found a fertile ground in our environment, producing fruits that many of its authors did not foresee."[78]

In an apparently united and homogeneous religious environment, the book had the effect of a bomb. It contributed to waking up the sleepy majority, and to warn it against the progressivist current, whose insidious manoeuvres were checked. "This book" wrote Bishop Sigaud "was a cry of alarm and a cauterizing iron. A cry of alarm that stopped thousands of faithful from following, in good faith, the errors and excesses of the Liturgical Movement that advanced as an overwhelming wave."[79]

"In the history of the Catholic Church" the same prelate commented subsequently "there are books that were graces given by God to His people. (...) They are graces because their content enlightens the intelligence with extraordinary lights. They are graces because they encourage the will to act in a way as to fulfil the will of God." Among these books, after having recalled the *Confessions* and *The City of God* by St Augustine, the *Imitation of Christ* and the *Spiritual Exercises* by St Ignatius, the *Treatise of true devotion* by St Louis Marie Grignion

---

[76] Ibid, p. 196.
[77] Ibid, p. 213.
[78] Ibid, p. 337.
[79] Archbishop Geraldo de Proença Sigaud, *A Encíclica "Mediator Dei* e um pouco de história da Igreja no "Brasil", O Legionário, no. 803, 28 December 1947.

de Montfort, Archbishop Sigaud was to also mention the work of Plinio Corrêa de Oliveira on the twentieth anniversary of its appearance: "On our own national level, and in due proportion, one can say that *In Defence of Catholic Action* was a book-grace".[80]

8. An "act of Kamikaze"

The author of the book was not unaware that the publication of a work of that nature would be equivalent to an act of kamikaze: It would certainly inflict a hard blow on rising progressivism, but it would also inevitably expose the *Legionário* group to criticism and retaliation, compromising its influence in Catholic spheres. This was exactly what happened from then on.

"It was a kamikaze act. Either progressivism or we would blow up. We did. In the catholic milieu, the book drew applause from some, furious irritation from others, and a profound bewilderment from the immense majority. The dark night of an unbearable, complete and endless ostracism descended upon those of my friends who continued faithful to the book. Forgetfulness and oblivion enveloped us when we were still in the flower of our youth: this had been the sacrifice foreseen and accepted. Dawn, as we will see, only returned in 1947. However, nascent progressivism received a blow from the book from which until today it has not yet recovered."[81]

In private the archbishop of São Paulo, José Gaspar de Afonseca e Silva, did not hide his anxiety for the movement guided by Plinio Corrêa de Oliveira, with the obvious support of the Apostolic Nuncio.[82] However, he died suddenly in an aircraft accident, while on his way to Rio de Janeiro, on 27 August 1943. His successor Archbishop Carlos Carmelo de Vasconcellos Motta,[83] even before

---

[80] Archbishop G. de Proença Sigaud, "Um livro que foi uma graça para o Brasil", Catolicismo, no. 150, June 1963.
[81] P. Corrêa de Oliveira, "Kamikaze", Folha de S. Paulo, 15 February 1969.
[82] C. Isnard O.S.B., *Reminescências*, p. 221.
[83] Carlos Carmelo de Vasconcellos Motta was born on 16 July 1890 in the city of Bom Jesus do Amparo (Minas Gerais). Ordained to the priesthood on 29 June 1918, he was consecrated Bishop of Diamantina on 30 October 1932. On 19 December 1935 he was raised to the archdiocese of São Luiz do Maranhão, which he held until 18 August 1944, when he was called to replace Archbishop José Gaspar de Afonseca e Silva, as archbishop of São Paulo. He governed the archdiocese until 1964 when he was transferred to Aparecida immediately after the Revolution of 31 March. In February 1946 he was raised to the Cardinal purple by Pius XII as titular of St Pancras. He died in Aparecida do Norte on 18 September 1982.

occupying the Episcopal see was warned in detail about the boiling situation in the Paulista capital.[84]

Archbishop Carlos Carmelo, whose vision was the opposite to that of the *Legionário*, was also of a different temperament to that of his predecessor: he was not a man to mince matters and he faced up to the situation. He imposed an "armistice" on the *Legionário* team[85] which acted as a disavowal of its directors. Plinio Corrêa de Oliveira lost his role of president of Catholic Action; Father Antônio de Castro Mayer, Vicar-General of the archdiocese, was demoted to curate of the parish of São José de Belém; Father Geraldo de Proença Sigaud was sent to Spain.[86] A stormy campaign of defamation followed against which Dr Plinio and his companions could not defend themselves publicly because of the "armistice" imposed on them by the archbishop. Finally, in December 1947, Plinio Corrêa de Oliveira was ousted from the direction of the *Legionário*. The issue of 29 February 1948, contained an editorial entitled *"Legionário em terceira fase"* (*Legionário* in its third phase) in which the beginning of a "new phase" of existence of the weekly was announced. The final motto of the unsigned article said everything: *"Incipit vita nova"*.[87] Not a word about Plinio Corrêa de Oliveira, who, with immense generosity, had dedicated fifteen years of his life to the *Legionário*. In that same year, the future Bishop Helder Câmara took over the role of ecclesiastical assistant of Brazilian Catholic Action.[88] The atmosphere was deeply altered.

Progressivism was already demonstrating the main lines of what would be its constant strategy in the subsequent years. Plinio Corrêa de Oliveira himself summarized it in these points:

"a) Flight from debate or doctrinal dialogue. The criticisms of my

---

[84] The new archbishop's informer was, it seems, the Benedictine Dom Paulo Marcondes Pedrosa whom we have already met as the founder of the Marian Congregation of Santa Cecília and of the *Legionário* (C. Isnard O.S.B., *Reminescências*, p. 223).

[85] "Let there be a total and complete armistice between the contending parties! We do not intend that this instruction be definite, but only as an emergency, while momentous subjects are being judged by the Episcopal commission of Catholic Action" (Cf. "Revista Eclesiástica Brasileira", no. 4, December 1944, p. 978). Cf. also "Armistício", O Legionário, no. 641, 19 November 1944.

[86] P. Corrêa de Oliveira, "Padre Sigaud", O Legionário, no. 711, 24 March 1946.

[87] O Legionário, no. 804, 29 February 1948.

[88] Bishop Helder Câmara had participated actively in the Brazilian Integralist Action, the fascist inspired movement of Plinio Salgado, becoming a member in 1937 of the supreme council of the AIB, composed of 12 members. When in 1946 the archbishop of Rio Jaime de Barros Camâra wanted to make him his auxiliary bishop, he met with difficulties from the Holy See, because of his previous political activity in the "Integralists". The Pope refused the nomination that only arrived six years later. During that period of time, Bishop Câmara completed his transition from Integralism to Progressivism.

book, made explicit in one or another of the religious press, were vague, poor in arguments and rich in passion. Sometimes they also appeared implicit or veiled in pronouncements of this or that ecclesiastical personality;

"b) Defamation and then a campaign of silence and ostracism. Fuelled by a defamatory campaign, totally verbal, the principal clergy and laity who had applauded my book were gradually reduced to silence, removed from their positions, and relegated to ostracism. Some were only able to free themselves from this ostracism by remaining definitively silent about the subject;

"c) Advance, as if nothing had happened. Having thus stifled the opposition, the only thing left to the innovative current of opinion was to continue their advance, discreetly but resolutely."[89]

The small group of the *Legionário* remained however compact and loyal during the storm: the oldest of its nine members was thirty-nine years old, the youngest twenty-two.[90] Starting from February 1945 this group used to meet, every evening without fail, in the office at 665 Martim Francisco Street, in a part of the city called Santa Cecília, anxiously analyzing the deterioration of the religious and political situation in Brazil and in the world.

Plinio Corrêa de Oliveira, intellectual guide of the group, made every effort to instil it with a profound and true interior life, convinced as he was that action and study should be nourished at the springs of prayer and sacrifice. He thus explained "interior life":

"A man must endeavour to be constantly analyzing himself. At every moment, he needs to know how his soul is: why is he acting in this or that way; if it is licit for him to proceed in this or that way; if to feel in this or that way in face of a certain event is according to Catholic morality. This effort is called 'life', because it is so intense and should be so continuous that, for man, it constitutes an existence that unfolds of its own accord on a higher and more profound plain than his external existence. This is what is called 'interior life', precisely because it demands that man be in the uninterrupted habit of analyzing himself and controlling himself, unceasingly acting and living 'within himself'."[91]

---

[89] P. Corrêa de Oliveira, *A Igreja ante a escalada da ameaça comunista. Apelo aos Bispos Silenciosos*, São Paulo, Editora Vera Cruz, 1976, pp. 48-9.

[90] Dr Plinio's eight companions were: José de Azeredo Santos, Paulo Barros de Ulhôa Cintra, José Fernando de Camargo, José Carlos Castilho de Andrade, Fernando Furquim de Almeida, José Gonzaga de Arruda, Adolpho Lindenberg, José Benedicto Pacheco Salles.

[91] P. Corrêa de Oliveira, "Pio XII", O Legionário, no. 553, 19 March 1943.

In study and prayer, in fraternal and daily life together, the group grew in unity and solidarity. This catacombal period, the eve of new struggles, lasted three years.[92] During this period, the old *Legionário* team never ceased its controversial battle against the errors taking root in the Catholic world. One of the main targets continued to be Jacques Maritain, object of critical essays written, not only by Plinio Corrêa de Oliveira,[93] but also by valiant polemicists such as Father Arlindo Vieira[94] and José Azeredo Santos.[95]

During this period of isolation and misunderstandings, among the great friends of the group, we find Father Walter Mariaux,[96] a prominent German Jesuit whom Dr Plinio described in this way:

---

[92] "The grim harvester took three combatants from our scanty ranks. The first was the polished, intrepid, noble son of Our Lady, our unforgettable José Gustavo de Souza Queiroz. I also remember with respect and nostalgia the ardent personality, while at the same time being silent and gentle, of a militant member of JOC (Catholic Workers Youth), Mrs Angelica Ruiz. And the fighting and distinguished figure of a model head of family, of this excellent surgeon that all of Santos admired, of this outstanding university professor, of this father of the poor called Antônio Ablas F.o" (P. Corrêa de Oliveira, "Nasce a TFP", Folha de S. Paulo, 22 February 1969). On José Gustavo de Souza Queiroz, Cf. ID., "Bemaventurados os puros, porque verão a Deus", O Legionário, no. 710, 17 March 1946.

[93] On 6 February 1944, Plinio Corrêa de Oliveira published and commented on in *Legionário* the full text of the letter sent by Maritain to the Brazilian newspaper *O Diario*, in answer to the criticisms of Father Arlindo Vieira, that had appeared on 31 October 1943 in the same *Legionário* (Cf. "Os 'direitos humanos' e *O Legionário*", O Legionário nos. 600 and 601, of 6 and 13 February 1944). Cf. also ID., "Desfazendo explorações maritainistas", Catolicismo, no. 42, June 1954, pp. 5–6; ID., "A Comunidade dos Estados Segundo as normas de Pio XII", Catolicismo, no. 43, July 1954, pp. 5–6; ID., "Tolerar o mal em vista de um bem superior e mais vasto", Catolicismo, no. 44, August 1954, p. 3.

[94] In Rio de Janeiro "the principal figure opposing Maritain was the cultured and intrepid Jesuit Arlindo Vieira" (P. Corrêa de Oliveira, *A Igreja ante a escalada da ameaça comunista*, p. 45). Father Arlindo Vieira was born in Capão Bonito, in the State of São Paulo on 19 July 1897. Having entered the Society of Jesus, he finished his studies in Rome and in Paray-le-Monial before returning to Brasil where he devoted himself to teaching and then to the missions of the people, travelling to the poorest and most abandoned areas of Brazil. He celebrated his last Mass in Diego Vasconcelos, on the feast day of the city's patron saint, 4 August 1963. After distributing Holy Communion, he collapsed on the altar, where he died leaving great emotion among those present and a fame of holiness that continues to surround his memory. "His eucharistic weeks will be the spiritual renewal of the parishes. The parish priests fight over having him. Not a few bishops in the interior of Minas Gerais, of São Paulo, of Rio de Janeiro make use of his good services. He knows how to captivate the heart of the people with his goodness. His eloquence excites. It is as if his words bring a veritable supernatural message" A. Maia S.J., *Crônica dos Jesuitas do Brasil centro-leste*, (São Paulo, Edições Loyola), p. 212. On Father Vieira Cf. Francisco Leme Lopes S.J., "A mensagem espiritual do P. Arlindo Vieira S.J. (1897–1963)", Verbum, no. 27, 1970, pp. 3–102; ID., "O P. Arlindo Vieira S.J., constante evocação", Verbum, no. 27, 1970, pp. 403–19.

[95] In September 1950, the magazine *Vozes* of Petropolis published an article by José Azeredo Santos, "O rôlo compressor totalitário e a responsabilidade dos católicos", in which Maritain's doctrines defended by Tristão de Athayde were criticized. In its December issue the *Revista Eclesiástica Brasileira* carried the article, explaining in a note that these were important and opportune questions examined with perspicacity and good sense. But in the month of March it was forced to publish a note by Cardinal Vasconcellos Motta which did not hide his disapproval of the article by Azeredo Santos.

"Blond, very tall, Herculean, exuberant health, ample gestures, the hands of a field marshal, he always gives a first impression of one who is robust and determined which little by little fills in with new psychological elements. I have never known a richer personality in contrasting elements that were, nonetheless, harmonic."[97]

In 1949 Father Mariaux, organizer of the Marian Congregation of the São Luiz school, was recalled to Europe by his superiors. Some of the members of the congregation that he directed turned therefore to the group that met at Martim Francisco Street under the guidance of Dr Plinio. Thus the "Grupo da Martim" was born. Prominent among them were the four Vidigal Xavier da Silveira brothers, Dr Luiz Nazareno de Assumpção Filho, Dr Eduardo de Barros Brotero, Prof Paulo Corrêa de Brito Filho and José Luiz Marinho Villac, future rector of the seminary of Campos.[98]

9. A star was lit in the night ....

In January 1947 the sudden and unexpected news arrived of the appointment of Father de Proença Sigaud as bishop of Jacarezinho.[99]

---

[96] Father Walter Mariaux, born in Ülzen in Germany on 21 December 1894, in 1913 joined the Society of Jesus and in 1926 became a priest. He began his apostolate with the Marian Congregations in Cologne (1929) and in Münster (1933). At the beginning of 1935, he transferred to Rome, to the Central Secretariate of the Marian Congregations. His open hostility to National Socialism made his return to Germany impossible. Thus in 1940 Father Mariaux was sent to develop the Marian apostolate in Brazil, where in that same year he met and joined the group of the *Legionário*. He returned to Germany in 1949, first to Hanover and then to Munich, where from 1953 he directed the *Paulus-Kreis*, the famous *Maior Latina* congregation and the national secretariate of the Marian Congregations. The magazine *Die Sendung* was the expression of his lay apostolate. He died in Munich on 30 April 1963. Under the pseudonym of Testis Fidelis, Father Mariaux published, *El Cristianismo en el Tercer Reich*, Buenos Aires, La Verdad, 1941, a well-documented and implacable analysis of National Socialist anti-Christianity. On Father Mariaux Cf. Walter Fincke, "P. Dr. Walter Mariaux S.J. ", Sendung, no. 16, 1963, pp. 97–108; Max von Gumppenberg S.J., "Walter Mariaux S.J. Ein Leben im Dienste der Kongregation", Korrispondenz", no. 13, 1963, pp. 177–81; Héja Gyula S.J., "Father Walter Mariaux S.J. (1894–1963) ", Acies Ordinata, nos. 31–2, 1962–3, pp. 390–5.
[97] P. Corrêa de Oliveira, "Em Itaicí", O Legionário, no. 609, 9 April 1944.
[98] Canon José Luiz Villac entered the seminary in 1950 (Dr Plinio was sponsor to his ordination to the priesthood). Over a period of ten years, he was director of the seminary of Jacarezinho and then that of Campos. Having moved to São Paulo, he is chaplain to the TFP and was able to assist Plinio Corrêa de Oliveira in the days of his last illness and death.
[99] Father de Proença Sigaud was consecrated bishop on 1 May 1947 by the Papal Nuncio. On this occasion, Plinio compared him to the great personages of the Brazilian episcopate such as Bishop Vital and Archbishop Duarte Leopoldo e Silva, "models of intrepidity and firmness, of combativity and holy audacity". "One can expect much from him as regards true and unbreakable grandeur of soul." P. Corrêa de Oliveira, "Dominus conservet eum", Legionário, no. 768, 27 April 1947.

A few months later, Father Antônio de Castro Mayer was nominated coadjutor of Octaviano Pereira de Albuquerque, Archbishop-bishop of Campos.[100] The two priests, shelved because of their support to the group of the *Legionário* and to the book *In Defence of Catholic Action*, were now honoured by a demonstration of trust by the Holy See that seemed to be a reparation. Plinio Corrêa de Oliveira recalled the episode with these words:

> "I still remember the day in January of 1947 when I gave the news to my friends that, according to an envoy, Pius XII had named Fr Sigaud as bishop of Jacarezinho. But how? What? Our joy was great, but our doubt even greater. Fr Sigaud, during the windstorm, had been sent as a missionary to far-away Spain. Would he return? Yes, he would. And our joy rose to Heaven as a hymn. A star was lit to shine in the night of our exile, upon the remains of our ship-wreck!
>
> "Contrary to all expectations, another joy awaited us the next year. As I arrived, one night in March of 1948, at our catacomb, a friend awaited me at the door full of joy. Canon Mayer who, during the storm, had gone from the high post of Vicar-General of the Archdiocese to become the parish priest of far-away, albeit interesting, Belenzinho, had just communicated to us his nomination as coadjutor-bishop of Campos. It is useless to tell with what jubilation we immediately went to congratulate him."[101]

On 20 November 1947 the encyclical *Mediator Dei*[102] on the sacred liturgy appeared. It aimed to correct the deviations in the liturgical movement by developing the Pontifical teaching already begun with the *Mystici Corporis*.[103] The *Legiónario* greeted it with joy, publishing the entire text of the important document.[104]

---

[100] On his death, in January 1949, Father de Castro Mayer became bishop of this important diocese of the state of Rio de Janeiro.

[101] P. Corrêa de Oliveira, "Nasce a TFP", Folha de S. Paulo, 22 February 1969.

[102] Pius XII, Encyclical *Mediator Dei* of 20 November 1947, in AAS, (1947), vol. 39, pp. 521–95. Cf. J. Froger, "L'encyclique Mediator Dei", La Pensée catholique, (1949), no. 7, pp. 56–76.

[103] Pius XII, Encyclical *Mystici Corporis* of 29 June 1943, in AAS, (1943), vol. 35, pp. 193–248. Cf. P. Corrêa de Oliveira, "Mystici Corporis Christi", O Legionário, no. 585, 24 October 1943; Father José Fernandes Veloso, "O 'liturgismo' condenado pelo Santo Padre Pio XII", O Legionário, no. 612 30 April 1944; Father Ascanio Brandão, "Falsos profetas", O Legionário, no. 616, 28 May 1944.

[104] P. Corrêa de Oliveira, "Notas e comentários à Encíclica *Mediator Dei*", O Legionário, no. 803, 28 December 1947. "The publication of the Encyclical *Mediator Dei* constitutes, for all, a cause for holy and vibrant jubilation" (Idem, "Fé, união e disciplina", O Legionário, no. 800, 7 December 1947). No. 803 was the last issue of the *Legionário* under the direction of Plinio Corrêa de Oliveira; it is likely that the publication of these comments on the *Mediator Dei* was the last straw that led to the dismissal of Dr Plinio and his team.

The next year, in the *Bis saeculari* Constitution,[105] Pius XII formulated a definition of "Catholic Action" that showed a clear analogy with that already expounded by Dr Plinio. In 1947, the Pontiff had issued a warning against the tendency to level out the various forms of apostolate, limiting them to Catholic Action alone. He had admonished that in the "magnificent world movement of lay apostolate, (...) we must avoid the error of those who seek to make all work for souls conform to a uniform pattern".[106] This way of acting, the Pontiff insisted, "is quite foreign to the traditions of the Church" which "favours a fruitful multiplicity of Catholic apostolate, manifested in various societies and institutions which all work intensely under the guidance and protection of the Supreme Head of the Church."

There is no text of Pius XII where we can read that Catholic Action is a "participation" in hierarchical apostolate.[107] "This apostolate always remains the apostolate of the laity, and it does not become hierarchical apostolate, even when it is exercised with a mandate of the hierarchy."[108] In order to avoid any misunderstanding and ambiguity, the Pope always uses the word "collaboration".

Against the apostolate of the laity as emancipation from the Holy Hierarchy Pope Pius XII stated:

"It would be a mistake to see in Catholic Action (...) something

---

[105] Pius XII, Apostolic Constitution *Bis Saeculari* of 27 September 1948. Cf. Ludger Brien S.J., *La constitution 'Bis saeculari', texte et commentaire*, 4th edn., Montréal, Secrétariat National des Congrégations Mariales, 1961. Bishop A. de Castro Mayer, *A Constituição Apostolica "Bis Saeculari Die"*. *Repercussões jurídicas. Esclarecimentos doutrinários*, (conference addressed in Piracicata on 9 December 1948), in *Las Congregaciones Marianas. Documentos Pontificios*, Zaragoza 1953; Cf. also Fr. Juan Bautista M. Ferre, O.C., *Catolicismo o Capillismo*, Madrid, Emamevica, 1957; ID., *La Acción Católica Piedra de escandalo*, Emamevica, Madrid 1958; Arturo Alonso Lobo O.P., *Que es y que no es la Acción Católica*, Impr. de Aldecoa, Madrid 1950; ID, *Laicología y Acción Católica*, Madrid-Buenos Aires, Studium, 1955; Fr. Cyrillus B. Papali O.C.D., *De apostolatu laicorum*, 2nd edn., Rome, Teresianum, 1962.

[106] Pius XII, Radiomessage to the Congress of Marian Congregations in Barcelona of 7 December 1947. "One must guard against those who, impelled by praiseworthy zeal, seek to make all work for souls conform to a uniform pattern. This they do because of a short-sighted view which is quite foreign to the traditions and gentle spirit of the Church, the heir of the doctrine of St Paul: 'Now there are diversities of graces, but the same Spirit' (1 Cor. 12:4). And just as in earthly armies various components and units ensure by their very diversity that harmonious co-operation which leads to victory, in the same way, side by side with other forms of zeal, however important and essential they may be, the Church desires and encourages the existence of organizations of lay apostolate. (...) She wishes them to prosper and develop according to their own organizations and methods, thus furnishing a clear proof that in the army of Christ there exists a fruitful multiplicity of Catholic apostolate, manifested in various societies and institutions which all work intensely under the guidance and protection of the Supreme Head of the Church" (ibid; Cf. IP, vol. IV, *Il Laicato*, p. 788).

[107] J.-G. Dubuc, *Les relations entre hiérarchie et laïcat*, p. 56.

[108] Pius XII, Speech to the II World Congress for the apostolate of the laity, of 5 October 1957, in IP, vol. IV, *Il Laicato*, pp. 528 sgg.

essentially new, a change in the structure of the Church, a new apostolate of laymen side by side with that of the priests and not subordinated to the latter. In the Church laymen have always collaborated in the apostolate of the Hierarchy in subordination to the Bishop and to him to whom the Bishop has entrusted the responsibility for the care of souls under his authority. Catholic Action has only given this collaboration but a new form and organization so that it may be better and more efficaciously exercised."[109]

"Recently what is called 'lay theology' has sprung up and spread to various places, and a new class of 'lay theologians' has emerged, which claims to be independent. Nevertheless, it is necessary to maintain to the contrary that there never has been, there is not now, and there never will be in the Church a legitimate teaching authority of the laity withdrawn by God from the authority, guidance and watchfulness of the sacred teaching authority. In fact, the very denial of submission offers a convincing proof and criterion that laymen who thus speak and act are not guided by the spirit of God and of Christ."[110]

Against the attribution of sacrificial power to the laity, the Pope stresses that:

"The priest-celebrant, putting on the person of Christ, alone offers sacrifice, and not the people, nor clerics, nor even priests who reverently assist. All, however, can and should take an active part in the Sacrifice. The Christian people, though participating in the Eucharistic sacrifice, do not thereby possess a priestly power, We stated in the Encyclical *Mediator Dei* on the sacred Liturgy. (...) For there are some who have not ceased claiming a certain true power to offer sacrifice on the part of all, even laymen, who piously assist at the sacrifice of the Mass. (...) It must be firmly believed that the 'priesthood' common to all the faithful, high and reserved as it is, differs not only in degree, but in essence also, from priesthood fully and properly so called, which lies in the power of offering the sacrifice of Christ Himself."[111]

Almost as if to bring an end to the period of ostracism, a letter of the Secretariat of State dated 26 February 1949, signed by the then

---

[109] Pius XII, Address to the directors of Italian Catholic Action, of 5 May 1951, in IP, vol. IV, *Il Laicato*, p. 879. Cf. also Pius XII, address to the World Congress of the apostolate of the laity, of 14 October 1951, in IP, vol. IV, *Il Laicato*, pp. 913 sgg.

[110] Pius XII, Address to cardinals and bishops for the canonization of Pius X, of 31 May 1954, in IP, vol. IV, *Il Laicato*, pp. 972 sgg.

[111] Pius XII, Address to the cardinals and bishops of 2 November 1954, in IP, vol. IV, *Il Laicato*, pp. 982 sgg.

Substitute Secretary of State, Archbishop Giovanni Battista Montini, officially communicated the praise and blessing of Pius XII to Plinio Corrêa de Oliveira for his book *In Defence of Catholic Action*.[112]

Plinio Corrêa de Oliveira's book was a reply in advance to many erroneous and dangerous theories that would develop in subsequent years. The liturgical and secularist deviations incubated in Catholic Action exploded in the end like a cancer in the post conciliar period, revealing a new conception of the Church itself. After all, already during those years, avant-garde theologians such as Fathers Yves Congar[113] and Karl Rahner[114] were making every effort to draw from the developments of Catholic Action a new egalitarian "theology of the laity", already involving female priesthood.[115]

10. A new flag: *Catolicismo*

In January 1951, Bishop Antônio de Castro Mayer founded, in Campos, the cultural monthly *Catolicismo*. The editorial group was co-ordinated by José Carlos Castilho de Andrade, former secretary of the editorial staff of the *Legionário*. Old contributors of the combative magazine were also Fernando Furquim de Almeida, who edited the section devoted to the history of the Church; Adolpho Lindenberg, author of the comments on international economy and politics; José de Azeredo Santos, who looked after philosophy and sociology in the column "Nova et Vetera". Plinio Corrêa de Oliveira opened the first

---

[112] This is the text of the letter sent by the Secretariat of State to Plinio Corrêa de Oliveira on 26 February 1949: "Illustrious Sir, Moved by your filial dedication and piety, you offered the Holy Father the book *Em Defesa da Ação Católica*, in which you reveal perfect care and persevering diligence. His Holiness is very pleased with you for having explained and defended Catholic Action – of which you have a complete knowledge and for which you have great esteem – with penetration and clarity so that it has become clear to all how important it is to study and promote this auxiliary form of the hierarchical apostolate. The August Pontiff hopes with all his heart that this work of yours results in rich and mature fruits and that from it you may harvest neither small nor few consolations. And as a pledge that it be so, he grants you the Apostolic Benediction. Meanwhile, with due consideration, I declare myself, Devotedly yours, J. B. Montini." In 1963 Archbishop Montini was elected Pope Paul VI.

The book had also received the approval of six archbishops and fifteen bishops of Brazil (Cf. *Em Defesa da Ação Católica. Aprovações e encomios de autoridades eclesiásticas*, São Paulo, 1983).

[113] Yves Congar, *Jalons pour une théologie du laïcat*, Paris, Editions du Cerf, 1953.

[114] Karl Rahner S.J., "L'apostolat des laïcs", tr. fr. Nouvelle Revue Théologique, 1, 1956, vol. 78, pp. 3–32.

[115] "Every time that someone is in legitimate and usual possession of any part of liturgical or legal power that goes beyond the fundamental right of every baptized person, this person is no longer lay in the normal sense, he no longer belongs to the simple 'people of God' (...). In this strictly theological sense, a woman can belong perfectly to the 'clergy', even if the range of power that she can receive is more limited than that of a man" (K. Rahner, op. cit., pp. 5–6).

issue of *Catolicismo* with an unsigned article destined to become the manifesto of the Catholic Counter-Revolution.[116] Underlining the meaning of the feast of Christ the King, he wrote:

"A heavenly King above all. But a King whose government is already exercised in this world. A King who by right possesses the supreme and full authority. The King makes laws, commands and judges. His sovereignty becomes effective when his subjects recognize his rights, and obey his laws. Jesus Christ has rights over us all: He made laws, he governs the world and will judge men. It is our responsibility to make the kingdom of Christ effective by obeying its laws. This kingdom is an individual fact, if it is considered in regards to the obedience every loyal soul gives to Our Lord Jesus Christ. In fact, the kingdom of Christ is exercised over souls; and therefore the soul of each one of us is a part of the territory under the jurisdiction of Christ the King. The kingdom of Christ will be a social fact if human societies obey him. It can therefore be said that the kingdom of Christ becomes effective on earth, in its individual and social sense, when men in the intimate of their souls and in their actions conform to the law of Christ and societies do so in their institutions, laws, customs, cultural and artistic aspects."[117]

Between 1951 and 1959, with comprehensive essays in *Catolicismo*, Plinio Corrêa de Oliveira cast the doctrinal foundations of what was to be his masterpiece: *Revolution and Counter-Revolution*. His view of the social sovereignty of Christ is antithetical to the Maritainian view which was gaining ground at the time and which the Brazilian thinker continued to make the object of much criticism. Originally, the intellectual contribution of Dr Plinio, apart from his editorials, was also expressed in a column entitled "Ambiences, Customs, Civilizations", where, through the analysis of pictures, photographs, drawings, fashions, he emphasized the values of Christian civilization and the process of dissolution that had struck at them by showing aspects that until then had been scarcely or never considered by the Counter-Revolutionary writers.[118]

Meanwhile *Catolicismo* began to extend its battle against Catholic Progressivism well beyond the confines of the diocese of Campos. The new magazine differed from the *Legionário* in a fundamental point: The latter was just a newspaper; the new publication began to become the organ of a movement.

---

[116] P. Corrêa de Oliveira, "A cruzada do século XX", vol. 78, Catolicismo, no. 1, January 1951.
[117] Ibid.
[118] A complete collection of "Ambientes, Costumes e Civilizações", containing 185 articles, was published in São Paulo in 1982 by the Artpress Papéis e Artes Gráficas.

Plinio Corrêa de Oliveira and his collaborators had begun to travel to various countries of South America and Europe to make contact with the Catholic and anti-communist circles of the whole world. We can only imagine Dr Plinio's emotion when in Rome for the first time, in the summer of 1950, on the occasion of the Jubilee. In the eternal City, he saw Father Castro e Costa, his old professor at the São Luiz School; he was welcomed with affection by the now Cardinal Aloisi Masella; he frequented the best Roman aristocratic society; finally he was received by the Holy Father and by Archbishop Giovanni Battista Montini, Substitute Secretary of State. During the audience, turning to him and to Bishop de Castro Mayer who was with him, Archbishop Montini said: "Professor, I want you to know that the letter I wrote you was not out of mere politeness. Each word was attentively weighed. I have the pleasure of declaring this here in the presence of Bishop Mayer."[119] He returned to Rome, and to Europe during the summer of 1952. On that occasion, he was invited to lunch by Otto von Hapsburg, in his house at Clairfontaine in France.[120] The son of two extraordinary parents such as the Emperor Karl and his wife Zita, the young Otto was a prince of great charm and intelligence, who failed to comply with the hopes of many counter-revolutionaries by subordinating the Catholic commitment to his political career, that culminated in his election to the European Parliament.[121]

Plinio Corrêa de Oliveira was united by a great affinity of thought to Prince Pedro Henrique of Orléans-Braganza, head of the Brazilian Imperial House.[122] Every time he came to São Paulo, Dom Pedro Henrique went to visit the "group of Catolicismo" always accompa-

---

[119] P. Corrêa de Oliveira, "E sobre ti está edificada a Igreja", Catolicismo, no. 151, July 1963.

[120] Cf. J. S. Clá Dias, *Dona Lucilia*, vol. II, p. 52.

[121] An outline of his political view in Otto de Habsbourg-Lorraine, *L'idée impériale. Histoire et avenir d'un ordre supranationale*, with a Preface by Pierre Chaunu, Nancy, Presses Universitaires de Nancy, 1989. To the archduke Otto, who in his book criticizes "the long-standing alliance between throne and altar" (p. 218) and denies the existence of an Islamic threat for Europe (pp. 207–09), the ideas of "Christianity" and "Revolution", typical of the counter–revolutionary vision, are essentially foreign.

[122] His Imperial and Royal Highness Pedro Henrique of Orléans-Braganza (1908–81), married to the Princess Mary Elizabeth of Bavaria, had twelve children. The first, Prince Luiz, born on 6 June 1938, is the current head of the Imperial House of Brazil and the legitimate dynastic heir to the rights of the Crown; he is followed in order of succession by Prince Bertrand, born in 1941, and Prince Antonio, born in 1950. The latter is married to Princess Christine de Ligne, by whom he has had four children, heirs in their turn to the Brazilian throne: Prince Pedro Luiz (1983), Prince Rafael (1986), Princess Amélia (1984) and Princess Maria Gabriela (1989). Cf. A. A. dos Santos, *Quém é quém na Família Imperial*, in *Parlamentarismo sim!*, São Paulo, Artpress, 1992, p. 259. "Considering the sombre and threatening panorama in which the country finds itself - Armando Alexandre dos Santos writes (...), Prince Luiz does not only represent the nostalgias of a glorious remote past, about which serious historians today unanimously agree, but he is also the depository of better days yet to come" (*A Legitimidade monárquica no Brasil*, p. 38).

nied by one of his sons. Two of them, Dom Luiz, the eldest, and Dom Bertrand, joined the circle of the disciples of Dr Plinio. Because of their names so laden with historical memory, and their piety and exemplary lives, they would distinguish themselves among the prominent members of *Catolicismo* and, later, of the TFP.

From 1953, the *Catolicismo* group began to promote "study weeks" for friends and propagandists of the newspaper. These managed to gather hundreds of young people from various states of Brazil. That same year saw the appearance of an important pastoral letter, dedicated to the *Problems of the modern apostolate*,[123] prepared by Bishop de Castro Mayer with Dr Plinio's collaboration. It was one of the first texts of formation for young people who identified themselves with the newspaper's way of thinking.

In January 1954, São Paulo celebrated the four hundredth anniversary of its foundation. It had become a city of 2,700,000 inhabitants expanding at a dizzy rate. On 25 January, the archbishop Carlos Carmelo Vasconcellos Motta inaugurated the new cathedral that had been begun forty years previously by Archbishop Leopoldo e Silva, in the Praça da Sé. In August of that year, the president, Getúlio Vargas, committed suicide. After the provisional presidency of João Café Filho, he was succeeded by Juscelino Kubitschek, the *"presidente bossa nova"* who promised to achieve "fifty years in five".[124] *Catolicismo* tried to dissipate that atmosphere of superficial optimism, denouncing the growing influence of Communism in Brazil and in the world, as well as the increase of immorality, which the world epidemic of Rock and Roll appeared to be the most obvious symptom.[125] While underlining the limits of liberal anti-communism[126] Plinio Corrêa de Oliveira continued to indicate Catholicism as being the only solution to the problems of the present time. At Christmas 1955, he wrote:

"What is Catolicismo? What is its place in the House of God? By

---

[123] Cf. Bishop Antônio de Castro Mayer, *Carta pastoral sobre problemas do apostolado moderno, contendo um catecismo de verdades oportunas que se opoêm a erros contemporaneos*, Campos, Bôa Imprensa Ltda., 1953.

[124] Cf. Maria Helma Simões Paes, *A década de 60.*, 2nd edn., (São Paulo, Editora Atica, 1993), p. 31. On Juscelino Kubitschek (1902–76), president from 1956 to 1961, Cf. the entry for Silvia Pantoja and Dora Flaksman in DHBB, vol. II, pp. 1698–717. Cf. also Juscelino Kubitschek, *Meu caminho para Brasilia: cinquenta anos em cinco*, Rio de Janeiro, Bloch Editores, 1978; Edgar Carone, *A quarta República*, São Paulo, Difel, 1980. Brasília, the new capital, begun in 1955, was inaugurated by Kubitschek and his deputy João Goulart on 21 April 1960. With them was Archbishop Helder Câmara who praised it as a "dream come true". J. Kubitschek, *Por que construi Brasília*, (Rio de Janeiro, Bloch Editores, 1975), pp. 284–5.

[125] P. Corrêa de Oliveira, "Primeiro marco do ressurgimento contra-revolucionário", Catolicismo, no. 86, February 1958.

answering this question, we will have found our own place next to Jesus. Our task is principally one of myrrh. A journal written for militant and practising Catholics ... we want them to be very salty salt, a light placed on the mountain top and very bright. Lord, this is how we collaborate. This is the Christmas present we gather during the whole year to offer Thee. Others will give Thee the incense of their innumerable works, capable of an inappreciable good. We fit into this great work by abundantly burning, in this beloved Brazil, the austere, but odiferous myrrh of the 'yes, yes; no, no'."[127]

In 1958, with the death of Pius XII an era came to an end. *Catolicismo* however did not deviate from the line of absolute loyalty to Catholic tradition that had formerly been that of the *Legionário*.

"Our *leitmotiv* should be that there is no salvation outside the Church for the temporal order of the West. We should desire a civilization that is totally, absolutely, minutely Roman, Catholic and Apostolic. The demise of intermediary political, social or cultural ideals is patent. One cannot stop along the way back to God. To stop is to retreat, to stop is to play the hand of confusion. We desire only one thing: complete Catholicism."[128]

The great goal that Plinio Corrêa de Oliveira had indicated in the first issue of the magazine brightened the horizon of the approaching years.

"And this is our objective, our great ideal. We advance toward the Catholic civilization that may arise from the ruins of today's world, as the civilization of the Middle Ages was born from the ruins of the Roman world. We advance to the conquest of this ideal with the courage, the same perseverance, the same will to face and overcome all obstacles with which the Crusaders marched toward Jerusalem. For, if our forebears were capable of dying to reconquer the Sepulchre of Christ, how could we – sons of the Church as they – not want to struggle and die to restore something that is infinitely more valuable than the most precious Sepulchre of the Saviour, that is, His Reign over the souls and societies He created and saved that they may love Him eternally?"[129]

---

[126] P. Corrêa de Oliveira, "O anti-comunismo e o reino de Maria", Catolicismo, no. 62, February 1956, pp. 1-2; ID., "Covadonga, monumento de uma epopéia negativista?", Catolicismo, no. 66, June 1956, pp. 1-2.

[127] P. Corrêa de Oliveira, "Apparuit benignitas et humanitas salvatoris nostri Dei", Catolicismo, no. 60, December 1955.

[128] P. Corrêa de Oliveira, "A grande experiença de 10 anos de luta", O Legionário, no. 666, 13 May 1945, then Catolicismo, no. 173, May 1965.

[129] P. Corrêa de Oliveira, "A cruzada do século XX".

Chapter IV

Revolution and Counter-Revolution

"If the Revolution is disorder,
the Counter-Revolution is the restoration of Order.
And by Order we mean the peace of Christ in the Reign of Christ.
That is, Christian civilization, austere and hierarchical,
fundamentally sacral, anti-egalitarian, and anti-liberal."

1. "Doctor of the Counter-Revolution"

Revolution and Counter-Revolution, the work inseparably linked to the name of Plinio Corrêa de Oliveira, appeared in April 1959, on the occasion of the one hundred and first issue of the magazine *Catolicismo*.[1]

The word "Revolution", that originally indicated the heavenly movement of the stars, assumed a new meaning in the eighteenth century, especially after the French Revolution. Since then the latter has been the archetype of all revolutions, even of those that preceded it historically. The study of revolutions is a basic theme of political thought today.[2] "Revolution" the philosopher

---

[1] P. Corrêa de Oliveira, *Revolução e Contra-Revolução*, Campos, Bôa Imprensa Ltda., 1959. The work had four editions in Brazil and numerous editions in the Spanish-speaking world, in France, in Germany, in the United States (*Revolution and Counter-Revolution*, 3rd edn., York (PA), The American Society for the Defense of Tradition, Family and Property, 1997), in Canada and in Italy. It was also distributed in Australia, the Philippines, the Republic of Ireland, South Africa, and in the United Kingdom.

[2] Cf. among others Karl Griewank, *Der neuzeitliche Revolutionsbegriff. Entstehung und Enwicklung Europäische Verlagsanstalt*, Frankfurt a. Main 1969; Jean Baechler, *Les phénomènes révolutionnaires*, Paris, PUF, 1970; Roman Schnur, *Revolution und Weltbürgerkrieg*, Berlin, Duncker u. Hamblot, 1983; *L'Europa moderna e l'idea di Rivoluzione*, edited by Carlo Mongardini and Maria Luisa Maniscalco, Rome, Bulzoni, 1990; Charles Tilly, *European Revolutions 1492–1932*, Oxford, Blackwell, 1993.

Augusto Del Noce states "is the key word for understanding our age"[3] and "analysis of the idea of revolution is the main problem of philosophy".[4] Wars and revolutions, observes Hannah Arendt, "have thus far determined the physiognomy of the twentieth century".[5] But, whereas wars belong to the more ancient phenomena of the past, "revolutions, properly speaking, did not exist prior to the modern age; they are the most recent of all major political data".[6]

It is with the Enlightenment that the term "revolution" changes its meaning, and comes to signify a phenomenon of epochal nature destined to deeply condition the course of history. Voltaire often speaks of a "revolution of spirits", a revolution of minds, of which the philosophers, the Enlightenment thinkers, were sowing the seeds. In 1769 he writes: "It has already been happening for the last fifteen years; and in another fifteen, after such a beautiful morning, the full day will come".[7] This concept of a real regeneration or palingenesis of society takes on its modern significance thanks to what happened in France between 1789 and 1795.[8]

For Plinio Corrêa de Oliveira, the Revolution does not mean the subversion of any established order, nor is the Counter-Revolution a generic reactionary attitude against a reality which one opposes. He wants to give these words the precise meaning which they were given, starting from the French Revolution, by the Pontifical Magisterium and that fruitful line of Catholic thought that, inspired

---

[3] A. Del Noce, *Lezioni sul marxismo*, (Milan, Giuffré, 1972), p. 8.
[4] A. Del Noce, *Tramonto o eclissi dei valori tradizionali*, (Milan, Rusconi, 1971), p. 156.
[5] Hannah Arendt, *On Revolution*, (London, Faber and Faber, 1963), p. 1.
[6] Ibid, p. 2.
[7] François Arouet de Voltaire, letter of 2 March 1769 in *Oeuvres*, edited by the m.se of Condorcet, Société Litteraire Typographique, (Kehl 1785–89), vol. XLVI, p. 274.
[8] On the French Revolution, apart from the classical summary by Pierre Gaxotte, *La Révolution française*, new edition edited by Jean Tulard, Bruxelles, Complexe, 1988 (in English: *The French Revolution*, translated and with an introduction by Walter A. Philips, London-New York, C. Scribner's & Son, 1932), Cf. the reprints of the studies by Augustin Cochin (1876–1916), *La Révolution et la libre pensée*, Paris, Copernic, 1976 (1924), and *Les sociétés de pensée et la démocratie moderne*, Paris, Copernic, 1978 (1925), which influenced the historical "revision" by François Furet, *Penser la Révolution française*, Paris, Gallimard, 1988; F. Furet – Mona Ozouf (edited by), *Dictionnaire critique de la Révolution française*, Paris, Flammarion, 1988. On the cultural origins of the French Revolution: P. Hazard, *The European Mind*; ID., *La pensée européenne au XVIII siècle, de Montesquieu à Lessing*, 3 vols., Paris, Boivin, 1946; Daniel Mornet, *Les origines intellectuelles de la Révolution*, Paris, Colin, 1933; Bernard Groethuysen, *Philosophie de la Révolution française*, Paris, Gallimard, 1956. On the religious aspect, Cf. the important work of Jean de Viguerie, *Christianisme et Révolution*, Paris, Nouvelles Editions Latines, 1986.

by it and often anticipating it, was called "counter-revolutionary".[9]

The most famous author is Count Joseph de Maistre,[10] the thinker from Savoy to whom we owe one of the first reflections on the Revolution of 1789. But this school of thought had a much larger range of names than those to which it is usually referred. Even before de Maistre, the Jesuit Pierre de Clorivière[11] sensed the depth of the French Revolution, drawing a surprising picture of it: In 1794 he writes "The Revolution we saw break out shows, as foreseen by the Sacred Scriptures, three main characteristics: it was sudden, it is great, it will be general".[12] Along these lines, in the nineteenth century, we come across authors such as Louis de Bonald,[13] Juan Donoso Cortés,[14] Karl Ludwig von Haller,[15] Cardinal Edouard Pie,[16]

---

[9] There is no organic and deep exposition of Catholic Counter-Revolutionary thinking; the subject is dealt with a heterogeneity of positions by: Fernand Baldensperger, *Le mouvement des idées dans l'émigration française (1789–1815)*, 2 vols., Paris, Plon, 1925; Dominique Bagge, *Les idées politiques en France sous la Restauration*, Paris, P.U.F., 1952; Jean-Jacques Oechslin, *Le mouvement ultra-royaliste sous la Restauration: son idéologie et son action politique (1814–1830)*, Paris, Librairie générale de droit et de jurisprudence, 1960; Jacques Godechot, *La contre-révolution, doctrine et action (1789–1804)*, Paris, P.U.F., 1961; R. Rémond, *Les Droites en France*, Paris, Aubier-Montaigne, 1982; Stéphane Rials, *Révolution et Contre-Révolution au XIX siècle*, Paris, Albatros, 1987; E. Poulat, *Antireligion et Contre-Révolution*, in ID., *L'antimaçonnisme catholique*, Paris, Berg International, 1994. Great use can also be made of a series of articles written by Prof F. Furquim de Almeida "Os católicos franceses no século XIX", Catolicismo, from no. 1, January 1951 up to no. 80, August 1957.

[10] The writings of Count Joseph de Maistre (1753–1821) are collected in the *Oeuvres complètes contenant ses oeuvres posthumes et toute sa correspondance inédite*, 14 vols, edn. *ne varietur*, ibidem 1924–8, Lyon, Vitte et Perrussell, 1884–6. In spite of the abundance of bibliography on the author, there is no complete study on De Maistre. For an introduction Cf. *The works of Joseph de Maistre*, ed. by Jack Lively, New York, Macmillan, 1965. Cf. also E.D. Watt, "The English Image of Joseph de Maistre", European Studies Review, 1979, vol. 4, pp. 239–59; Richard Lebrun, *Joseph de Maistre: An Intellectual Militant*, Kingston-Montreal, McGill-Queen's University Press, 1988.

[11] Of Father Pierre Joseph Picot de Clorivière (1735–1820), Cf. the *Etudes sur la Révolution*, in *Pierre de Clorivière, contemporain et juge de la Révolution*, edited and with introduction by René Bazin, Paris, J. de Gigord, 1926 (now P. de Clorivière, *Etudes sur la Révolution*, Escurolles, Fideliter, 1988). Cf. also the large section on Pierre Monier-Vinard, S.J., *Clorivière*, in DSp, vol. II (1953), col. 974–9. Clorivière was the last Jesuit to have pronounced his solemn vows in France before the suppression of the Society of Jesus and he was its restorer after 1814. The cause for his beatification has been introduced.

[12] P. de Clorivière, *Etudes sur la Révolution*, p. 115.

[13] On Viscount Louis-Ambrois de Bonald (1754–1830), of whom the *Oeuvres Complètes* in three volumes (Paris 1859) have come out with Migne, Cf. the classic volume by H. Moulinié, *De Bonald. La vie, la carrière politique, la doctrine*, Paris, F. Alcan, 1916; Cf. also Mary Hall Quinlan, *The Historical Thought of the Viscount de Bonald*, Washington, Catholic University of America Press, 1953; Robert Spaemann, *Der Ursprung der Soziologie aus dem Geist der Restauration. Studien über L. G. A. de Bonald*, Munich, Kösel, 1959; C. Constantin, *sub voce*, in DTC, vol. II,1 (1910), col. 958–61.

[14] On Juan Donoso Cortés, Marquess of Valdegamas (1809–53), see the introductory study that Carlos Valverde premised to his edition of the *Obras completas*, Madrid, BAC, 1970, vol. I, pp. 1–166 (with an ample bibliography). The letter addressed by Donoso Cortés to Cardinal Fornari on 19 June 1852 may be considered one of the clearest manifestos of the Catholic Counter-Revolution of the nineteenth century. The original text is in J. Donoso Cortés, *Obras completas*, vol. II, pp. 746–62.

Bishop Charles Freppel[17] and, at the beginning of our century, Mgr Henri Delassus,[18] a gallant apologist whom Plinio Corrêa de Oliveira held in particular esteem. We should not forget that next to these authors there was also the teaching of the Popes, especially that of the venerable Pius IX and of St Pius X, whose letter *Notre Charge Apostolique* of 1910, which contains all his thinking, can be defined, according to Dom Besse, as "the Counter-Revolution in action".[19]

The thinking of the Counter-Revolutionaries is, in this sense, related to, but distinct from, that of the Conservatives[20] who have Edmund Burke[21] as their precursor, and is rather commingled with

---

[15] Karl Ludwig von Haller (1768-1854) is the author of the *Restauration der Staats-Wissenschaft, oder Theorie des natürlich geselligen Zustands; der Chimäre des Küstlich-bürgerlichen entgegensetzt*, 6 vols, Winterthur, Steiner, 1816-34. On Haller, see Michel de Preux, *Ludwig von Haller. Un légitimiste Suisse*, Sierre, A la Carte, 1996.

[16] Of Cardinal Edouard-Louis Pie (1815-80) Cf. the *Oeuvres de Monseigneur l'Evêque de Poitiers* (10 editions, the last in Paris, 10 vols., J. Ledars 1890-4). Cf. also Mgr Louis Baunard, *Histoire du Cardinal Pie; Evêque de Poitiers*, 2 vols., Poussielgue, Oudin, 1886, and the studies by Etienne Catta, *La doctrine politique et sociale du Cardinal Pie*, Paris, Nouvelles Editions Latines, 1959 and by Theotime de Saint-Just, *La royauté sociale de Notre-Seigneur Jésus-Christ, d'après le cardinal Pie*, Chiré en Montreuil, Ed. Sainte Jeanne d'Arc, 1988.

[17] Bishop Charles Freppel (1827-91) was adviser to the Vatican Council I, where he upheld the infallibility of the Pope, and from 1869 was bishop of Angers where in 1875 he founded the Catholic University. Cf. his *Oeuvres polémiques*, in 10 vols. (Paris, Palme, 1874-8) and *La Révolution française*, Paris, Trident, 1987 (1889).

[18] Mgr Henri Delassus (1836-1921), ordained to the priesthood in 1862, he exercised his ministry in Lille where, from 1874, he was owner, director and principal editor of the "Religious weekly of the diocese of Cambrai" which, with the creation of the diocese of Lille took the name of "Religious weekly of the diocese of Lille" and "he made it one of the bastions of the struggle against liberalism, modernism and all the forms of the Anti-Christian conspiracy in the world" (E. Poulat, *Intégrisme et catholicisme intégral*, (Tournai, Casterman, 1969), pp. 258-9). He was a member of "Sodalitium Pianum" and St Pius X raised him to domestic prelate in 1904, to apostolic protonotary in 1911 and to the role of dean of the chapter of the Cathedral of Lille in 1914, acknowledging, on the occasion of his priestly jubilee, his zeal in defending Catholic doctrine (*Actes de Pie X*, (Paris, Maison de la Bonne Presse, 1936), t. VII, p. 238). His main works are *Le problème de l'heure présente: antagonisme de deux civilisations*, cit., then reworked in *La conjuration antichrétienne: le temple maçonnique voulant s'élever sur les ruines de l'Eglise catholique*, 3 vols, with a letter of introduction by Cardinal Rafael Merry del Val, Paris, Desclée, 1910.

[19] Dom Jean Martial Besse, *L'Eglise et les libertés*, (Paris, Nouvelle Librairie Nationale, 1913), p. 53.

[20] Cf. Peter Viereck, *Conservatism*, in EB, vol. 27 (1986), pp. 476-84; ID., *Conservatism from John Adams to Churchill*, Westport, Greenwood Press, 1978; John Weiss, *Conservatism in Europe, 1770-1945*, London, Thames and Hudson, 1977; Klaus Epstein, *The Genesis of German Conservatism*, Princeton, Princeton University Press, 1966; Russell Kirk, *The Conservative Mind: from Burke to Eliot*, Washington (DC), Regney, Gateway, 1986 (1953).

[21] The official birth of international conservatism dates to the publication of the work by Edmund Burke (1729-97), *Reflections on the Revolution in France* in 1790. On Burke there is a vast amount of literature. We confine ourselves to mentioning the works by Alfred Cobban, *E. Burke and the Revolt against the Eighteenth Century*, London, Allen and Unwin, 1978 (reprint of the 1929 edition), and *The Debate on the French Revolution (1789-1800)*, (2nd edn.), London, Adam and Charles Black, 1960, and recently Crawford B. Macpherson, *Burke*, New York, Oxford University Press, 1980; Michael Freeman, *Edmund Burke and the critique of political radicalism*, Oxford, Basil Blackwell, 1980.

that of the so-called Ultramontanes, rivals of Catholic Liberalism and intransigent defenders of the Papal Primacy during the nineteenth century. These included Louis Veuillot[22] in France, St Antonio Maria Claret[23] in Spain and, in England, the great converts such as Cardinal Henry Edward Manning[24] and Father Frederick William Faber.[25]

To these many names of intellectual exponents, we must add at least that of a statesman who symbolizes the Catholic Counter-Revolution of the nineteenth century: the president of Ecuador, Gabriel García Moreno,[26] whose figure is rich in analogies with that of Plinio Corrêa de Oliveira.

Revolution and Counter-Revolution is thus part of a Catholic trend that has its own history and physiognomy within modern history. This line of thinking is characterized by a complete adhesion to the Pontifical Magisterium in all its expressions and by an in-depth meditation on the historical process initiated by the French Revolution. Plinio Corrêa de Oliveira's work is not however a repetition of the previous Counter-Revolutionary thought, but a masterful reworking and development of it, that makes the author an authentic "doctor" of this school in the twentieth century. In fact, he, on the one hand, reworked and arranged, with an extraordinary capacity for synthesis, the previous thinking; on the other he enriched it with new and unexplored dimensions.

2. Christianity in the Pontifical Magisterium

Revolution and Counter-Revolution is founded on an historical and philosophical premise in complete harmony with the Magisterium of

---

[22] On Louis Veuillot Cf. note 41 of chap. II, and among his works, "L'illusion libérale", in *Oeuvres*, vol. 10, pp. 315–61.

[23] St Antonio Maria Claret (1807–70). Founder of the Congregation of the Missionary Sons of the Immaculate Heart of Mary, archbishop of Cuba (1849–57), confessor of Queen Isabel II in Madrid, then among the protagonists of Vatican Council I, where he defended Papal infallibility. He was beatified by Pius XI in 1934 and canonized by Pius XII on 7 May 1950. Cf. *Escritos autobiograficos y espirituales*, Madrid, BAC, 1959 and the entry for Giuseppe Maria Viñas, in BSS, vol. II (1962), col. 205–10.

[24] On Cardinal Henry Edward Manning (1808–92), Cf. David Newsome, *The convert cardinals: John Henry Newman and Henry Edward Manning*, London, Murray, 1993.

[25] On the Oratorian Father Frederick William Faber (1814–63), Cf. Ronald Chapman, *Father Faber*, London, Burn and Oates, 1961.

[26] Gabriel García Moreno (1821–75), during his presidency he signed a concordat with the Holy See (1863), considered the model for the Catholic Concordats of the nineteenth century and he consecrated the Republic of Ecuador to the Sacred Heart (1873). "His existence was a constant battle against the opposing political powers who tended towards de-christianization and for this he was the object of profound hatred by his enemies who had him assassinated at the entrance to the Cathedral of Quito" (Silvio Furlani, sub entry, in DTC, vol. V (1950), col. 1936). Cf. also Alphonse Berthe, C. SS. R, *Garcia Moreno. Président de l'Equateur, vengeur et martyre du droit chrétien*, 2 vols., Paris, Téqui, 1926.

the Church: the necessity of not only single individuals to conform to the law of Christ, but also societies and states, over which the Redeemer exercises exclusive sovereignty. Fruit of this work of Christianization of social life is Catholic civilization.[27] "Catholic civilization is to the Church as water is to the fountain or light to its source."[28] For the Brazilian thinker, the Christian peoples form an authentic family in the most genuine sense of the word. Just like the family, Christianity too is united by a community of life: the supernatural life that makes every believer an adoptive child of Christ. "The concept of Christendom is a projection, in the natural sphere, of the great supernatural reality that is the Mystical Body of Our Lord Jesus Christ."[29]

In his encyclical *Il fermo proposito* of 11 June 1905, St Pius X had stressed that "the civilization of the world is Christian. The more completely Christian it is, the more true, more lasting and more productive of genuine fruit it is",[30] and in the letter *Notre Charge Apostolique* of 25 August 1910 he recalled:

"Civilization has not yet to be founded, nor has the new State to be built in the clouds. It existed and exists; it is Christian civilization; it is the Catholic City. The only question is that of re-establishing it and restoring it without delay on its natural and divine foundations against the continually repeated attacks of the wicked utopia of revolution and impiety: *Omnia instaurare in Christo* (Eph. 1:10)."[31]

In his turn, Leo XIII teaches that Christian civilization had its concrete historical expression, medieval Christendom.

"There was once a time when the philosophy of the Gospels

---

[27] On Medieval Christianity and the idea of Christianity generally, Cf.: Bernard Landry, *L'idée de chrétienté chez les scholastiques du XIII siècle*, Paris 1929; Alois Dempf, *Sacrum Imperium*, Munich-Berlin, Oldenbourg, 1929; Christopher Dawson, *The Making of Europe – An introduction to the history of European unity*, London, Sheed and Ward, 1932; Jean Rupp, *L'idée de chrétienté dans la pensée Pontificale des origines à Innocent III*, Paris, Les Presses Modernes, 1939; Luigi Prosdocimi, *Cristianità medievale e unità giuridica europea*, in Various authors *Storia d'Italia. Dalla civiltà latina alla nostra Repubblica*, (Novara, De Agostini, 1980), vol. IV, pp. 288–312 with ample bibliography. For a general view of Medieval civilization Cf. also Hilaire Belloc, *Europe and the Faith*, with an introduction by Douglas Woodruff, London, Burn and Oates, 1962 (1920); Raffaello Morghen, *Medioevo cristiano*, Bari, Laterza, 1962; Giorgio Falco, *La santa romana repubblica. Profilo storico del Medioevo*, Milan-Naples, Ricciardi, 1968; Leopold Genicot, *Le Moyen Age*, 3rd edn., Tournai, Casterman, 1978.

[28] P. Corrêa de Oliveira, "O crime de Hitler", O Legionário, no. 547, 31 January 1943; Cf. also ID., "Civilização cristã", O Legionário, no. 546, 24 January 1943.

[29] P. Corrêa de Oliveira, "Cristandade", O Legionário, no. 732, 18 August 1946.

[30] St Pius X, Encyclical *Il fermo proposito*, in ASS, (1905), vol. 37, p. 745.

[31] St Pius X, Letter *Notre Charge Apostolique*, 25 August 1910, p. 612.

governed the states. Then it was that the power and divine virtue of Christian wisdom had permeated the laws, institutions, and customs of the people; imbuing all ranks and relations of civil society. Then, too, the religion instituted by Jesus Christ, firmly established in befitting dignity, flourished everywhere thanks to the favour of princes and the legitimate protection of magistrates. Then the Priesthood and the Empire were happily united in concord and friendly interchange of good offices. So organized, civil society bore fruits beyond all expectation, whose remembrance is still, and always will be, in renown, registered as it is in innumerable documents that no artifice of the adversaries can destroy or obscure."[32]

Plinio Corrêa de Oliveira comments: "This luminous reality made from an order and divine perfection that is supernatural and heavenly rather than natural and earthly was called Christian Civilization, produced from Christian culture, which in its turn is the child of the Catholic Church."[33] Medieval Christendom was, then, the human society that in history achieved the Catholic ideal with the greatest perfection. If Maritain had written that "there is only one Catholic Church; there can be various Christian civilizations, various Christendoms",[34] the Brazilian thinker affirms rather with force that "Christendom was not just any order, or merely one of many possible orders. It was the realization, in the circumstances inherent to the times and places, of the only authentic order among men, namely, Christian civilization."[35]

The origin of the term and of the concept of the "Middle Ages"[36] is linked to a historiographical vision that was meant to describe a millennium of Western history like a long "night", a dark parenthesis between the "light" of the pagan world and the "rebirth" of the modern era; the Enlightenment thinkers of the eighteenth century will draw on this concept, already present in Petrarch[37] and in Italian humanism. In this way, as Eugenio Garin observes, "the contrast between the dark ages and the enlightening rebirth will foment a controversy of four centuries, from the fourteenth to the seventeenth centuries, ideally linking Humanism and Enlightenment".[38]

---

[32] Leo XIII, Encyclical *Immortale Dei*, of 1 November 1885, in AAS, 1885, vol. XVIII, p. 169.
[33] P. Corrêa de Oliveira, "A cruzada do século XX".
[34] J. Maritain, *Humanisme intégral*, p. 442.
[35] P. Corrêa de Oliveira, *Revolution and Counter-Revolution*, p. 41.
[36] G. L. Burr, "How the Middle Ages got their Names", American Historical Review, 1911–12, vol. 18, pp. 710 sgg.; Etienne Gilson, "Notes sur une frontière contestée", Archives d'histoire doctrinale et litteraire du moyen age, 1958, vol. 25, p. 65; Ludovico Gatto, *Viaggio intorno al concetto di Medioevo*, Rome, Bulzoni, 1977; Pietro Zerbi, *Il Medioevo nella storiografia degli ultimi vent'anni*, Milan, Vita e Pensiero, 1985.

The "black legend" about the Middle Ages, re-launched by Marxist historiography, has definitively collapsed, and no serious historian would be prepared today to consider the Middle Ages as a parenthesis of obscure barbarism.[39] The term Middle Ages has lost every semantic aspect of a negative sign, to simply indicate that historical age when all society, in its institutions, in its laws, in its customs, allowed itself to be shaped by the Catholic Church. For this reason Benedict XV defines medieval Europe as a homogeneous civilization directed by the Church[40] and Pius XII states that "it is right to recognize that the Middle Ages and its mentality had a note of authentic Catholicism: the indisputable certainty that religion and life form, together, an indissoluble whole".[41]

All medieval society conformed harmoniously to the natural order laid down by God himself when he created the universe and to the supernatural order inaugurated with the Redemption and inspired by the Church. This was the great civilization that slowly but strongly emerged from the chaos of the Barbarian age under the influence of the natural and supernatural energies of the people that were baptized and ordered in Christ. Writes Plinio Corrêa de Oliveira:

"The conversion of the Western peoples was not a superficial phenomenon. The seed of supernatural life penetrated the inner most part of the soul, and the formerly rough, lascivious and superstitious barbarian tribes gradually formed themselves according to the likeness of Our Lord Jesus Christ. The supernatural society –

---

[37] Francesco Petrarca was the first to mark a divide between the "*antiqua*", Roman age and the "*nova*" age, following the Middle Ages: Cf. *Epistolae de rebus familiaribus*, VI, 2; XX, 8 etc. Wallace K. Ferguson, in *Il Rinascimento nella critica storica* (It. tr., Bologna, Il Mulino, 1968, pp. 20–3), considers him "the first to express that concept of 'dark ages' which was destined to dominate for centuries in the interpretation of the Middle Ages and to provide the dark background from which the light of the Renaissance would emerge" (p. 21); Cf. also Theodor E. Mommsen, *Petrarch's Conception of the 'Dark Ages'*, in *Medieval and Renaissance Studies*, edited by E. F. Rice Jr., (New York, Cornell University Press, 1959), pp. 226–42; Eugenio Garin, *Rinascite e rivoluzioni. Movimenti culturali dal XIV al XVIII secolo*, (Bari, Laterza, 1976), pp. 4–47.

[38] E. Garin, *Rinascite e rivoluzioni*, p. 15.

[39] Marco Tangheroni, "La 'leggenda nera' sul Medioevo", Cristianità, no. 34–35, February-March 1978, p. 6–9; Régine Pernoud, *The Glory of the Medieval World*, London, D. Dobson, 1950; ID., *Pour en finir avec le Moyen Age*, Paris, Editions du Seuil, 1977; Raymond Delatouche, *La chrétienté médiévale*, Paris, Téqui, 1989; Jacques Heers, *Le Moyen Age, une imposture. Vérités et légendes*, Paris, Perrin, 1993.

[40] Benedict XV, Encyclical *Pacem Dei munus* of 23 May 1920, in AAS, 1920, vol. 12, p. 216.

[41] "We – stated John Paul II in his turn – are still the heirs of long centuries during which a civilization was formed in Europe inspired by Christianity. (...) During the Middle Ages, from a certain cohesion of the entire continent, Europe built a luminous civilization of which many testimonies remain" (Speech to the EEC in Brussels on 21 May 1985, Osservatore Romano, 22 May 1985).

the Church – thus spread its hierarchical structure throughout Europe. And from the mists of Scotland to the slopes of Vesuvius, dioceses, monasteries, cathedrals, conventual and parochial churches flourished, and, around them, the flocks of Christ. (...) From these vitalized human resources were born the kingdoms and the noble stirps, courteous customs and just laws, the guilds and chivalry, scholasticism and universities, the gothic style and the minstrels chant."[42]

What were the causes of the decline of medieval civilization? In his encyclical *Immortale Dei* Leo XIII writes that "the harmful and lamentable rage for innovation which rose to a climax in the sixteenth century threw first of all into confusion the Christian religion, and next, by natural sequence, invaded the precincts of philosophy, whence it spread among all the classes of society".[43] The religious, intellectual, and the political and social fields are the three fields assailed by the dissolutive process that the Pope calls "new jurisprudence". This is a declared "enemy" of the Church and of Christianity, which, in turn, is described by Pius XII in these terms:

"It is to be found everywhere and among everyone; it can be both violent and astute. In these last centuries, it has attempted to disintegrate the intellectual, moral, and social unity in the mysterious organism of Christ. It has sought nature without grace, reason without faith, freedom without authority, and, at times, authority without freedom. It is an 'enemy' that has become more and more apparent with an absence of scruples that still surprises: Christ yes; the Church no! Afterwards: God yes; Christ no! finally, the impious shout: God is dead; and, even, God never existed! And behold now the attempt to build the structure of the world on foundations which we do not hesitate to indicate as the main causes of the threat that hangs over humanity: economy without God, law without God, politics without God."[44]

This enemy will be the specific object of Plinio Corrêa de Oliveira's study. After demonstrating the nature and modality of action of the enemy, he will propose an efficacious reaction for destroying it and for restoring Christian civilization.

In summarizing the unshakeable nature of the antagonism between the Church and its mortal enemy, he writes:

---

[42] P. Corrêa de Oliveira, *A grande experiencia de 10 anos de luta.*
[43] Leo XIII, Encyclical *Immortale Dei*, in IP, *La pace interna delle nazioni.*
[44] Pius XII, Speech *Nel contemplare* of 12 October 1952, in DR, vol. XIV, p. 359.

"This terrible enemy has a name: it is called Revolution. Its profound cause is an explosion of pride and sensuality that has inspired, not one system, but, rather, a whole chain of ideological systems. Their wide acceptance gave rise to the three great revolutions in the history of the West: the Pseudo-Reformation, the French Revolution, and Communism."[45]

3. The great crisis of the Christian West

Revolution and Counter-Revolution offers first of all a view of our age that can be assumed in a word that is today dramatically topical: crisis.[46]

"The many crises shaking the world today – those of the State, family, economy, culture, and so on – are but multiple aspects of a single fundamental crisis whose field of action is man himself. In other words, these crises have their root in the most profound problems of the soul, from whence they spread to the whole personality of present-day man and all his activities."[47]

Thus it is man who is at the centre of Dr Plinio's work; man, the rational creature composed of body and soul who is today in the throes of a profound crisis.

For all the multiplicity of the factors of this crisis, it still preserves five essential characteristics:

1. *It is universal*, in as much as there is no people who is not affected by it, to a greater or lesser extent.

2. *It is one,* in the sense that there is not a series of autonomous crises that have no connection with one another, but a same crisis today affects the whole of what was once Christendom.

3. *It is total,* because it takes place in a whole series of problems so profound as to spread to all the forces of the soul and to all the fields of action of man.

4. *It is dominant,* because it is like a queen who controls forces and events that are apparently chaotic.

---

[45] P. Corrêa de Oliveira, *Revolution and Counter-Revolution*, p. 3.

[46] "During our time – John Paul II affirmed in Santo Domingo on 12 October 1992 – a cultural crisis of unexpected proportions is observed. Certainly today's cultural foundation offers a good number of positive values, many of them the fruit of evangelization; but at the same time, it has eliminated fundamental religious values and introduced deceptive conceptions, that are not acceptable from a Christian point of view" (John Paul II, Speech *Nueva Evangelización, Promoción humana, Cultura cristiana. "Jesucristo ayer, hoy y siempre"* of 12 October 1992, in suppl. to "L'Osservatore Romano" no. 238 of 14 October 1992, IV, pp. 21-2).

[47] P. Corrêa de Oliveira, *Revolution and Counter-Revolution*, p. 9.

5. *It is a process,* that is, a long system of causes and effects, born in the deepest areas of the Western soul and culture, that, from the fifteenth century to our days, have been producing progressive convulsions.

4. The historical stages of the Revolution

The historical stages of this process that has been going on for a number of centuries are the three great revolutions of the history of the West: Protestantism, the French Revolution and Communism. Plinio Corrêa de Oliveira thus summarized this process:

"1) The Pseudo-Reform was a first revolution. It sowed the spirit of doubt, religious Liberalism and ecclesiastic Egalitarianism, even if to different extents, in the various sects that originated from it.[48]

"2) It was followed by the French Revolution, which was the triumph of egalitarianism in two fields. In the religious field, under the form of Atheism, enticingly labelled as Secularism. And in the political sphere, with the false theory that every inequality is an injustice, every authority a danger and freedom is the supreme good.[49]

"3) Communism is the transposition of these maxims to the socio-economic field."[50]

For Plinio Corrêa de Oliveira the origins of this process date to the fourteenth century, when in Christian Europe a transformation of

---

[48] On protestantism, fundamental is the criticism by Jaime Balmes, *El protestantismo comparado con el catolicismo*, 2 vols., Madrid, BAC, 1967, 1842–4. The developments of Protestantism should be followed especially in the English sects of the seventeenth century and in the movement that erupted in the English Revolution. For Plinio Corrêa de Oliveira, the English Revolution of the seventeenth century occupies a prominent position in the tragic history of the crisis of the West. "Along these lines, along with the variants that always exist when history repeats itself, Charles I is really a pre-figure of Luis XVI, Cromwell a precursor of Robespierre or Saint-Just, and the English revolution a foretaste of the French Revolution" (P. Corrêa de Oliveira, "Figuras que encarnam concepções de vida", Catolicismo, no. 77, May 1957). On Protestant sects generally, Cf. R. de Mattei, *Alta ruet Babylon – L'Europa settaria del cinquecento*, Milano, IPL, 1977. Among those who openly criticize the French Revolution, there are many Protestant authors today. Cf. Aa. Vv., *Révolution et christianisme. Une appréciation chrétienne de la Révolution française*, Lausanne, L'Age d'Homme, 1992; and particularly Jean Marc Berthoud, of whom Cf. "La Révolution française et les Révolutions", Résister et Construire, no. 8–9, July-November 1989.

[49] For an overall view of the French Revolution, seen in its essence and in its true causes, in the light of the thinking of Plinio Corrêa de Oliveira, Cf. *Despreocupados ... rumo à Guilhotina. A autodemolição do Ancien Régime*, edited by J. S. Clá Dias, São Paulo, Edições Brasil de Amanhã, 1993.

[50] P. Corrêa de Oliveira, *Revolution and Counter-Revolution*, p. 4.

mentality begins that becomes increasingly clearer during the fifteenth century.

> "The thirst for earthly pleasures became a burning desire. Diversions became more and more frequent and sumptuous, increasingly engrossing men. In dress, manners, language, literature, and art, the growing yearning for a life filled with delights of fancy and the senses produced progressive manifestations of sensuality and softness. Little by little, the seriousness and austerity of former times lost their value. The whole trend was toward gaiety, affability, and festiveness. Hearts began to shy away from the love of sacrifice, from true devotion to the Cross, and from the aspiration to sanctity and eternal life. Chivalry, formerly one of the highest expressions of Christian austerity, became amorous and sentimental. The literature of love invaded all countries. Excesses of luxury and the consequent eagerness for gain spread throughout all social classes."[51]

This moral atmosphere contained the aspiration to an order of things that was fundamentally different from that of the Middle Ages. It is in this mood, in these "tendencies", that the great doctrinal errors and the historical disturbances of the subsequent centuries took root.

5. The depths of the Revolution

The Brazilian thinker distinguishes three depths in the Revolution. These, chronologically, overlap to a certain extent.

The deepest level is that of the *tendencies*. When the disorderly tendencies of man refuse to conform to an order of things that should guide them and correct them, they begin by modifying mentalities, ways of being, customs and artistic expressions.

From these deep strata, the crisis passes into the ideological terrain. It is the *revolution in the ideas*. Dr Plinio recalls the phrase used by Paul Bourget in his famous work *Le démon du Midi*: "One must live as one thinks, under pain of sooner or later ending up thinking as one has lived".[52] Inspired by the intemperance of the rebel tendencies, new doctrines appear. In the beginning, they at times seek a *modus vivendi* with the old ones, expressing themselves in such a way as to maintain a semblance of harmony with them. Generally, however, this does not take long to break out into a declared struggle.

---

[51] P. Corrêa de Oliveira, *Revolution and Counter-Revolution*, p. 14.
[52] Paul Bourget, *Le démon de midi*, Paris, Librairie Plon, 1914, vol. II, p. 375.

The *revolution in the facts* follows the *revolution in the ideas* when it begins to transform, by bloody or unbloody means, the institutions, laws and customs in the religious realm as well as in temporal society.[53]

6. The role of passions in the revolutionary process

The revolutionary process, considered as a whole, and also in its main episodes, is understood by the Brazilian thinker as the development, in stages, and through continuous metamorphosis, of dissolute tendencies of Western and Christian man and of the errors and movements that these foment.

The deepest cause of this process is, for Plinio Corrêa de Oliveira, an explosion of pride and sensuality that inspired a whole chain of ideological systems and a whole series of actions resulting from them.

"Pride leads to hatred of all superiority and, thus, to the affirmation that inequality is an evil in itself at all levels, principally at the metaphysical and religious ones. This is the egalitarian aspect of the Revolution. Sensuality, *per se*, tends to sweep aside all barriers. It does not accept restraints and leads to revolt against all authority and law, divine or human, ecclesiastical or civil. This is the liberal aspect of the Revolution. Both aspects, which in final analysis have a metaphysical character, seem contradictory on many occasions. But they are reconciled in the Marxist utopia of an anarchic paradise where highly evolved mankind, "emancipated" from religion, would live in utmost order without political authority in total freedom. This, however, would not give rise to any inequality."[54]

The Counter-Revolutionary authors of the nineteenth century, such as de Maistre, de Bonald and Donoso Cortés, described well the Revolution in its process of doctrinal errors. What characterizes the work of Plinio Corrêa de Oliveira is rather his attention to "the passions" and their influence on the strictly ideological aspects of the revolutionary process.[55]

Conforming to the use of various spiritual authors, when he speaks of "passions" as the supports of the Revolution, the author refers to the disordered passions of the human soul.[56] And, in keeping with

---

[53] P. Corrêa de Oliveira, *Revolution and Counter-Revolution*, p. 27.
[54] P. Corrêa de Oliveira, *Revolution and Counter-Revolution*, p. 3.

everyday language, he includes among the disordered passions all impulses toward sin existing in man as a result of Original Sin and of the triple concupiscence denounced by the Gospel: that of the flesh, the eyes and the pride of life.[57]

The Revolution has therefore its first origin and its most intimate driving force in disordered passions. Just like typhoons and cataclysms, it has immense strength, but this is directed at destruction.[58]

7. The speeds of the Revolution

The revolutionary process appears with two different speeds. The first, rapid, is destined to apparent failure, at least at immediate level. The second, that is much slower, is usually crowned with success.

The most extreme revolutionary movements can be traced back to the first speed: movements such as the Anabaptists in the sixteenth century and the Jacobin and anarchical currents of the nineteenth and twentieth centuries. To the second speed we can trace the moderate currents of Protestantism and Liberalism that, advancing in successive stages of dynamism and inertia, favour the decline towards the same point of arrival.

The failure of the extremists is only apparent: they create a fixed point of attraction that, because of its radicalism, fascinates the moderates. Society ends up going slowly along the road on which the most radical intended to bring it.

---

[55] H.-D. Noble, *Passions*, in DTC, vol. XI,2 (1932), col. 2211–41; Aimé Solignac, *Passions et vie spirituelle*, in DSp, vol. XII,1 (1984), col. 339–57. Passions may be understood in the metaphysical sense (Cf. St. Thomas Aquinas, *Summa Theologica*, I-IIae, q. 23 art. 2-4) and in the psychological sense. H.-D. Noble defines passion as "a unique act of the sensitive appetite that essentially includes an affectionate tendency and a psychological reaction" (col. 2215). cf.also Gérard Blais, *Petit traité pratique des passions humaines*, Sherbrooke (Canada), Editions Paulines, 1967; Antonio Eymieu (1861–1933), *Le gouvernement de soi-même – Essai de psychologie pratique*, Paris, Perrin, 1910. In investigating relationships between ideas, sentiments and acts, Eymieu establishes some great psychological laws, the first of which is that the idea drives towards the act of which it is the portrayal. The second principle is that the action excites the sentiment of which it should be the normal expression. The third is that the passion intensifies to the maximum point and uses human psychological forces for its own ends.

[56] The [disordered] tendencies produce moral crises, erroneous doctrines, and then revolutions. (...) The latter then lead ... to new crises, new errors, and new revolutions. (...) The fact is that disordered passions, moving in a crescendo analogous to the acceleration of gravity and feeding upon their own works, lead to consequences which, in their turn, develop according to a proportional intensity. P. Corrêa de Oliveira *Revolution and Counter-Revolution*, pp. 30-1.

[57] Cf. 1 John 2:16. P. Corrêa de Oliveira, *Revolution and Counter-Revolution*, pp. 46-7.

[58] P. Corrêa de Oliveira, *Revolution and Counter-Revolution*, p. 29.

8. The agents of the Revolution: Freemasonry and sects

The simple dynamism of passions and human errors, states Plinio Corrêa de Oliveira, is insufficient to explain the victorious march of the Revolution. This success demands the drive and direction of shrewd and conscious agents who direct a revolutionary process that is in itself chaotic: these are above all the anti-Christian sects, of any kind.

All the sects and secret forces whose aim is the destruction of the Church and Christian civilization can be considered as Agents of the Revolution. The mother sect, around which the others are organized, is Freemasonry.[59] It, as is seen clearly from the Pontifical documents, and especially from the encyclical *Humanum Genus* by Leo XIII, has as its "ultimate purpose, the utter overthrow of that whole religious and political order of the world which the Christian teaching has produced, and the substitution of a new state of things in accordance with their ideas, of which the foundations and laws shall be drawn from mere Naturalism".[60]

From 1931, Plinio Corrêa de Oliveira began to deal with the problem of the occult action of Freemasonry and the secret forces.[61] The Brazilian thinker referred often to the "secret forces" that operate in history, but precisely because of the importance which he attributed to the problem, he did not want to belong to the band of fanciful researchers that are so frequent in this delicate sector of research. He always faced this matter with seriousness and equilibrium, following a school that includes such great authors as Father Augustin

---

[59] The first condemnation of Freemasonry dates to the constitution *In eminenti* of Clement XII of 24 April 1738. The excommunication was confirmed and renewed by Benedict XIV with the constitution *Providas* of 18 May 1751 and by Pius VII with the constitution *Ecclesiam a Jesu Christo* of 13 September 1821. Leo XII ratified and sealed the previous decrees with the apostolic constitution *Quo graviora* of 13 March 1825; Pius VIII spoke in the same sense with the encyclical *Traditi* of 21 May 1829, as did Gregory XVI with the encyclical *Mirari Vos* of 15 August 1832, and Pius IX with the encyclical *Qui pluribus* of 9 November 1846 and numerous other interventions. The last great papal document regarding the Freemasons is the encyclical *Humanum Genus* by Leo XIII of 20 April 1884 (in AAS, 1906, vol. XVI, pp. 417-33). Since then Popes included the condemnation in canons 684, 2335 e 2336 of the Code of Canon Law in force from 1917 to 1983. In the New Code of Canon Law that came into force on 29 November 1983, Freemasonry is not expressly mentioned as it was in the previous Code. The Sacred Congregation for the Doctrine of the Faith, in a document of 26 November 1983, did however confirm that "the negative judgement of the Church with regard to Masonic associations remains unchanged, because their principles have always been considered irreconcilable with the doctrine of the Church and therefore enrolling in them remains forbidden. The faithful who belong to Masonic associations are in a state of sin and cannot receive Holy Communion" (L'Osservatore Romano, 27 November 1983).

[60] Leo XIII, Encyclical *Humanum genus*.

[61] P. Corrêa de Oliveira, "A Igreja e o Judaismo", A Ordem, no. 11, January 1931, pp. 44-52.

Barruel,[62] Jacques Crétinau-Joly,[63] Father Nicolas Deschamps[64] and, during our century, after Mgr Delassus, Mgr Ernest Jouin[65] and Count Léon de Poncins.[66] These authors, and others, documented in an incontestable manner the existence of an insidious anti-Christian conspiracy in history.

"The production of a process as consistent and continuous as that of the Revolution amid the thousand vicissitudes of centuries fraught with surprises of every kind seems impossible to us without the action of successive generations of extraordinarily intelligent and powerful conspirators. To think that the Revolution could have reached its present state in the absence of such conspirators is like believing that hundreds of letters thrown out a window could arrange themselves on the ground to spell out a literary piece, Carducci's *Ode to Satan*, for instance."[67]

Actually, the real problem for Plinio Corrêa de Oliveira is not so much to reveal the identity of the conspirators but, much more important, to show the profound nature of the Revolution and the mechanisms thanks to which it advances: in fact the agents can change, but the revolutionary process, its mechanisms and its anti-Christian goal do not change.

If the classic denunciation of the secret forces is focused on their channels of infiltration and of control of the social body, especially as

---

[62] Augustin Barruel S.J. (1741–1820), *Mémoires pour servir à l'histoire du jacobinisme*, 4 vols., London, Fauche, 1797–8. In the same year, the *Mémoirs* of Barruel were translated from the French by the Hon Robert Clifford, with the title, *Memoirs illustrating the history of Jacobinism*, 4 vols., London 1797–8.

[63] Jacques Crétinau-Joly (1803–75), historian of the Vendée and of the Society of Jesus, using documentary material received from the Holy See, outlined in *L'Eglise Romaine en face de la Révolution*, (2 vols., Paris, Plon, 1859), the situation of the struggles between the Catholic Church and the Revolution in the period that goes from the Pontificate of Pius VI to the beginning of that of Pius IX. The work was reprinted by the Cercle de la Renaissance Française (2 vols., Paris, 1976).

[64] Nicolas Deschamps S.J. (1797–1872), *Les Sociétés Secrètes et la Société ou philosophie de l'histoire contemporaine*, 2 vols., Avignon, Fr. Séguin aîné, 1854, then Paris, Oudin, 1882, enriched by a third volume of documents and by an *Introduction sur l'action des sociétés secrètes au XIX siècle* by Claude Jannet.

[65] Ernest Jouin (1884–1932) parish priest of the Church of St Augustin in Paris, in 1912 launched the "Revue Internationale des Sociétés Secrètes", the famous RISS, (published until 1939) which, due to the seriousness of the documentation and the expertise of its collaborators, was an study tool of great value. Cf. Joseph Sauvêtre, *Un bon serviteur de l'Eglise, mgr. Jouin (1844-1932)*, Paris, Casterman, 1936.

[66] Léon de Poncins (1897–1975), *Les forces secrètes de la Révolution*, Paris, Bossard, 1928; with Emmanuel Malynski, *La guerre occulte*, Paris, Beauchesne, 1936; *La Franc-maçonnerie d'après ses documents secrets*, Chiré-en-Montreuil, Diffusion de la Pensée Française, 1972; *Christianisme et franc-maçonnerie*, Chiré-en-Montreuil, Diffusion de la Pensée Française, 1975. In English: *Freemasonry and the Vatican: a struggle for recognition*, London, Britain Publishing, 1968.

regards the political and financial nerve-centres of modern States, Plinio Corrêa de Oliveira's work, as Fernando Gonzalo Elizondo rightly observes, introduces a new dimension:

> "It is the study and denunciation of the masonic techniques of governing the souls. The profound explanation of the knowledge and manipulation of the disorderly tendencies, of the creation of ambiences, of the spreading, whether by the media or by other means, of a mentality that, becoming generalized, guarantees the successful advance of revolutionary ideas and facts."[68]

9. The anarchical goal of the Revolution

> "The effervescence of the disordered passions arouses, on the one hand, hatred for any restraint and any law, and, on the other, hatred for any inequality. This effervescence thus leads to the utopian conception of Marxist anarchism, in which an evolved humanity, living in a society without classes or government, could enjoy perfect order and the most complete liberty, from which no inequality would arise. As can be seen, this ideal is simultaneously the most liberal and the most egalitarian imaginable."[69]

The anarchical utopia of Marxism consists in a state of things in which the human personality would have reached such a high level of progress that it would be possible for it to freely develop in a society without a State or a government.

The Revolution is destroying in modern man the notion of sin, the very distinction between good and evil and, *ipso facto*, it denies the Redemption of Our Lord Jesus Christ which, without sin, becomes incomprehensible and loses any logical relation with history and life.[70]

---

[67] P. Corrêa de Oliveira, *Revolution and Counter-Revolution*, p. 38. An entire section of the work *Despreocupados rumo à Guilhotina* is dedicated to Freemasonry and secret societies, pp. 265–317.

[68] Fernando Gonzalo Elizondo, "El deber cristiano de la militancía contrarrevolucionaria", Verbo, nos. 317–18, September-October 1993, p. 840, pp. 825–40

[69] P. Corrêa de Oliveira, *Revolution and Counter-Revolution*, p. 54. "In this society – which would live in complete order despite not having a government – economic production would be organized and highly developed, and the distinction between intellectual and manual labour would be a thing of the past. A selective process, not yet determined, would place the direction of the economy in the hands of the most capable, without resulting in the formation of classes. These would be the only and insignificant remnants of inequality. But, since this anarchic communist society is not the final term of history, it seems legitimate to suppose that these remnants would be abolished in a later evolution" (ibid, p. 54).

[70] P. Corrêa de Oliveira, *Revolution and Counter-Revolution*, p. 66.

By placing all its trust in the individual, as happens during its liberal phase, or in collectivity, as happens during its socialist phase, the Revolution idolizes man, trusting in his possibility of "self-redemption" through a radical social transformation.

The anarchical goal of the Revolution gets confused with the utopia of a universal Republic where all the legitimate differences between peoples, families, social classes, would be dissolved in a confused and seething mixture:

"The utopia toward which the Revolution is leading us is a world whose countries, united in a universal republic, are but geographic designations, a world with neither social nor economic inequalities, run by science and technology, by propaganda and psychology, in order to attain, without the supernatural, the definitive happiness of man."[71]

10. The metaphysical values of the Revolution

Two notions, conceived as metaphysical values, express the spirit of the Revolution: absolute equality and complete liberty. They are served by two passions: pride and sensuality. "It is in these sad depths that one finds the junction between these two metaphysical principles of the Revolution, namely, equality and liberty, which are mutually contradictory from so many points of view."[72]

The claim to think, feel and do all that unbridled passions demand is the essence of Liberalism. Actually the only freedom that it safeguards is that of evil, opposing in this Catholic civilization, that rather gives good all support and all freedom, but limits as much as possible the action of evil.

Plinio Corrêa de Oliveira dwells therefore on this radical egalitarianism, showing its consequences in the religious, political and social spheres. The denial of every inequality leads, at metaphysical level, to the refusal of the principle of identity and of non-contradiction. It results in "egalitarian" pantheism, because if the real is without specific inequalities and identity, the difference between men and God also collapses and everything is confusedly deified. The Gnostic aspect of the Revolution lies in this pantheism. A fundamental trait of Plinio Corrêa de Oliveira's thinking was, on the contrary, love of the

---

[71] Ibid, p. 67. The "religious" premises of this utopia are well described by Thomas Molnar in his *Utopia. The perennial heresy*, New York, Sheed and Ward, 1967.

[72] P. Corrêa de Oliveira, *Revolution and Counter-Revolution*, p. 51.

concrete, of individuality, of distinctions. He made his own the fundamental principle of Thomism according to which the specific object of the human intelligence is not the undefined being, but the "*quidditas rei sensibilis*",[73] the specific essences of the real. It is through the direct experience of the specific essences that man can reach knowledge of the universe and even the formulation of the first principles.

The essence, explains St Thomas in *De ente et essentia*, is the object of the definition of the thing,[74] what it is exactly. All that exists has its own essence because it is distinct from the reality that surrounds it and is not confused with it. The essence of the being is therefore its specific unity that distinguishes it from the multiplicity of the real.[75]

The first property of the reality that we know are the essences and, with them, not the unity but the inequality of the real. Or, to be more precise, we know the one through the many. Plinio Corrêa de Oliveira states:

"St Thomas teaches that the diversity of creatures and their hierarchical gradation are a good in themselves, for thus the perfections of the Creator shine more resplendently throughout creation.[76] He says further that Providence instituted inequality among the angels[77] as well as among men, both in the terrestrial paradise and in this land of exile.[78] For this reason, a universe of equal creatures would be a world in which the resemblance between creatures and the Creator would have been eliminated as much as possible. To hate in principle all inequality is, then, to place oneself metaphysically against the best elements of resemblance between the Creator and creation. It is to hate God".[79]

11. The "*philosophia perennis*" of Plinio Corrêa de Oliveira

Plinio Corrêa de Oliveira unhesitatingly defined himself as a convinced Thomist, conforming in this to the Magisterium of the

---

[73] The "*actus essendi*", too luminous for created intelligence, cannot be the real ground of the philosophical speculation of man, whose main object of knowledge is the "essences". The primacy of the "*actus essendi*" over essence is certainly an undeniable given of Thomism. But when the affirmation of this primacy leads to an exaggerated controversy against the alleged scholastic "essentialism", it risks degenerating into an attitude of an existentialistic type (Cf. C. Fabro, C.P.S., *Introduzione a San Tommaso*, Milan, Ares, 1983, pp. 100–03).

[74] St Thomas Aquinas, *De ente et essentia*, chap. II.

[75] St Thomas Aquinas, *Summa Theologica*, I, q. 11, a. 1.

[76] Cf. St Thomas Aquinas, *Summa contra gentiles*, II, 45; *Summa theologica*, I, q. 47, a. 2.

[77] Id., *Summa theologica*, I, q. 50, a. 4.

[78] Ibid, I, q. 96, a. 3 and 4.

[79] P. Corrêa de Oliveira, *Revolution and Counter-Revolution*, p. 50.

Church that in the last century, from Leo XIII[80] to John Paul II,[81] never ceased to point to the *Doctor Communis Ecclesiae* as the point of reference for the philosophical studies of Catholics. Contrary to many neo-Thomists of the twentieth century, anxious to build a bridge between the *philosophia perennis* and modern thinking,[82] the Brazilian thinker always stressed the incompatibility between the philosophy of the being and the orientation of "modern" philosophy, from Descartes[83] to Kant, from existentialism to modern nihilism, seeing in this the progressive itinerary of human intelligence towards metaphysical suicide.

The Summa Theologica, that summarizes, according to Pius XII, "the spiritual universe of the greatest genius of the Middle Ages",[84] is for Pius XI, "heaven as seen from earth".[85] Next to St Thomas, whose *Summa* he knew and widely commented upon, Plinio Corrêa de Oliveira placed St Bonaventure,[86] whose philosophy has well been described as "the most medieval of the philosophies of the Middle Ages".[87] The Brazilian thinker set out to recompose the vault of that

---

[80] Leo XIII may be considered the promoter of the rebirth of Thomism in modern times, with the encyclical *Aeterni Patris* of 4 August 1879, in which he declared St Thomas to be the sole official teacher in the Catholic schools of every level. On this important document, Cf. Various authors, *Le ragioni del tomismo. Dopo il centenario dell'enciclica "Aeterni Patris"*, Milan, Edizioni Ares, 1979.

[81] John Paul II, "Il Centenario dell'Aeterni Patris", Speech given at the Angelicum on 18 November 1979, L'Osservatore Romano, 19–20 November 1979.

[82] Cf. for example Antonin-Dalmace Sertillanges O.P., *Saint Thomas d'Aquin*, 4th edn., Paris, Alcan, 1925. An extreme case of deviation from Thomism, through the assumption of the *apriori* of Kant and of the existentialism of Heidegger is that of the Jesuit Karl Rahner (*Geist im Welt*, 1st edn., Innsbruck, Rauch, 1939) clearly denounced by the Stigmatine father Cornelio Fabro in *La svolta antropologica di Karl Rahner*, Milan, Rusconi, 1974. Of Fr Fabro, *Catolicismo* published in 1963 an article, translated by the *Osservatore Romano*, in which the author stressed the impossibility of establishing a bridge between true Christian philosophy, which can never deny the notion of divine transcendence, and the modern philosophical schools founded on the "principle of immanence", C. Fabro C.P.S., "Filosofia moderna e pensamento cristão", Catolicismo, no. 151, July 1963, p. 6.

[83] On the abandonment of the metaphysical in modern thinking, Cf. C. Fabro, C.P.S., *Introduzione all'ateismo moderno*, 2 vols., Rome, Studium, 1969; Tomas Tyn, O.P., *Metafisica della sostanza. Partecipazione e analogia entis*, (Bologna, Edizioni Studio Domenicano, 1991), pp. 243–384.

[84] Pius XII, Speech of 25 September 1949, in DR, vol. XI, p. 217.

[85] Pius XI, Address to the Angelicum of 12 December 1924, in *Xenia Thomistica*, Rome, 1925, vol. III, p. 600.

[86] On this aspect of the philosophy of St Bonaventure, Cf. J. M. Bissen, O.F.M., *L'exemplarisme divin selon Saint Bonaventure*, Paris, Vrin, 1929; E. Gilson, *Le philosophie de Saint Bonaventure*, Paris, Vrin, 1953; Efrem Bettoni O.F.M., *San Bonaventura di Bagnoregio*, Milan, Biblioteca Francescana, 1973; Francesco Corvino, *Bonaventura da Bagnoregio francescano e pensatore*, Bari, Dedalo, 1980.

[87] Thus Jacques Guy Bougerol O.F.M., at the end of the congress on St Bonaventure of Rome, on 26 September 1974, cit. in Leonardo Piazza, *Mediazione simbolica in San Bonaventura*, (Vicenza, Edizioni L.I.E.F., 1978), p. 65.

arch of thought which had its two pillars in the two great doctors of the Church, placed by Sixtus V on the same level of holiness of doctrine and of authority of Magisterium: *"Hi enim sunt duae olivae et duo candelabra* (Apoc. 11:4)".[88]

The "sapiential" vision of Plinio Corrêa de Oliveira is linked to the profound and lapidary sentences on "Wisdom" of St Thomas and of St Bonaventure. If the Angelic Doctor affirmed that *"Sapientia est ordinare et iudicare"*,[89] the Seraphic Doctor echoed him by writing that *"Sapientia diffusa est in omni re"*.[90]

"Omnia in mensura et numero et pondere disposuisti",[91] recites in its turn the Sacred Scripture. The Belgian philosopher De Bruyne stresses the exceptional importance of this verse on which is based that which defines the "sapiential" aesthetics of the Middle Ages.[92] Plinio Corrêa de Oliveira, recalls one of his disciples,

> "instinctively lived this sapiential aesthetics ever since his first vision of things. He slowly made them explicit until they became the corner stones of the Counter-Revolutionary doctrine, of what he many times called 'the total image' of the Counter-Revolution".[93]

Dr Plinio invited his disciples to deepen their knowledge of the notion of *"analogia entis"* and the theory of participation, as well as the cognitive and metaphysical value of the symbol. Plinio Corrêa de Oliveira's vision, like that of the Middle Ages, is that "The world unfolds itself like a vast ensemble of symbols, like a cathedral of ideas. It is the most richly rhythmical conception of the world, a poly-

---

[88] Sixtus V, Bull *Triumphantis Jerusalem.*

[89] St Thomas Aquinas *Summa Theologica*, I, q. 1, a. 6, c.; q. 79, a. 10, ad 3.

[90] St Bonaventure, *Hexäemeron*, col. 2, no. 21 (V, 340 a).

[91] "But Thou hast ordered all things in measure, and number and weight" (Wisd. 11:21).

[92] Edgar De Bruyne, *L'esthétique du Moyen Age*, (Louvain, Editions de l'Institut Supérieur de Philosophie, 1947), p. 11. Cf. also ID., *Etudes d'esthétique médiévale*, 3 vols., Brugge, De Tempel, 1946. "Under whatever aspect we consider it, there exists in reality but one mediaeval vision of the world, whether it expresses itself in works of art or in defined philosophical concepts: that, namely, which St Augustine drew with a masterhand in his *De Trinitate*, and which is directly referable to the words of the Book of Wisdom (11:21): *omnia in mensura, et numero, et pondere disposuisti."* E. Gilson, *The Spirit of Mediaeval Philosophy*, (Notre Dame-London, University of Notre Dame Press, 1991), p.101.

[93] Miguel Beccar Varela, Letter to the author.

[94] Johan Huizinga, *The Waning of the Middle Ages*, Harmondsworth, Penguin Books, 1965. "Medieval man effectively lived in a world populated with meanings, connections, supernatural senses, manifestations of God in things, in a nature that continuously spoke in a heraldic language (...) because it was the sign of a superior truth. (...) In its symbolic vision, nature, even in its most fearful aspects, becomes the alphabet with which the Creator speaks to us of the order of the world, of the supernatural goods, of the steps to be taken to move in the world in an orderly way to acquire the heavenly prizes. (...) Early Christianity had educated to the symbolic translation of the principles of faith." Umberto Eco, *Arte e bellezza nell'estetica medievale*, (Milan, Bompiani, 1978), pp. 68–9. A fresco of the medieval symbolic cosmos is painted by Marie-Madeleine Davy in *Initiation à la symbolique romaine*, Paris, Flammarion, 1977.

phonic expression of eternal harmony".[94] For medieval man nothing exists without meaning: *"nihil vacuum neque sine signo apud Deum"*[95] and everything that exists is made in such a way as to awaken the thought and memory of God. "The glory of the divine model is in every creature (...). Thus, every being is a path that leads to the model, he is a vestige of the wisdom of God".[96]

St Bonaventure offers us an itinerary of the soul to God "through the signs" of the sensible world that, with characteristics that are always different and unequal, address us with a single divine appeal. The truth of things consists in showing the supreme truth, the model cause. It is this similarity between the creature and the Creator that consents us to raise ourselves from things to God.[97] "The human intellect was created to ascend gradually – like the steps of a ladder – up to the supreme Principle that is God."[98]

Among the classical "proofs" of the existence of God, Plinio Corrêa de Oliveira especially appreciates the "fourth way",[99] understanding it however as a method of formation and a psychological process that shapes the human soul, rather than an abstract philosophical syllogism.

The "fourth way" that leads to God, the most perfect being, through the perfections in which all creation, in different measures and degrees, shares is that in which the platonic aspect is greatest. It shows God not just as an efficient cause and a final cause, but also as the model cause of creation and it contemplates the order of creation as a universe of harmony and beauty, a reflection of the uncreated divine Beauty.

"The beauty of God is reflected in the hierarchical and harmonic ensemble of all these beings in such a way that there is not, in a certain sense, a better way of knowing the infinite and uncreated beauty of God than by analyzing the finite and created beauty of the universe considered, not so much in each being, but in their ensem-

---

[95] St Ireneus, *Adversus haereses*, books V, l. IV, c. 2.
[96] St Bonaventure, *Hexäemeron*, col. 12, nn. 14–15.
[97] This likeness, as Etienne Gilson observes, does not imply a participation of things in the essence of God. "The real likeness that exists between the Creator and his creatures is a likeness of expression. Things are to God as signs are to the meaning that they express; they are therefore a sort of language and the entire universe is only a book in which everywhere one reads the Trinity." E. Gilson, *La philosophie au Moyen Age*, (Paris, Payot, 1952), p. 442.
[98] St Bonaventure, *Breviloquium*, p. 2, c. 12 (V, 230 a).
[99] *"Quarta via sumitur ex gradibus qui in rebus inveniuntur"*. Of all the Thomist proofs, as Gilson observes, the fourth is that which has caused the greatest number of different interpretations (E. Gilson, *Le thomisme*, (Paris, Vrin, 1972), p. 82). Cf. C. Fabro C.P.S., "Sviluppo, significato e valore della IV via", Doctor Communis, no. 7, 1954, pp. 71–109; ID., "Il fondamento metafisico della quarta via", Doctor Communis", no. 18, 1965, pp. 49–70, now both in *L'uomo e il rischio di Dio*, (Rome, Studium, 1967), pp. 226–71.

ble. God is reflected, nonetheless, in a masterpiece that is higher and more perfect than the Cosmos. It is the Mystical Body of Christ, the supernatural society we venerate with the name Holy Roman Catholic, Apostolic Church. She herself constitutes a whole universe of harmonic and variegated aspects that sing and reflect, each in its own way, the holy and ineffable beauty of God and the Word Incarnate. By contemplating the universe, on the one hand, and Holy Mother Church, on the other, we can elevate ourselves to the consideration of the holy, infinite and uncreated beauty of God."[100]

Modern philosophy, starting from Kant, has reduced beauty to a purely subjective element. According to the *philosophia perennis*, the beautiful is rather a transcendental property of the being, that is a perfection that belongs to every thing in as much as it is, without exceptions. Being the property of the being, the *pulchrum* (the beautiful) is linked with the transcendental attributes of the true, because it likes what is known by the intellect, and of good because the object of the beautiful satisfies the sensitive appetite. The beautiful is the radiance of the true and of good,[101] it is indeed a summary of truth and good.[102] "Beauty is like a synthesis of transcendental things. Literally, it is the excellence of intelligibility of an object whose parts splendidly in harmony (unity), fascinate the intelligence (truth) and attract desire (good)."[103] The beautiful, as St Bonaventure affirms, embraces all causes and is common to them. The glory of God, ultimate end of man and of history, is the contemplation of His Beauty, and it is what constitutes the happiness of man. If, indeed, the soul, knowing the true, moves towards the end that is the divine Good, it does so with even greater enthusiasm when it perceives God through the beauty of things created. Plinio Corrêa de Oliveira was an ardent champion of the "beautiful" as a weapon of the Counter-Revolution of the twentieth century.

If it is true that the *pulchrum* is another name for the *verum* (the

---

[100] P. Corrêa de Oliveira, "O Escapulário, a Profissão e a Consagração interior", speech at the 3rd National Congress of the Carmelite Tertiary Order (São Paulo, 14–16 November 1958), Mensageiro do Carmelo, special edition of 1959.

[101] Cf. Leo J. Elders, *La metafisica dell'essere di san Tommaso d'Aquino in una prospettiva storica*, It. tr., (Vatican City, Libreria Editrice Vaticana, 1995), vol. I, p. 167. On the "*pulchrum*" in St Thomas, Cf. *Summa Theologica*, I, q. 5, a. 4; I, q. 39, a. 8; IIIae, q. 27, a. 1 to 3.

[102] "Beauty in created order is the splendour of all the transcendents united, of the being, of the one, of the true and of the good; or, to be more precise it is the splendour of a harmonious unity of proportion in the integrity of the parts (splendor, proportio, integritas, Cf. I, q. 39, a. 8)" R. Garrigou-Lagrange O.P., *Perfections divines*, (Paris, Beauchesne, 1936), p. 299.

[103] François-Joseph Thonnard A.A., *Précis de Philosophie*, (Tournai, Desclée, 1966), p. 1227.

true) and for the *bonum* (the good), its replacement with the *horridum* (the horrendous) is only one aspect, one that is more insidious because it is less noticed, of that process of destruction of every quality of the Being that characterizes the Revolution. The hatred of the Revolutionary forces for human beauty, the image of divine beauty, is shown in this love for the horrendous. The Revolution wants to destroy every form of *pulchrum* in the life of man to make it more difficult, if not impossible, to reach God through his creatures.

12. Ambiences, Customs, Civilizations

In *Revolution and Counter-Revolution* Plinio Corrêa de Oliveira writes that

"Given that God established mysterious and admirable relations between, on the one hand, certain forms, colours, sounds, perfumes, flavours and, on the other, certain states of soul, it is obvious that, through the arts, mentalities can be profoundly influenced and persons, families and peoples can be induced to form a profoundly revolutionary state of spirit."[104]

This passage is fundamental for understanding the special contribution of Plinio Corrêa de Oliveira to the magazine *Catolicismo* in the column "Ambiences, Customs, Civilizations", whose extraordinary importance was not understood by everyone.

The ambience is the harmony that results from the affinity of various beings gathered in the same place, and it exercises a profound influence on men.

"Men formed ambiences in their image and likeness, ambiences in which their customs and civilization are reflected. But the opposite is also true to a large extent: the ambiences themselves formed, in their image and likeness, men, customs and civilizations."[105]

Proof of the importance of the ambience for the balanced development of natural and supernatural life is constituted by the wisdom with which God organized the great ambience called creation in which we are immersed, formed by the living beings who surround us: plants, animals, and which has at its head man, the image and likeness of God.

---

[104] P. Corrêa de Oliveira, *Revolution and Counter-Revolution*, p. 63.
[105] P. Corrêa de Oliveira, "Sêde prudentes como as serpentes e simples como as pombas", *Catolicismo*, no. 37, January 1954.

The interpretation and comments of the physiognomy of exceptional men, saints or revolutionaries, in this sense, were a constant note of the thought of Plinio Corrêa de Oliveira. In fact a man's way of being is expressed in his physiognomy, in his behaviour, in his features and even in his clothes, whose change in history is linked to the change of human personalities and types.[106] "Society, as it were," Pius XII affirmed "speaks with the clothes it wears; with its clothes it reveals its secret aspirations and it uses it, at least in part, to construct or destroy its future".[107] In turn, the Brazilian thinker notes:

> "If clothing should be in accordance with the user and with the circumstance in which it is used, there must be a harmony between a man's eminence and the eminent position he has attained. But God does not only have eminent men as children. Every human creature, no matter how modest, has an inherent dignity that is natural and unalienable. And even more so, immeasurably so, is the dignity of the least, the least noticed son of the Church, as a Christian, that is, as one baptized, as a member of the Mystical Body of Our Lord Jesus Christ."[108]

The same applies for art, for urban planning, for architecture which are the result of a group of ideas, tendencies, aspirations and psychological attitudes.[109] He counters the ancient medieval order, which expresses the harmony of scholastic philosophy,[110] with the modern Babel.

> "But the typical sounds of the immense modern Babels, the noise of the machines, the brouhaha and voices of men who toil in search of gold and pleasure; who no longer know how to walk, but run; who no longer know how to work without becoming exhausted; who are unable to sleep without tranquilizers nor to have fun without stimulants; whose laugh is a frenetic and sad grimace; who no longer know how to appreciate the harmonies of real music, but only the cacophony of jazz; all of this is but the excitation of disorder of a society that will only find true peace when it will have found the true God once again."[111]

---

[106] P. Corrêa de Oliveira, "Indumentária, hierarquia e igualitarismo", Catolicismo, no. 133, January 1962; Cf. also Id., "O hábito e o monge", Catolicismo", no. 62, February 1956.
[107] Pius XII, *Discorso di Gran Cuore* of 8 November 1957, in DR, vol. XIX, p. 578.
[108] P. Corrêa de Oliveira, "Dignidade e distinção para grandes e pequenos", Catolicismo, no. 33, September 1953.
[109] P. Corrêa de Oliveira, "O espírito cristão e o espírito pagão manifestados pela arquitetura", Catolicismo, no. 7, July 1951.
[110] Cf. Erwin Panofsky, *Gothic architecture and Scholasticism*, Latrobe, Archabbey Press, 1951.
[111] P. Corrêa de Oliveira, "Tranquilidade da ordem, excitação na desordem", Catolicismo, no. 110, February 1960.

Just like clothes, so language, gestures and ceremonial are also elements that have a great cultural and pedagogical importance for the common good of peoples.[112] It is a natural social "liturgy" that is expressed in order and in magnificence.

In the firmament of the Church there is harmony between apparently contradictory extremes such as the solitary vocation of the monk, inspired by a total renunciation of the world, and the splendour of the Pontifical ceremonies that used to once express the greatest pomp of which the world was capable.

"No, there is no contradiction between one order of values and another, except in the mind of the egalitarian, servants of the Revolution. On the contrary, the Church shows its sanctity precisely because with equal perfection, with the same supernatural genius, it knows how to organize and stimulate the practice of virtues that shine in the obscure life of the monk and those that sparkle in the sublime ceremonial of the Papacy. Even more than this, one balances the other. We could almost say that one extreme (in the good sense of the term) compensates the other and is reconciled. The doctrinal basis where these two holy extremes meet and harmonize is very clear.

"God, Our Lord, gave creation to us to serve as a means to reach Him. Thus, culture and art, inspired by Faith, emphasize the beauties of irrational creation and the splendours of the talent and virtue of the human soul. This is what is called culture and Christian civilization. In this way, men are formed in truth and beauty, in the love of the sublimity, of hierarchy and of order that reflect in the universe the perfection of Him who made it. Thus, creation in fact helps towards our salvation and the divine glory. But, on the other hand, they are contingent and ephemeral. Only God is absolute and eternal. It is our duty to remember this. This is why it is good to keep a distance from created beings so that by despising them we only think of the Lord. According to the first way, that is, by considering everything creation is, we arrive at God. According to the second, we arrive at God by considering what it is not. The Church invites her children to go by either path simultaneously, that is, by considering the spectacle of its pomps as well as by the abnegation

---

[112] P. Corrêa de Oliveira, "Têm os simbolos, a pompa e a riqueza uma função na vida humana?", Catolicismo, no. 82, October 1957. Cf. also, on the subject of the ceremonial of the pontifical power, the two studies "As cerimonias da posse de Eisenhower à luz da doutrina católica", and "Por que o nosso mundo pobre e igualitário se empolgou com o fausto e a magestade da coroação?", Catolicismo, no. 27, March 1953, and no. 31, July 1953.

that only She knows how to inspire and to effectively bring about."[113]

13. The Counter-Revolution and Catholic civilization

In his masterpiece, Plinio Corrêa de Oliveira does not confine himself to an implacable denunciation of evil. He also tries to outline the only therapy that can defeat it. If the essence of the revolutionary spirit consists in metaphysical hatred for any inequality and any law, the Counter-Revolution will find this strength above all in metaphysical love for the truth, inequality and moral law.

> "If the Revolution is disorder, the Counter-Revolution is the restoration of order. And by order we mean the peace of Christ in the Reign of Christ, that is Christian civilization, austere and hierarchical, fundamentally sacral, anti-egalitarian and anti-liberal."[114]

The Counter-Revolution is not a return to the past, nor is it a generic reaction, but one "waged against the Revolution as it is in fact today. Therefore, it has to be waged against the revolutionary passions as they are inflamed today, revolutionary ideas as formulated today, revolutionary ambiences as seen today".[115]

Just like the Revolution, the Counter-Revolution is also a process that knows different phases and speeds. In the journey from error to truth, however, the fraudulent metamorphoses of the Revolution are not allowed. If the Revolution hides its ultimate aim from its followers, the progress towards the good is obtained from men by making it known and loved in its completeness. The Counter-Revolution is "conservative" only if it means to preserve what is presently good and deserves to live. It is "traditionalist", but has nothing in common with the pseudo-traditionalism that preserves certain styles or customs, only out of an archaeological love of ancient things. The true Counter-Revolutionary apostle must make his own the regulations established by St Pius X, according to which Catholics must not "veil the more important precepts of the Gospel out of fear of being perhaps less heeded or even completely abandoned," even if, the holy Pontiff added "it will not be alien to prudence, when proposing the truth, to make use of a certain temporization when it is a matter of enlighten-

---

[113] P. Corrêa de Oliveira, "Pobreza e fausto: extremos harmonicos no firmamento da Igreja", Catolicismo, no. 96, December 1958.
[114] P. Corrêa de Oliveira, *Revolution and Counter-Revolution*, p. 75.
[115] Ibid, p. 74.

ing men who are hostile to our institutions and entirely removed from God."[116]

In the actual state, Plinio Corrêa de Oliveira concludes, a Counter-Revolutionary is whoever:

"1) Knows the Revolution, order and the Counter-Revolution in their respective spirits, doctrines, and methods.

"2) Loves the Counter-Revolution and Christian order, and hates the Revolution and 'anti-order'.

"3) Makes of this love and this hatred the axis around which revolve all his ideals, preferences, and activities."[117]

14. The driving force of the Counter-Revolution

If the most powerful driving force of the Revolution is the dynamism of human passions, provoked by a metaphysical hatred against God, against the Truth and against Good, there exists a symmetrical Counter-Revolutionary trend that aims at controlling passions by subordinating them to will and reason. The driving force of the Counter-Revolution is to be found in the spiritual strength coming to man from the fact that God governs his reason, the reason dominates will and the latter finally dominates sensibility. He is the servant of God but, exactly for this reason, he is master of himself.

Such a spiritual strength cannot be conceived without considering supernatural life, that raises man above the miseries of fallen nature. In this spiritual strength, for Plinio Corrêa de Oliveira, lies the most profound dynamism of the Counter-Revolution.

"It may be asked what value can be attributed to this dynamism. We reply that, in theory, it is incalculable, and it is certainly superior to that of the Revolution: '*Omnia possum in eo qui me confortat*' (Phil. 4:13).

"When men resolve to co-operate with the grace of God, the marvels of history are worked: the conversion of the Roman Empire; the formation of the Middle Ages; the reconquest of Spain, starting from Covadonga; all the events that result from the great resurrections of soul of which peoples are also capable. These

---

[116] St Pius X, Encyclical *Jucunda Sane*, of 12 March 1904, in ASS, vol. XXXVI, p. 524.

[117] P. Corrêa de Oliveira, *Revolution and Counter-Revolution*, p. 81. He distinguishes between "actual" counter-revolutionaries who have the full picture and "potential" counter-revolutionaries who grasp the clash only in some particular aspect. They must be conquered to the full Counter-Revolution.

resurrections are invincible, because nothing can defeat a people that is virtuous and truly loves God."[118]

15. The Counter-Revolution and the Church

If the Revolution is a process that aims at destroying all Christian temporal order, it is obvious that its ultimate target is the Church, "The Mystical Body of Christ, the infallible teacher of the Truth, the guardian of Natural Law, and, therefore, the ultimate foundation of temporal order itself".[119] The Revolution is an enemy that has risen against the Church to prevent it from fulfilling its mission to save souls not only while exercising its direct spiritual power, but also its indirect temporal power. The Counter-Revolution that rises in defence of the Church

"is not destined to save the Spouse of Christ. Supported as she is on the promise of her Founder, she does not need men to survive. On the contrary, it is the Church that gives life to the Counter-Revolution, which, without her, is neither feasible nor even conceivable".[120]

In Plinio Corrêa de Oliveira's view, the Counter-Revolution is not an end in itself but a compliant instrument of the Church. In its turn the Church does not identify with the Counter-Revolution, nor does it need to be saved by it.

"The Church is the soul of the Counter-Revolution. If the Counter-Revolution is the struggle to extinguish the Revolution and to build the new Christendom, resplendent with faith, humble with hierarchical spirit, and spotless in purity, clearly this will be achieved, above all, by a profound action in the hearts of men. This action is proper to the Church, which teaches Catholic doctrine and leads men to love and practise it. Therefore, the Church is the very soul of the Counter-Revolution."[121]

The exaltation of the Church is the ideal of the Counter-Revolution.

"If the Revolution is the opposite of the Church, it is impossible to

---

[118] P. Corrêa de Oliveira, *Revolution and Counter-Revolution*, p. 104. On this idea R. de Mattei, "La vita interiore fondamento della Contro-Rivoluzione", Lepanto, nos. 132–3, July–August 1993.
[119] P. Corrêa de Oliveira, *Revolution and Counter-Revolution*, p. 114.
[120] Ibid, pp. 115–16.
[121] Ibid, p. 117.

hate the Revolution (considered in its entirety and not just in some isolated aspect) and to combat it without *ipso facto* having the ideal of exalting the Church."[122]

The Church is therefore a fundamental Counter-Revolutionary force, but it does not identify with the Counter-Revolution: its true force lies in being the Mystical Body of Our Lord Jesus Christ.

Nevertheless, the scope of the Counter-Revolution goes beyond, in a certain sense, the ecclesiastical sphere, because it involves a reorganization of all temporal society from its foundations. This social restoration is inspired by the doctrine of the Church, but on the other hand it involves numerous concrete and practical aspects that regard specifically civil order.

> "And in this respect, the Counter-Revolution goes beyond the ecclesiastical ambit, though always intimately bound to the Church in every matter that has to do with her Magisterium and indirect power."[123]

Plinio Corrêa de Oliveira's work ends with an offering of filial devotion and unlimited obedience to "sweet Christ on earth", infallible summit and foundation of the truth, His Holiness John XXIII,[124] and with a filial consecration of his work to Our Lady:

> "It was the Immaculate Virgin who crushed the head of the Serpent, the first, the major, the eternal revolutionary, the instigator and foremost upholder of this Revolution, as of any before or after it. Mary is, therefore, the Patroness of all those who fight against the Revolution.
>
> "The universal and all-powerful mediation of the Mother of God is the counter-revolutionaries' greatest reason for hope. And, at Fatima, she already gave them the certainty of victory when she declared that, even after an eventual surge of communism throughout the world, 'finally, my Immaculate Heart will triumph!'
>
> "We beseech the Virgin, therefore, to accept this filial homage, a tribute of love and an expression of absolute confidence in her triumph."[125]

---

[122] Ibid.

[123] Ibid, p. 118.

[124] In the Italian edition of 1972, and in subsequent editions, the conclusion was maintained in the same terms, replacing the name of John XXIII, with that of the then reigning Pontiff Paul VI.

[125] P. Corrêa de Oliveira, *Revolution and Counter-Revolution*, p. 167.

16. Beyond the frontiers of Brazil: a school of thought and action

Some of the main themes touched by Plinio Corrêa de Oliveira were also dealt with by other contemporary Catholic thinkers, generically defined "traditionalists". It is sufficient here to recall the names of the Belgian philosopher, Marcel de Corte,[126] of the French founder of the Cité Catholique, Jean Ousset,[127] of the Italian philosopher, Augusto Del Noce,[128] of the Swiss historian, Gonzague de Reynold,[129] of the Spanish thinker, Francisco Elías de Tejada.[130]

Revolution and Counter-Revolution was not however just an intellectual work, but also the living germ of a movement that was destined to develop and spread throughout the world. Plinio Corrêa de Oliveira differs from many other contemporary traditionalist intellectuals precisely because of the role that he attributed to the living thought, destined to be communicated through personal action and to be organized in the apostolate of conquest. This unprecedented union of thought and action was not understood by some traditionalist circles, used to reconciling the Counter-Revolutionary doctrine with a political procedure inspired by various theories. This occurred above all in France, after the experience of Action Française.

France, "eldest daughter of the Church", was the fatherland of the Catholic Counter-Revolution that here produced its most penetrating minds, from Father Pierre de Clorivière to Mgr Henri Delassus. But

---

[126] Of Marcel de Corte (1905–94), Cf. *Philosophie des moeurs contemporaines*, Brussels, Editions Universitaires, 1944; *L'homme contre lui même*, Paris, Nouvelles Editions Latines, 1962. On de Corte Cf. Miguel Ayuso Torres, Danilo Castellano, Juan Vallet de Goytisolo, "In memoriam Marcel de Corte", Verbo, nos. 327–8, 1994, pp. 761–94.

[127] Jean Ousset (1914–94), *Pour qu'il règne,* Paris, Dominique Martin Morin, 1986. Ousset's work, that appeared for the first time in 1957, had numerous editions in France and many translations. The movement of La Cité Catholique, founded by Ousset in 1947, became in 1963 Office International des Oeuvres de Formation Civique et d'Action Culturelle selon le Droit Naturel et Chrétien. It had its greatest intellectual development in Spain, with the magazine *Verbo* directed by Juan Vallet de Goytisolo. Cf. Estanislao Cantero, "A los treinta anos", Verbo, nos. 301–02, January–February 1992, pp. 7–16.

[128] On Augusto Del Noce (1910–89), author, apart from the already mentioned works, of *L'epoca della secolarizzazione* (Milan, Giuffré, 1970) and *Il suicidio della Rivoluzione* (Milan, Rusconi, 1979), Cf. Rocco Buttiglione, *Augusto Del Noce. Biografia di un pensiero*, Casale Monferrato, Piemme, 1991; R. de Mattei, "Augusto Del Noce y el suicidio de la Revolución", Verbo, nos. 337–8, 1995, pp. 871–86.

[129] Of Count Gonzague de Reynold (1880–1970), Cf. especially *L'Europe tragique*, Paris, Spes, 1934; *La formation de l'Europe*, 10 vols., Paris, Plon, 1944–52.

[130] Of Francisco Elias de Tejada (1917–78), Cf. *La monarquía tradicional*, Madrid, Rialp, 1954. On this figure, Cf. the recent study by M. Ayuso Torres, *La filosofia jurídica y política di Elías de Tejada*, Madrid, Fundación Francisco Elías de Tejada, 1994.

between the end of the nineteenth and the beginning of the twentieth century, under the influence of Charles Maurras[131] and with the birth of Action Française, there was a "turning point" in the French traditional thinking in a positivistic and naturalistic sense.[132] One of its exponents, Louis Dimier, during lessons held in 1906 at the Institute of Action Française, numbered among the "masters of the Counter-Revolution" such authors as Sainte-Beuve, Balzac, Taine, Renan and even the Socialist Proudhon.[133] This was happening in the same years when within the Church the social modernism of Sillon condemned by St Pius X was developing. The analogy between Modernism and Action Française did not escape a Counter-Revolutionary author such as Augustin Cochin who thus summarized it:

"By pressing the movement to its end, the Modernist would like to set the Church in the place of God. Even today there are those who put the body before the spirit and order before the end: Maurras defends the body for the order that it presents; Le Roy[134] compromises the spirit; it is the same doctrine: intellectual with Le Roy, materialist with Maurras."[135]

Initially some Counter-Revolutionary Catholics such as a Father de

---

[131] Charles Maurras (1869–1952), founder of the newspaper and movement of Action Française, exercised great influence over various generations of French intellectuals. An ample view of his work in Eugen Weber, *L'Action française*, Paris, Stock, 1964. Cf. also Robert Havard de la Montagne, *Histoire de l'Action Française*, Paris, Amiot-Dumont, 1950; Colette Capitan Peter, *Charles Maurras et l'idéologie d'Action Française*, Paris, Seuil, 1972; Victor Nguyen, *Aux origines de l'Action française. Intelligence et politique à l'aube du XXe. siècle*, Paris, Fayard, 1991.

[132] The "turning point" was well described by Rafael Gambra Ciudad in *La monarquía social y representativa en el pensamiento tradicional*, (Madrid, Rialp, 1964), pp. 21–31, and in the entry *Tradicionalismo*, in GER, vol. XXII (1975), pp. 671–3. Gambra distinguishes between the right-wing, Catholic and counter-revolutionary traditionalism and left-wing traditionalism that, influenced by Comte, leads, through Taine and Renan, to Action Française. Cf. also R. de Mattei, "Augustin Cochin e la storiografia contro-rivoluzionaria", Storia e Politica", vol. 4, 1973, pp. 570–85.

[133] Louis Dimier, *Les maîtres de la contre-révolution au XIX siècle*, Paris, Nouvelle Librairie Nationale, 1907, pp. 115–35 (Balzac), pp. 161–84 (Sainte-Beuve), pp. 187–208 (Taine), pp. 209–230 (Renan), pp. 279–303 (Proudhon).

[134] Edouard Le Roy (1870–1954), follower of Bergson, was the philosopher who tried to give a doctrinal base to modernism. Many works by Father Garrigou-Lagrange were written precisely to disprove its fundamental agnosticism.

[135] A. Cochin, *Abstraction révolutionnaire et réalisme catholique*, (Paris-Lille, Desclée de Brouwer, 1960), pp. 54–5. "The method of Action Française – observes Stéphane Rials – does not ignore transcendency, but it effects a utilitarian treatment of it through a positivist interpretation. The Humanity of Comte becomes the Nation of Maurras. Transcendence is bent to the horizontal dimension, immanence is idolized, Providence is denied" (*Révolution et Contre-Révolution au XIX siècle*, pp. 48–9).

Pascal[136] and a Dom Besse,[137] collaborated with Action Française, appreciating its dynamism and the efficiency of its intervention. It was however a strictly procedural collaboration, conditioned by the loyalty of the Church movement. But Action Française, in its evolution from political movement to school of thought, saw the doctrine of Maurras prevail over the Counter-Revolutionary doctrine.[138]

The prudent attitude of St Pius X, who summarized his judgement on Maurras' writings in the formula *damnabiles non damnandos*, is a point of reference that cannot be eliminated.[139] Pius X approved Maurras' condemnation, but postponed its public promulgation judging it to be inopportune at a moment of open conflict with the French government. Maurras' followers stressed the second term of the formulation, which however only shows a contingent judgement, of a diplomatic nature, indicating an opportunity and not an evalua-tion. In St Pius X's *damnabiles* lies all the substance of a clear doctrinal judgement, which today does not permit any true Catholic to look on Maurras as a model.

Plinio Corrêa de Oliveira's judgement of Action Française, expressed a number of times in the *Legionário* was coherent with the

---

[136] Of Father Georges de Pascal (1840–1918), see among others, *Enseignement social, vues sociales d'un homme de tradition*, Paris, Rondelet, 1899; *Révolution et Contre-Révolution, le centenaire de 1789 et les conservateurs catholiques*, avec une lettre de M. le Marquis de La Tour du Pin, Paris, Impr. de Saudaux, 1898. Cf. A. de Lavalette Mobrun, *Le père de Pascal*, Paris, Jouve, 1918.

[137] Jean-Martial Besse (1861–1920), Benedictine historian and scholar, in 1909 held the profes-sorship of Syllabus in the *Institut d'Action Française*. On him, apart from *L'Eglise et les libertés*, Cf. *Eglise et Monarchie*, Paris, Jouve, 1910; *Le catholicisme libéral*, Paris, Desclée, 1911; *Les Religions laiques*, Paris, Nouvelle Librairie Nationale, 1913.

[138] This aspect was noted by Jean Madiran: "The generation of Catholics that were formed in a Catholic way, and who became part of Action Française by virtue of a "compromise for action", was succeeded by a generation that had a Maurrasian formation and was no longer sensitive to what could have been irritating and in any case unacceptable for a Christian, in Maurras' school of thought". J. Madiran, *L'Intégrisme, histoire d'une histoire*, (Paris, Nouvelles Editions Latines, 1964), p. 97.

[139] On 2 January 1914 the Congregation of the Index judged that five books of Maurras (*Chemin de Paradis, Anthinea, Les amants de Venise, Trois idées politiques, L'avenir de l'intelligence*) and the magazine *L'Action Française* directed by him deserved condemnation. St Pius X consid-ered it opportune to postpone the promulgation of the decree of 29 January 1914, but the excommunication was then pronounced by Pius XI in 1926. In 1939, after the signature, by the directors of Action Française, of a declaration of submission, the sanctions regarding the news-paper were removed by Pius XII (Cf. Decree of the Holy Office of 10 July 1939; response of the Sacred Penitentiary of 24 July of the same year; the condemnation of the writings of Maurras listed by the Index remained in force). Cf. also Lucien Thomas, *L'Action française devant l'Eglise. De Pie X à Pie XII*, Paris, Nouvelles Editions Latines, 1965; Michael Sutton, *Nationalism, positivism and catholicism: the politics of Maurras and French Catholics*, London, Cambridge University Press, 1982; Oscar. L. Arnal, *Ambivalent alliance. The Catholic Church and the Action Française. 1899–1939*, Pittsburgh, University of Pittsburgh Press, 1985; André Laudouze, *Dominicains français et Action Française*, Paris, Les Editions Ouvrières, 1989.

position of the Magisterium of the Holy See.[140] Apart from affinities or convergences at a strictly political level, there was a basic incompatibility between the doctrine of the Church and that professed by the heads of Action Française.

Beside the problems with Maurras,[141] in some circles of post-war French traditionalist culture there were traces of old errors such as Jansenism and Gallicanism. The latter being hostile to that Roman Catholic spirit which is, first and foremost, the universality and the capacity to understand good, wherever it appears and with the legitimate modalities proper to every reality. But what characterized these circles was above all a defeatist mentality, that could ill agree with the combative and hope-filled theories of *Revolution and Counter-Revolution*.[142]

Strange as it may seem, in Europe, *Revolution and Counter-Revolution* had its deepest influence, apart from in the Iberian peninsula, above all in Italy, a country without a traditionalist culture in the strict sense of the term.

European Counter-Revolutionary thought in fact summed up its vision in the formula "Throne and Altar", that is in loyalty to the Church and to the dynasties that in the course of history embodied Catholic tradition. However, in Italy, after the elimination of the pre-unification dynasties by the Piedmont of the Savoys and the subsequent invasion of Rome of 1870, the breach opened between the Papacy and the House of Savoy left no room for Counter-Revolutionary legitimism. Even after the fall of the monarchy, the monarchists occupied Liberal-Nationalistic positions, while the Catholics were diverted towards the Christian Democratic Party, responsible for the transfer to the left of the post-war Catholic world.[143] In this way, in the land chosen by Providence for the See of

---

[140] When the excommunication was revoked by Pius XII, he ended the controversy with these words: "There is no greater pretence than to be more Catholic than the Pope. Rome has spoken: the case is judged. Let no one be unconditionally enthusiastic or unduly rigorous" (P. Corrêa de Oliveira, "Action Française", O Legionário, no. 359, 30 July 1939). Cf. also ID., "A Action Française e a Liga das Nações", O Legionário, no. 276, 26 December 1937; ID., "Action Française", O Legionário, no. 349, 21 May 1938.

[141] Cf. for example the special issue of the magazine *Itinéraires*, no. 122, April 1968, dedicated to Maurras, with articles by Jean Madiran, Henri Charlier, Jean Ousset, Pierre Gaxotte, Roger Joseph, V. A. Berto, Henri Rambaud, Gustave Thibon, Jean-Baptiste Morvan, Jacques Vier, Louis Salleron, Georges Lafly, Marcel de Corte.

[142] A description of this mentality in the small book *La mano che estingue, la voce che addormenta*, edited by the Ufficio Tradizione, Famiglia, Proprietà, Rome 1996.

[143] For an analysis of this itinerary, Cf. R. de Mattei, *Il centro che ci portò a sinistra*, Rome, Fiducia, 1994 and the manifesto of the Centro Culturale Lepanto "Prodi il Kerensky italiano?", Il Tempo and Il Giornale of 14 May 1996. Cf. also Giovanni Cantoni, *La lezione italiana*, Piacenza, Cristianità, 1980.

Peter, an authentically Catholic political action was lacking and the strongest and best organized Communist Party of the West, following the lesson of Antonio Gramsci, was able to develop the strategy of the historical compromise. This brought about, in May 1996, the rise to power of the Neo-Communists.

While Italy was in the throes of political agitation, the group of Alleanza Cattolica was born around the principles of *Revolution and Counter-Revolution* that had been translated and published by Giovanni Cantoni.[144] It was followed, in 1973, by the birth of the magazine *Cristianità*. Subsequently other groups and movements were inspired by *Revolution and Counter-Revolution*, among which figures the Centro Culturale Lepanto, founded in Rome in 1982.[145]

17. Nobility and Analogous Traditional Elites in face of the IV Revolution

Nobility and Analogous Traditional Elites[146] may be considered the ideal continuation and development of *Revolution and Counter-Revolution*.

In an essay entitled *Revolution and Counter-Revolution Twenty Years After*,[147] Plinio Corrêa de Oliveira describes the appearance, after the Communist Revolution, of a less ideological and more tendencial IV Revolution that programmes the extinction of the old

---

[144] The first Italian translations of the work, for the edizioni dell'Albero, dates to 1969. The second, with an introductory essay by G. Cantoni, *L'Italia tra Rivoluzione e Contro-Rivoluzione,* appeared in 1972 for the editions of *Cristianità*. The third, with an afterword by Plinio Corrêa de Oliveira entitled *Rivoluzione e Contro-Rivoluzione vent'anni dopo*, in 1977. "In this work – wrote Giovanni Cantoni in his introduction – are all the elements that permit us to define it as an expression in the form of a thesis of counter-revolutionary thinking in the age of the cultural Revolution." (Introduction, p. 49). Of G. Cantoni Cf. also *Plinio Corrêa de Oliveira al servizio di un capitolo della dottrina sociale della Chiesa: il commento del Magistero alla "parabola dei talenti"*, Cristianità, no. 235, November 1994.

[145] The Centro Culturale Lepanto, founded in Rome in 1982 by the author of these pages, made its mark in Italy and in Europe because of its doctrinal interventions on themes such as the New Concordat (1985), the Treaty of Maastricht (1992), the Islamic danger (1993), the legalization of homosexual marriage (1994), the denunciation of collaboration between Catholics and neo-Communists in Italy (1995-6).

[146] P. Corrêa de Oliveira, *Nobreza e elites tradicionais análogas*. Eng. tr. *Nobility and Analogous Traditional Elites in the Allocutions of Pius XII*, York (PA), The American Society for the Defense of Tradition, Family and Property, 1993. The book was also translated into Spanish, Italian, and French. It has received the approval of various personalities among whom four cardinals, Mario Luigi Ciappi, Silvio Oddi, Alfons Maria Stickler and Bernardino Echeverría, and two famous theologians, Fathers Raimondo Spiazzi and Victorino Rodríguez.

[147] P. Corrêa de Oliveira, *Revolution and Counter-Revolution Twenty Years After* in *Revolution and Counter-Revolution*, pp. 123–66 (with an update to the III part by the same Plinio Corrêa de Oliveira).

models of reflection, volition and sensibility to arrive more rapidly at the ultimate goal of the Revolution: the establishment, on the ruins of Christian civilization, of a "tribal" and anarchical society, obedient to the Prince of Darkness. The return of the human model presented by the "traditional elites" can be, according to the Brazilian thinker, the main antidote to this extreme decline of society. If the Sorbonne Revolution, in 1968, was an explosion of universal importance, that accelerated the unhealthy germs of proletarianization of society, the impulse to continuous perfection, that characterized the Middle Ages and the following centuries, could today be reborn if the nobility found within it the meaning of their historical mission.

"Should the twentieth-century noble remain aware of this mission and, animated by Faith and love for a well-understood tradition, do everything to fulfil it, he will achieve a victory of no less grandeur than that of his ancestors when they held back the barbarians, drove Islam beyond the Mediterranean, or smashed through the gates of Jerusalem under the command of Godfrey of Bouillon."[148]

In the conclusion of his last book, Plinio Corrêa de Oliveira thus describes the ruinous prospect of the long Revolutionary process:

"This process has advanced relentlessly, from the waning and fall of the Middle Ages to the initial joyful triumphs of the renaissance; to the religious revolution of Protestantism, which remotely began to foment and prepare the French Revolution and, even more remotely, the Russian Revolution of 1917. So invariably victorious has been its path despite uncountable obstacles that one might consider the power that moved this process invincible and its results definitive.

"These results seem definitive indeed if one overlooks the nature of this process. At first glance it seems eminently constructive, since it successively raised three edifices: the Protestant Pseudo-Reformation, the liberal-democratic republic, and the Soviet socialist republic.

"The true nature of this process, however, is essentially destructive. It is Destruction itself. It toppled the faltering Middle Ages, the vanishing Old Regime, and the apoplectic, frenetic, and turbulent bourgeois world. Under its pressure the former U.S.S.R. lies in ruins – sinister, mysterious, and rotten like a fruit long-since fallen from the branch.

"*Hic et nunc*, is it not true that the milestones of this process are

---

[148] P. Corrêa de Oliveira, *Nobility and Analogous Traditional Elites*, p. 116.

but ruins? And what is the most recent ruin generating but a general confusion that constantly threatens imminent and contradictory catastrophes, which disintegrate before falling upon the world, thus begetting prospects of new catastrophes even more imminent and contradictory. These may vanish in turn, only to give way to new monsters. Or they may become frightful realities, like the migration of Slavic hordes from the East to the West, or Moslem hordes from the South to the North.

"Who knows? Will this actually happen? Will this be all? Will it be even worse than this?

"Such a picture would discourage all men who lack Faith. Those with Faith, however, can already hear a voice coming from beyond this confused and grim horizon. The voice, capable of inspiring the most encouraging confidence, says: 'Finally, my Immaculate Heart will triumph'."[149]

18. The judgement of an eminent contemporary theologian of *Revolution and Counter-Revolution*

Among the judgements passed on *Revolution and Counter-Revolution*, that of Father Anastasio Gutiérrez, eminent canonist of the Claretian order and consultor of various Vatican departments, is profound and detailed. Among other things, he writes:

"Revolution and Counter-revolution is a masterly work whose teachings should be disseminated far and wide so as to penetrate the conscience, not only of all those who consider themselves truly Catholic, but I would say even more, of all other men of good will. In it, the latter would learn that salvation can be found only in Jesus Christ and His Church; the former would feel confirmed and fortified in their Faith and psychologically and spiritually forewarned and immunized against the cunning process that employs many of them as useful idiots or fellow travellers.

"Its analysis of the revolutionary process is impressive and revealing on account of its realism and profound understanding of history, from the end of the Middle Ages in decadence, which paved the way for the paganizing renaissance and the pseudo-reformation, thence for the terrible French Revolution, and, soon after, atheistic Communism.

"That historical analysis is not only external. The actions and

---

[149] P. Corrêa de Oliveira, *Nobility and Analogous Traditional Elites*, pp. 130–1.

reactions it deals with are also explained in light of the human psychology, both the individual psychology and the collective psychology of the masses. However, it is necessary to recognize that someone directs this profound and systematic de-Christianization. Man undoubtedly tends toward evil – pride and sensuality – but were not someone holding the reins of these disorderly tendencies and sagaciously co-ordinating them, they most probably would not have produced such a constant, skilful, and systematic action, which, tenaciously maintained, profits even from the ups and downs caused by the resistance and natural 'reaction' of the opposing forces.

"*Revolution and Counter-Revolution* also foresees, although using caution in its prognoses and by means of hypotheses, the next possible evolution of the revolutionary action and, in turn, that of the Counter-Revolution.

"The book abounds in perspicacious sociological, political, psychological, and evolutive insights and observations, not few of which are worthy of an anthology. Many of them outline the intelligent 'tactics' that favour the Revolution and those that may and should be used in a general counter-revolutionary 'strategy'.

"In sum, I would dare to affirm that this is a prophetic work in the best sense of the word. It should be taught in the Church's centres of higher education so that at least the elite classes become fully aware of a crushing reality about which, I believe, they do not have a clear notion. (...) This book is an authentic product of Christian wisdom."[150]

---

[150] P. Anastasio Gutiérrez C.M.F., Letter to Juan Miguel Montes, on 8 September 1993.

Chapter V

Tradition, Family, Property

"In idealism, zeal.
In manners, courtesy.
In action, dedication without limits.
In the presence of the enemy, prudence.
In the fight, pride and courage.
And with courage, victory."

1. A consistent and inseparable block ...

Having reached full maturity, Plinio Corrêa de Oliveira decided to give the family of souls that surrounded him and shared his ideals the form of an association. On 26 July 1960 the Sociedade Brasileira de Defesa da Tradição, Família e Propriedade[1] was founded in São Paulo, the first of a series of associations inspired by his thinking that were gradually founded throughout five continents.[2]

The trilogy, Tradition, Family, Property, apart from indicating the associations founded and inspired by Plinio Corrêa de Oliveira, summarizes his conception of the world which in turn reflects the foundations of the social doctrine of the Church.[3]

Real tradition, the Brazilian thinker writes, presupposes two principles:

---

[1] The beginning of the public activity of the TFP dates to 25 July 1963, when the association officially took over all the activities that had up to then been controlled by Prof Plinio Corrêa de Oliveira personally, and by his collaborators of the group of *Catolicismo*. Up to his death, Plinio Corrêa de Oliveira was president of the Brazilian TFP while the vice-president, also until his death, was Prof Fernando Furquim de Almeida (1913-81).

[2] TFP, similar bodies or representative bureaux were founded in Argentina, Chile, Uruguay (1967), Perú (1970), Colombia, Venezuela, Spain (1971), Ecuador, United States (1973), Bolivia, France, Portugal (1974), Canada (1975), Italy (1976), South Africa (1980), Germany, Australia (1982), Costa Rica (1983), New Zealand (1985), Philippines (1986), Paraguay (1987), The United Kingdom (1989), India (1992), Poland (1995), Japan, Guatemala (1996).

[3] Its "fundamental lines – as Pius XII states – were and still are the same: the family and property as the basis of personal provision; then, as complementary factors of security, local bodies and professional unions, and lastly the State". Pius XII, Christmas radiomessage of 24 December 1955, in DR, vol. XVII, pp. 437-8.

"a) that every authentic and living order of things has within itself an on-going impulse towards improvement and perfection;

"b) that, for this reason, true progress does not consist in destroying, but, rather, adding; it does not consist in breaking links, but continuing ever higher.

"In short, tradition is the sum of the past with the present having an affinity with it. Today should not be the denial of yesterday, but its harmonic continuation."[4]

Tradition, from the Latin "*tradere*", does not therefore mean mere attachment to the past, but transmission of a wealth of values from one generation to another.[5] "The tradition we represent is Catholic Tradition. It is a tradition full of life. An ardent natural and supernatural life."[6] In order to develop, what is alive needs a favourable environment. The natural environment for the transmission and development of values is the family which, as the Church teaches, is "the fundamental cell, the constituent element of the community of the State".[7] But to survive and develop, the family, in its turn, needs a material foundation that guarantees its life and freedom. For this reason, Pius XI, in his encyclical *Quadragesimo anno*, states that "Man's natural right of possessing private property, and transmitting it by inheritance, must remain intact and inviolate, and cannot be taken away by the State".[8]

Max Delespesse, a famous Belgian progressivist, in a book with the significant title: *Tradition, Famille, Propriété. Jésus et la triple contestation* (Tradition, Family, Property. Jesus and the threefold contestation), notes:

---

[4] P. Corrêa de Oliveira, "TFP. Tradição", Folha de S. Paulo, 12 March 1969. Cf. also ID., *Nobility and Analogous Traditional Elites*, pp. 52–3.

[5] Pius XII taught well how there is no real progress outside tradition. "The word itself is etymologically synonymous with advancement and forward movement – synonymous, but not identical. Whereas, in fact, progress means only a forward march, step by step, in search of an uncertain future, tradition also signifies a forward march, but a continuous march as well, a movement equally brisk and tranquil, in accordance with life's laws (...). As the word itself implies, tradition is a gift handed down from generation to generation, the torch that at each relay one runner places in and entrusts to the hand of the next, without the race slowing down or coming to a halt. Tradition and progress complement each other so harmoniously that, just as tradition without progress would be a contradiction in terms, so progress without tradition would be a foolhardy proposition, a leap into darkness." Speech to the Roman aristocracy and nobility of 19 January 1944, in *Nobility and Analogous Traditioinal Elites*, p. 53.

[6] P. Corrêa de Oliveira, Speech of 3 January 1992, Catolicismo, no. 494, February 1992.

[7] Pius XII, Address to French fathers of families of 18 September 1951, in DR, vol. XIII, p. 242.

[8] Pius XI, Encyclical *Quadragesimo anno* of 15 May 1931, in AAS, 1931, vol. 23, pp. 190–216. Cf. Denz.-H, no. 3728.

"Certain superficial observers might be amazed at the trinomial tradition-family-property, as if these really did not go together. In fact, the union of these three terms is not at all casual. (...) Tradition, family, property is a coherent block that one accepts or refuses, but whose elements cannot be separated."[9]

The most radical refusal of this doctrinal block was expressed, during our time, by Socialism and Communism whose basic principles, according to the Russian mathematician Igor Chafarevitch,[10] may be summed up in these points:

a) abolition of private property;
b) abolition of the family;
c) destruction of religion;
d) equality, suppression of social hierarchy.

The formula TFP, Plinio Corrêa de Oliveira affirms in his turn, comprises "the three great principles denied by modern collectivism", which opposed it with a similarly significant trinomial: "massification – servitude – hunger".[11]

2. New methods of apostolate

What unmistakably characterizes the Brazilian TFP and the other TFPs in the world inspired by Plinio Corrêa de Oliveira was not just the coherence of the vision of the world, but also the surprising new methods of apostolate.

From the very beginnings of its activity, the TFP found itself struggling against the conspiracy of silence imposed on its initiatives by the mass-media. In order to reach public opinion directly, Plinio Corrêa de Oliveira invented great publicity campaigns in which the young people of the TFP, through the use of megaphones, banners, slogans and music, attracted the attention of the people in the streets. On 30 March 1965, in the Viaduto do Chá, the most crowded thoroughfare of São Paulo, the great red standards with the rampant lion made their first appearance, which, in 1969, were to be followed by the red capes, idealized by Dr Plinio himself. These standards and capes today distinguish throughout the world the public apostolate of the TFP. Plinio Corrêa de Oliveira always stressed the importance of this

---

[9] Max Delespesse, *Tradition, Famille, Propriété. Jésus et la triple contestation*, (Paris, Fleurus, 1972), pp. 7, 8.
[10] Igor Chafarevitch, *Il socialismo come fenomeno storico mondiale*, It. tr. (Milan, La Casa di Matriona, 1980), p. 267.
[11] P. Corrêa de Oliveira, *Nobility and Analogous Traditional Elites*, p. 109.

standard-bearing apostolate which "produces in public opinion a vivifying and healthy shock that symbolizes the counter-offensive of the good".[12]

In the conversion process, not only does the logical factor intervene, but also psychological and supernatural factors, because it is above all the grace of God that works in the soul of man, attracting him towards adhesion to the truth and the practice of virtue. It is in fact through the "shock" of grace that the change from the old man to the new man, of which St Paul speaks in his letters, takes place.[13]

Dom Chautard teaches how a Catholic Institution worthy of this name must be penetrated by interior life, which is the condition of fruitfulness of action.[14] The great development of external activities led to the birth among the TFP followers of the desire for particularly quiet areas, where they could build spiritual buttresses that would prevent them from falling into an excess of activism. Thus, next to the traditional centres, the "hermitages"[15] were born: places of study and prayer characterized by greater meditation and a precise rule of life.

The establishment of areas where there was an atmosphere filled with seriousness and supernatural spirit responded to the requirement, always stressed by Dr Plinio, to fight the Revolution not just on the level of ideas, but also on that deeper one of the tendencies. In this same dimension, at a moment in time when the Revolution was spreading through the human type of the hippies and the punks, he invented special "ceremonial clothes". They had the scapular of Our Lady of Mount Carmel and the cross of St James, whose symbolic meaning was similar to that of the red capes used in public activities. These clothes, which because of their original style cannot neither be traced to traditional religious clothes, or even less to military uniforms, are worn in special circumstances to express a chivalrous spirit as opposed to modern moral degeneration.

Among the new means of propaganda, Dr Plinio also invented the "caravans", formed by groups of young followers, who carry out an

---

[12] P. Corrêa de Oliveira, "Obstáculo à corrida para o caos", Catolicismo, no. 517, January 1994. According to what history teaches us, writes Plinio Corrêa de Oliveira, "it seems that the great conversions usually occur by a fulminating thrust of the soul caused by grace on the occasion of a given internal or external fact". *Revolution and Counter-Revolution*, p. 100.

[13] Eph. 4:21–4.

[14] Dom J.-B. Chautard, *The Soul of the Apostolate*, pp. 82–6.

[15] The word "hermitage" is owed to Fabio Vidigal Xavier de Silveira, director of the Brazilian TFP, who died in 1971. A few years before his death, when visiting the famous Hermitage "dei Carceri" of Assisi, he was enthusiastic about the supernatural spirit that characterized it and had applied the use of this term, in everyday language, to the office where he worked.

"itinerant" apostolate from one end of the immense country to the other. From October 1970 to 1995, they covered the whole Brazilian territory for a total of 5,031,360 kilometres, carrying out 23,199 campaigns in cities of all the states of Brazil and distributing 1,741,080 books and leaflets published by the association. This was a completely new propaganda tool, which made it possible to contact the general public while avoiding the filter of the media. The request for the works published, enormous for Latin America, confirmed the validity of Dr Plinio's initiative.

For years, the TFP regularly promoted Study Weeks of Anti-Communist Formation (SEFAC) during which, with conferences prepared with the help of audio-visual aids, a precise criticism of Communism was developed and the opposing Catholic doctrine was clearly expounded. These formation courses of the TFP were for young people from Brazil and every part of the world, a precious occasion to get to know each other, exchange opinions and live in a fraternal atmosphere.

Next to the commitment of the followers in the strict sense, called members or volunteers, a new form of apostolate has taken hold in recent years: that of the *Correspondentes e Esclarecedores* (Supporters and Friends).[16] These latter spread the counter-revolutionary deals within the family and professional environments where they work. At the end of the 1980s, through the modern technique of direct mail, that makes it possible to communicate by post with tens of thousands of supporters, the TFP acquired new efficient tools of apostolate. Some of the campaigns they promoted even managed to create new movements of opinion and radically change situations in various fields.

3. The left-wing evolution of the Brazilian clergy and the birth of the CNBB

On 14 October 1952, twenty archbishops met in Rio de Janeiro to arrange the foundation of the Conferência Nacional dos Bispos do Brasil (CNBB) in order to "co-ordinate and subsidize religiously

---

[16] Plinio Corrêa de Oliveira himself thus defined the role of the Supporters: "Our supporters have the mission to fight in this great battle of public opinion, with their example, their behaviour, with all that transpires from their being true Catholics. And it is what a true counter-revolutionary must do and say, facing the wave of perdition that is dragging the modern world. We are doing this. We must give a good example again every time, repeat the same words, know how to proclaim our ideals on high and raise high our standards". Meeting with the Supporters of 7 September 1989.

oriented activities, as well as those concerned with charity, philan-thropy and social work" throughout the national territory.[17] Bishop Helder Câmara, who had become auxiliary bishop of Rio de Janeiro, was nominated the first secretary and entrusted with the preparatory work for the project of the CNBB.[18] Starting from 1954 the Episcopal organization, prevailing over the individual dioceses, became the unofficial "voice" of the Church in Brazil.[19] Within it, Bishop Câmara[20] appeared as the figure destined to assume, at least in part, the "charismatic" role formerly held by Cardinal Leme in the reli-gious renewal of the Thirties. It was during this period that the "turn to the left" of the Brazilian episcopate occurred thanks to the new Papal Nuncio Armando Lombardi (1954–66), who favoured the nomi-nation of progressivist bishops, collaborating with Bishop Câmara in preparing the most "advanced" social declarations.[21]

In May 1956, the conference of the bishops of the Northeast, orga-nized by Bishop Câmara in Campina Grande (Paraíba), in the presence of the President of the Republic Kubitschek who concluded the proceedings, denounced the "terrible injustices" of the country, announcing that the bishops would take the "side of the oppressed, to co-operate with them in a work of promotion and redemption".[22] The

---

[17] Cf. M. Kornis, D. Flaksman, *Conferencia Nacional dos Bispos do Brasil (CNBB)*, in DHBB, vol. II, pp. 884-9. "Archbishop Giovanni Montini, Vatican Secretary of State and future Pope Paul VI, greatly influenced Pope Pius XII to have the organization approved." ibid, p. 884.

[18] Sergio Bernal, *La Iglesia del Brasil y el compromiso social*, (Rome, Pontificia Università Gregoriana, 1986), p. 46.

[19] One of its important dignitaries, Cardinal Aloisio Lorscheider, would even define it as the unofficial spokesman for the Vicar of Christ. cf. *O Povo* of Fortaleza, 16 February 1981.

[20] Bishop Câmara "by now holds a power in fact, if not by right, far superior to that of the cardinal of Rio, Cardinal Jaime Câmara, first figure of the national Church". Richard Marin, *Dom Helder Câmara. Les puissants et les pauvres*, (Paris, Les Editions de l'Atelier, 1995), p. 83. "In the Episcopal kaleidoscope, Bishop Helder Câmara is a standard-bearer (...). He sums up in his person the whole evolution of a Church in rupture with traditional social order." Charles Antoine, *L'Eglise et le pouvoir au Brésil. Naissance du militarisme*, (Paris, Desclée de Brouwer, 1971), p. 77.

[21] "Convinced of the need for a renewal of the Church in the country and that it could be done through the CNBB, Bishop Lombardi held weekly meetings with Bishop Câmara and attended several meetings of the CNBB where he supported most avant-garde social declarations." M. Kornis, D. Flaksman, *Conferência Nacional dos Bispos do Brasil (CNBB)*, p. 885. "A great friend of Bishop Helder Câmara, with whom he had lunch once a week, a staunch ally of those developing the new strategies of Brazilian Catholicism, he presided, during his nunciature, over the creation of 48 dioceses, 11 archbishoprics and 16 prelatures. During these ten years, 109 bishops and 24 archbishops were nominated, who today represent the majority of the country's episcopate." Marcio Moreira Alves, *A Igreja e a política no Brasil*, (São Paulo, Editora Brasiliense, 1979), p. 80. Marcio Moreira Alves observes that the nominations of conservative bishops in Brazil are all previous to 1955, the date of the beginning of the nunciature of Archbishop Lombardi; since then, with the sole exception of Bishop José Angelo Neto, nomi-nated in 1960, all the bishops have been of clearly progressivist tendencies (ibid).

[22] R. Marin, op. cit., p. 84. From its first meetings held in Bélem (1953) and Aparecida (1954) the CNBB proposed the question of "Land Reform".

question of "social justice" and of "land reform" was destined to become the strong point of the CNBB, especially from 1958, with the new pontificate of John XXIII.

After the establishment of the CNBB, two events of continental importance had great influence on the action of the Brazilian hierarchy: the creation, in 1955, at the initiative of Bishop Câmara, of the CELAM (Latin American Episcopal Council) and the Cuban Revolution of 1959.[23]

"As the point of departure for the irruption of politics in the heart of the ecclesiastical institution" writes Pierre Vayssière "we find the CELAM, an organ for linking the various episcopates of the continent, created in 1955 at the initiative of Bishop Helder Câmara."[24] At the end of the 1960s, a group of South American theologians began to formulate a "liberation theology"[25] whose spirit penetrated the Second General Assembly of the CELAM, held in Medellin in 1968, in the presence of Paul VI.[26] The new theological current which stated that it wanted to apply in Latin America the directives of Vatican Council II, presented the mission of Jesus Christ as being preeminently the work of social and political liberation. It used social science, and especially Marxist methodology, as a tool for "freeing the oppressed classes". In this situation, the theologian became,

---

[23] Cf. José Oscar Beozzo, *A Igreja no Brasil*, in *A Igreja Latino-Americana às vésperas do Concilio*, (São Paulo, Edições Paulinas, 1993), pp. 46–77. Cf. also J.F. Regis de Moraís, *Os bispos e a política no Brasil*, São Paulo, Cortez Editora, 1982; Thomas C. Bruneau, *The Church in Brazil*, Austin, University of Texas Press, 1982; *A Igreja nas bases em tempo de transição (1974–1985)*, edited by Paulo José Krischke and Scott Mainwaring, Porto Alegre, L&PM Editores, 1986; C. Antoine, "L'épiscopat brésilien dans les décennies du dévelopement", Etudes, no. 1–2, June-July 1986, pp. 15–26; J. O. Beozzo, *A Igreja do Brasil. De João XXIII a João Paulo II de Medellin a Santo Domingo*, Petrópolis, Vozes, 1994.

[24] Pierre Vayssière, *Les révolutions d'Amérique Latine*, (Paris, Seuil, 1996), p. 263.

[25] Its first systematic wording, of 1971, is the work of the Peruvian theologian Gustavo Gutiérrez. Born in 1928 and trained at the University of Louvain, Father Gutiérrez was for many years Visiting Professor at the University of Michigan, exercising, as Pierre Vayssière (op. cit., p. 358) observes, an important influence in the university world of North America. Among the theologians who laid the foundations for liberation theology, we recall the Jesuits Jon Sobrino and Juan L. Segundo, the Franciscan Leonardo Boff and Bishop Helder Câmara "who although not a theologian by profession, gave a very great contribution to the development of liberation theology with his words and with his actions". Battista Mondin, *I teologi della liberazione*, (Milan, Borla, 1977), p. 36. Apart from the support given by Bishop Câmara, the thematic and organizational development of the movement was supported by bishops such as Leonidas Proaño in Ecuador, Oscar Romero in Salvador, Sergio Méndez Arceo and Samuel Ruiz in Mexico, Zambrano Camader in Colombia. On liberation theology cf. also Armando Bandera O.P., *La Iglesia ante el proceso di liberación*, Madrid, BAC, 1975; Father Miguel Poradowski, *El marxismo en la teologia*, Madrid, Speiro, 1976; Alfonso Lopez Trujillo, *De Medellin a Puebla*, Madrid, Editorial Catolica, 1980.

[26] Cf. B. Mondin, *I teologi della liberazione*, p. 31. "It is with the meeting of the CELAM in Medellin, that liberation theology acquires its right to citizenship." R. Vidales, "Acquisizioni e compiti della teologia latino-americana", Concilium, no. 4, 1974, p. 154.

according to the formula of Gramsci, an "organic intellectual of the proletariat",[27] whose main function is to bring closer the "kingdom of justice on earth".[28]

This same period saw the Cuban Revolution which "to the Latin-American imagination represents the paradigm of every future revolution" appearing "as a detonator capable of triggering a giant explosion whose continental shock wave would upset the conservative regimes, thus obtaining the 'second independence' of Latin-America".[29] The revolutionary guerrilla warfare, according to the Castro–Guevara plan, managed to encompass about twenty countries of Central and South America, bringing the continent to the edge of chaos.

In the religious and civil life of Brazil and of Latin America, the religious left-wing tendency spread rapidly through a process "that was supported by members of the episcopate and by Catholic Action in the workers' and university environments and was demonstrated in the birth of Grassroot Ecclesial communities".[30] At the beginning of 1962, inside the *Juventude Universitaria Católica* (JUC), a document called "Estatuto Ideológico" (Ideological Statute) was approved; it advocated "socialism" and the "Brazilian revolution". From the JUC and the JEC (*Juventude Estudantil Católica*),[31] the two student associations of Catholic Action, a new organization was born, Ação Popular,[32] which advocated an open revolutionary action to overthrow the foundations of Brazilian society.[33] It intended to stand beside the "socialist current that is transforming modern

---

[27] José Francisco Gómez, "El intelectual orgánico según Gramsci y el teologo de la liberación en América Latina", Christianismo y Sociedad (Mexico), no. 91, 1987, pp. 102–04.

[28] Alvaro Delgado, "Le clergé en révolte", La Nouvelle Revue Internationale, no. 4, April 1973, pp. 70–1, pp. 65-75.

[29] P. Vayssière, *Les révolutions d'Amérique Latine*, p. 127, 174.

[30] Michael Sievernich, *Théologie de la Libération* in DSp, vol. XV, 1991, p. 501.

[31] The JUC and the JEC, which were the two student branches of the Brazilian Catholic Action (ACB), were recognized by the ecclesiastical hierarchy in 1950 and in fact they were dissolved with the end of the ACB in 1966.

[32] Cf. Haroldo Lima, Aldo Arantes, *Historia da Ação Popular da JUC ao PC do B*, São Paulo, Editora Alfa-Omega, 1984, and the entry Ação Popular (AP) of Mônica Kornis, Dora Flaksman, in DHBB, vol. I, pp. 16-17. The first national co-ordinator of the new organization was Herbert José de Souza and its main ideologist the Jesuit Father Henrique de Lima Vaz. The *Basic Document* of January 1963 stated: "Ação Popular opts for a policy of revolutionary preparation. They try to mobilize the people by developing their levels of consciousness as regards capitalism (national or international) and feudalism". In P. J. Krischke, *A Igreja e as crises políticas no Brasil*, (Petropolis, Vozes, 1979), p. 85. "It would be difficult to establish a difference between such a statement and the official guidelines of the marxist parties. The difference means, nevertheless, that it had its origins in sectors having access to the people through the vast ecclesiastical network of parishes, schools, institutions of social welfare, etc." (ibid).

[33] Cf. Aloizio Augusto Barbosa Torres, "Ação Popular, Capítulo deplorável na historia do Brasil Católico", Catolicismo, no. 183, March 1966.

history", by adhering to the "avant-garde role of the Soviet Revolution".[34]

Plinio Corrêa de Oliveira saw in this itinerary, that he had in fact foreseen, the logical development of the progressivism he had fought during the 1930s and 1940s. It was to be opposed by the TFP, which he considered to be the legitimate development of the former Catholic movement, in absolute loyalty to the perennial Magisterium of the Church.

The religious life of Brazil, according to a contemporary historian, was by now destined to vacillate between two poles: the progressivist pole and that represented by the TFP.[35]

4. "Land Reform": a matter of conscience

From the beginning of the 1950s, a biased campaign organized by the Marxist inspired mass-media began to present Brazil as the land of injustice and social imbalances, of the great unproductive landed estates and the miserable *favelas* (shantytowns) on the outskirts of the upper-class neighbourhoods of the big cities. "Land Reform" was presented as the only means capable of satisfying the elementary requirements of justice crushed by the owners. This presentation of the problem was based on false doctrinal premises and on a similarly false vision of the Brazilian socio-economic situation.

Actually, the greatest unproductive estate of Brazil and of the world is that composed of the immense area of lands belonging to the State. About 50 percent of Brazilian territory is today made up of lands that belong to the federal, state and municipal authorities of the country.[36] It is, therefore, difficult to understand, except in the light of a Marxist ideology, a "Land Reform" that, rather than distributing public lands, wants to confiscate the private lands which, in spite of everything, have made Brazil the second country in the world, after the United States, in foodstuffs production.

The "Land Reform", demanded by the Communist Party since the 1920s, caught on especially in the circles of the Catholic left, of the

---

[34] H. Lima, A. Arantes, op. cit., p. 37.

[35] Oscar de Figuereido Lustosa O.P., *Presencia da la Iglesia en la sociedad brasileña*, in *Manual de Historia de la Iglesia*, edited by Quintín Aldea and Eduardo Cardenas, Editorial Herder, Barcelona 1987, vol. X, pp. 1334–5. "In the middle of the two groups is the majority of the Christian group (bishops, priests, laymen), the conservatives and the liberals, who on several occasions vacillate between approving reactionary ideas and supporting certain progressivist demands." ibid, p. 1335.

[36] At the beginning of the 1960s the percentage of public land was much higher.

Top: Plinio's parents: the lawyer João Paulo Corrêa de Oliveira and Dona Lucilia Ribeiro dos Santos.
Below left: Plinio Corrêa de Oliveira on the day of his First Communion.
Below right: João Alfredo Corrêa de Oliveira, Plinio's great-uncle and president of the Council of Ministers during the Empire, author of the famous Golden Law that, in 1888, abolished slavery in Brazil.

"My mother taught me how to love the Church..."

Top: Two photographs of Dona Lucilia: in 1912 in Paris in her younger years and in 1968 in São Paulo a few days before her death. *Left:* The Salesian Church of the Sacred Heart where she would go for her daily devotions.

Three photographs of Plinio
Corrêa de Oliveira at different
periods of his life.

Top left: With honours, a graduate
of the Law School.
Top right: At only 24 years of age,
member of the Constitutional
Assembly.
Right: In his professor's gown at
the university in the 40's.

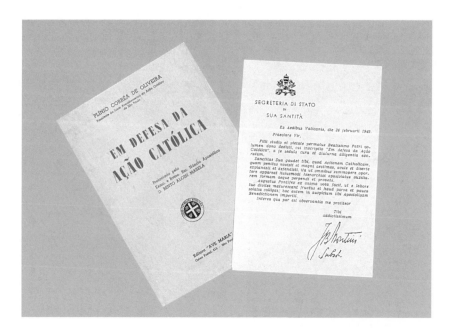

Top: Plinio Corrêa de Oliveira's first book *In Defence of Catholic Action*. It earned him a letter of praise written by Archbishop Montini (future Paul VI) in the name of Pius XII.

Below: Two ecclesiastics who supported Plinio Corrêa de Oliveira's apostolate in Brazil: The Most Reverend Duarte Leopoldo e Silva, archbishop of São Paulo and the Apostolic Nuncio, who would later become a cardinal, Benedetto Aloisi Masella, who is holding a copy of *Legionário*.

*Above: Revolution and Counter-Revolution,*with numerous editions in several languages, is Plinio Corrêa de Oliveira's *magnum opus* and has inspired thousands of Catholics around the world.

Below: One of the first public campaigns of the Brazilian TFP against divorce.

Plinio Corrêa de Oliveira always supported the "Church of Silence" persecuted under the Communist regime. Great defenders of the Faith such as Cardinal Josef Slipyj and Cardinal Josef Mindszenty eulogized the the work of Dr Plinio and the TFPs.

Left: Cardinal Slipyj is received at the Brazilian TFP's head-quarters.
Below: Cardinal Mindszenty is received by the Venezuelan TFP at Caracas airport.

Plinio Corrêa de Oliveira's action encompassed the great world events of the XX century.

Top: A TFP delegation in front of the walls of the Kremlin, where the communist flag still flies, in 1990, when a petition signed by five million people in favour of the independence of Lithuania was delivered to Gorbachev.
Below: The American TFP at an anti-abortion demonstration in Washington, D.C.

Top: Requiem Mass for Plinio Corrêa de Oliveira celebrated by Cardinal Stickler in Rome.

Above: The Mother of Good Counsel of Genazzano (Rome) to whom Dr Plinio had a very special devotion.

Left: A view of the cortege taking his mortal remains to a cemetery in São Paulo on 5 October 1995.

university and media intelligentsia and in those of high finance.[37] From the union of these forces, in 1960, at the suggestion of the Christian democrat governor of the State of São Paulo, Carvalho Pinto, a project of "Land Revision" was born. It was also supported by the CNBB. The left-wing propaganda presented the rural situation as explosive, due to the discontent of the farm workers. It demanded the expropriation of the so-called unproductive landowners in order to distribute the land to the workers. The goal was to eliminate every form of large and medium-sized rural property, to reduce agricultural properties to minimal dimensions, ultimately driving the country into hunger.

On 10 November 1960, a large manifesto published on the front page of the most important newspapers of Brazil announced the launching of Plinio Corrêa de Oliveira's book *Reforma Agraria. Questão de Consciência (Land Reform – A Matter of Conscience).*[38] The first part of the work was written by Dr Plinio himself. However, the text was submitted for theological review to Bishop Antônio de Castro Mayer and to Bishop Geraldo de Proença Sigaud, respectively bishops of Campos and of Jacarezinho, so they could be co-authors. The second part of the book was written by the economist Luiz Mendonça de Freitas. It was of a strictly technical nature, and demonstrated how Brazil produced in abundance both for its needs and for development, without its economy being in any way limited by the presence of the large estates.

Because of the clarity of its reasoning, the fame of its authors, and also because of its widespread distribution, the book immediately became a "national case". Its discussion spread from the squares to the newspapers, the radio, the television and to the halls of Congress. "The book produced a shock not just in Brazil, but in all the international press. It also provoked strong reactions from the Brazilian episcopate."[39] While, in August 1961, a left-wing political exponent, João Goulart,[40] who intended making "Land Reform" his strong point, rose

---

[37] Cf. Gileno De Carli, *História da Reforma Agraria*, Brasília, Gráfica Brasiliana, 1985.

[38] Cf. Various Authors, *Reforma Agraria. Questão de Consciência*, São Paulo, Editora Vera Cruz, 1960, had numerous editions in Brazil, Argentina (1963), Spain (1969), Colombia (1971), totalling some forty-one thousand copies. It was followed by a positive programme of agrarian policies by the same authors, the *Declaration of Morro Alto* that had two editions in Portuguese.

[39] José Luis Gonzalez-Balado, *Câmara, l'évêque rouge?*, (Québec, Editions Paulinas, 1978), p. 53.

[40] On João Goulart (1919–76), cf. the entry of Marieta de Morais Ferreira, César Benjamim, in DHBB, vol. II, pp. 1504–21. In his message to Congress in March 1962, Goulart demanded reforms in the banking system, in public administration, in taxes and "Land Reform, the great Brazilian aspiration" which he describes as "an irresistible idea-force" (*Message to the National Congress*, Rio de Janeiro, 1962, pp. XI–XII). "Land Reform can no longer be postponed (...) other reforms are also imperative" (*Folha de S. Paulo*, 2 May 1962). "His main concern was Land Reform. He lived for this. It really was his fixed idea" recalls his widow Maria Teresa Goulart. *Manchete*, 1 April 1978.

to power, Bishop Helder Câmara, general secretary of the CNBB and auxiliary bishop of Rio, announced that the reform project was "a document inspired by the principles of the social doctrine of the Church".[41] Brazilian public opinion did not, however, follow its bishops on this dangerous road that opened the doors to the Communist agenda for the country. The reaction of the people was not long in being made manifest, ending up in the military movement that in 1964 over-threw the President of the Republic Goulart.[42] "In the doctrinal preparation of the movement"[43] "a decisive role" was played by the "book-symbol against Land Reform"[44] distributed by the TFP.

The fall of Goulart sent shock-waves around the world, and made it impossible for a Marxist-type Revolution to triumph in Brazil. The repercussions from the political field soon spread to the ecclesiastical field. In April 1964 Bishop Helder Câmara left his position with the CNBB, becoming archbishop of Olinda and Recife, while Cardinal Vasconcellos Motta was transferred from the archdiocese of São Paulo to that of Aparecida. In the same year the leaders of the CNNB were replaced by moderates. Archbishop Helder Câmara was replaced as secretary by Bishop José Gonçalves, auxiliary bishop of the cardinal of Rio, Jaime Câmara; while the archbishop of Ribeirão Preto, Agnelo Rossi, was elected as president of the organization. He replaced Cardinal Vasconcellos Motta as archbishop of São Paulo.

The "coup" that, under the presidency of Marshal Castelo Branco, brought the military to power is known in Brazil as the "Revolution of 64".[45] It clamped down on the Communist organizations, but it was not able to set up a programme of positive psychological and cultural recovery. While in the moderate circles the illusion of having finally averted the Communist danger spread, the left-wing exponents began infiltrating the university and secondary school teaching environments and the media.

---

[41] On 30 April a document of the central commission of the CNBB was published. Cf. "La Documentation Catholique", no. 1403 (July 1963), col. 899–906.

[42] On 19 March 1964, a great *"Marcha da Família com Deus pela liberdade"*, gathered 500,000 people in São Paulo. Eleven days later the army intervened. Goulart was forced to leave Brazil while another mass demonstration, in Rio, on 2 April, gathered a million people in support of the new regime.

[43] Thomas Niehaus, Brady Tyson, *The Catholic Right in contemporary Brazil: the case of the Society for the Defense of Tradition, Family and Property*, in *Religion in Latin America. Life and Literature*, edited by Lyle Brown and William Cooper, (Waco (Texas), Markharm Press Fund, 1980), p. 399. According to Georges-André Fiechter also, the TFP "played an important role in mobilizing the people against Goulart in 1964". *Le régime modernisateur du Brésil, 1964-1972. Etude sur les interactions politico-économiques dans un régime militaire contempo-rain*, (Leiden, A. W. Sijthoff, 1972), p. 175. Cf. also Emanuel de Kadt, *Catholic Radicals in Brazil*, (London, Oxford University Press, 1970), p. 98.

[44] M. Moreira Alves, *O Cristo do Povo*, (Rio de Janeiro, Ed. Sabía, 1968), p. 271.

On 30 November 1964 Marshal Castelo Branco signed an *Estatuto da Terra* (Statute of the Land) in the same style and spirit as the "Land Reform" of Goulart. The implementation of the document was, however, slow and steady, from its promulgation to the *Primeiro Plano Nacional de Reforma Agrária* – PNRA (*First National Plan of Land Reform*) launched by the Sarney government in October 1985. And for twenty years Plinio Corrêa de Oliveira opposed it rigorously and tirelessly.

When, in February 1980, the general assembly of the CNBB, gathered in Itaicí, issued a document entitled *Igreja e problemas da terra* – IPT (*The Church and the land problem*) in favour of "Land Reform", Plinio Corrêa de Oliveira replied with his book *Sou católico: posso ser contra a Reforma Agrária? (I am Catholic: can I be against Land Reform?*), demonstrating the contrast between the Magisterium of the Church and the document of the Episcopal Conference and denouncing its obvious Socialist and Marxist formulation.[46] Another book by the Brazilian thinker in defence of private property and free enterprise appeared in 1985,[47] as the country was being swept by a movement of violent rural demonstrations, with the invasion and occupation of privately owned lands.[48] The urgency of the "Land Reform" was justi-

---

[45] Between 1964 and 1984, Generals Humberto Castelo Branco (1964–7), Arthur da Costa e Silva (1967–9), Emilio Garrastazu Medici (1969-74), Ernesto Geisel (1974–9), João Baptista Figuereido (1979-84) succeeded one another in power in Brazil. The ideological base of the regime founded in 1964 was the doctrine of "national security" elaborated in the Escola Superior de Guerra, widely known as "Sorbonne". The doctrine of "national security" developed a concept of global war to be fought on various fronts (economic, political, psychological) to guarantee Brazil's role as a power. Cf. T. E. Skidmore, *The Politics of Military Rule in Brazil 1964-1985*, New York, Oxford University Press, 1988.

[46] P. Corrêa de Oliveira, Carlos Patricio del Campo, *Sou católico: posso ser contra a Reforma Agrária?*, São Paulo, Editora Vera Cruz, 1981. Carlos Patrício del Campo, was born in Santiago of Chile in 1940 and graduated in agrarian engineering, he then specialized at Berkeley; teacher of Agronomy at the Catholic University of Chile, since 1972 he collaborates with the financial and administrative department of the Brazilian TFP. Four editions were printed, totalling 29,000 copies of his book and distributed among the intellectual elites of Brazil and especially among the land owners. During this period the TFP distributed two issues of *Catolicismo* (no. 402 of June 1984 and no. 406-07 of October–November 1984) dedicated to re-awakening Brazilian public opinion from its lethargy.

[47] P. Corrêa de Oliveira, C. P. del Campo, *A propriedade privada e a livre iniciativa, no tufão agro-reformista*, São Paulo, Editora Vera Cruz, 1985. 1986, see also, with a preface by Plinio Corrêa de Oliveira, the publication of the work by C. P. del Campo, *Is Brazil sliding toward the extreme Left? Notes on the Land Reform Program in South America's largest and most populous country* (New York, The American Society for the Defense of Tradition, Family and Property, 1986), in which the author documents how at the root of "Land Reform" there are no serious economic evaluations, but only an ideological stand corrupted by an egalitarian and socialist spirit.

[48] P. Corrêa de Oliveira, "Invasões, reforma agrária e temas conexos", Folha de S. Paulo, 21 April 1986.

fied by the occupation of the land,[49] rare up to 1985, but increasingly more widespread after the appearance of the PNRA.

The aim of the new book was to give the farm owners knowledge of their rights, to urge them to protect themselves with prudence and energy in order to avoid, once again, the implementation of the confiscatory "Land Reform".[50] Its socialist nature is revealed especially by the economic sanctions suffered by those who are dispossessed: public authorities pay, often with great delay and with devaluated money, a price for dispossession that is vastly inferior to the price of the land. But "Land Reform" is also socialist due to the fact that the manual labourer to whom the land is transferred becomes, in fact, not a small landowner, but a member of a state farm co-operative, who holds the property rights of the land. He thus becomes an employee of the State. In this sense "present agrarian legislation harms, as we see it, both the landowner and the manual labourer in the field. Everything benefits the State. And this is socialism".[51]

Plinio Corrêa de Oliveira's battle against "Land Reform" forms part of a constant defence of private property and free enterprise that makes the Brazilian thinker the greatest apostle in our century of the social doctrine of the Church on this specific point.

Today one tends to forget that private property is a fundamental point of Catholic doctrine[52]: "Christian conscience" confirms Pius XII "cannot acknowledge the justice of a social order that denies or makes practically impossible or vain the natural right of ownership both of consumer goods and of production goods".[53]

Plinio Corrêa de Oliveira always stressed the importance of this doctrinal point, the least understood by the modern world that is so

---

[49] According to statistics of the Brazilian government itself and research of expert institutes, a good part, sometimes the majority, of the invaders of the land were not native agricultural workers, but often city dwellers and even small land owners.

[50] In 1988 the TFP published a manifesto, "Ao término de décadas de luta cordial, alerta da TFP ao Centrão" (*Folha de S. Paulo*, 28 April 1988), that traces the results of almost three decades of struggle against "Land Reform", recalling how from the very beginning it had foreseen that the Land Reform movement would have provoked analogous movements in the building and city sectors, as well as in that of industrial and commercial businesses. *Reforma agrária. Questão de consciência*, pp. 157-8.

[51] P. Corrêa de Oliveira, "Reforma Agrária: oportuno pronunciamento do Presidente da TFP", Catolicismo, no. 429, September 1986.

[52] Popes Leo XIII in the encyclical *Rerum Novarum* of 15 May 1891, Pius XI in the encyclical *Quadragesimo anno* of 15 May 1931, John XXIII in the encyclical *Mater et Magistra* of 15 May 1961, John Paul II in the encyclical *Centesimus annus* of 1 May 1991, authoritatively teach how property is a natural and inalienable right of man. St Thomas Aquinas states that "it is lawful", indeed "it is necessary for human life to possess its own goods", and that private property is a development of the natural right owed to human reason. *Summa Theologica*, IIa-IIae, q. 66, a. 2, reply e ad 2.

[53] Pius XII, Radiomessage of 1 September 1944, in DR, vol. VI, p. 275.

full of egalitarianism and selfishness.[54] Since the Thirties he had seen the attack on private property as "a profound upheaval of the whole social body" that opened the doors "to all communist embryonic forms".[55]

It should be noted that Plinio Corrêa de Oliveira was not, as some might believe, or allow themselves to believe, a landowner. Although a descendant of agricultural dynasties, his family had lost, since the Twenties, any wealth derived from land. This absolute lack of personal interests to be defended testifies to the nobility of his struggle at a time when many of the main owners of urban and rural properties of the country decisively supported the left-wing groups and parties.

5. The condemnation of Communist infiltration in the clergy

Between the Sixties and the beginning of the Seventies, the international left launched an offensive of great importance in Latin America. It intended using the progressivist clergy and Catholic circles for undermining the still rather conservative political regimes. However it found its way blocked by Plinio Corrêa de Oliveira and the TFP.

When, in July 1968, there came to light a disturbing document by the Belgian priest Joseph Comblin,[56] professor in the Theological Institute of Recife, Plinio Corrêa de Oliveira decided the moment had come to act openly against Communist infiltration now widespread among the clergy. He addressed a letter to Archbishop Câmara, archbishop of Recife, where he denounced in the Comblin document

"the call to subversion in the country, to revolution in the Church, (...) the calumny against the Civil Authority, Ecclesiastical

---

[54] P. Corrêa de Oliveira, "Liberdade, trabalho ou propriedade", Folha de S. Paulo, 2 October 1968; "Propriedade privada", Folha de S. Paulo, 30 May 1971; "Papas e propriedade privada", Folha de S. Paulo, 6 June 1971. The Brazilian thinker did not ignore the social function of private property: "Free enterprise and individual property are irreplaceable to increase production. This is its principal function. Man will strive his best at work as long as he knows that he can accumulate, to his own advantage, the fruits of his labour and pass them on to his children. If this incentive is lacking, if all his work - excepting his wage - returns to the collectivity, he becomes a civil servant. That is why underproduction and, therefore, hunger is an inevitable evil of collectivist regimes". ID., "Função social", O Jornal, 30 September 1972.

[55] P. Corrêa de Oliveira, "A causa do comunismo", O Jornal, 5 February 1936.

[56] Joseph Comblin was born in 1923 in Brussels and, after having completed his studies in Louvain and Malines where he was ordained to the priesthood in 1947, he was transferred, in 1958, to Latin America where he taught Theology and Pastoral activity in numerous institutes and universities. Among his most famous works, in which man is defined as a "revolutionary animal", cf. *Théologie de la Révolution*, Paris, Editions Universitaires, 1970.

Hierarchy, the Armed Forces and the Judiciary, and the presentation of a grossly falsified idea of the national reality".[57]

"Of all the campaigns organized by the Tradition, Family and Property movement" according to abbé Antoine "the most spectacular was undoubtedly that of July 1968."[58] In two months, between July and August, the TFP activists collected over one and a half million signatures against Communist infiltration in the Church in the streets of 158 cities of Brazil. Among the signatures were those of 19 archbishops and bishops, numerous ministers, and of dozens of congressmen and politicians. Abbé René Laurentin, who was travelling through Brazil, recalls:

> "Highly mobile teams collected signatures just about everywhere: in the railway stations, the airports, and in other public places. The authors of this initiative quite kindly canvassed me in a supermarket in Curitiba. They were holding a standard of red velvet with an upright lion. They invited me to sign 'against Communism'."[59]

The petition was officially presented to the Vatican on 7 November 1969. No reply ever arrived from the Holy See, but progressivism in Brazil suffered a momentary check and Father Comblin was forced to abandon the country.

In January 1969, on the occasion of a conference held for the students of Harvard, Archbishop Câmara proposed the admission of Communist China to the UN and the integration of Cuba into the Latin-American system. The response from the TFP was immediate:

> "In a significant article that appeared in the daily newspaper *O Estado de São Paulo*" recalls Sebastião A. Ferrarini in his book *La presse et l'archevêque rouge* "the president of the national council of the TFP (...) expresses his entire disagreement with the disturbing proposals of the prelate who, to his way of thinking, follows

---

[57] Catolicismo, no. 211, July 1968.

[58] C. Antoine, *L'Eglise et le Pouvoir au Brésil*, p. 144. "The direct occasion for the explosion of the operations is the publication of a reserved study made by the Belgian theologian Father Joseph Comblin, at the request of Archbishop Câmara. (...) Officially launched on 10 July, the campaign finally ended on the following 12 September. During this period the TFP activists collected 1,600,000 signatures in the streets of 158 towns of the country" (ibid, pp. 144–5). According to Marcio Moreira Alves: "The greatest campaign that they (the TFP activists) undertook, against Archbishop Helder Câmara and his friends, obtained, according to the organizers, 1,600,368 signatures, among which were those of 19 archbishops and bishops, of numerous ministers, of dozens of congressmen and politicians" (*A Igreja e a política no Brasil*, p. 230). "Brazil has become the centre of activity of reactionary circles of the Latin-American Church" the ultra-progressivist Alvaro Delgado notes alarmed. *Le clergé en révolte*, p. 72.

[59] René Laurentin, *L'Amérique latine à l'heure de l'enfantement*, (Paris, Seuil, 1970), p. 132.

Marx's example by making a typical inversion of values by giving primacy to the economy."[60]

It was after this analysis by Professor Corrêa de Oliveira that Archbishop Câmara was labelled in Brazil, and then throughout the world, as the "red archbishop".[61]

After 70 days of campaign, 40 caravans of followers had visited 514 cities and distributed 165 thousand copies of *Catolicismo*.

6. In face of the Communist threat against the Church

In September 1970 the Marxist Salvador Allende rose to power in Chile, thanks also to the collaboration and complicity of the Christian Democrats and large sectors of the clergy. What was happening in Chile had a meaning that extended well beyond the boundaries of that country and was to constitute a precedent of world importance. Since 1967 a young leader of the Brazilian TFP, Fabio Vidigal Xavier da Silveira (1935–71), in a book dedicated to *Frei the Chilean Kerensky*,[62] had denounced the role played by the leader of the Christian Democrat Eduardo Frei,[63] and by his followers, in the Communization of Chile. On the same theme a series of important articles by Plinio Corrêa de Oliveira appeared in the *Folha de S. Paulo* and, in 1973, a manifesto of the Chilean TFP was published. It developed a central idea: Communism would not have come to power in Chile if Catholic public opinion had not been ideologically intoxicated and confused.

In 1977, Plinio Corrêa de Oliveira had the summary of a book of the Chilean TFP prepared. This book denounced the collaboration of a large part of the Chilean episcopate and clergy with the Marxist experiment of Salvador Allende. The first part of the study, published

---

[60] Sebastião Antonio Ferrarini, *A Imprensa e o Arcebispo vermelho (1964–1984)*, (São Paulo, Edições Paulinas, 1992), p. 63. In an interview granted to Oriana Fallaci in August 1970, Câmara declared he was "in agreement with the analysis of the capitalist society" made by Marx, hoping for "a society that is remade from scratch on Socialist foundations and without shedding blood". O. Fallaci, *Intervista con la storia*, 4th edn., (Milan, Biblioteca Universale Rizzoli, 1980), pp. 577, 583.

[61] Among the bishops who on that occasion kept their distance from the TFP, the Brazilian public was amazed to see Bishop Vicente Scherer and the cardinal of Salvador, Eugenio Sales. cf. Catolicismo, no. 212/214, August–October 1968.

[62] Fabio Vidigal Xavier da Silveira, *Frei o Kerensky Chileno*, São Paulo, Editora Vera Cruz, 1967.

[63] Eduardo Frei (1914–82), disciple in Paris of Maritain, tried to put into practice the Christian Democrat political utopia through a "Revolution in freedom" which had one of its main supports in "Land Reform". Cf. Pierre Letamendia, *Eduardo Frei*, Paris, Beauchesne, 1989; Fabio V. da Silveira, *Frei o Kerensky Chileno*.

under the title *The Church in face of the rise of the communist threat. An Appeal to the Silent Bishops*,[64] written by Plinio Corrêa de Oliveira, analyzed the positions taken by the Brazilian ecclesiastical hierarchy in favour of Communism. The work of the Brazilian thinker showed how communist infiltration of Catholic circles had begun forty years previously. Symptoms of the drama of the situation were the scandalously pro-communist poems of Pedro Casaldáliga, bishop of São Felix de Araguaia. The book concluded with a passionate appeal to the "silent bishops", that they abandon their reserve and speak out. "In the hands of the Silent Ones" wrote Corrêa de Oliveira "God gave all the means to still remedy the situation: they are numerous, and hold well-placed and prestigious positions."[65]

Silence was once again the only eloquent answer![66]

Towards the end of the 1970s the political atmosphere in Brazil changed profoundly following the gradual liberalization of the regime, the so-called *Abertura Politica*.[67] The process began under the government of President Ernesto Geisel and was completed under that of General João Batista Figueredo. In this phase the Catholic left renewed its attempt to conquer the society under the leadership of new personages, among whom figured the cardinal-archbishop of São Paulo, Paulo Evaristo Arns[68] and the cardinal-archbishop of Fortaleza, Aloísio Lorscheider.[69]

7. A tribalistic and Communist conception of the mission

In his appendix to *Revolution and Counter-Revolution* Plinio Corrêa de Oliveira denounced in 1977 the birth of new "tribalistic" currents within the Catholic Church.

They "intend to transform the noble, bone-like rigidity of the eccle-

---

[64] Cf. P. Corrêa de Oliveira, *A Igreja ante a escalada da ameaça comunista. Apelo aos Bispos Silenciosos*, São Paulo, Editora Vera Cruz, 1976. Published in June 1976, the book had four editions totalling 51,000 copies.

[65] Ibid, p. 86.

[66] During the same period, the contributor to *O Estado de S. Paulo* in Rome, the Italian journalist Rocco Morabito, made known in an article that: "it was possible to find, on tables in the Vatican, some copies of the book by Plinio Corrêa de Oliveira". O Estado de S. Paulo, 8 April 1977.

[67] President Geisel revoked the Institutional Act 5 (AI–5) which he himself had promulgated, which guaranteed control of Parliament by the military. He abolished the death penalty and censorship on radio and television and permitted the return of some political exiles. A clear analysis of the factors that influenced the process of *Abertura Politica* was presented by Prof Plinio Corrêa de Oliveira in *Sou católico: posso ser contra a Reforma Agraria?*, pp. 47–55. President Figueredo subsequently proclaimed an amnesty for political crimes and promulgated a law on the reorganization of the parties.

siastical structure – as Our Lord Jesus Christ instituted it and twenty centuries of religious life moulded it – into a cartilaginous, soft, and amorphous texture of dioceses and parishes without territories and of religious groups in which the firm canonical authority is gradually replaced by the ascendancy of Pentecostal 'prophets', the counterparts of the structuralistic-tribalistic witch doctors. Eventually, these prophets will be indistinguishable from witch doctors".[70]

In the same year, in a book entitled *Indigenous tribalism, a comunist-missionary ideal for Brazil in the XXI century*,[71] the Brazilian thinker analyzed thirty-six documents published by the new progressivist missiology, denouncing their infiltration into the structure of the Church.

By upsetting the traditional Catholic conception – according to which the aim of the Catholic missions is to bring civilization with the faith – the new missiological current saw tribalism as the chance to effect a utopian "kingdom of God" on earth. This "tribalization" process appears as the natural result of the break-up of the Christian civilization hoped for by progressivist theology. If in fact, as St Pius X affirms, no true civilization is possible outside Christianity, the denial of the civilizing mission of the Church inevitably involves regression to the tribal living of savages.

---

[68] Cardinal Paulo Evaristo Arns, a Franciscan, was nominated by Paul VI archbishop of São Paulo on 22 October 1970 and cardinal on 2 February 1973. In May of the same year he sold the Episcopal palace of São Paulo, moving to the area of Sumaré. From the beginning of his episcopate he made "Land Reform" and the campaign for human rights his banner. He considered the legalization of the Brazilian Communist Party "inevitable" and promoted the creation of the Partido dos Trabalhadores (PT) which united the exponents of left-wing trade unionism. He always supported the most progressivist theologians of Brazil and of Latin America. After the publication on 30 October 1975 of the *Declaração de Itaicí*, an Episcopal document with an open Communist tendency, the TFP had a message published in the press, *Não se iluda, Eminência*, in which Professor Corrêa de Oliveira thus addressed the archbishop of São Paulo: "However, do not fool yourself, Eminence. The people continue to fill the churches and to frequent the sacraments. (...) Attitudes like those of the signatories of the Itaicí document open up an increasingly larger gap. This gap is not between religion and the people, but, rather, between the Paulista Episcopate and the people. The Ecclesiastical Hierarchy, exactly in the measure in which it omits fighting communist subversion, isolates itself from the national context." Catolicismo, nn. 299–300, November–December 1975.
[69] Bishop Aloísio Lorscheider, a Franciscan, was secretary general (1968-71) and president (1971-9) of the CNBB. Nominated by Paul VI as archbishop of Fortaleza (1973) and cardinal (1976), from 1975 he was both president of CELAM and the CNBB.
[70] P. Corrêa de Oliveira, *Revolution and Counter-Revolution*, pp. 162–3.
[71] Cf. P. Corrêa de Oliveira, *Tribalismo indígena, ideal comuno-missionário para o Brasil no século XXI*, São Paulo, Editora Vera Cruz, 1977. New caravans of the TFP, visiting 2,963 cities, distributed 76,000 copies of the book printed in seven successive editions. On "modern" missiology cf. also the essay by Father M. Poradowski on *El marxismo en la teología de misiones* in his book *El marxismo en la teología* (cit.) and by the same author, "Tribalismo y pastoral misionera", Verbo, nos. 185–6, May–June 1980, pp. 567–78.

"We should emphasize that the greatest problem raised by these deliria" Dr Plinio wrote "does not lie in the missionaries themselves, nor in the indians. The problem is to know how this philosophy could have arisen in Holy Mother Church with impunity, thus poisoning seminaries, deforming missionaries, and perverting missions. And all this with such strong ecclesiastical backing."[72]

Two years later, when Sandinismo took power in Nicaragua, it seemed that the hour of victory of "liberation theology" had arrived. "The liberators" recalls Cardinal López Trujillo "transformed Nicaragua into a political testing ground they earnestly and enthusiastically supported. (...) Triumphant Sandinismo became the avant-garde of the people's Church...."[73] In Brazil, liberation theology had its media leaders in Fathers Leonardo and Clodoveo Boff, respectively a Franciscan and a Servite, protected by the cardinal of São Paulo, Paulo Evaristo Arns.

At the end of February 1980 in a suburb of São Paulo, an international Congress of Theology was held. It was organized by the "Ecumenical Association of Theologians of the Third World" and brought together liberation theologians of forty-two countries, among whom were bishops, priests, religious and "committed" lay people. Cardinal Arns was nominated Honorary President of the Congress, dedicated to *The Ecclesiology of Grassroot Communities*.

The closing session of the meeting celebrated an open apologia of the Sandinista revolution in Nicaragua, by now the "theological site"[74] of "liberation theology". This homage to Sandinismo took place in the theatre of the Catholic university with the participation of the "Commander" Daniel Ortega, then the Marxist president of Nicaragua, of Father Miguel d'Escoto, of the "chaplain" of the Revolution Father Uriel Molina and of Frei Betto, the Dominican famous for the condemnation inflicted on him for terrorism.

The atmosphere became almost unreal when Bishop Pedro Casaldáliga, wearing a Sandinista guerrilla uniform given to him by the Nicaraguan delegation, stated: "Dressed as a guerrilla I feel as if I had put on the robes of a priest." Amidst applause, he then solemnly added that he would try to honour this "sacrament of liberation" with "facts, and if necessary with blood".

---

[72] P. Corrêa de Oliveira, *Tribalismo indígena*, p. 48.
[73] A. Lopez Trujillo, "La Teología de la Liberación: datos para su historia", Sillar, no. 117, January–March 1985, p. 33.
[74] Javier Urcelay Alonso, "Sandinismo en Nicaragua: ¿uma revolución liberadora? ", Verbo, nos. 256–60, October–December 1987, pp. 1171–92. Cf. also *Nicaragua. Les contradictions du sandinisme*, edited by P. Vayssière, Paris, Presses du CNRS, 1988.

The TFP distributed a special issue of *Catolicismo*, containing a report on the "Sandinista night" and a further denunciation of Communist infiltration in Catholic circles. This was a complete illustrated report on what had happened, with the full transcript of the speeches made, followed by an introductory analysis and clear comments by Plinio Corrêa de Oliveira.[75]

8. A denunciation of the revolutionary character of the Grassroot Ecclesial communities

During this same period, liberation theology, although condemned by John Paul II in Puebla, found its strongest expression in the Grassroot Ecclesial Communities (GEC), indicated by the media as the great emergent power in Brazil. In the name of the Gospel, they advocated class struggle and social transformations with a Marxist stamp for the country.

The most effective condemnation of the revolutionary action of the Grassroot Ecclesial Communities, was the book *The Grassroot Communities, many speak of them but few know them – the TFP describes them*, that appeared in August 1982 and was immediately distributed throughout the country.[76] The study, a work by the brothers Gustavo Antônio and Luis Sérgio Solimeo, was preceded by a section written by Plinio Corrêa de Oliveira, in which the president of the TFP, in presenting *The goals of the GEC in the Brazilian context*, demonstrated how the CNBB was exercising the role of a "Fifth branch of government" in Brazil by using GECs as their tool.[77] The work went on to analyze the *Genesis, organization, doctrine and*

---

[75] Cf. Catolicismo, no. 355, July–August 1980.
[76] P. Corrêa de Oliveira; Gustavo Antonio Solimeo e Luis Sérgio Solimeo, *As CEBs ... das quais muito se fala, pouco se conhece. A TFP as descreve como são*, São Paulo, Vera Cruz, 1982. Six editions of this work have been printed with a total of 72,000 copies plus a further cartoon-style edition of 180,000 copies. Cf. P. Corrêa de Oliveira, "Suspeita estapafúrdia e juízo temerário", Folha de S. Paulo, 30 September 1982. Cf. also Antonio Augusto Borelli Machado, "Le comunità ecclesiali in Brasile: una crociata senza croce", Cristianità, no. 92, December 1982.
[77] Plinio Corrêa de Oliveira insists that the modern State, especially Brazil is not only dominated by the traditional powers (Executive, Legislative and Judiciary), but also by two other branches that are as "informal" as they are influential: the media and the episcopate. "In a recent book, I affirmed that there are only three branches in Brazil, the Executive, Legislative and Judiciary. But, today, there are two others that are perceptibly more influential in face of public opinion. The 4th Power is the Media, whose prestige relies more on the credulity of the naive than on the adhesion of truly cultured readers. The 5th Power is the CNBB, who – save in rare instances and honourable exceptions – has much more influence over the gullible than on true men of Faith." (P. Corrêa de Oliveira, "Prevenindo para tonificar", Folha de S. Paulo, 5 July 1983). Cf. ID., "Ditatorialismo publicitário centrista", Folha de S. Paulo, 10 August 1983.

action of the GECs, using a vast documentation. The subversive nature of the Grassroot Communities was clear as they promoted invasion of urban and rural properties, revolts in the factories, intimidation and unrest of every kind, with the aim of overthrowing the present socio-political regime in Brazil. Plinio Corrêa de Oliveira defined the GECs' effort as "crusade without a cross".[78]

> "Essentially the GECs are a political crusade (...) that does not exclude the possibility of going from a legal civil struggle to that of violence, whenever there is no other way to impose the reforms envisioned."[79]

The Spanish historian Ricardo de la Cierva, in his book *Jesuítas, Iglesia y Marxismo*, thus describes the main aspects of the TFP study:

> "The ideological key of the Grassroot Communities is almost always liberation theology. (...) Although their promoters consider them as a series of isolated points, the TFP scholars demonstrate that actually they form a perfectly co-ordinated network that starts from the left wing of the Episcopal Conference. (...) One of the keys of the Grassroot Communities consists in their schismatic tendency to form a new Church in opposition to the institutional Church."[80]

The Spanish historian is also amazed at the support given by the institutional Church to these protesting communities:

> "The Conference of Bishops of Brazil is the most numerous in the world. It is composed of a 'silent majority' generally dominated by a tendencially left-wing and liberationist minority that does not exceed sixty bishops but which often drags the 'moderates' in favour of its decisions. (...) It is this same left-wing of the Brazilian episcopate that controls the movement of the Grassroot Communities that has introduced into Brazilian society a completely new form of doing politics, to the point that the Communities as a whole have been converted into an 'emerging electoral force'."[81]

On 6 August 1984, the Sacred Congregation for the Doctrine of the Faith published the Instruction, *Libertatis Nuntio*,[82] in which "libera-

---

[78] P. Corrêa de Oliveira, *As metas das CEBs*, in *As CEBs* ..., p. 86.
[79] Ibid, p. 88.
[80] Ricardo de la Cierva, *Jesuítas, Iglesia y Marxismo, 1965–1985. La Teología de la liberación desenmascarada*, (Madrid, Plaza & Janés Editores, 1986), pp. 116-18.
[81] Ibid, pp. 118–19.
[82] Congregation for the Doctrine of the Faith, Instruction *Libertatis Nuntio* of 6 August 1984, in AAS, vol. 76, 1984, pp. 890-9; Denz.-H, nos. 4730–41.

tion theology" was irrevocably condemned. On 22 March 1986, this document was followed by a second one on Christian liberty and liberation, *Libertatis conscientia*,[83] which was presented as a "positive" intervention on the same theme. The two documents, approved by John Paul II, constitute a single message that put an end to the claims of the new theological current and of the movement of the "Grassroot Ecclesial Communities" inspired by it.

The doctrinal and practical contribution of the TFP to the struggle against "liberation theology" in Latin America is undeniable. Ten years after this denunciation campaign, one of the forerunners of "liberation theology", Father Joseph Comblin, denounced so many times by the TFP, confessed in a 1993 interview that by now "the GECs are marginalized, thrashed, and fulminated everywhere. Today, they are but minorities without influence in the milieu of local churches".[84]

9. The TFP in the world: the development of the anti-communist epic

By the end of the Seventies, the TFP's range of action had been extended throughout Latin America and from here it spread, ever more incisively, to the United States and Europe. The prominent role of the associations that followed Plinio Corrêa de Oliveira was to oppose the psychological war being waged on all continents by Communism and to counter it with the integrity of Catholic doctrine.

In December 1981, while the media of the whole world were supporting the newly-elected French president Mitterand, the TFP, then in 13 countries around the world, published Plinio Corrêa de Oliveira's message to the Western nations entitled *What Does Self-Managing Socialism Mean for Communism: a Barrier? Or a Bridgehead?*.[85] In examining Mitterand's programme in the light of

---

[83] Congregation for the Doctrine of the Faith, Instruction *Libertatis conscientia* of 22 March 1986, in AAS, vol. 79, 1986, pp. 554–9; Denz.-H, nos. 4750–76. This instruction was preceded by a note of the Congregation for the Doctrine of the Faith (AAS, vol. 77, 1985, pp. 756–62), in which the book of the theologian Leonardo Boff O.F.M., *Church: charism and power*, New York, Crossroad, 1985, was condemned.

[84] Cit. in "Expoente da 'teologia da libertação' confessa o fracasso das comunidades eclesiais de base", Catolicismo, no. 505, January 1993.

[85] P. Corrêa de Oliveira, *O socialismo autogestionário: em vista do comunismo, barreira ou cabeça-de-ponte?* The message, which occupied six pages, appeared on 9 December 1981 in *The Washington Post* (USA) and in the *Frankfurter Allgemeine Zeitung* (RFT) and was later released by 187 publications in 53 countries and 14 languages, totalling 34,767,900 copies. In the United Kingdom the full text was published in *The Observer*, a one-page summary in *The Guardian*, and a communiqué in *The Daily Telegraph*. Cf. also P. Corrêa de Oliveira, *Autogestion socialiste: les têtes tombent à l'entreprise, à la maison, à l'école*, Paris, Tradition, Famille, Propriété, 1983.

the great categories of *Revolution and Counter-Revolution* the Brazilian thinker showed how between the French Revolution and self-managing Socialism there existed "a whole genealogy of revolutions: 1848, 1871 and that of Sorbonne in 1968".[86]

The author of the message demonstrated that the self-managing programme aimed at breaking society up into autonomous cells, through transformation not only of industrial, commercial and rural enterprises, but also of the family, the school, and all social life, thus upsetting the private life of every individual.

The basic themes that Plinio Corrêa de Oliveira touched upon were evidently not of purely French importance.[87] The aim of the intervention, which concluded with the historical text in which St Pius X hoped France might once again shine like the first born daughter of the Church, was to open the eyes of international public opinion.

It is difficult to measure the effects of this historical text that was distributed throughout the world. In fact, after that, Mitterand's programme underwent a rapid decline in popularity and the French president was forced to renounce, at least in part, the reforms of his original project.

Between the neo-Socialism of Mitterand and the *perestroika* launched by Gorbachev[88] in 1985, there is an historical and ideological continuity. In both cases we see an attempt of Marxism to free itself from its statist wrapping to hasten the march towards that self-managing type of society Plinio Corrêa de Oliveira had described in the appendix to the third part of *Revolution and Counter-Revolution.*

The new step in the revolutionary process had its first spectacular result on 9 November 1989 with the fall of the Berlin Wall. While Poland, East Germany, Czechoslovakia and Hungary were breaking away from the Soviet bloc, Plinio Corrêa de Oliveira launched a petition drive to collect signatures in support of Lithuanian independence, left to its fate by the West. With 5,218,000 signatures collected in less than three months, the "Pro Lituania libera" campaign entered the

---

[86] P. Corrêa de Oliveira, "Autogestão, dedo e fuxico", Folha de S. Paulo, 11 December 1981.
[87] Another man, symbol of socialism at the beginning of the 80s, was Felipe Gonzalez in Spain. The Spanish TFP raised its voice in alarm with the book *España, anestesiada sin percibirlo, amordazada sin quererlo, extraviada sin saberlo. La obra del PSOE*, Madrid, Editorial Fernando III el Santo, 1988.
[88] On the "liberalization" of *Glasnost* (1985) and of *Perestroika* (1986), perhaps the greatest propaganda movement of the history of Communism, cf. the critical observations of Françoise Thom, *Le moment Gorbatchev*, Paris, Hachette, 1989; Mario Furlan, *I volti di Gorbaciov*, Milan, Greco Editori, 1990; Hubert Bassot, *Du nouveau à l'Est? Niet*, Paris, Pierre Téqui, 1993; Hans Huyn, *Tromperie sur les étiquettes*, Lausanne, Documentation chrétienne, 1993.

Guinness Book of Records as the largest petition drive in history. The delivery of the microfilm of the signatures took place with great solemnity on 4 December 1990 in the Lithuanian Parliament.[89] On 27 August 1991, the independence of Lithuania was finally recognized by the Western countries and by the Soviet Union itself on the following 6 September. The same happened a short time later with the other Baltic States.

The collapse of the Iron Curtain and the events taking place in Eastern Europe posed new questions about the future development of *perestroika*, but they also offered the confirmation, so tragically obvious, of the failure of the Communist utopia.[90] In a manifesto entitled, *Communism and Anti-communism on the Threshold of the Millennium's Last Decade*, published in over 50 of the world's largest newspapers in early March 1990, Plinio Corrêa de Oliveira, with his usual perspicacity, observed:

"All this current commotion of European geography is demonstrated here and there in different circumstances and meanings; but they are dominated by one general meaning that incorporates them and penetrates them like a great common impulse: it is Discontent. (...) A furious fire is spreading throughout the Soviet empire, breaking it up: these are the flames of a gigantic 'discontent'. Discontent of those who do not agree to anything but who are physically prevented from speaking, moving, rising, in short of demonstrating an efficacious dissidence. (...) Probably the most widespread and total Discontent that history has ever known. (...) If the Discontent in the Soviet world developed in this way without meeting any obstacles of greater entity along its way, there would be no need for the political observer to be very clever to grasp the final point of arrival: the destruction of Soviet power in all its immense empire, that was up to yesterday surrounded by the Iron Curtain, and the rising, from the depths of the ruins that are thus accumulated, of a single, immense, thun-

---

[89] A delegation composed of eleven members of the different TFPs, led by Dr Caio V. Xavier da Silveira, director of the TFP-bureau in Paris, personally delivered to President Vytautas Landsbergis, on 4 December 1990 in Vilnius, the microfilm of the monumental petition drive.

[90] "Communism's strength lies in its unlimited capacity for destruction, its weakness in its incapacity to construct and to create. (...) If communism may be defined as a movement which destroys everything but itself in its first phase and which paralyzes society in its second, then I believe in its third phase it will begin to self-destruct." Carlos Franqui, *From Paralysis to Self-Destruction*, in *Debates on the future of Communism*, edited by Vladimir Tismaneanu e Judith Shapiro, (London, Macmillan, 1991), p. 19.

dering cry of indignation from the enslaved and oppressed people."[91]

Two years later, in an interview with *Diário Las Américas* of Miami of 14 May 1992, Plinio Corrêa de Oliveira stated:

"Perhaps the day is not far off when the debatable authenticity of communism's retreat will show that it was but a metamorphosis, and that the decomposed larva flies away as the 'pretty' butterfly of self-management.... Self-management is what the theoreticians and supreme leaders of communism, from Marx and Engels to Gorbachev, always presented as the most extreme and expressive form of communism, its quintessence. (...) Communism, apparently defeated, would thus have spread throughout the world. In this, then, would the prophecies of Fatima be confirmed when they warned: if men do not amend their lives, Russia will spread its errors throughout the world!"[92]

10. 1994: An overall view of the world

The last public manifesto prepared by the Brazilian thinker appeared on 9 December 1994 in the *Folha de S. Paulo*. It was addressed to the participants of the American summit who had gathered in Miami from 9 to 11 December that year and outlined an impressive picture of the international situation at the twilight of the century. The final words renewed that confidence in the victory of Christian civilization that had always been a dominant note in the apostolic commitment of Plinio Corrêa de Oliveira and of the TFP. We give here the complete text of this document, which appears almost like his historical testament:

The TFPs of the three Americas

1. Convey their concerns regarding

---

[91] P. Corrêa de Oliveira, *Communism and Anti-communism on the Threshold of the Millennium's Last Decade*, in *The Wall Street Journal*, 27 February 1990. The manifesto was published for the first time in *Folha de S. Paulo* of 14 February 1990. In that same month Dr Plinio wondered: "I ask, in effect: Gorbachev, plus perestroika, plus the fall of the 'Iron Curtain,' plus the visit of the Russian head of state to John Paul II, and plus the Gorbachev–Bush meeting on the glorious waters of Malta, upon which once the ships of the crusaders reflected, does not all this constitute a colossal manoeuvre involving the whole world in the clutches of a policy of convergence and self-management that will bring every nation within two steps of communism?" P. Corrêa de Oliveira, "Um comentário atual, uma antiga previsão", Folha de S. Paulo, 9 February 1992.

[92] P. Corrêa de Oliveira, Interview in *Diário Las Américas*, 14 May 1992. "Gorbachev, – he affirmed in another interview – did not put an end to the communist regime, but rather liberated it from the cancer of statism." *Expreso* (Ecuador), 31 May 1992.

– The bewildering indifference, passivity, and even complicity of sundry ecclesiastical, political, intellectual, media, and financial circles toward the ineffectual communist regime in the land once called the Pearl of the Antilles and toward its aged inspirer and head, Fidel Castro.

– The inconsistent double-standard applied by several institutions and governments of the Americas in their liberal, even conciliatory, policy toward Cuba's regime, on the one hand, and their adamant, even armed, opposition to Haiti's former regime on the other.

– The clever metamorphosis undertaken by countless figures of the far left after the fall of the Berlin Wall, who – without repudiating their revolutionary past nor renouncing their egalitarian goals – have attained powerful political posts simply by changing labels and adopting new methods of action.

– The way such individuals exploit their political power to promote a virtual cultural revolution that deals a radical blow against fundamental principles of Christian civilization by numbing the wholesome reaction of public opinion.

– The destructive potential as detonators for socio-economic chaos displayed by Latin American terrorist and guerrilla groups supported by outside forces.

– The continuing spiritual crisis afflicting the Roman Catholic Church – with its inevitable consequences for civil society – and the concurrent progress made by sects, animist religions, and even satanic movements.

2. Deplore

– The arrogance with which homosexual militants claim alleged 'rights' in direct opposition to the laws of God and of nature.

– The unspeakable pressure exerted by international institutions and social factions within the Americas on behalf of abortion, contraception, divorce, concubinage, euthanasia, and other evils destructive of the family, as typified by the UN conference in Cairo.

– The experimentation on human embryos and analogous genetic and eugenic experimentation, which brutishly ignore elemental religious and ethical principles.

– The escalating drug trade and the schemes to legalize such deadly addictions.

– The ominous collaboration of the media in spreading the poison of anti-Christian 'values' that corrode the very soul of civilization.

3. Profess grave reservations regarding

– The reckless rapidity with which certain political circles seek to hasten hemispheric integration, in ways that blur, if not obliterate, state borders, cultural characteristics, and even national sovereignties.

– The apparent lack of appreciation in these circles regarding the highly dubious consequences of such analogous social engineering as the Maastricht Treaty, which is strongly opposed by millions of Europeans.

– The inordinate, media-induced confidence and irrational fascination for economic development as the answer to all our problems, the profound spiritual and moral roots of which are routinely relegated to an inferior plain.

– The frenzied hopes which some place in the emergence of a cyber-civilization, in utter disregard of its inherent perils and the serious detriments derived from the psychological, moral, and cultural transformations it would inevitably entail.

– The ever-escalating political, social, and economic influence of non-governmental organizations (NGOs), many of which have specifically revolutionary agendas (such as those promoting a return to tribalism, antithetical to Christian civilization), as was evident at the 1992 Earth Summit in Rio de Janeiro, and the international largesse lavished on these NGOs.

– The imposition of draconian reductions – budgetary and otherwise – on noble armed forces of the hemisphere in the illusion of new national and international realities.

– The strident voices accusing some armed forces of violating the human rights of communist guerrillas – voices so strangely silent in the face of the violent crimes perpetrated by revolutionary terrorists against urban and rural populations in important countries such as Colombia and Peru.

4. Publicly call on the leaders of our hemisphere assembled in Miami to

– Openly discuss, in depth and detail, these and other sensitive and urgent problems impacting the future of the Americas, welcoming constructive debate without fear of disagreement.

– Propose sound solutions to these problems in full accord with the authentic Christian traditions that embody the legitimate aspirations of the peoples of the Americas.

– Adopt with all due diligence the political, economic, and educational measures needed to effect the immediate normalization of the situation of the Cuban people.

5. View with hope

– The dawning of a wholesome rejection of the anti-Christian Revolution on so many fronts by a growing number of the peoples of this hemisphere, particularly among the poor and working classes.

– The awakening of public opinion to the onslaught of television and other media outlets as conduits of immorality, which is particularly destructive to our children and youth.

– The rejection by the electorate of avowedly leftist presidential candidates in Brazil, Mexico, Colombia, Peru, Argentina, and El Salvador.

– The loss of face of 'liberation theology' and the collapse of its base communities, even among the most impoverished segments of the population.

– The waning of the West's ideological obsession with egalitarianism, so advantageous to socialism and communism.

– The excellent prospects – solidly based on the firm foundation of Christian civilization – that these developments have opened for co-operation between Latin America, on the one hand and the United States and Canada, on the other.

Accordingly, the TFPs of the three Americas

– Affirm their deep and abiding conviction that, when men resolve to co-operate with the grace of God, the unfolding of history generates marvels. This is the lesson bequeathed us by pre-medieval and medieval Europe, which, beginning with decadent Latin populations and hordes of barbarian invaders, attained, under every point of view, a religious, cultural, and economic level without precedent.

– Proclaim their unwavering certainty that despite the moral upheavals, material crises, and pitfalls of every kind being prepared for the Americas by the enemies of the Church and Christian civilization, we shall witness the resplendent resurgence of Christendom throughout the Americas, as forseen by Our Lady of Fatima in 1917 when she promised: *In the end, my Immaculate Heart will triumph!*[93]

11. Plinio Corrêa de Oliveira as "Father" and "Founder"

From the foundation of the Brazilian TFP until his death, over a period of 35 years, Plinio Corrêa de Oliveira personally wrote, or indirectly inspired, hundreds of manifestos, declarations, press releases, open letters, collections of signatures, messages of every kind, in his name and on behalf of the TFPs of the whole world.[94]

---

[93] P. Corrêa de Oliveira, *As Americas rumo ao 3° milênio: convicções, apprensões e esperanças das TFP do continente*, Catolicismo, no. 528, December 1994, En. tr. *The Americas on the Dawn of the Third Millennium: Convictions, Apprehensions, and Hopes of the Hemispheric TFPs*, published in the *Washington Post* on 6 December 1994.

[94] Up to the last days of his life, he held four conferences per week for all the members of the TFP resident in São Paulo, as well as numerous meetings of formation and study. The total number of conferences held by Dr Plinio with the members of the TFP exceeds twenty thousand.

In the last part of his life, when he displayed incredible activity, he increasingly appeared to be a man with a deep interior life, conforming to the model outlined by St Paul: "It is no longer I who live, but Christ who lives in me".[95] In him, action was always the external effusion of the supernatural life from which he drew from reciting the rosary, daily Holy Communion and above all the constant protection of the faculties of the soul.

What struck his collaborators was the presence in him of apparently contrary virtues, such as simplicity and prudence, extreme combativity, as well as great amiability and sweetness. The affection and devotion of his disciples, who loved to be considered his children, grew increasingly around his paternal figure. The declaration of the TFP, which appeared on 3 November 1995, one month after his death, renders this touching testimony:

> "In the midst of the modern tempest, his example of life, his unalterable faith, his intense piety, were, and continue to be now that God has called him back to himself, the spiritual support of all the members of the Brazilian TFP, as indeed of the autonomous and fellow TFPs. Many people owe him the immense grace of perseverance in the Faith; many others, who were wandering misled on the tortuous roads of the world, owe their return to the straight path to his words, his dedication and sacrifice.
>
> "His solicitude for each and every member of the groups of the TFP was almost unlimited, and we can say that there is not a member or a volunteer who did not feel he was their true father.
>
> "His fatherly attention reached its peak when there was a risk to the spiritual good of those whom Providence had in some way entrusted to him, never missing an occasion to offer a word of advice, a gesture of attention or a word of encouragement."[96]

The TFP's declaration recalls how Plinio Corrêa de Oliveira was favoured by Providence with a particular gift: the discernment of the intentions and secrets of the heart. The capuchin, Bishop Vital Maria Gonçalves de Oliveira,[97] the figure in the Brazilian clergy who was

---

[95] Gal. 2:20.

[96] "Um homem de Fé, pensamento, luta e ação", Catolicismo, no. 539–40, November–December 1995.

[97] On Bishop Vital, cf. note 5 of chap. II.

most loved by Plinio Corrêa de Oliveira, affirmed that he had a special form of psychological penetration, inherited from his mother, with which he discerned people's good and bad intentions. Dr Plinio had a similar aptitude, capable of penetrating the psychology and mentality of a person, by conversing with him or even just by examining his photograph. This capacity was born of natural talents but also of a special supernatural light. This should not cause any surprise: in fact the Church teaches that the natural faculties of man are elevated and reflected by virtues and by the gifts of the Holy Spirit, necessary – says Leo XIII – for the "just man who lives the life of grace".[98]

12. Between misunderstandings and slander

During his long life, Plinio Corrêa de Oliveira had great admirers, especially in the ecclesiastic field.[99] Among these were distinguished defenders of the faith such as Cardinals Slipyj[100] and Mindzsenty, eminent cardinals such as Aloisi Masella, Pizzardo, Staffa, Ciappi, Echeverría Ruíz, Stickler, Oddi, and theologians of international fame, such as Fathers Anastasio Gutiérrez, Victorino Rodríguez, Antonio Royo Marín.

"All who desire to live a godly life in Christ Jesus" warns St Paul, however "will be persecuted."[101] It is difficult to find the founder of a Catholic Institution who has not suffered slander and persecutions. An obvious example is St Ignatius who was accused of being an "enlightened person" and underwent eight trials before the foundation

---

[98] Leo XIII, Encyclical *Divinum illud munus*, of 9-5-1897, in IP, *Le fonti della vita spirituale*, p. 51.

[99] Neither Plinio Corrêa de Oliveira, nor his work was ever officially censored by the Church. Nor can the critical note of the Brazilian Episcopal Conference published on 19 April 1985, as a press release and not as an ecclesiastical decree, be considered censorship. Cf. the reply of the TFP that appeared in *Folha de S. Paulo* and other dailies on 24 April 1985; cf. also G. A. Solimeo e L. S. Solimeo, *Analyse par la TFP brésilienne d'une prise de position de la CNBB sur la 'TFP et sa famille d'âmes'*, Paris, Société Française pour la Défense de la Tradition, Famille et Propriété, 1989; cf. also *The NCBB note on the Brazilian TFP: Unfounded statements, Biased and impassioned assessments*, London, Tradition, Family, Property – Bureau for the United Kingdom, 1997.

[100] The Ukrainian Cardinal Josef Slipyj was the guest of the TFP in São Paulo on 26 September 1968. Prof Plinio Corrêa de Oliveira, on that occasion, gave a reception in his honour, with the participation of important members of the clergy, of the Armed Forces and of Paulista society. Cf. *Catolicismo*, no. 215, November 1968.

[101] 2 Tim. 3:10–13.

of his order. Even after pontifical approval, the School of Theology of Paris, which three centuries before had condemned the mendicant orders, criticized the "novelty" of the Society of Jesus, accusing it of disturbing the religious peace and of having been born to destroy rather than to build. The same Society of Jesus was suppressed by the Pontifical authorities from 1773 to 1814, in the critical years that saw the explosion of the French Revolution.[102]

One moment spread by word of mouth, the next amplified by the media, slander is an ancient arm of the Revolution, which uses it to try to demolish the credibility of its opponents. "Lie, Lie, something will remain", was the notorious motto attributed to Voltaire.

Even more than his thinking, Plinio Corrêa de Oliveira's work suffered misunderstandings and slander. The slander which refers to the very person of the founder of the TFP, may be summarized in the accusation of having wanted to establish, within this association, a cult to his person and to that of his mother, Dona Lucilia.[103] The principal misunderstandings concern his specific vocation and that of the TFP: the struggle to defend and restore Christian social order, according to the great comission of the Pontifical Magisterium.

These accusations came from the most varied sectors, but mainly from two opposite ones: the Socialist-Communists,[104] and from some

---

[102] On the suppression of the Society of Jesus, with the brief *Dominus ac Redemptor* of Clement XIV, of 22 July 1773, cf. Paul Dudon S.J., *De la suppression de la Compagnie de Jésus (1758-1773)*, in "Revue des questions historiques", vol. 132, 1938, pp. 75-107. "The real cause" of this suppression, Henri de Bonald wrote in 1827, "was resentment against religious and monarchical power, which found solid support in that order that educated young people". H. de Bonald, *Risposta a nuove offese contro una celebre Compagnia*, It. tr., (Imola, Tip. Galeati, 1827), p. 52.

[103] On this claim of "improper" veneration of Prof Plinio Corrêa de Oliveira, cf. the work published by the TFP in his defence: A. A. Borelli Machado; A. Sinke Guimarães; G. A. Solimeo; J. S. Clá Dias, *Refutação da TFP a uma investida frustra*, São Paulo, Sociedade Brasileira de Defesa da Tradição, Família e Propriedade, 1984, vol. I, pp. 155-229; and the two press releases "A TFP afirma sua posição doutrinária e interpela opositor", Folha de S. Paulo, 17 August 1984; and "Voltando as costas a uma controvérsia", Folha de S. Paulo, 28 August 1984.

[104] During the month of February 1976, in four successive transmissions of its programme *Escucha Chile*, Radio Moscow attacked the Chilean TFP with regard to the book *The Church of Silence in Chile* which it had just published. On 20 November 1984, the newspaper *Izvestia*, official voice of the Soviet government, showed its full solidarity with the publicity attack which targeted the Asociación Civil Resistencia, sister association of the TFP in Venezuela, and the TFP Bureau in Caracas.

circles of the "traditionalist" right.[105] This really defamatory typhoon was ably channelled by the so-called "anti-Cult movement". Back in 1985, Plinio Corrêa de Oliveira revealed its totalitarian and anti-Christian nature in an introduction he wrote to a study on "brainwashing".[106]

One of the first and most violent "media uproars"[107] started in Rio Grande do Sul in 1975 while the TFP was involved in spreading the Pastoral Letter of Bishop de Castro Mayer *On the Indissolubility of Marriage*. This same Brazilian bishop intervened openly in defence of the defamed association with a letter of protest from which we give here a meaningful passage:

"This campaign is the vehicle for such injustice that I cannot abstain from formulating my protest against it. A protest, in my case, is all the more imperious since, considering my relationship with the TFP, the campaign strikes at my honour as a bishop of Holy Mother Church. (. . .)

If, then, the TFP were subversive, nazi-fascist, and a disturber of public order; if it separated, against the natural order, children from their parents, what should be said of a bishop who maintains constant contact with this Society, who knows every aspect of its activities, and accepts, willingly, the society's offer of spreading our pastoral letter against divorce which stands up for the rights of

---

[105] Prof Massimo Introvigne raises an hypothesis that he defines as "disturbing" or perhaps "malicious": "Particularly, but not only, in France, in recent years, various 'Lefebvrian' and 'Sedevacantist' publications have conducted campaigns against 'cults' with particularly violent tones. If it were just, or mainly, a case of the defence of traditional Catholic doctrine, there would be no cause for wonder. But, in point of fact, this literature makes its own the arguments of the lay anti-cult movement, and willingly attacks realities of the Catholic world such as the TFP and Opus Dei. Therefore, a legitimate suspicion assails us that the anti-cult movement uses certain 'Lefebvrian' and 'Sedevacantist' groups as advance troops, as wreckers, to throw into the fray, for the first bayonet charge; and, naturally, to be sacrificed at the opportune moment, since, by adopting the usual criteria of the anti-cult movement, these groups can be easily, in turn, disqualified as 'cults' when, and to the extent, necessary". M. Introvigne, *'Sette' e 'diritto di persecuzione': le ragioni di una controversia*, in G. Cantoni, M. Introvigne, *Libertà Religiosa, 'Sette' e 'Diritto' di persecuzione*, (Piacenza, Cristianità, 1996), p. 106.
[106] The study appeared in number 409 (January 1985) of *Catolicismo* with the title "'Lavagem cerebral' – um mito ao serviço da nova 'Inquisição terapêutica'". Cf. also David G. Bromley, *The Brainwashing. Deprogramming Controversy: Sociological, Psychological, Legal and Historical Perspectives*, New York-Toronto, The Edwin Mellen Press, 1983. In May 1987, the *American Psychological Association* in turn declared the theory of "brainwashing" applied to religious movements as "non scientific". Cf. M. Introvigne, "L'Opus Dei e il movimento anti-sette", Cristianità, no. 229, May 1994.
[107] The term was coined by Dr Plinio himself to indicate the organized public calumny that was being moved against the TFP.

God over human society? Such a bishop would be an accomplice and even be in collusion with them."[108]

The most virulent attacks against the TFP were subsequently dealt in France (1979),[109] Venezuela (1984),[110] again in Brazil (1993)[111] and in Spain (1995). This last persecution, promoted by the already mentioned "Anti-Cult movement", resulted in the "kidnapping" of a young Spanish member of the TFP, Santiago Canals Coma, whom they wanted to "de-programme" with brutal methods to "restore him" to his family.[112]

On that occasion Father Antonio Royo Marín, one of the greatest contemporary theologians, felt it his duty to publicly intervene in defence of the Spanish TFP with these words:

"There have been many occasions that have given me the opportunity of knowing the TFP thoroughly as well as several of its principal members around the world, including its organization, how it is run, its fights, its growth and its victories. They are all exemplary practising Catholics. They attend Mass, receive Communion daily, pray the fifteen Mysteries of the Rosary every day as well as other pious devotions, all of which are traditional and commonly practised within Holy Mother Church. They do not perform any strange or obsolete ceremony, but rather they all are in total harmony with the most authentic Roman Catholic spirit.

---

[108] Letter of Bishop Antônio de Castro Mayer published in no. 294, June 1975, of *Catolicismo*. The TFP reacted in turn with the document *A TFP em legitima defesa*, published in the newspapers and in the special issue (June 1975) of the same magazine.

[109] This was an anonymous libel, as calumnious as it was superficial and lacking in that logic which is the pride of French intelligence, to which the TFP replied with a work in two volumes entitled *Imbroglio, Détraction, Délire. Remarques sur un Rapport concernant les TFP*, Paris, Association Française pour la Défense de la Tradition, de la Famille, de la Propriété, 1979. In spite of this response-document, the libel, known as "rapport Joyeux" from the name of the person subsequently discovered to be its author, continued to be quoted and spread in semi-clandestine publications against the TFP.

[110] This persecution led, with a governmental decree of 13 November 1984, to the closure in Venezuela, of the Asociación Civil Resistencia, an autonomous body, but linked to the TFPs in 14 countries. In 1985, to defend itself from other attacks, the TFP published a work by Plinio Corrêa de Oliveira, *Guerreiros da Virgem – A réplica da Autenticidade, A TFP sem segredos*, São Paulo, Editora Vera Cruz, 1985 and the book by A. Sinke Guimarães, *Servitudo ex Caritate*, São Paulo, Artpress, 1985.

[111] The TFP replied with an article entitled "Usando o mesmo realejo, mais uma vez investe contra a TFP o tablóide de Zero hora. A TFP se defende", that appeared in *Correio do Povo* of 19 February 1993.

[112] Santiago Canals Coma, *¿Renace la persecución religiosa en España? Historia de un secuestro*, Zaragoga, Editorial Ramiro el Monje, 1996. "Before God – testifies the same kidnapped person – I affirm solemnly that I never heard a word or witnessed a gesture of Prof Plinio Corrêa de Oliveira which did not bring me closer to God our Lord, to the Most Blessed Virgin and to the Roman Pontiff. In the end, to the Holy Roman Catholic and Apostolic Church, our beloved Mother, whose invisible head is Our Lord Jesus Christ." ibid, p. 17

They have a great veneration for the Holy Father who they consider the Vicar of Christ and His supreme representative in the world. They are deeply devoted to the Virgin Mary and are convinced that, in the end, her Immaculate Heart will triumph throughout the world as promised at Fatima."[113]

The underlying theme of the accusations is the disparaging qualification of "cult", of which in numerous writings the TFPs have shown to be groundless.[114] Among the illustrious personages who defended the TFP from this slander, surreptitiously directed against the Catholic Church itself, are Cardinal Alfons Stickler[115] and Cardinal Bernardino Echeverría Ruíz. The latter, in a letter to the President of the French Chamber Philippe Séguin, expressed his "profound perplexity before this injurious amalgam aimed at an upright association composed of Catholics animated by a great love for God and their fellow men".[116]

13. Proper and improper cult according to the Church

The accusations of improper "veneration" of Plinio and Dona Lucilia by secularists and progressivists are difficult to understand, but even more so when they come from Catholic circles, especially the "traditionalist" ones.

In fact the twentieth century was the era of the deifying of man, enthroned on altars once dedicated to God. Politicians, sportsmen, singers have all been objects of a cult that can be defined as "fanatic" precisely because its extravagant character has made it stray into idolatry. If an improper form of veneration rendered to men exists, there are also proper forms of veneration such as that reserved for saints or, on a natural level, to particularly distinguished men. Veneration, in its essence, is an act of esteem and in its wider significance is nothing more than the expression of an interior sentiment with which one man recog-

---

[113] "Vehemente desmentido del Padre Royo Marín a la indigna campaña de calumnias contra T.F.P.-Covadonga", *La Vanguardia* of 27 July 1995. Father Antonio Royo Marín O.P., Preacher General of the Dominican Order, is author of 26 works of theology and Catholic doctrine. His defence of the Church and the Papacy was rewarded with the medal "Pro Ecclesia et Pontifice" given to him by Pope John Paul II.

[114] Cf. the important book by G.A. Solimeo and L.S. Solimeo, *La nouvelle inquisition athée et psychiatrique. Elle taxe de secte ceux qu'elle veut détruire*, Paris, Société Française pour la Defense de la Tradition, Famille et Proprieté, 1991, and the similarly clear related contribution by Benoît Bemelmans, *Le rapport Guyard à la lumière de la doctrine catholique et du droit français*, Paris, Société Française pour la défense de la Tradition, Famille et Propriété, 1996. This work is a clear refutation of the *Rapport* on the cults in France, launched by the *Assemblée nationale* in December 1995.

[115] Cf. the preface to this book.

[116] Text in B. Bemelmans, *Le Rapport Guyard*, pp. 17–18.

nizes the excellence of another.[117] The excellence of the saints renders them worthy of a form of worship called *dulia* or veneration, different and inferior to the supreme cult of adoration or *latria* due only to the Most Holy Trinity and to the humanity of Jesus Christ. The Catholic Church in defining the precise areas of this veneration admits its legitimacy against the heretical negation of the devotion to the saints.[118]

Only the Church can establish, in an infallible manner, who is a "saint" and publicly promote his cult. It is lawful however to render, to those who have died in odour of sanctity, a "private" veneration, whose existence is after all a requirement of the ecclesiastical authorities for the processes of beatification and canonization. "Let us honour the servants" pronounced Pope John XV in the most ancient canonization procedure of the Church "so that the honour may return to the Lord, who said 'He who receives you receives me' (Mt. 10:40)."[119] *Lumen Gentium* says:

> "Every genuine testimony of love to the saints by nature tends to and terminates in Christ himself, 'the crown of all saints', and through him in God, who in his saints is recognized as admirable and is glorified."[120]

This private cult is none other than the demonstration of devotion that spontaneously flows from the hearts of the faithful before the Church officially pronounces on the merits. Such expressions of devotion, authorized by the Church, are not born suddenly on the morrow of the death. The "odour of sanctity" often surrounds the future saint when he is still alive: it was so for almost all the great saints in the Church, and it is so today for personages that have not yet been canonized. Such is the case of Padre Pio, around whom, while yet alive, an atmosphere of enthusiastic veneration was created, to the point that some even spoke of "fanaticism".[121]

---

[117] Luigi Oldani, *Culto*, in EC, vol. IV, 1950, col. 1040, col. 1040–4.

[118] The legitimacy and utility of the cult of the saints was defined by the Council of Trent in its XXV session (Denz.-H, nos. 1821–4). Cf. also P. Sejourné, *Saints (culte des)*, in DTC, vol. XIV, 1939, col. 870–978; Justo Collantes S.J., *La fede della Chiesa cattolica*, (Vatican City, Libreria Editrice Vaticana, 1993), pp. 577–90.

[119] John XV, Encyclical *Cum conventus esset*, of 3 February 993 to the bishops and abbots of France and of Germany for the canonization of Bishop Ulrich of Augusta, in Denz.-H, no. 675.

[120] Vatican Council II, Dogmatic Constitution *Lumen Gentium*, of 21 November 1964, in Denz.-H, no. 4170.

[121] "The groups of Padre Pio" in particular were stamped as fanatics because of their "veneration" and were denounced for superstition and disobedience by the ecclesiastical authorities. They are still active and widespread. This did not prevent the opening on 20 March 1983, at the request of the Polish episcopate, of the cause for the beatification of the Capuchin from Pietrelcina which is still in process. Cf. Rino Cammilleri, *Storia di Padre Pio*, (Casale Monferrato, Piemme, 1993), pp. 169–82.

To confine ourselves to just one other example, it is sufficient to recall the clamorous enthusiasm that surrounded Don Bosco during his journey to Paris in 1883. Blessed Don Rua made this explicit statement during the Process for the Cause of Beatification:

"If he went into a church to hold a conference, so great was the crowd that gathered that he had to be accompanied by three or four people to open a way for him to reach the pulpit; and often guards had to be put at the doors, to avoid the danger of an accident caused by the crush. If he was seen in the squares or in the streets, he was promptly surrounded by an immense crowd, who knelt in the full light of day to implore his blessing. At his residence, there was a continuous press of people, who considered themselves fortunate to see a saint."[122]

We do not intend to deduce the holiness of Plinio Corrêa de Oliveira from the demonstrations of admiration and devotion of his disciples, but just to emphasize the full harmony of these expressions of enthusiasm with the doctrine and practice of the Church.

We can understand in this perspective, apart from the tributes of affection that surrounded Dr Plinio even while living, the special veneration that was born within the TFP towards the mother of the founder, Dona Lucilia, after her death.

Dona Lucilia Ribeiro dos Santos led a hidden life until 1967, when for the first time, because of a serious illness that had struck her son, many friends filled her house and were received by her. In this difficult period, she, then ninety-one years old, extended to the companions of Dr Plinio a welcome that betrayed, as he himself recalls, "her maternal affection, her Christian resignation, her unlimited goodness of heart and the fascinating kindness of the beautiful times of the São Paulo of yesteryear".[123] Young people were enchanted by her character that was so simple and affectionate: "The faint and beautiful light of both dusk and dawn were always to be found in her smile".[124]

A few months later, on 21 April 1968, Dona Lucilia died.[125] For sixty years she had offered an example of a daily exercise of virtue, from which her son drew strength and example. She showed that

---

[122] Giovanni Battista Lemoyne, *Vita di San Giovanni Bosco*, (Turin, Società Editrice Internazionale, 1977), p. 528. Cf. also *Don Bosco nella storia della cultura popolare*, edited by Francesco Traniello, Turin, SEI, 1987.

[123] Cf. *O Estado de S. Paulo*, 22 August 1979.

[124] J. S. Clá Dias, *Dona Lucilia*, vol. III, p. 187.

[125] Dona Lucilia died on the eve of completing 92 years, on 21 April 1968. "With her eyes wide open, understanding perfectly well the solemn moment that approached, she raised herself up a bit, made a big sign of the cross and, with entire peace of soul and confidence in the Divine mercy, she slept in the Lord." J. S. Clá Dias, *Dona Lucilia*, vol. III, p. 201.

perfection in ordinary life which is the secret of the "little way" outlined by Saint Thérèse of Lisieux.[126] Even within the home, a "little way" to holiness is in fact possible and, according to all those who knew her, Dona Lucilia's long life was a living example of this.

The comparison between Lucilia Ribeiro dos Santos and the Carmelite of Lisieux is not surprising. Without the publication of *The Story of a Soul,* no one would have ever imagined the heights of holiness and love of God attained by a nun during the ordinary life of a convent, who died at the age of twenty-four. In the case of Dona Lucilia it was not a book that revealed the splendours of her soul to us, but the life of her son, as a mirror that reflects and develops her virtues.

After her death, someone in the TFP thought of appealing to the intercession of Dona Lucilia and, spontaneously and mysteriously, a private cult began to flourish around her tomb.[127]

To ask someone's intercession clearly does not signify officially proclaiming their holiness. A great contemporary theologian and spiritual guide such as Father Royo Marín, after carefully studying the

---

[126] "In my little way there is only room for ordinary things. It is necessary that what I do, little souls can also do." St Thérèse of the Child Jesus, *Gli scritti*, (Rome, Postulazione Generale dei Carmelitani Scalzi, 1979), no. 227, pp. 216-217). On the "little way", cf. André Combes, *Introduction à la spiritualité de S. Thérèse de l'Enfant Jésus. Etudes de théologie et histoire de la spiritualité*, Paris, Vrin, 1946.

[127] The Brazilian TFP was accused of having wanted to promote an improper cult to the mother of its founder through the recital of some litanies addressed to her (for an exhaustive refutation of these accusations cf. G. A. Solimeo, *Un comentário anti-TFP. Estudo acerca de um Parecer concernente a uma Ladainha*, appendix to *Refutação da TFP a uma investida frustra*, pp. 391-463). In fact, for some time, a litany with invocations to Dona Lucilia circulated among some volunteers of the association. This had been composed by two youths in late 1977. The litany was prohibited by Prof Corrêa de Oliveira as soon as he heard about it due to the impropriety of its language and the strangeness of expression, clearly due to the young age and inexperience of its authors. Father Vitorino Rodríguez, after examining it, commented: "Various invocations are rather naïve, others too extravagant or technical and others quite ambiguous, hence the misunderstanding. For all these reasons I think it was opportune that Doctor Plinio prohibited them. Nevertheless, I think that it is an exaggeration to describe some invocations as heterodox or blasphemous, without considering the relativity of the language used in them" (*Refutação da TFP a uma investida frustra*, p. 395). If the Association, moreover, had wished to promote and organize such a cult, it would have done so in quite a different way, more suited to it. After all, what should we think about a young nun, who invoked and had her fellow sisters invoke their spiritual director who had just died with a series of litanies, in which, calling him "St Claude", she defined him as: "mirror of all virtues", "living image of perfection", "stream of divine consolations", "field of the Paradise of the Church", "lily planted in virgin earth", "shrine of graces", "whose tongue was like the voice of the Holy Spirit" , "sun of perfection", "seed of the Gospel", "voice of the apostles", "torch of the world", "shield of the Catholic faith"? The litanies are those that Margaret Mary Alacoque composed and had recited in the convent for her spiritual director, Claude de la Colombière, who had just died. The nun would become a great saint and her spiritual director would be canonized by the Church, but only many years after the litanies were prepared. The censors of the Court that examined the cause of beatification of the two saints did not judge that this fact would have damaged their canonization. They thus demonstrated that wisdom of the Church which its children so often lack when animated by zeal rather than by true charity and love for good.

biography of Dona Lucilia, did not however hesitate to state that this work describes "the life of a real saint, in every sense of the word".[128]

14. A specific vocation: the "consacratio mundi"

Throughout its history, the TFP, presided over by Plinio Corrêa de Oliveira, defended itself from the numerous violent attacks launched against it. These rebuttals provided an excellent occasion for defining its physiognomy in an increasingly precise manner.

What then is the TFP? It is foremost a school of thought that draws from a wide intellectual patrimony, rich in both speculative and operational principles.

> "What is necessary in the TFP's school of thought? First of all, a total and enthusiastic adhesion to the doctrine of the Holy Roman Catholic and Apostolic Church as expressed in the teachings of the Roman Pontiffs and the ecclesiastical Magisterium in general (attributing to each document, according to its nature, the fullest deference decreed by Canon Law). Then, an adhesion to a whole series of theoretical or theoretico-practical principles that were deduced, with scrupulous logical rigour, from Catholic doctrine or the analysis of reality – whether present or historical – according to the methodology and criteria carefully elaborated in the TFP, and whose foundations are to be mostly found in the aforementioned treatise *Revolution and Counter-Revolution.* Finally, an adhesion to a series of operative principles developed through an attentive analysis of their practical application over a period of decades of acting in common. Such principles also have their foundations outlined in *Revolution and Counter-Revolution* (Part II, Chap. V to XI). The ensemble of these principles constitute the fundamental patrimony of the TFP's school of thought."[129]

The term "school of thought" does not however fully cover the vocation of the TFP, which even if born as a simple civic association, in

---

[128] J. S. Clá Dias, *Dona Lucilia*, vol. I, p. 9. "The real question is: Was Dona Lucilia a real saint, in the fullest sense of the word? In other words, did her Christian virtues reach the heroic degree indispensably required for someone to be acknowledged by the Church with a beatification or canonisation? In face of the rigorously historical data with which this biography provides us in such abundance – concludes Father Royo Marín – I dare to answer a resounding 'yes', and without any vacillation." ibid, vol. I, p. 11.

[129] P. Corrêa de Oliveira, *A réplica da autenticidade*, pp. 132-3.

over thirty years has been characterized, ever more profoundly, as a family of souls not without similarities to a religious family.

The relation established over the years between Dr Plinio and the members of the TFP is in fact similar to that existing between the founder of a religious institution and his disciples. What is the current position of this family of souls with respect to the ecclesiastical authorities? "It is that of the full liberty that the Church itself gives to simple germinating nuclei or to Catholic societies being born."[130] Vatican Council II in fact declared the freedom of association within the Church, affirming that "the laity have the right to establish and direct associations".[131] "There is no reason" comments Father Anastásio Gutiérrez "for denying this freedom aimed at Christian perfection and lay apostolate: indeed these goals are explicitly admitted for the freedom of association."[132]

For Canon Law the TFP is a private association of lay persons subjected *in rebus fidei et morum* (in matters of Faith and Morals) to the vigilance that the Church exercises over all its faithful, taken individually or associated between each other. The juridical nature of these civic associations does not change because religious practices are exercised within them and because their members adopt forms of life similar to those of the consecrated life.[133]

> "Given this situation, the TFP and its family of souls have a special characteristic. As an association, the TFP is an exclusively civic society. Its members, taken individually, are free to practice what they want as Catholics. Thus the TFP appears as a place where these Catholics, considered individually, live their religion according to the common practises that the Church has always proposed to its faithful."[134]

---

[130] A. Sinke Guimarães, *Servitudo ex caritate*, p. 266.

[131] Vatican Council II, Decree *Apostolicam Actuositatem* on the Apostolate of the laity of 18 November 1965, no. 19.

[132] A. Gutiérrez C.M.F., entry *Istituti di perfezione cristiana*, in DIP, vol. V, 1988, col. 85, cols. 75–106.

[133] In the book *Refutação da TFP a uma investida frustra*, we read that: "the TFP may be considered as a *confraternitas laicalis*, that is, as an association of Catholics with religious objectives, which is not set up or controlled by the ecclesiastical authorities and whose members therefore direct it freely according to its by-laws" (vol. I, pp. 319-320). Cf. also Comissão de Estudos da TFP, *A TFP: uma vocação, TFP e famílias, TFP e famílias na crise espiritual e temporal do século XX*, São Paulo, Artpress, 1986, vol. I, pp. 271–2; A. Sinke Guimarães, *Servitudo ex caritate*, cit., pp. 157-160. "Thus – commented Dr Plinio – the TFP is perfectly well defined as a civic entity under civil law, and as a *confraternitas laicalis* under ecclesiastical law, at least until in-depth studies of the new Code of Canon Law indicate a more adequate terminology" (P. Corrêa de Oliveira, *A réplica da autenticidade*, p. 219). On the nature of the TFP as regards Canon Law cf. also G. A. Solimeo and L. S. Solimeo, *Analyse par la TFP brésilienne d'une prise de position de la CNBB sur la 'TFP et sa famille d'âmes'*.

[134] A. Sinke Guimarães, *Servitudo ex caritate*, pp. 159–60.

It should be noted that what distinguishes lay associations from ecclesiastical associations is not their goal, which in both cases is religious, but the fact that they are or are not established at ecclesiastical level.

The aim of the TFP, expressed by Article 1 of its statutes, consists in working for the restoration of the fundamental principles of natural and Christian order. This aim is no different from the mission of "to restore all things in Christ"[135] and "consecrate the world"[136] so often referred to by the Pontiffs of this century and which Vatican Council II, in the Decree *Apostolicam Actuositatem*, defines "*instaurationem Ordinis temporalis*" (the restoration of temporal order).[137] John Paul II himself, quoting the Council[138] affirms that "it is the special task of the lay faithful to bring the truth of the Gospel to influence the reality of social, economic, political and cultural life. They have the specific task of the sanctification of the world from within by undertaking secular activity".[139] With these words he simply confirms what was already said by Vatican Council II: "The lay person receives, through the grace of God, a specifically lay vocation which destines him to seek holiness and to exercise an apostolate which deals with temporal themes ordered according to God."[140]

Plinio Corrêa de Oliveira, who since the Thirties has argued with progressivism for the improper role it attributed to the laity with respect to the clergy, was paradoxically accused of exaggerating, at the expense of the clergy, the role of the laity in the service of the Church. The reality is quite different.

According to Catholic doctrine, spiritual and temporal order are distinct realities, but not separate ones, as is already implicit in the recommendation of Our Lord to render to Caesar what is Caesar's and to God what is God's.[141] The liberal principle of the separation of the two spheres, however, penetrated, after the French Revolution, into Catholic circles. The result was that, while in some political sectors it was imagined that there would be a temporal restoration which would disregard grace and the supernatural, in other ecclesiastical sectors, on the contrary, the role of nature, reason and of man's free co-operation with divine grace tended to be minimized. These were the two errors of naturalism and supernaturalism destined to explode

---

[135] St Pius X, Letter *Notre Charge Apostolique*.
[136] Cf. Pius XII, Speech of 5 October 1957 for the World Congress of the Apostolate of the Laity, in DR, vol. XIX, pp. 459–60.
[137] Cf. J. Collantes S.J., *La fede della Chiesa cattolica*, p. 320.
[138] Cf. Vatican Council II, Constitution *Lumen Gentium*, no. 31.
[139] John Paul II, Speech to United States bishops of 2 July 1993, L'Osservatore Romano, 4 July 1993.
[140] Vatican Council II, Constitution *Lumen Gentium*, no. 316.
[141] Luke 20:25; Mark 12:17; Matt. 22:21.

after the pontificate of Pius XII. These ambiguities were translated into unilateral and arbitrary exaggerations of the role of the laity or, *per diametrum*, of the clergy in society. The Magisterium of the Church, to which Plinio Corrêa de Oliveira constantly conformed, indicates the path to a harmonious balance.

The action of the laity does not derive from a natural tendency to action, but from the characteristics of Baptism and Confirmation, which impose the duty of apostolate,[142] which is none other than the exercise of Christian charity that is the duty of all men.[143]

The laity form a holy nation, they are consecrated to God with Baptism and with Confirmation, they are called to honour God with the holiness of their lives and with their participation in the worship of the Church. They have a special mission to "consecrate" the temporal order to God. "Dignity, consecration, a mission that Sacred Scripture and Tradition summarize and indicate with one word: royal priesthood of the faithful."[144] Plinio Corrêa de Oliveira, on this point, always echoed the Church's doctrine.

"Our modern mentality" observes a contemporary Catholic writer "finds it difficult to understand how in the past the laity were able to play an important role in the spiritual field without the clergy taking offence."[145] He recalls the cases of St Benedict and St Francis of Assisi, who founded and directed their orders without ever reaching priesthood. Likewise, St Ignatius preached his *Exercises* and gathered his first followers much before becoming a priest. We could give other examples, such as that of the famous Baron de Renty,[146] a lay gentleman and father of a family who spiritually directed some monasteries of nuns.

The monks of the early centuries were mostly lay as were the military orders of Knights Hospitallers of the Middle Ages, as well as the teaching institutes founded after the seventeenth century.

"According to the traditional doctrine of the Church" states John

---

[142] Pius XI, Letter *Ex officiosis litteris* of 10 November 1933 in IP, *Il laicato*, p. 532.

[143] Pius XI, Letter *Vos Argentinae Episcopos* of 4 December 1930, in IP, *Il laicato*, p. 320.

[144] P. G. Rambaldi S.J., "Sacerdozio gerarchico e sacerdozio non gerarchico", Civiltà Cattolica, vol. 102, 1951, no. II, pp. 354–5, pp. 345–57.

[145] Daniel Raffard de Brienne, *L'Action catholique*, (Paris, Renaissance Catholique, 1991), p. 8.

[146] On Baron Gaston de Renty (1611–49), a number of times superior of the Society of the Most Holy Sacrament and promoter of the Catholic renaissance in France in the seventeenth century, cf. the famous biography by Father Jean Baptiste Saint-Jure S.J., *La vie de monsieur Renty, ou le modèle d'un parfait chrétien*, Paris, Le Petit, 1651, and recently Yves Chiron, *Gaston de Renty. Une figure spirituelle du XVIII siècle*, Montsûrs, Editions Résiac, 1985; Raymond Triboulet, *Gaston de Renty, 1611–1649*, Paris, Beauchesne, 1991; Id., entry in DSp, vol. XIII (1987), coll. 363–9.

Paul II "consecrated life by its nature is neither lay nor clerical,[147] and for this reason 'lay consecration', be it male or female, is a state in itself complete of profession of the evangelical counsels.[148] Therefore, for the person and for the Church, it has its own special value, that is independent of the sacred ministry."[149]

In this perspective, the TFP, next to the married members and followers, has many who have renounced marriage choosing a state of life which is neither priestly, nor religious. Perfect chastity, Pius XII teaches in the encyclical *Sacra Virginitas*, is not reserved only for the religious, it can also be advised for the simple laity, "men and women".[150] The invitation to perfect chastity is after all constantly recommended by the Church as a choice that achieves a state of life that is superior to marriage, finalized in a mission of works of charity, or teaching, or apostolate.[151]

John Paul II has also often stressed the importance of continence and chastity in Christian life. The Christian who is coherent with the Gospel

"must insist on high ideals, even if they go against current opinion". "Jesus Christ (...) said that the way of continence, of which he himself is a witness with his life, not only exists and is possible, but it is particularly valid and important for the Kingdom of Heaven. And this is how it should be, since Jesus Christ chose it for himself."[152]

The specific vocation of the TFP, that of lay people who work for the "*consecratio mundi*", may cause confusion because of its novelty and uniqueness within the Church. On the other hand, "St Anthony probably did not have many forerunners when he left for the desert", writes Father Henry, stressing the fact that the Holy Spirit can raise up something that is "completely unprecedented in the Church".[153] In fact, according to the theologians, no merciful work exists for whose

---

[147] Cf. *Code of Canon Law*, can. 588, §. 1.

[148] Cf. Vatican Council II, Decree on the renewal of religious life *Perfectae caritatis*, no. 10.

[149] John Paul II, Apostolic Exhortation *Vita Consecrata*, of 25 March 1996, suppl. to *L'Osservatore Romano*, 26 March 1996.

[150] Pius XII, Encyclical *Sacra Virginitas* of 25 March 1954, p. 163.

[151] To preserve the virtue of chastity, the TFP recommends great vigilance. It especially warns its young people against going to beaches, mixed swimming pools, discos, places of dissipation, and promiscuity that put their purity at obvious risk. This vigilance, an expression of genuine Catholic spirit, is one of the points that irritates most the so-called "anti-cult movement", ideologically dependant on Freudian pan-sexualism.

[152] John Paul II, Audience of 31 March 1982, in *Insegnamenti*, vol. I, 1982, p. 1047.

[153] A. M. Henry O.P., *Obéissance commune et obéissance religieuse*, suppl. to "La vie spirituelle", 15-9-1953, b. 26, VI, 1953, p. 258.

accomplishment a religious order cannot be established.[154] This is why the Church contains in its maternal bosom a marvellous variety of orders, congregations and religious families, even secular ones, each of which, in responding to the various requirements of the times and souls, demonstrate the different aspects of radicality of the Gospel and of the life of the Church.[155] All refer back to the charism of their founder.[156]

> "Whether or not they are canonized" comments Father Olphé-Galliard "the founders are bearers of a charism that enables them to give rise to a spiritual family destined to carry forward the lymph of their holiness. The authenticity of the latter is recognized both by the fruitfulness of their foundation, and by the example of their personal experience."[157]

What his biographers said about St Pancomius and his disciples has been repeated about many founders: "After God, he was their Father".[158] "Imitation of the founder" as Father Olphé-Galliard notes again "has nothing to do with the cult of the personality generated in honour of certain modern ideologies."[159] It emanates from that principle of mediation according to which every paternity comes from God.[160]

It cannot be denied that Plinio Corrêa de Oliveira has the characteristics of a Founder. A Founder not because he wanted to impose this role upon himself, but because he is thus recognized by thousands of Catholics all over the world. A Founder in the broad sense, not so

---

[154] Paul Philippe, *Les fins de la vie religieuse selon saint Thomas d'Aquin,* (Atenas, Fraternité de la Très-Sainte-Vierge Marie, 1962), p. 88.

[155] Pius XII, in his Address to the I World Congress for the Apostolate of the Laity of 14 October 1951 (in DR, vol. XII, pp. 291–301), insists on this great liberty that the Church allows the faithful in choosing the road which best suits them.

[156] The expression "charism of the founders" entered the official language of the Magisterium with the *Evangelica Testificatio* no. 11 (1971). It indicates the gifts of nature and grace bestowed on the founder of a spiritual family for achieving his mission. On "founders" cf. Juan Maria Lozano, C.M.F., *El fundador y su familia religiosa. Inspiración y carisma,* Madrid, Publicaciones Claretianas, 1970; Fabio Ciardi, *I fondatori uomini dello spirito. Per una teologia del carisma del fondatore,* Rome, Città Nuova, 1982; ID., *In ascolto dello spirito. Ermeneutica del carisma dei fondatori,* Rome, Città Nuova, 1996; A. Sinke Guimarães, *Servitudo ex Caritate,* pp. 184–210; Elio Gambari S.M.M., J. M. Lozano C.M.F., Giancarlo Rocca S.S.P., entry *Fondatore,* in DIP, vol. IV (1977), coll. 96–101; Michel Olphé-Galliard S.J., entry *Fondatore,* ibid, coll. 102–08; G. Damizia, sub entry, in EC, vol. 5, 1950, pp. 1474–5; J. F. Gilmont, "Paternité et médiation du fondateur d'Ordre", Revue d'Ascétique et de Mystique, vol. 40, 1964, p. 416, pp. 393–426; Francisco Juberías, C.M.F., "La paternidad de los fundadores", Vida Religiosa, vol. 32, 1972, pp. 317–27.

[157] M. Olphé-Galliard S.J., entry *Fondatore,* col. 102.

[158] Ibid, col. 103.

[159] Ibid.

[160] Eph. 3:5.

much of a specific order, but of a spiritual and intellectual school and of a style of life of open fight against the Revolution.

"*Novum militiae genus ortum nuper auditur in terris ....*"[161] "Now we hear that a new kind of knight has appeared on the earth ...." The words of St Bernard can be well applied to the disciples of Plinio Corrêa de Oliveira, who thus summarizes the contemporary version of the chivalrous style of long ago: "In idealism, zeal. In manners, courtesy. In action, dedication without limits. In the presence of the enemy, prudence. In the fight, pride and courage. And with courage, victory."[162]

---

[161] St Bernard of Clairvaux, *De Laude novae militiae*, in Franco Cardini, *I poweri cavalieri del Cristo*, (Rimini, Cerchio, 1994), p. 132.
[162] P. Corrêa de Oliveira, "Estilo", Folha de S. Paulo, 24 September 1969.

Chapter VI

Passion of Christ, Passion of the Church

*"How many are living in union with the Church
at this tragic moment as tragic as the Passion;
at this crucial moment in history, when mankind
is opting for Christ or against Christ?"*

1. Credo in unam sanctam, catholicam et apostolicam Ecclesiam

Credo in unam, sanctam, catholicam et apostolicam Ecclesiam.
These words of the *Creed* are certainly those that most deeply
resounded in the heart of Plinio Corrêa de Oliveira, during the century
in which he lived. He himself recalls how his love for the Church and
the Papacy always inspired his struggle in defence of Christian civilization and how it progressively increased from his distant childhood.

> "I still recall the catechism lessons in which the Papacy was
> explained to me, its divine institution, its powers, its mission. My
> heart of a child (I was about nine years old) was filled with admi-
> ration, with rapture, with enthusiasm: I had found the ideal to
> which I would dedicate my whole life. From then to now, my love
> for this ideal has only grown. And I pray to Our Lady that she ever
> increase it in me, until my dying breath. I desire that the last act
> of my intellect may be an act of faith in the Papacy; that my last
> act of love may be an act of love for the Papacy. Thus, in fact, I
> would die in the peace of the elect, well united to Mary my Mother,
> and through her to Jesus, my God, my King and my excellent
> Redeemer."[1]

It is difficult to understand the profound meaning of these words in an
age characterized by a general coldness and indifference towards

---

[1] P. Corrêa de Oliveira, "A perfeita alegria", Folha de S. Paulo, 12 July 1970, It. tr. in *Il
crepuscolo artificiale del Cile cattolico*, (Piacenza, Cristianità, 1973), p. 21.

ecclesiastical institutions. They were written at the beginning of the 70s, at a time when the crisis of the Church seemed to reach its climax.

In the Appendix to *Revolution and Counter-Revolution,* the author noted how in 1959, when his work first appeared, the Church was still considered a great spiritual power against the expansion of the Communist world. In the following years, the decisive centre of the struggle between the Revolution and the Counter-Revolution moved from temporal society to inside spiritual society. "The Holy Church" wrote Plinio Corrêa de Oliveira after the Council "is now this centre. In her, progressivists, crypto-communists, and pro-communists confront anti-progressivists and anti-communists."[2]

To those who asked him why fight the errors pervading the faithful, when there were so many others outside the Catholic ranks, Plinio Corrêa de Oliveira replied from as early as the 50s: "If the enemy is storming the walls, everyone must unite. But if it has penetrated the citadel, then it is not enough to fight outside the walls, but also within the walls".[3]

2. The Jubilee of 1950: triumph or incipient crisis?

The Holy Year of 1950 was the last historical moment in which the Church appeared in all the power it derived from being the Seat of Truth. While Europe was recovering with difficulty from the moral and material devastation of the war, the Jubilee offered an extraordinary image of the militant Catholic Church. The climax of the Holy Year was the proclamation of the dogma of the Assumption of Mary into Heaven on 1 November 1950.

A witness narrates that, from the dawn of that day, St Peter's Square, still immersed in silence, "was transformed into a huge limitless sea, into which an unending and uninterrupted flow of people crowded".[4] Every people and every nation were represented in that

---

[2] P. Corrêa de Oliveira, *Revolution and Counter-Revolution*, p. 151.
[3] P. Corrêa de Oliveira, "Razões e contra-razões em torno de um tema efervescente", Catolicismo, no. 71, November 1956; ID., "Indulgentes para com o erro, severos para com a Igreja", Catolicismo, no. 72, December 1956; ID., "Não trabalha pela concordia senão quem luta contra o erro", Catolicismo, no. 73, January 1957; Cunha Alvarenga (=José de Azevedo Santos), "Infiltrações comunistas em ambientes católicos", Catolicismo, no. 61, January 1956. Along the same lines are three articles on modernism, that appeared in numbers 81, 82, 83 (Sept.-Oct.-Nov. 1957) with the titles "O cinquantenario da Pascendi"; "Por orgulho repelem toda sujeição" and "Revivem nos modernistas o espirito e os metodos do Jansenismo".
[4] Sister Pascalina Lehnert, *Pio XII. Il privilegio di servirlo*, It. tr. (Milan, Rusconi, 1984), p. 172.

immense undulating crowd, while the singing and prayers melted harmoniously into each other. Preceded by the white procession of the bishops in cope and mitre, the Pope appeared on the gestatorial chair. After imploring the assistance of the Holy Spirit, Pius XII solemnly defined "to be a divinely revealed dogma: that the Immaculate Mother of God, the ever virgin Mary, having completed the course of her earthly life, was assumed body and soul into heavenly glory".[5] The whole world, linked by radio to the teeming square, exulted.

"It seemed like a vision, and yet it was reality: until late at night, Pius XII blessed, because the crowd never ceased to call him even after the window was closed, for one stream of people that left the square, another took its place. Everyone wanted to be blessed again before that wonderful day came to an end."[6]

However the symptoms of an incipient crisis were not lacking. On 12 August of that same year, the Pontiff published the encyclical *Humani Generis*, to denounce the "poisonous fruits" produced by "novelties in almost every field of technology".[7] The encyclical condemned the relativism of those who believed they "could reconcile Catholic dogmas with any kind of philosophy or theory, whether immanentism, idealism, existentialism or any other system".[8] This relativism, which had already characterized the modernism condemned by St Pius X, was now strengthened under the guise of "*nouvelle théologie*" (new theology).[9] Its exponents were Jesuit theologians, influenced by the thinking of Teilhard de Chardin, such as Fathers Henri de Lubac and Jean Daniélou, and Dominicans, who proposed a revolutionary inter-

---

[5] Pio XII, *Munificentissimus Deus*, in Denz-H., no. 3903. Cf. also the text in AAS, 42, 1950, pp. 767–70.
[6] Suor P. Lehnert, *Pio XII*, p. 174.
[7] Pius XII, Encyclical *Humani generis*, of 2 August 1950 in Denz-H., no. 3890 (nos. 3875–99) and in AAS, vol. 42, 1950, pp. 561–77. On this important document, Cf. Various authors, *La encíclica Humani Generis*, Madrid, C.S.I.C., 1952; R. Garrigou-Lagrange O.P., *La struttura dell'enciclica Humani Generis*, in ID., *Sintesi tomistica*, (Brescia, Queriniana, 1953), pp. 541–54; Mgr Pietro Parente, *Struttura e significato storico e dottrinale della enciclica Humani Generis*, in ID., *Dio e i problemi dell'uomo*, (Rome, Belardetti, 1955), vol. II, pp. 611–36. Cf. also J. de Aldama, "Pio XII y la Teología nueva", Salmaticensis, no. 3, 1956, pp. 303–20.
[8] Pius XII, Encyclical *Humani generis*, in Denz-H., no. 3882.
[9] The denomination is of Pius XII in the address *Quamvis inquieti* of 17 September 1946, in DR, vol. VIII, p. 233. The necessity of the condemnation of the "nefarious germ of modernism" resurfacing in the dogmatic, biblical and social fields, emerged, ten years later, from many of the "pre-preparatory votes" of the Council sent by the bishops to Rome (Cf. *Acta et Documenta Concilio Oecumenico Vaticano II Apparando, Series I (Antepraeparatoria), Appendix Voluminis II. Pars I*, (Typis Plyglottis Vaticanis 1961), pp. 218–19). Thomas M. Loome thus comments: "Teilhard de Chardin, Congar and de Lubac are among those deemed worthy of the Council's attentions. And from one bishop we find the rather curt suggestion: 'Doctrina J. Maritain damnetur'". *Liberal catholicism*, p. 25.

pretation of the theology, like Fathers Marie-Dominique Chenu and Yves Congar. All these would play a forefront role in the religious life of the following years and would then be elevated to the Cardinal purple.

The incipient crisis of the Church emerges for example from the correspondence of those years between two religious, now beatified: Don Giovanni Calabria, founder of the Poor Servants of Divine Providence, and Cardinal Ildefonso Schuster, archbishop of Milan. "For years" writes Don Calabria "with growing insistence, I hear the lament of Jesus in the depths of my heart: my Church!"[10] "May God preserve the Holy Father Pius XII" answers Cardinal Schuster in his turn "because I already pity his successor. The storm is raging and who will ever dare take command of the boat?"[11]

3. The announcement of Vatican Council II

The death of Pius XII and the election of John XXIII in October 1958 marked an historic turning-point. The pontificate of John inaugurated a new style of government, "completely unusual in carrying out the papal role in the last two centuries".[12] Among the first acts of his pontificate was to enlarge the college of cardinals by naming new ones, whose number had been fixed at seventy by Sixtus V. There was a certain amazement that the first on the list was the archbishop of Milan, Giovanni Battista Montini, whose banishment from Rome had been seen as a punishment for strong divergence of views with Pius XII.[13]

On 25 January 1959, in the Benedictine monastery of St Paul's without the walls, John XXIII announced to the cardinals present and to the whole world his desire to convoke an ecumenical Council. The announcement "had the effect of a fanfare blast inside and perhaps even more outside the Church".[14]

---

[10] Letter of Don Giovanni Calabria to Cardinal Schuster of 21 November 1948, in *L'epistolario Cardinal Schuster-don Calabria (1945-1954)*, edited by Angelo Majo and Luigi Piovan, (Milan, NED, 1989), p. 30.
[11] Letter of Cardinal Schuster to Don Calabria of 20 July 1951, in op. cit., p. 93. When in 1953 Our Lady wept in Syracuse, the Cardinal commented: "even the most holy Virgin weeps over the evils of the Church and concerning the chastisement that hangs over the world" (Letter of Cardinal Schuster to Don Calabria of 6 October 1953, in op. cit., p. 160).
[12] Daniele Menozzi, *La Chiesa cattolica e la secolarizzazione*, (Turin, Einaudi, 1993), p. 174.
[13] Silvio Tramontin, *Un secolo di storia della Chiesa*, vol. II, p. 259. Mgr Hubert Jedin in his turn defines as "surprising" the nomination of Mgr Montini on 1 November 1954 to archbishop of Milan, as successor to Cardinal Schuster. *Il Concilio Vaticano II*, in HKG, It. tr., vol. X, 1, p. 123.
[14] H. Jedin, *Il Concilio Vaticano II*, p. 108.

The next day, in a Message to the Ambrosian diocese, Cardinal Montini greeted the event with enthusiasm:

"This Council will be the greatest that the Church has ever celebrated in its twenty centuries of history, because of the spiritual and numerical confluence, in the total and peaceful unity of its hierarchy; it will be the greatest for the catholicity of its dimensions, truly involving the whole geographical and civil world. History unfolds with immense and timeless visions before our eyes."[15]

4. Would the Council condemn Communism?

If in Rome and in Europe few had an idea of the approaching crisis, in Brazil Plinio Corrêa de Oliveira, commenting on the announcement of the Council, expressed in January 1962 in *Catolicismo* the hope that it would bring an end to the terrifying confusion that was spreading among Catholics. "This confusion is gradually taking on truly apocalyptic proportions in Brazil and throughout the world, and, to my way of thinking, constitutes one of the greatest calamities of our days."[16] The focus of attention of the Brazilian thinker in this important article was the problem of relations between Catholicism and Communism.

"Due to its inherently atheistic and materialistic nature, communism cannot but have in mind the complete destruction of the Catholic Church, the natural guardian of the moral order which is inconceivable without the family and property."[17]

In keeping with its premises, Communism cannot be limited to one State or a group of States. "It is much more than a political party. It is a philosophical sect that has its own vision of the cosmos."[18] Its doctrine implies a conception of the world that is antithetic to the Catholic one. Every attempt at "coexistence" is therefore, for the Brazilian thinker, doomed to failure.

"Within each country, as on the international scene, communism is in a state of inevitable, constant and multi-faceted struggle with the Church and those States who refuse to be swallowed by the marxist sect. This fight is as implacable as that existing between Our Lady

---

[15] G. B. Montini, *Discorsi e scritti sul Concilio (1959–1963)*, edited by A. Rimoldi, (Brescia-Rome, Quaderni dell'Istituto Paolo VI, 1983), p. 25.
[16] P. Corrêa de Oliveira, "Na perspectiva do proximo Concilio", Catolicismo, no. 133, January 1962.
[17] Ibid.
[18] Ibid.

and the Serpent. For the Church, which is indestructible, this fight will only end with the final crushing of the communist sect, not only in the West but throughout the world, including in the most hidden dens of Moscow, Peking and others. (...)

"Having said this, one cannot admit that the coexistence of Christian and communist nations is capable of the stability, composure and coherence inherent to the International Law that should rule Christian nations. Because International Law presupposes upright dealings among the peoples. Now, uprightness presupposes the acceptance of a morality. And it is inherent to communist doctrine to say that morality is purely empty bourgeois principle."[19]

On the other hand, the teaching mission of the Church consists not only in teaching the truth, but also in defining and condemning errors. The analysis and condemnation of the doctrine and practice of Communism should have constituted, according to Plinio Corrêa de Oliveira, one of the central points of the Vatican Council that was about to open. This conviction was moreover shared by hundreds of Council Fathers throughout the world. In the pre-preparatory phase of the Council, 378 bishops had asked that it should deal with modern atheism and, in particular, with Communism, indicating the solutions for facing the danger.[20] The Vietnamese archbishop of Hué, for example, defined Communism as "the problem of problems", the paramount issue of the day: "to discuss other problems ... is to follow the example of the theologians of Constantinople who bitterly discussed the sex of angels while the Islamic armies were threatening the very walls of the city".[21]

Among the bishops consulted by the Holy See to receive advice and suggestions, there were also the Brazilians Bishop de Castro Mayer and Archbishop de Proença Sigaud. The latter has the merit of an answer in which, because of the extent of its perspectives and the logical concatenation, it is not hard to see the influence of Dr Plinio, with whom he had a longstanding solidarity.

"I note that the principles, doctrine and spirit of the so-called Revolution infiltrate the clergy and the Christian people, as in the past the principles, doctrine, spirit and love for paganism infiltrated medieval society causing the Pseudo-Reformation. Many among the clergy no longer perceive the errors of the Revolution or resist

---

[19] Ibid.
[20] Mgr Vincenzo Carbone, "Schemi e discussioni sull'ateismo e sul marxismo nel Concilio Vaticano II. Documentazione", Rivista di Storia della Chiesa in Italia, vol. XLIV, 1990, pp. 11–12, pp. 10–68.
[21] *Acta et Documenta Concilio Oecumenico Vaticano II apparando*, Series II, vol. II, pars III, (Rome, Tipografia Poliglotta Vaticana, 1968), pp. 774–6.

them. Other members of the clergy love the Revolution as a good cause. They propagate it and co-operate with it. They persecute its adversaries by obstructing and slandering their apostolate. Most pastors keep silent, others are imbued with the errors and spirit of the Revolution and favour it overtly or covertly, as was the case during the time of Jansenism. Those who denounce and refute these errors are persecuted by their own colleagues, who brand them as 'fundamentalist'. From the seminaries of the Eternal City itself, seminarians come out with their minds full of revolutionary ideologies. They describe themselves as 'Maritainists', or 'followers of Teilhard de Chardin', or 'Christian socialists', or 'evolutionists'. The priests fighting the Revolution are highly unlikely to be raised to Episcopal rank, whereas those who favour it frequently are raised to Episcopal office."[22]

"Communism has created the science of the revolution. Its main weapons are unruly and systematically fomented human passions. The Revolution uses two vices as forces to destroy Christian society and to build a Godless one: sensuality and pride. These disordered and violent passions are being purposefully unleashed under the iron discipline of leaders for a specific aim: to destroy the foundations of the City of God and build the City of Man. Even a totalitarian tyranny is condoned, and misery tolerated, as long as the order of the Antichrist is established."[23]

The reference to the unruly passions clearly alludes to the fundamental theory of *Revolution and Counter-Revolution*. Confronted with the revolutionary process, which finds its ultimate expression in Communism, the Brazilian bishop did not hesitate to state: "The Church should organize a systematic fight against the Revolution throughout the world."[24]

---

[22] *Acta et Documenta Concilio Oecumenico Vaticano II apparando*, Series I, vol. II, pars VII, (Rome, Tipografia Poliglotta Vaticana, 1961), pp. 181–2.

[23] Ibid, pp. 184–5.

[24] Ibid, p. 182. "In my modest opinion – wrote Archbishop Sigaud again – the Church must organize, at world level, a systematic struggle against the Revolution. I do not know if this is already happening. The Revolution proceeds in just this way. An example of this organized and systematic activity is the worldwide simultaneous and uniform establishment of 'Christian democracies' in many nations after the great war. This ferment penetrates all lands. Congresses are held, an International is created, and everywhere slogans are raised saying: 'let us make the Revolution, before the others do!' It is the Revolution done with the consent of the Catholics. According to my modest opinion, if the Council wants to produce healthy fruits, it must first of all meditate on the condition of the Church today which, like Christ, is living its Good Friday, delivered unprotected to its enemies, as Pius XII said in his speech to young Italians. We must consider the mortal war that is waged against the Church in all fields; we must discover the enemy, discern his strategy and his battle tactics, meditate on his logic, psychology and dynamics, in order to decide with certainty on the individual battles of this war, to organize the counter-offensive and direct it with security" (ibid).

5. The Council of "*Aggiornamento*"

On the morning of 11 October 1962 there were over 2,500 Council Fathers gathered in St Peter's Basilica.[25] The solemn ceremony was watched, thanks to television, by millions of people all over the world. In the overflowing Basilica, the choir sang the Credo and then the Magnificat, while the procession of the Fathers solemnly advanced. At the head were the superiors of the religious orders, the abbots general, and the prelates nullius; then the bishops, archbishops, the patriarchs, the cardinals and, in the gestatorial chair, lastly John XXIII.

The incomparable image of St Peter's Basilica, the presence of the Vicar of Christ and of the successors of the Apostles, made that ceremony a majestic spectacle. Never as in this moment did the Church demonstrate its universal, hierarchical and anti-egalitarian character.

"The opening of the Second Vatican Council" commented Plinio Corrêa de Oliveira "provides us with the occasion to meditate with particular attention upon a truth which we see on a daily basis, but which, nevertheless, modern man, a son of the Revolution, refuses to acknowledge. Just and harmonic inequality is to such an extent at the core of the great works of God that Our Lord Jesus Christ, when founding the masterpiece of creation which is His Mystical Body, the Holy Catholic Church, made it an unequal society. This society has a monarch who is the Pope and who has total and direct jurisdiction over all the bishops and faithful. Each diocese has spiritual Princes whose duty it is, in union and communion with the Pope, to govern the faithful. And there is the Clergy which, under the direction of the Bishops, rule over the various parishes of Christians."[26]

The inaugural speech of the Pope, pronounced in Latin and transmitted live by the media world-wide was, as Father Wenger

---

[25] On Vatican Council II the most recent and complete overall work is the *Storia del Concilio Vaticano II*, directed by Giuseppe Alberigo, (Bologna, Peeters-Il Mulino, 1995), of which up to now only one volume has been published. Among the abundant bibliography, Cf. also: René Laurentin, *L'enjeu du Concile*, 4 vols., Paris, Seuil, 1962–6; Antoine Wenger A.A., *Vatican II*, 4 vols., Paris, Editions du Centurion, 1963; Giovanni Caprile S.J., *Il Concilio Vaticano II*, 5 vols., Rome, Civiltà Cattolica, 1965–9; Gianfranco Svidercoschi, *Storia del Concilio*, Milan, Ancora, 1967; Henri Fesquet, *Diario del Concilio*, Milan, Mursia, 1967; Ralph M. Wiltgen S.V.D., *Le Rhin se jette dans le Tibre: le Concile inconnu*, Paris, Editiòns du Cèdre, 1976; *La Chiesa del Vaticano II (1958–1978)*, in *Storia della Chiesa*, begun by Augustine Fliche and Victor Martin, then directed by Jean Baptiste Duroselle and E. Jarry, Cinisello Balsamo, Edizioni San Paolo, 1994, vol. XXV/1, with ample bibliography on sources and studies.
[26] P. Corrêa de Oliveira, "O Concilio e o igualitarismo moderno", Catolicismo, no. 142, October 1962, p. 7.

observes, was the key to understanding the Council.[27] "The speech of 11 October was the true charter of the Council. More than an agenda, it established the spirit. More than a programme, it gave the orientation."[28] The novelty was not so much in the doctrine but in the psychological optimistic spirit with which relations between the Church and the world were set: sympathy and "openness".

In his speech John XXIII criticized the prophets of doom[29] and stressed how from the assembly "a Magisterium with a mainly pastoral character" would emerge. According to the Pontiff, the Council proposed to formulate the perennial teaching of the Church in language suitable to the new times. The aim, according to a term destined to become fashionable, was that of *"aggiornamento"* (modernization).[30] If the Council of Trent passed into history as the Council of the Counter-Reformation, "it is likely that Vatican II will be known in the future as the Council of Aggiornamento".[31]

The first session of the Council lasted from 11 October to 8 December 1962. On the eve of the opening of the Council, Plinio Corrêa de Oliveira arrived in Rome accompanied by a large group of friends and disciples of the Brazilian TFP.[32] He stayed there until 21 December, following all the work of the session, which ended without reaching any decision. His feelings continued to be very different from the widespread optimism of the time. "This voyage" he wrote to his mother "is the fruit of long reflection. (...) I could never, under any point of view, give up rendering to the Church, to whom I have dedicated my life, this service at a point in history that is as sad as the Death of Our Lord."[33] In the same letter Plinio states that "never has the siege of the external enemies of the Church been so strong, and never has the action of its internal enemies been so generalized, so co-ordinated and so audacious."

---

[27] A. Wenger, *Vatican II*, vol. I, p. 39.

[28] Ibid, p. 38.

[29] *Documentation Catholique*, 4 November 1962, col. 1380.

[30] John XXIII, speeches of 11 September 1960 and 28 June 1961.

[31] Christopher Butler O.S.B., *L'aggiornamento del Concilio Vaticano II*, in *La teologia dopo il Vaticano II*, edited by John M. Miller C.S.C., (Brescia, Morcelliana, 1967), p. 3, pp. 3–16. "Aggiornamento", according to Dom Butler means, even etymologically, "modernization": *"La chiesa doveva essere modernizzata"* (ibid).

[32] Among those who came to Rome were: Prof Fernando Furquim de Almeida, the young prince Bertrand of Orléans-Braganza, Luiz Nazareno da Asumpção, Paulo Brito, Fabio Xavier da Silveira, Carlos Alberto Soares Corrêa, Sergio Brotero. The latter had travelled earlier by ship bringing with him twenty trunks of Catholic propaganda material, which included copies in various languages of *Revolution and Counter-Revolution* by Dr Plinio and *On the Problems of Modern Apostolate* by Bishop de Castro Mayer.

[33] Cit. In J.S.C. Dias, *Dona Lucilia*, vol. III, p. 117.

Plinio Corrêa de Oliveira, who had good knowledge of the revolutionary process, knew with what ease an organized minority can take over an assembly and impose their views on a passive and confused majority. It had happened during the French Revolution and it happened again during Vatican Council II, not by chance defined by some as "the Eighty-nine of the Church". From the beginning, a limited group of bishops from Central Europe, among whom Cardinals Lercaro, Liénart, Frings, Koenig, Doepfner, Suenens, Alfrink, assisted by their "experts",[34] organized themselves into an efficient structure.[35] It had its expression in the weekly meetings of the *Domus Mariae*, during which information was exchanged or initiatives were co-ordinated "and when necessary the pressures to be exercised on the assembly".[36] Only in a later period, when the progressivist minority in the Assembly became a majority, did the defenders of Tradition start to get organized.

The Brazilian prelates played an important role in Rome. If among the leaders of the progressivist group Archbishop Helder Câmara[37] had distinguished himself, on the opposite front, arrayed in the front line were Bishop Antônio de Castro Mayer and Archbishop Geraldo de Proença Sigaud.

During the first session of the Council, Plinio Corrêa de Oliveira installed a secretariat in Rome which actively followed the work of the assembly and offered a constant service especially to the Brazilian prelates closest to him. Around them, a group of conservative bishops and theologians soon formed, among whom Bishop Luigi Carli, Archbishop Marcel Lefèbvre, and a group of teachers from the Lateran University, such as Mgr Antonio Piolanti and Archbishop Dino Staffa. They met on Tuesday evenings at the General Curia of

---

[34] The activity of the Council Fathers was flanked by that of the "experts": the official ones or *"periti"*, who assisted at the general congregations without the right to vote, and the private ones, sent by some bishops as advisers. Among the latter were theologians such as Fathers Chenu, Congar, Daniélou, De Lubac, Häring, Küng, Rahner, Ratzinger, Schillebeeckx, who would carry out roles of great influence. Cf. J. F. Kobler, "Were theologians the engineers of Vatican II?" Gregorianum, vol. LXX, 1989, pp. 233–50.

[35] "The reality of the Council – according to Cardinal Siri – is this: it was the struggle between the *Horatii* and *Curiatii*. They were three and three, in the Council four and four. On that side: Frings, Liénart, Suenens, Lercaro. On this side: Ottaviani, Ruffini, Browne and myself" (Benny Lai, *Il Papa non eletto. Giuseppe Siri, cardinale di Santa Romana Chiesa*, (Rome-Bari, Laterza, 1993), p. 233). On the origins of what Father Wiltgen calls "the World Alliance" (*Le Rhin se jette dans le Tibre*, cit., p. 128), Cf. also Dom Helder Câmara, *Les conversions d'un évêque*, pp. 152–3.

[36] R. Aubert, *Organizzazione e funzionamento dell'assemblea*, in *La Chiesa del Vaticano II*, p. 177.

[37] "This man – recalls Cardinal Suenens – carried out a fundamental role behind the scenes, even if he never spoke during the Conciliar sessions." Léon J. Suenens, *Ricordi e speranze*, (Cinisello Balsamo, Edizioni Paoline, 1993), p. 220.

the Augustinians to examine, with the help of theologians, the schema presented each time in the assembly.

Later, on 22 October 1963, at a religious institute of Via del S. Uffizio, the first meeting of the group that would take the name of Coetus Internationalis Patrum[38] was held. The bishops taking part in the meeting, about thirty, decided that they would meet regularly. Archbishop Geraldo de Proença Sigaud was nominated secretary, and was in his turn assisted by the efficient office of the secretariat made available by the members of the TFP present in Rome.

Plinio Corrêa de Oliveira, who, after his return to São Paulo, daily followed the proceedings of the assembly, understood the depth of the change taking place, which was not only to be read between the lines of the theological language, but was also expressed in significant gestures, destined to have a profound impact on the people. The Council wanted to be pastoral and not dogmatic, but in the century of "heresy in action", practice can have a revolutionary importance ideas may not have.

John XXIII died after four years of pontificate on 3 June 1963. Only eighteen days later, on 21 June, Cardinal Giovanni Battista Montini, archbishop of Milan, was elected Pope and took the name of Paul VI. In his first radiomessage, he assured that the main part of his pontificate would be dedicated to continuing the Vatican Ecumenical Council II.

Although worried about the likely course of events, Plinio Corrêa de Oliveira wished to demonstrate in *Catolicismo* "our unconditional adhesion, our limitless love, our entire obedience, not only to the Apostolic See, but also to the august Persons of he who occupied it yesterday and occupies it today", not without recalling that the latter was the same prelate who in 1949 had sent him a kind commendation on behalf of Pius XII.[39]

On 30 June 1963, when the Pope, after the Pontifical Mass, put down his mitre and put on the tiara, for the last time after many centuries the solemn formula resounded: "Receive the tiara adorned with three crowns, and know that you are the father of princes and kings, the ruler of the world, the Vicar of our Saviour Jesus Christ, to whom be all honour and glory throughout the centuries." Among Paul VI's first decisions was, in fact, to abolish the *flabelli*, the baldachin, the gestatorial chair and, with the tiara, the actual ceremony of Pontifical coronation.

---

[38] On the Coetus Internationalis: R. M. Wiltgen, *Le Rhin se jette dans le Tibre*, pp. 147-8; R. Laurentin, *Bilan de la troisième session*, in *L'enjeu du Concile*, vol. III, p. 291; R. Aubert, *Organizzazione e funzionamento dell'assemblea*, pp. 177-9; V. A. Berto, *Notre-Dame de joie. Correspondance de l'abbé Berto, prêtre. 1900-1968*, (Paris, Editions du Cèdre, 1974), pp. 290-5; ID., *Pour la Sainte Eglise Romaine. Textes et documents*, Paris, Editions du Cèdre, 1976.

[39] P. Corrêa de Oliveira, "... E sobre ti está edificada a Igreja", Catolicismo, no. 151, July 1963.

The second session of the Council, which was from many aspects the most important, began on 29 September and ended on 4 December with the approval of the constitution *Sacrosanctum Concilium* on the liturgy. At the beginning of the second session, for the first time the question of Communism was presented in the assembly.[40]

6. The freedom of the Church in the Communist State

The pontificate of John XXIII, and then the opening of the Council, seemed to have inaugurated a new climate of a "thawing" among realities already defined by the Magisterium as antithetic.[41]

On 7 March 1963 John XXIII had received in audience at the Vatican Alexis Adjubei, son-in-law of Kruschev and director of *Izvestia*.[42] The encyclical *Pacem in terris*,[43] which had appeared on 11 April 1963, was presented to public opinion as a basis for future collaboration between movements of Christian inspiration and movements of Socialist inspiration. From the French philosopher Roger Garaudy to the inspirer of the

---

[40] On the relations between the Church and Communism during the Council Cf. R. M. Wiltgen S.V.D., *Council News Service*, 2 vols., Rome, Divine Word News Service, 1963; ID., *Le Rhin se jette dans le Tibre*, pp. 269–74; A. Wenger, *Vatican II*, vol. I, pp. 187–346; vol. II, pp. 297–316; G. F. Svidercoschi, *Storia del Concilio*; Philippe Levillain, *La mécanique politique de Vatican II*, (Paris, Beauchesne, 1975), pp. 361–439; V. Carbone, *Schemi e discussioni sull'ateismo e sul marxismo*; Andrea Riccardi, *Il Vaticano e Mosca 1940–1990*, (Rome-Bari, Laterza, 1993), pp. 217–304.

[41] On the *Ostpolitik*, whose premises date to the Twenties (A. Wenger, *Rome et Moscou 1900–1950*, Paris, Desclée de Brouwer, 1987), Cf. Giancarlo Zizola, *Giovanni XXIII. La fede e la politica*, (Rome-Bari, Laterza, 1988), pp. 55–211; A. Riccardi, *Il Vaticano e Mosca*, pp. 217–64. In 1976, Father Alessio Ulisse Floridi, member for 15 years, as "Sovietologist", of the college of writers of La Civiltà Cattolica, published a book on *Mosca e il Vaticano* (Milan, La Casa di Matriona, 1976) in which he analyzed the Vatican *Ostpolitik* from an unusual angle: that of Soviet "dissension", showing how those who should have been the beneficiaries of the policy of détente were actually its victims. Later, in recalling the participation in Vatican Council II of the "observers" of the patriarchate of Moscow, whose bond of direct dependence on the Kremlin was known, he remarked: "It is certain, that on the part of the Kremlin there was a deep interest in preventing any possible attempt of the Council to condemn Communism officially. (...) The Orthodox Church put aside its reservations regarding the Council only after it appeared clear that the Council would not condemn Communism" (On the subject of "dissension" and "*ostpolitik*", Interview with Father Alessio U. Floridi edited by R. de Mattei, Cristianità, no. 32, December 1977). Cf. also Dennis J. Dunn, *Détente and Papal-Communist relation, 1962–1978*, Boulder (Colorado), Westview Press, 1979; Mireille Maqua, *Rome-Moscou. L'Ostpolitik du Vatican*, Louvain-la-Neuve, Cabay, 1984.

[42] A few days later, the secretary of the PCI, Togliatti, in full election campaign, officially proposed a collaboration between Catholics and Communists, affirming that "religious utopia" can serve as a revolutionary impulse on the road of socialism (Cf. *Rinascita*, 30 March 1963). In Italy, in the elections of 29 April 1963, the PCI increased its votes by a million, which came above all from Catholic circles seduced by the "dialogue" between the Holy See and the Soviet regime.

[43] Text in AAS, vol. 55, 1963, pp. 257–304.

Italian "historical compromise" Franco Rodano, many theorists of the convergence between Catholics and Communists were to refer to it.[44] The Kremlin had meanwhile made it known that if in the sittings of the Council the Communist problem was debated, the ecclesiastical observers of the Greek-Schismatic Russian Church would withdraw from the assembly. This threat contributed to paralyzing the ecclesiastical circles for whom ecumenism was an imperative of that hour.

The attitude of the Communist governments with regard to the Catholic Church and all other religions was evolving from open persecution to a limited tolerance that permitted a restricted freedom of worship and of word. In the first session of the Council, some conservative prelates with whom Plinio Corrêa de Oliveira was in contact agreed with him on the fact that it was not lawful for Catholics to have an agreement with the Communist regime, even at the price of the concession of a certain freedom of worship. However they believed that it was not easy to demonstrate the theory. He therefore devoted himself to a new study, that appeared in August 1963 in *Catolicismo* with the title *The Church and the Communist State: the Impossible Coexistence*.[45] In the work, dedicated to the problem of the lawfulness of the "peaceful coexistence" between the Church and the Communist regime, the author unequivocally demonstrated that Catholics cannot accept any *modus vivendi* with Communism that involves renouncing the defence of the right to private property, decreed by the seventh and tenth Commandments. The essay, translated into Spanish, French and Italian, was distributed to the 2,200 Council Fathers and 450 journalists from all over the world who were present in Rome, raising an echo that reached beyond the Iron Curtain.[46] On 4 January 1964, a

---

[44] On Roger Garaudy (*De l'anathème au dialogue*, Paris, Plon, 1955), Cf. P. Corrêa de Oliveira, "Garaudy esboça nova aproximação" and "A manobra Garaudy", Folha de S. Paulo, 8 and 15 March 1970; on Franco Rodano, (*Questione democristiana e compromesso storico*, Rome, Editori Riuniti, 1977) Cf. A. Del Noce, *Il cattolico comunista*, Milan, Rusconi, 1981. Cf. also Gianfranco Morra, *Marxismo e religione*, Milan, Rusconi, 1976.

[45] Cf. P. Corrêa de Oliveira, "A liberdade da Igreja no Estado comunista", Catolicismo, no. 152, May-August 1963; ibid., no. 161, May 1964; then with the title *Acordo com o regime comunista: para a Igreja, esperança ou autodemolição?*, São Paulo, Editora Vera Cruz, 1974. En. tr. *The Church and the Communist State: the Impossible Coexistence*, New Rochelle (NY), The Foundation for a Christian Civilization, 1978.

[46] The study was violently attacked in Poland by the Catholic-Communist movement Pax in its publications *Kierunki* (no. 8 of 3 January 1964) and *Zycie i Mysl* (nos. 1-2 of 1964). The magazine *Wiez* of Warsaw also aligned with Pax. In France, the famous Catholic newspaper of Paris *L'Homme Nouveau* (5 March 1964) defended the work which was however attacked by the progressivist publication *Témoignage Chrétien* (no. 1035 of 1964). On the Polish "anomaly", that is, on that singular historical model of co-existence of the Catholic Church and the Communist State in Poland, Cf. Giovanni Barberini, *Stato socialista e Chiesa cattolica in Polonia*, Bologna, CSEO, 1983; Norbert A. Zmijewski, *The Catholic-marxist ideological dialogue in Poland, 1945-1980*, Aldershot (England), Darmouth Publishing Company, 1991.

complete version of the text appeared in the Roman daily *Il Tempo*, arousing the attention of the public opinion of the Eternal City. The book had numerous editions world-wide in various languages and was accorded a letter of approval signed by Cardinal Giuseppe Pizzardo, Prefect of the Sacred Congregation of Seminaries and Universities, and by Archbishop Dino Staffa, secretary of the same department, later a cardinal. In this letter it was hoped for "the widest circulation for this compact pamphlet, which is a most faithful echo of all the documents of the supreme Magisterium of the Church".

The core of the study is a theory of Pius XII that was dear to Plinio Corrêa de Oliveira:

"The good or evil to souls depends and is infiltrated by the form given to society, whether consistent or not with divine law. That is to say, it depends on whether men, all called to be vivified by the grace of Christ, in the earthly contingencies during the course of life, breathe the healthy and vivid breath of truth and moral virtue, or the deadly and often lethal bacillus of error and depravation."[47]

Temporal order can in fact exercise a profound action, forming or deforming, over the soul of the people and of individuals. The Church cannot renounce rectifying this order, not even with the pretext of "spiritual" aims.

"By renouncing the teaching of the precepts of the Decalogue which are at the basis of private property (seventh and tenth commandments), the Church would present a disfigured image of God Himself. Such a condition would be gravely prejudicial to the love of God, the practice of justice and the full development of the faculties of man, and, as a consequence, to his sanctification."[48]

The Magisterial mission of the Church has after all as its object a teaching that is an indivisible whole. "The Church, in its teaching function cannot accept a half silence, a half oppression, to obtain a half freedom. It would be a complete betrayal of its mission."[49]

During the general congregation of 20 October 1963, the Fathers were presented, at the initiative of a group of French prelates, with a

---

[47] Pius XII, Radiomessage *La solennità della Pentecoste* of 1 June 1941, in AAS, vol. 33, 1941, p. 197.

[48] P. Corrêa de Oliveira, *The Church and the Communist State: the Impossible Coexistence*, p. 13. The exactness of this theory was demonstrated by the last dramatic events in Russia and in the former countries of the Warsaw Pact, in which decades of Communist dominion produced so many and significant damages to the faculties of man, from which he still has not managed to free himself.

[49] Ibid, p. 39.

"message for humanity" prepared by the Dominicans Chenu and Congar. The message aroused various criticisms in the hall, among which that of containing no mention of the "Church of Silence". It was especially criticized by the Ukrainian bishops in exile, who subsequently presented a statement which called the world's attention to the absence of their Metropolitan Josef Slipyj from the Council, deported to Siberia over seventeen years previously, while the Council Assembly saw the participation of two observers from the Patriarchate of Moscow whom they defined as "meek and useful instruments in the hands of the Soviet government".[50]

The distribution of the *Freedom of the Church in the Communist State* was connected to two other important initiatives: on 3 December 1963, Bishop Antônio de Castro Mayer officially delivered to Cardinal Amleto Cicognani, Secretary of State, a petition signed by 213 Council Fathers of 54 different nationalities, in which the Holy Father was asked to provide for the elaboration and study of a schema of conciliar constitution where:

"1. Catholic social doctrine is expounded with great clarity and the errors of Marxism, Socialism and Communism are denounced from a philosophical, sociological and economic point of view.

"2. Those errors and that mentality that prepare the spirit of Catholics to accept Socialism and Communism and that renders them disposed towards them be dispelled."

These errors and mentality, according to the authors of the text, "have their origin in the French Revolution".[51] The Counter-Revolutionary style of the petition was evident and revealed how the text of the document was inspired by Plinio Corrêa de Oliveira.[52]

Bishop Geraldo de Proença Sigaud, on his part, on 3 February 1964 personally delivered to Paul VI a petition signed by 510 prelates of 78

---

[50] G. F. Svidercoschi, *Storia del Concilio*, pp. 164–5. Two days after the publication of this document, on 23 November, Mgr Willebrands, on behalf of the Secretariate of the Union between Christians, during a press conference, defended the Russian observers, who had "demonstrated a sincerely religious and ecumenical spirit", while regretting the communiqué of the Ukraine bishops. On 9 February of the following year, Cardinal Slipyi was suddenly released from prison and arrived in Rome; the same occurred, during the early months of 1965, for the archbishop of Prague, Josef Beran.

[51] R. M. Wiltgen S.V.D., *Council News Service*, vol. I, p. 79. Cf. the text of this petition, Catolicismo, no. 157, January 1964.

[52] Father Wiltgen made it known that "a short time before the delivery of the petitions, a sixteen page article entitled *The Church in the Communist State: the Impossible Coexistence*, written by Dr Plinio Corrêa de Oliveira, a lay Catholic university professor in Brazil, had been distributed to each Council Father. The article supplies the doctrinal proofs to show that to admit that the Church can exist and enjoy its essential freedom in a Communist state is against Catholic principles". *Council News Service*, cit., vol. I, p. 79.

countries that implored the Pontiff, in union with his bishops, to consecrate the world, and Russia explicitly, to the Immaculate Heart of Mary.[53] Once again, the contribution of Dr Plinio to the elaboration of the text was decisive.

The petitions presented by two Brazilian bishops and the book by Plinio Corrêa de Oliveira were, as he pointed out in *Catolicismo*, an organic whole. "As a whole, the three documents constitute, each one in its own right, three distinctly important episodes in the fight against the greatest enemy of the Holy Father, of the Catholic Church and of Christianity."[54]

7. The silence on Communism: a failed Council?

Marxism and Communism were at the centre of the discussion of the schema on the Church in the modern world, during the third session of the Council that opened on 14 September 1964. The discussion was influenced by the encyclical of Paul VI *Ecclesiam Suam*, which had appeared two months previously, on 6 August 1964. In it the Pontiff deplored the ideological systems denying God and oppressing the Church in the world, but hoped "that they may one day open with the Church a positive dialogue, different from the present one, necessarily to be deplored and lamented".[55] "For the first time" observes a contemporary historian "the policy of dialogue with non-believers and socialist regimes entered an encyclical."[56]

In the general examination of the Council schema, which omitted every reference to Communism, the theme was touched upon by many Fathers with different emphases. Cardinal Josef Frings, in the name of the German and Scandinavian bishops, asked that the word Communism not be used, to avoid every appearance of political interference and connection with capitalism.[57] On the opposite front, The Most Reverend Yu Pin, archbishop of Nanking, in the name of seventy Council Fathers, demanded the addition of a new chapter, or at least of a solemn declaration on Communism to satisfy the expectations of those peoples who were groaning under the Communist yoke.[58]

---

[53] The text of the historical document, Catolicismo, no. 159, March 1964.
[54] P. Corrêa de Oliveira, "A margem de três documentos providenciais", Catolicismo, no. 259, March 1964, p. 3.
[55] AAS, vol. LVI (1964), no. 10, pp. 651–4.
[56] A. Riccardi, *Il Vaticano e Mosca*, p. 269.
[57] *Acta Synodalia sacrosancti concilii oecumenici Vaticani II*, Typis Poliglottis Vaticanis, 1978, vol. III, pars V, p. 510.
[58] *Acta Synodalia*, vol. III, pars V, p. 378.

On 7 April 1965, while the schema was being revised, Paul VI set up a Secretariat for non-believers, with the aim of promoting "dialogue" with them. The presidency of the body was entrusted to the Austrian Cardinal König, who had often acted as intermediary between the Holy See and Communist Governments.

On 14 September 1965 the fourth and final session of the Council began.[59] On 21 September, after the report by Mgr Garrone, the debate was opened on the schema of the "Pastoral Constitution" concerning relations between the Church and the world. The text in the possession of the Fathers made no explicit reference to Communism. In fact, according to the editors of the document, a condemnation would have been in contrast with the pastoral character of Vatican II and constitute an obstacle to the "dialogue" with the Communist regimes.

The Lebanese patriarch Maximos IV Saigh maintained that, to save mankind from atheism, rather than condemning Marxism, it was necessary to denounce the causes that provoke atheistic Communism. He proposed "a dynamic mysticism and a vigorous social morality and demonstrated that in Christ is the source of the effort of the workers towards their true liberation".[60] The Yugoslavian Cardinal Seper showed himself to be contrary to a condemnation of atheistic Communism, stating that partial responsibility for modern atheism was to be attributed to those Christians who obstinately continued to defend the established order and immobilism of the social structures. "We therefore proclaim that that rigid conservatism and that immobilism that some never cease to attribute to the Catholic Church is alien to the true evangelical spirit."[61] Even more explicit was Cardinal König, who invited the Catholics, in the countries subjected to Communism, to testify to the living God by sincerely collaborating in the economic and social progress of the regime, to demonstrate that from religion greater energies than atheism can flow. However protests and censorship were not lacking from Archbishop Geraldo de Proença Sigaud,[62] Bishop de Castro Mayer[63] and other prelates such as the Italian Cardinal Ermenegildo Florit and the Czechoslovak Jesuit Bishop Pavel Hnilica, ordained in hiding and only recently arrived in the West.

---

[59] Paul VI announced two decisions that caused commotion: the establishment of a synod of bishops that would offer the Pope, at regular intervals, the contribution "of its advice and collaboration" and his acceptance of the invitation to visit the UN on the occasion of the twentieth anniversary of its foundation. R. Aubert, *Il Concilio*, p. 323.

[60] *Acta Synodalia*, 1977, vol. IV, pars II, p. 451.

[61] G. F. Svidercoschi, *Storia del Concilio*, pp. 595–6.

[62] *Acta Synodalia*, vol. IV, pars I, p. 555.

[63] *Acta Synodalia*, vol. IV, pars I, pp. 371–2. P. Corrêa de Oliveira, "Lucida e relevante intervenção do bispo-diocesano no Concilio", Catolicismo, no. 179, November 1965, p. 8.

"It is necessary to speak" Bishop Elko, Ruthenian eparch of Pittsburg (United States) affirmed "of dialectic materialism, as of a plague in today's society and to condemn it as we should, so that future centuries will not consider us responsible for fear and pusillanimity, if we have only dealt with it indirectly."[64] "Every time an Ecumenical Council has met" said Cardinal Antonio Bacci in his turn "it has always solved the great problems which were stirring at that time and condemned the errors of the day. To remain silent on this point I believe would be an unpardonable lacuna, indeed a collective sin. (...) This is the great theoretical and practical heresy of our time; and if the Council does not deal with it, it may seem a failed Council!"[65]

8. A new relationship of the Church with the world

On 9 October 1964, after concluding the discussion on atheism, the *Coetus Internationalis Patrum* presented a petition in which it was asked that "...after paragraph no. 19 of the schema *The Church in the modern world*, which deals with the problem of atheism, a new and suitable paragraph that deals expressly with the problem of Communism be added".[66]

If Vatican II has an eminently pastoral character, the petition affirmed "what problem is more pastoral than this: to prevent the faithful from becoming atheists through Communism?" If the Council had remained silent on a problem of such importance, this silence, in the minds of the faithful, would have been the same "as a tacit abrogation of all that the last Supreme Pontiffs had said and written against Communism". The existence of pronouncements of so many Popes is not a reason for ignoring the problem, because "greater force and effectiveness is given to the question by the solemn consensus of the whole Council"; nor "can it happen that the Christians of the Church of Silence have in the future greater sufferings than what they now endure".[67]

---

[64] *Acta Synodalia*, vol. IV, pars II, p. 480.
[65] *Acta Synodalia*, vol. IV, pars II, pp. 669-70.
[66] On the whole business Cf. A. Wenger, *Vatican II. Chronique de la quatrième session*, pp. 147-73; R. Wiltgen, *Le Rhin se jette dans le Tibre*, pp. 272-8; V. Carbone, *Schemi e discussioni*, pp. 45-68. The text of the petition in *Acta Synodalia*, vol. IV, pars II, pp. 898-900. Cf. also P. Levillain, *La mécanique politique de Vatican II*, pp. 343-60.
[67] The text of the proposal may be found in the study *Il comunismo e il Concilio Vaticano II*, by Bishop Luigi M. Carli, in the book by Don Giovanni Scantamburlo, *Perché il Concilio non ha condannato il comunismo? Storia di un discusso atteggiamento*, (Rome, L'Appennino, 1967), pp. 177-240. Cf. also G. F. Svidercoschi, *Storia del Concilio*, pp. 604-05.

The petition was delivered to the General Secretariat by Archbishop Geraldo de Proença Sigaud and by Archbishop Marcel Lefèbvre, into the hands of the Frenchman Mgr Glorieux. He, however, did not transmit it to the commission that was working on the schema, with the pretext of not wanting to hinder their work. The petition had been signed by all of 454 prelates of 86 countries who were astounded when, on Saturday 13 November, they received the new text in the hall without any mention of their requests. On the same day, Bishop Carli addressed a letter of protest to the Council, denouncing the licence of the commission that had ignored a document of such great importance. In spite of the protests, on 15 November, Mgr Garrone affirmed that the "way of proceeding" of the commission agreed with the "pastoral scope" of the Council, with the "expressed desire" of John XXIII and of Paul VI and with the level of discussions which had been held in the hall on this subject.[68] Mgr Carli confirmed his appeal while the scandal exploded in the press.[69]

On 3 December, the Coetus Internationalis Patrum addressed a final appeal to the Council Fathers that they should vote against the schema as a whole, seeing how it was no longer possible to obtain partial amendments. In fact, 131 Fathers voted against the section on atheism while 75 voices pronounced themselves against the pastoral Constitution *Gaudium et Spes,* on the Church in the modern world. This Constitution, by reversing the position of the *Syllabus,* as Cardinal Ratzinger observed,[70] wished to be a completely new definition of the relations between the Church and the world.

On 5 December, in the presence of Paul VI, an interconfessional

---

[68] Ibid, p. 607.

[69] The controversy came to the attention of Paul VI who did not deem it necessary to intervene with his weight to rectify the serious irregularities. On 26 November, in the study of the Pope on the third floor of the Apostolic Palace, Cardinals Tisserant and Cicognani met with Monsignors Garrone, Felici and Dell'Acqua. Before the meeting began, Cardinal Tisserant had delivered to the Pope a letter in which among other things he declared: "Anathemas have never converted anyone and even if they were useful at the time of the Council of Trent, when princes could force their subjects to pass over to Protestantism, they are of no use today when each one has the sense of his own independence. As I already told your Holiness, a Conciliar condemnation of Communism would be considered by most people as a political move, and this would bring immense damage to the authority of the Council and of the Church itself. Cit. in V. Carbone, *Schemi e discussioni,* p. 58.

[70] Cardinal Ratzinger defines *Gaudium et Spes* as "a revision of the Syllabus of Pius IX, a sort of counter-syllabus (...) to the extent that it represents an attempt at an official reconciliation of the Church with the world that evolved after 1789", *Les principes de la Théologie catholique,* (Paris, Téqui, 1982), pp. 425–427. "This constitution – comments Mgr Jedin in his turn – was greeted with enthusiasm but its later history has already demonstrated that, at the time, its significance and importance had been widely overestimated and it had not been understood how deeply that 'world' it was wished to gain for Christ had penetrated into the Church", *Il Concilio Vaticano II,* p. 151.

prayer meeting took place, the first in which a Pontiff participated, during which representatives of all the religious confessions present recited passages from the Sacred Scripture.[71] On the afternoon of Monday 6 December, *L'Osservatore Romano* published the decree that abolished the *Index of forbidden books* and changed the "Holy Office" into the "Congregation for the Doctrine of the Faith", affirming that "because charity excludes fear, the defence of the faith will now be better provided for by promoting its doctrine".[72] A public embrace between Paul VI and the Greek-Schismatic Metropolitan Meliton of Heliopolis, who had come from Constantinople, ratified the cancellation by the Catholic Church of the excommunication of the "Orthodox" Church in 1054. In his homily Paul VI recalled that the Council had produced the encounter between "the religion of man" and the "religion of God", not failing to cause "amazement and scandal".[73]

On 7 December the last public session of Vatican Council II was held. In the presence of the Pope, the secretary general of the Council Mgr Pericle Felici proposed the first four documents for the approval of the Fathers: the pastoral Constitution *Gaudium et Spes*; the decrees *Ad Gentes* on the missionary activity of the Church and *Presbyterorum Ordinis* on priestly ministry, and the declaration *Dignitatis Humanae* on religious freedom.

Vatican Council II had closed without an explicit condemnation of Communism. The fact was of such importance as "to confirm the rumour of an explicit agreement between the Patriarchate of Moscow and the Holy See".[74] The Council's silence on Communism did in fact constitute a dramatic omission by the historical assembly. The closing ceremony of the Council took place on 8 December 1965. It, recalls Hubert Jedin with a certain bitterness in his memoirs, "did not correspond to the concept that I had of the solemnity due to an Ecumenical Council. It was a show and as such a concession to the era of the masses and the media".[75]

We can imagine the anxiety of Plinio Corrêa de Oliveira in face of the conclusions of the Council and, perhaps, his perplexity over the fact that the two Brazilian prelates close to him and Archbishop Lefèbvre himself had signed the group of Conciliar Acts, including

[71] Cf. G. Caprile, *Il Concilio Vaticano II*, vol. V, pp. 453–7.
[72] AAS, vol. 57, 1965, pp. 952–5.
[73] A. Wenger, *Les trois Rome*, (Paris 1991), p. 190. The text of the homily in *Acta synodalia*, vol. IV, pars VII, pp. 654–62; It. tr. in G. Caprile, *Il Concilio Vaticano II*, vol. V, pp. 501–05.
[74] A. Riccardi, *Il Vaticano e Mosca*, p. 281.
[75] Mgr H. Jedin, *Storia della mia vita*, it. tr., (Brescia, Morcelliana, 1987), p. 321.

the documents that they had opposed in the hall.[76] What is certain is that he assumed an attitude of respectful silence, waiting for the facts to confirm what he already foresaw.

"Presided over by John XXIII and later by Paul VI" he wrote in 1990 "the Vatican Ecumenical Council II was the largest in the history of the Church. It was agreed that all the major topics of the day related to the Catholic cause would be discussed. That the attitude of the Church toward Her greatest adversary at that time be among these topics was essential – absolutely essential! In Her nearly two-thousand-year history, the Church had never encountered such a powerful, brutal and cunning adversary, so completely opposed to Her doctrine. A discussion of contemporary problems facing religion that fails to deal with communism would be as flawed as a world medical conference convened to study today's major diseases that omits any reference to AIDs ...

"This is what Vatican *Ostpolitik* accepted from the Kremlin."[77]

9. The "resistance" to the Vatican *Ostpolitik*

The Vatican *Ostpolitik* had numerous critics all over the world, beginning with those who should have been its beneficiaries and who rather stated that they were its victims: the Christians of Eastern Europe. The most significant demonstration of public dissent in the Catholic field was however, without a doubt, the historical declaration of resistance published in 1974 in 21 daily papers of various countries by the TFPs then in existence in Europe and in the world. The author and first signatory of the historical declaration was Prof Plinio Corrêa de Oliveira.

In 1972 "détente" had received an extraordinary impulse from Nixon's journeys to China and Russia.[78] The aim of the policy devel-

---

[76] At first Archbishop Lefèbvre seemed to deny that he had signed these documents (*Itinéraires*, April 1977, pp. 224, 231). His signature is however shown by the *Acta synodalia*, vol. IV, pars VII, p. 809, 823. Mgr Carbone, in charge of the historical Archives of Vatican II, checked that the authentic signature is shown on the originals (D. Menozzi, *La Chiesa cattolica e la secolarizzazione*, p. 224). The importance of the signature is underlined by the magazine *Sedes Sapientiae* no. 131, winter 1990, pp. 41–2 and no. 35, winter 1991, and by abbot Georges de Nantes, "Situation tragique de l'Eglise", La Contre-Réforme Catholique au XXe. siècle, no. 266, July 1990, and nos. 280, 281, 282, February–March, April, May 1992.

[77] P. Corrêa de Oliveira, *Communism and AntiCommunism on the Threshold of the Millennium's Last Decade*.

[78] According to Plinio Corrêa de Oliveira, "it can be said without exaggeration that, from the time of the bolchevization of Russia, Communism had not had a victory comparable" to that granted it by the détente: "even the catastrophic concessions of Roosevelt at Yalta were not equal in harmfulness to the deepest results of the 'collapse of the ideological barriers' brought about by the Nixon–Kissinger team". "A crise louca", Folha de S. Paulo, 18 August 1974.

oped by the American president and his secretary of state Kissinger at world level was identical to the policy that Willy Brandt, the German Socialist Chancellor, was developing at the European level: the idea of a "convergence" between the Western and Communist blocs. The sole result of this policy of collaboration, based on the privileged axis Washington–Moscow, was to postpone for twenty years, thanks to economic aid, the inevitable crumbling of the Communist empire, while Soviet aggressiveness continued to increase in proportion to the assistance received from the West.

In the ecclesiastical field, Archbishop Agostino Casaroli,[79] "minister of Foreign Affairs" of Paul VI, followed a policy of entente with Communism similar to that of Brandt and Kissinger. One of the most illustrious victims of Vatican *Ostpolitik* was Cardinal Mindszenty, primate of Hungary and hero of the anti-communist resistance who, in 1974, was removed by Paul VI from the archdiocese of Esztergom and exiled to Rome, to facilitate the approaches between the Holy See and the Hungarian Communist government.[80]

> "In view of the general devastation" wrote Plinio Corrêa de Oliveira "Cardinal Mindszenty has risen as the great non-conformist, the author of the great international case, of an unbreakable refusal that saves the honour of the Church and of the human race. By his example – with the prestige of his roman purple intact on the robust shoulders of a courageous and abnegated shepherd – he showed Catholics that it is not licit for them to go along with the multitudes that bend their knee to Belial."[81]

A few days later, on 10 April 1974 an extensive declaration of the Brazilian TFP appeared as an advertisement in the *Folha de S. Paulo*

---

[79] Born near Piacenza in 1914, Agostino Casaroli was ordained to the priesthood in 1937 and in 1940 entered the service of the Secretariat of State, where he spent his entire ecclesiastical career. In 1963 he received from John XXIII the order to go to Budapest and to Prague to explore the possibilities of re-establishing contacts with those governments. This was the beginning of a long series of journeys in the Eastern Communist countries that led him to effect, especially under Paul VI, the Vatican policy known as *Ostpolitik*. In 1979, John Paul II nominated him cardinal, prefect of the Council for the Public Affairs of the State and his Secretary of State, a position he occupied until 1 December 1990. Cf. Alleste Santini, *Casaroli, l'uomo del dialogo*, Cinisello Balsamo, Edizioni San Paolo, 1993.

[80] Of Cardinal József Mindszenty Cf. le *Erinnerungen*, Frankfurt, Ullstein and Berlin, Propyläen, 1974. When on 5 February 1974, the news of his removal was made public, Cardinal Mindszenty issued a communiqué in which he declared that he had never renounced his role of archbishop nor his dignity of Primate of Hungary, stressing that "the decision had been taken solely by the Holy See" (ibid, p. 372).

[81] P. Corrêa de Oliveira, "Ao grande criador do caso imenso", Folha de S. Paulo, 31 March 1974. Cf. also ID., "La gloria, la alegria, la honra", Folha de S. Paulo, 10 February 1974; "Ternuras que arrancarian lágrimas", Folha de S. Paulo, 13 October 1974; "Conforme queira Budapest", Folha de S. Paulo, 20 October 1974.

entitled *The Vatican policy of détente towards the Communist govern-ments. For the TFP: to withdraw? or to resist?.*

That same year, on the occasion of a journey to Cuba, Archbishop Casaroli had affirmed that "the Catholics who live in Cuba are happy under the Socialist regime" and that "the Catholics and, in general, the Cuban people, haven't the least difficulty with the Socialist government".[82] This episode is recalled in the declaration of the TFP next to others that are no less significant: the journey to Russia in 1971 of Mgr Willebrands, president of the Secretariat for the Union of Christians, to meet the "Orthodox" bishop Pimen, a man trusted by the Kremlin; and the support of Cardinal Silva Henríquez, arch-bishop of Santiago of Chile, for the Marxist leader Salvador Allende.

Faced with these facts, Plinio Corrêa de Oliveira, in the name of the TFP, wrote with respectful, but, at the same time, very strong language:

"The Vatican policy of détente toward the Communist governments creates a situation which affects anti-Communist Catholics deeply, but much less, however, as anti-Communists than as Catholics. For at any moment a supremely embarrassing objection may be put to them: Does not their anti-Communist action lead to a result that is precisely opposed to the one intended by the Vicar of Christ? And how can one consider a Catholic to be consistent if he moves in an opposite direction from the Pastor of Pastors? This question leads all anti-Communist Catholics to a consideration of these alterna-tives: To cease the struggle? Or to explain their position?

"To cease the fight, we cannot. And we cannot cease it because of a duty of our conscience as Catholics. For if it is a duty of every Catholic to promote good and fight evil, our conscience imposes on us the responsibility of propagating the traditional doctrine of the Church, and of fighting Communist doctrine. (...)

"The Church is not, the Church never was, the Church will never be such a prison for consciences. The bond of obedience to the successor of Peter, which we will never break, which we love to the depth of our soul, to which we give the best of our love, this bond we kiss at the very moment at which, triturated by sorrow, we affirm our position. And kneeling, gazing with veneration at the figure of His Holiness Paul VI, we express to him our fidelity.

---

[82] Cf. *O Estado de S. Paulo*, 7 April 1974. During the journey, that took place between 27 March and 5 April 1974 at the invitation of the Cuban episcopate, Archbishop Casaroli had talks with members of the government and with Fidel Castro. The next year he was in the German Democratic Republic and from 30 July to 1 August 1975 he participated, as special delegate of Paul VI, in the Conference on "security" of Helsinki, signing the final act in the name of the Holy See.

"In this filial act we say to the Pastor of Pastors: Our soul is yours, our life is yours. Order us to do whatever you wish. Only do not order us to stay idle in face of the assailing red wolf. To this, our conscience is opposed."[83]

The obedience of the ecclesiastical hierarchy, imposed on us by the catechism and by our very faith, is not unconditional; it certainly has limits, as all theologians affirm. The *Dizionario di Teologia Morale* edited by Cardinals Roberti and Palazzini explains as an example:

"It is clear that it is never lawful to obey a Superior who commands something that is contrary to divine or ecclesiastical laws; in that case the words of St Peter should be repeated: we must obey God rather than men (Acts 5:29)."[84]

This legitimate "disobedience" of an order unjust in itself in matters of faith and morals can be extended, in particular cases, even as far as public resistance to the ecclesiastical authorities. Arnaldo V. Xavier da Silveira, in a study dedicated to the public resistance to the decisions of the ecclesiastical authority,[85] proved it well, offering examples of saints, doctors of the Church and illustrious theologians and canonists that demonstrate how — in the case of "imminent danger for the faith"[86] (St Thomas Aquinas) or of "the aggression of souls"[87] (St Robert Bellarmine) in the doctrinal field — it is legitimate for the faithful to exercise a right of even public resistance to the ecclesiastical authorities.

---

[83] P. Corrêa de Oliveira, "The Vatican Policy of Distension Toward the Communist Governments", Crusade for a Christian Civilization (New York), Vol. 4, no. 3, September 1974. The document was published in full, Catolicismo, no. 280, April 1974, and in 36 Brazilian newspapers and then copied in 73 more between newspapers and magazines of eleven countries, without receiving the slightest objection concerning its orthodoxy and its canonical correctness.

[84] D. Gregorio Manise O.S.B., entry *Obbedienza*, in DTM, p. 1115.

[85] Arnaldo Vidigal Xavier da Silveira, *La nouvelle Messe de Paul VI: qu'en penser?*, (Chiré-en-Montreuil, Diffusion de la Pensée Française, 1975), pp. 319–34.

[86] According to St Thomas Aquinas, there exists a right to publicly resist, in given circumstances, a decision of the Roman Pontiff. In this regard the Angelic doctor states: "if the faith were endangered, a subject ought to rebuke his prelate even publicly. Hence Paul, who was Peter's subject, rebuked him in public, on account of the imminent danger of scandal concerning faith, and, as the gloss of Augustine says on Gal 2:11, 'Peter gave an example to superiors, that if at any time they should happen to stray from the straight path they should not disdain to be reproved by their subjects'". *Summa Theologica*, II–II, 33, 4, 2.

[87] Another great theologian, the Jesuit cardinal St Robert Bellarmine, champion of the rights of the Papacy in its struggle against Protestantism, affirms: "just as it is lawful to resist the Pontiff who attacks the body, so it is also lawful to resist him who attacks souls, or who disturbs civil order, or, above all, he who should attempt to destroy the Church. I say it is lawful to resist him by not doing what he orders and preventing the implementation of his will; it is not however lawful to judge him, punish him and depose him because these acts belong to a superior", *De Romano Pontefice*, II, 29.

Hence the lawfulness of a position of "resistance": "This resistance is not separation, it is not revolt, it is not harshness, it is not irreverence. On the contrary, it is fidelity, it is union, it is love, it is submission."[88] Referring to the position of St Paul towards St Peter when St Paul "resisted him to his face",[89] Plinio Corrêa de Oliveira wrote: "In the sense in which St Paul resisted, our state is one of resistance".[90] This position of resistance was expressed publicly by all the Associations for the Defence of Tradition, Family and Property, and sister associations then in existence in America and Europe.

Twenty years after the Council, the *Instruction on some aspects of "liberation theology"*, of the Sacred Congregation for the Doctrine of the Faith,[91] which defined Marxism as "a shame of our time", seemed to prove the validity of the position of "resistance" to the *Ostpolitik* of the TFP and of the anti-communist Catholics of the whole world.[92]

10. The denunciation of the modernist "dialogue"

While following the encyclical *Ecclesiam suam* the word "dialogue" passed from mouth to mouth, in December 1965 Plinio Corrêa de Oliveira published another important study: *Unperceived Ideological Transhipment and Dialogue*.[93] In it the author denounced the use of the term "dialogue" as a technique of persuasion that, in the strategy

---

[88] P. Corrêa de Oliveira, "The Vatican policy of distension".
[89] Gal. 2:11.
[90] P. Corrêa de Oliveira, "The Vatican policy of distension".
[91] Congregation for the Doctrine of the Faith Instruction *Libertatis nuntius*.
[92] The declaration was greeted by Plinio Corrêa de Oliveira as "the jet of cold and benevolent water of a firemen's hose. (...) For those who felt distressed in face of this spectacle, for the moment tragic but which can soon become apocalyptic – commented Plinio Corrêa de Oliveira — to see that a body such as the Holy Congregation for the Doctrine of the Faith declare, in black and white, the incompatibility of Catholic Doctrine with Marxism is like for someone who is inside a fire to feel unexpectedly the jet of cold and benevolent water from a fireman's hose. And I who, as the president of the national council of the Brazilian TFP, was the first to sign the mentioned declaration of resistance to the Vatican *Ostpolitik*, have in justice to demonstrate, at this moment, the joy, gratitude and above all the hope that I feel from within the fire at the arrival of this relief. I know that there are brothers in the faith outside the ranks of the TFP, especially outside Brazil, who abstain from demonstrating similar sentiments, mainly because they think that just one hose is insufficient to quench the fire. I too think that one hose will not quench a fire. But this does not prevent me from greeting it as a benefit. All the more because I do not have proofs of the fact we will remain with only this hose. Was the instruction of Cardinal Ratzinger not unexpected? Does not one unexpected step invite us to expect others in the same direction, they too more or less unexpected?", P. Corrêa de Oliveira, "Un primo ostacolo agli errori diffusi dalla 'teologia della liberazione'", Cristianità, no. 117, January 1985.
[93] Cf. P. Corrêa de Oliveira, *Baldeação ideologica inadvertida e dialogo*, São Paulo, Editora Vera Cruz, 1965, En. tr. *Unperceived Ideological Transhipment and Dialogue*, Crusade for a Christian Civilization, Vol. 12 no. 4, October–December 1982; It. tr. *Trasbordo ideologico inavvertito e dialogo*, Naples, Edizione de L'Alfiere, 1970.

of Marxist conquest, occupies a position not inferior to its classical one of violence.

Silvio Vitale, in his preface to the Italian edition of the essay, thus summarized the analysis carried out by Doctor Plinio:

"With dialogue, Communism grasps the opportunity to induce the Catholic interlocutor to place himself on a level of Hegelian relativism: the dialogue takes place between persons who, in a confrontation between theses and antitheses, implicitly aim at a synthesis that includes and exceeds the first. This position is fully coherent with Communism. (...) Vice-versa it is fatal for the Catholic because he, in accepting this kind of dialogue, eventually contradicts the existence of truth and good as absolutes, unchangeables, transcendents. (...) The imprudent interlocutor starts out convinced that he can arrive at the truth and therefore at unity through his own undertaking to persuade the adversary. Then he begins to consider the supreme end of the conversation not to be the truth but unity. Subsequently he will end up believing that there are no objective truths and errors, so it is not necessary to convince to obtain unity. In fact he convinces himself that only in function of 'relative truths' and contingencies can he effectively assert himself and progress. At this point, having fallen completely into the hands of the Irenist utopia, he is dominated completely by the aim of coexistence at any cost with the adversary."[94]

Few analyses of Hegelian dialectics equal the work of the Brazilian thinker, in which metaphysical depth is accompanied by a great capacity for psychological and linguistic analysis. He recalls how, according to St Thomas, one of the reasons for which God permits errors and evil is so that, by contrast, the splendour of truth and good stand out all the more.[95] Now, how can one make this contrast be noticed, other than by the open and categorical denunciation of how much falsity and evil this censurable error contains? With this denunciation, imposed by the evangelical "yes, yes; no, no", a healthy conflict is produced in the soul of whoever is listening, by eliminating ambiguities and uncertainties and driving towards adhesion to total truth.

Plinio Corrêa de Oliveira places an absolute incompatibility against every Irenistic tendency:

"Communism cannot accept the coexistence with anyone who, contrary to itself, professes a philosophy based on the recognition

---

[94] Silvio Vitale, Preface to P. Corrêa de Oliveira, *Trasbordo ideologico*, pp. 6–7.
[95] St Thomas Aquinas, *Contra Gentes*, III, 71.

of the truth and the good as absolute, immutable, transcendent values existing in a perfect way in the divine essence."[96]

11. True and false ecumenism

The Irenistic mentality of compromise with error is typical of a psychological utopian disposition that hopes for an era without contrasts or controversies.

Plinio Corrêa de Oliveira demonstrates, in *Unperceived Transhipment*, that on the religious level, the Irenistic dialogue promotes interconfessionalism, weakens all religions and projects them into a condition of absolute confusion.

"Two forms of ecumenism should be pointed out. One type seeks – in order to lead souls to the one flock of the one Shepherd – to reduce as much as possible the number of arguments pure and simple and polemics in favour of argument-dialogue and other forms of interlocution. This ecumenism is amply based on numerous pontifical documents, especially those of John XXIII and Paul VI. But another type of ecumenism goes further and seeks to extirpate any and all militant character from the relations of the Catholic Religion with others. This extreme ecumenism is evidently founded upon relativism or religious syncretism, whose condemnation is found in two documents of St Pius X, the encyclical *Pascendi* against Modernism, and the Apostolic Letter *Notre Charge Apostolique* against the Sillon."[97]

Accordingly, all religions are accepted as "relative" truths and ordered among themselves according to a Hegelian dialectic schema. This second type of ecumenism drives souls towards a single and universal religion: the artificial and false "religion of Man".

"We observe that extreme ecumenism produces tragic confusion among Catholics as well as the separated brethren, be they schismatics, heretics or otherwise. This confusion is certainly one of the most tragic of our confusion filled age. Indeed, today there is no greater danger in the religious field than relativism. It threatens all religions, and any true Catholic or separated brother who seriously professes his own religion should fight it. This can only be done by the effort each one makes to maintain the natural and proper meaning of his belief against the relativistic interpretations that

---

[96] P. Corrêa de Oliveira, *Unperceived Ideological transhipment*, p. 38.
[97] Ibid, p. 28.

deform and undermine it. The ally of the true Catholic in this fight would be the Jew or the Mohammedan who allows not the slightest doubt about what unites or separates us. It is this kind of attitude that keeps relativism out of the fields it attempts to enter. Further, it is only once this attitude is adopted that interlocution in its various modes, including argument pure and simple and polemics, can help to unite souls. 'Good accounts make good friends,' says the proverb. Likewise, only clarity in thinking and expressing what one thinks really leads to unity. Exaggerated ecumenism, which tends to make everyone hide or underestimate his real discrepancies with others, leads to a regime of *maquillage*, which can only favour relativism, the most powerful common enemy of all religions."[98]

12. The postconciliar crisis explodes

The thirty years that passed from the end of Vatican Council II to the death of Plinio Corrêa de Oliveira in São Paulo on 3 October 1995 provide the occasion for many reflections on the course of what was defined the "conciliar" or "postconciliar" Church. The problem was interestingly deformed by the media after the explosion of the so-called "Lefèbvre case", from the name of the French archbishop[99] who from 1976 entered into open conflict with the Holy See on the

---

[98] Ibid., p. 29. "When one day the history – so dark and confused! – of the religious crisis, of the serious socio-economic reflections igniting the Catholic world will be written – the Brazilian thinker would write ten years later on the occasion of the visit of John Paul II to the Lutheran temple in Rome – the fatal action of ecumenism will be brought to light. Psychologists will be disconcerted by its great capacity for expansion. In effect, the ecumenical myth exerts a peculiar capacity to blind those who allow themselves to be bewitched by it. (...) Do they not see the danger lying in ambush at the end of this path, that is the formation, at world level, of a sinister supermarket of religions, philosophies and systems of all orders, in which truth and error will appear divided, mixed and haphazardly placed? The only thing absent from the world will be – if it be possible to arrive to this point – the complete truth: that is the Roman, Catholic, Apostolic Faith, without stain or alteration", P. Corrêa de Oliveira, "Lutero: no e poi no!", Lepanto, no. 22, January 1984.

[99] Archbishop Marcel Lefèbvre was born in Turcoing (Lille) on 29 November 1905 and died in Martigny on 25 March 1990. A student in the French seminary in Rome, he was ordained to the priesthood on 21 September 1929 by Bishop Liénart, bishop of Lille. In 1930 he joined the Congregation of the Holy Spirit mostly carrying out missionary apostolate in French Africa. He was consecrated bishop on 18 September 1947, nominated apostolic delegate for Francophone Africa and on 4 September 1955, archbishop of Dakar. He left this position in 1962, assuming the title of archbishop-bishop of Tulle. From 1962 to 1968 he was superior general of his Congregation. In 1970, he established the Priestly Fraternity of St Pius X in the diocese of Friburg in Switzerland, with the approval of Bishop Charrière, ordinary of the place. Starting from 1974 he began his dispute with the Holy See which would lead to his suspension *a divinis*, following the priestly ordinations of 29 June 1976, and to the excommunication *latae sententiae*, after the consecration of four bishops on 30 June 1988. Cf. "Il Regno documenti", no. 600, 1 September 1988, pp. 477–88.

subject of the New Mass and the Conciliar reforms.[100] However, under the pontificate of Paul VI, and well before the questions concerning Archbishop Lefèbvre, the subject of the "crisis of the Church"[101] had become a focus point for discussion, exciting the intervention of the greatest theologians and philosophers of the time.

The historian Hubert Jedin, who had collaborated at the Council as an "expert" with Cardinal Frings, after having tried to oppose the idea of a "crisis of the Church" at the end of the Sixties, was then forced to recognize its existence in a famous conference entitled *History and crises of the Church*, published in Italian by the *L'Osservatore Romano*.[102] On 17 September 1968, Mgr Jedin presented the German Episcopal Conference with a memorandum in which were illustrated five phenomena relative to the current crisis of the Church:

"1. the increasingly widespread insecurity in the faith, caused by the free distribution of theological errors from the cathedrae, in books and essays;

"2. the attempt to transfer into the Church forms of parliamen-

---

[100]Archbishop Marcel Lefèbvre, after distinguishing himself among the exponents of the conservative wing during the Council, had signed the Acts of the historical assembly and in his letters to the members of the Congregation of the Holy Spirit – of which he was superior general – he had demonstrated a moderately positive evaluation on the Conciliar reforms. In these documents Archbishop Lefèbvre not only recalled the timeliness of the liturgical renewal desired by the assembly, but even, while expressing his reserves, exhorted to welcome the positive elements of the Council, affirming that in its work it had enjoyed special graces "for bringing about reforms and adaptations in the Church, whose only scope is to lead to a more perfect sanctification and make the purest evangelical spirit live anew", Archbishop M. Lefèbvre, *Lettres pastorales et écrits*, (Escurolles, Fideliter, 1989), p. 217. He subsequently expressed his criticisms in the works *Un évêque parle. Ecrits et allocutions, 1963–1975*, Paris, Dominique Martin Morin, 1975; *J'accuse le Concile*, Martigny, Editions Saint-Gabriel, 1976; *Lettre ouverte aux catholiques perplexes*, Paris, Albin Michel, 1985; *Ils l'ont découronné*, Escurolles, Editions Fideliter, 1987. "It is difficult – observes Daniele Menozzi – to explain the reasons for this change of line on the basis of the documentation up to now available" (D. Menozzi, *La Chiesa cattolica e la secolarizzazione*, p. 202).

[101]The bibliography on this subject is vast. See especially: Joseph Cardinal Ratzinger, *The Ratzinger Report. An exclusive interview on the State of the Church*, San Francisco, Ignatius Press, 1986; Romano Amerio, *Iota unum. Studio delle variazioni della Chiesa cattolica nel secolo XX*, Milan-Naples, Riccardo Ricciardi Editore, 1985; Mgr Rudolf Graber, *Athanasius und die Kirche unserer Zeit*, Abensber, Verlag und Druck Joseph Kral, 1973. Cf. also Dietrich von Hildebrand, *Das Trojanische Pferd in der Stadt Gottes*, Regensburg, J. Habbel, 1969; ID, *Der verwüstete Weinberg*, Regensburg, J. Habbel, 1973; abbot Georges de Nantes, *Liber Accusationis*, delivered to the Holy See on 10 April 1973, It. tr., Rome, Arti Grafiche Pedanesi, 1973; Father Cornelio Fabro C.P.S., *L'avventura della teologia progressista*, Milan, Rusconi Editore, 1974; Bernardo Monsegú C.P., *Posconcilio*, 3 vols., Madrid, Studium, 1975–1977; Wiegand Siebel, *Katholisch oder konziliar – Die Krise der Kirche heute*, München-Wien, A. Langen-G. Müller, 1978; Cardinal Giuseppe Siri, *Getsemani – Riflessioni sul Movimento Teologico contemporaneo*, Rome, Fraternità della Santissima Vergine, 1980; George May, *Der Glauben in der nachkonziliaren Kirche*, Wien, Mediatrix Verlag, 1983.

[102] H. Jedin, "Kirchengeschichte und Kirchenkrise", Aachener Kirchenzeitung, 29 December 1968 e 5 January 1969, It. tr. L'Osservatore Romano, 15 January 1969.

tary democracy through the introduction of the right to participate on all three levels of ecclesiastical life, in the universal Church, in the diocese and in the parish;

"3. desacralization of the priesthood;

"4. free 'structuring' of the liturgical celebration in place of the fulfilment of the Opus Dei;

"5. ecumenism as protestantization."[103]

In that same 1968, in a speech which was a to be a landmark, Paul VI stated:

> "the Church finds herself in an hour of disquiet, of self-criticism, one might even say of self-destruction. It is like an acute and complex interior upheaval, which no one expected after the Council. (...) The Church is also being wounded by those who are part of her."[104]

He returned to the subject stating that he had the feeling "that the smoke of Satan has entered the temple of God through some crack" and precisely "through windows that ought to be open to the light."[105] "It was thought that after the Council the history of the Church would enter a sunny day. It entered instead a cloudy, stormy, dark, sceptical, and uncertain day."[106]

Among the theologians and philosophers, even of progressivist extraction, who admitted and denounced the spreading of this crisis, we recall just some significant pronouncements:

Cardinal Henri de Lubac, former exponent of the *"nouvelle théologie"*:

> "It is a new Church, different from that of Christ, which they desire to establish; they desire to effect an anthropocentric society, threatened by an immanent apostasy; we are at the mercy of a general movement of stumbling and surrender, of Irenism and of accommodation."[107]

---

[103] H. Jedin, *Storia della mia vita*, pp. 326-7.

[104] Paul VI, Speech to Lombard Seminary in Rome, of 7 December 1968, in *Insegnamenti di Paolo VI*, (Rome, Tipografia Poliglotta Vaticana, 1968), vol. VI, pp. 1188-9. The majority of Catholics, wrote Dr Plinio, would like to know "what is this smoke, what are these ideological labels and human instruments that are used by Satan as sprays for this smoke? What does this demolition consist of and how does one explain that this demolition is, oddly, an auto-demolition?", P. Corrêa de Oliveira, "Clareza", Folha de S. Paulo, 16 August 1978.

[105] Paul VI, Address for the ninth anniversary of his coronation of 29 June 1972, in *Insegnamenti*, vol. X, pp. 707-08.

[106] Ibid.

[107] Cardinal Henri de Lubac S.J., Speech to the International Congress of Theology in Toronto, August 1967, cit. in B. Monsegù, *Posconcilio*, vol. III, p. 371.

The Rt Rev Rudolf Graber, bishop of Regensburg:

"What happened then, over 1600 years ago (the Arian crisis), is being repeated today, but with two or three differences. Today, Alexandria represents the whole Church, shaken to its foundations." "Why is so little done to strengthen the pillars of the Church to avoid its collapse? If there is still someone who is convinced that the events that are taking place within the Church are marginal, or that they are transitory difficulties, it means that he is unrecoverable. But the responsibility of the heads of the Church is even greater, if they do not deal with these problems or if they believe that they can remedy the evil with some patchwork. No: here we are dealing with everything; here we are dealing with the Church; here we are dealing with a sort of Copernican revolution that has exploded in the very bosom of the Church, of a gigantic revolution in the Church."[108]

The Stigmatine father Cornelio Fabro, adviser to the Congregation for the Doctrine of the Faith:

"Thus the Church, a bit at a time, as regards the decision of the Pastors, has slipped into a situation of a lack of guidance which, both in the field of doctrine and in that of discipline, operates with growing disintegration. (...) The terrible words of the Gospel – 'You were like sheep without a shepherd' – must be applied in a large scale to the present situation of the Church."[109]

The Passionist father Enrico Zoffoli, member of the Pontifical Academy of St Thomas Aquinas:

"Today the Church is involved in overcoming perhaps the most serious of all crises: the storm that erupted because of modernism is still raging after almost a century. (...) The confusion of the faithful is universal, distressing, and the common disapproval reaches its climax when they hear, from the men of the Church, speeches and receive advice, assist at some of their rites, note an attitude that is so strange and unseemly, as to raise the suspicion that Christianity is an enormous deception. For this and more, are they not even tempted to atheism?" "The consequences are disastrous. (...) There is no truth that, under some aspect, does not become as if it were falsified. Some are denied, others unspoken, others derided, others adjusted in an unrecognizable way."[110]

---

[108] Mgr R. Graber, *Athanasius und die Kirche unserer* Zeit, It. tr. Sant'Atanasio *e la Chiesa del nostro tempo*, (Brescia, Civiltà, 1974), p. 28, 79.
[109] C. Fabro C.P.S., *L'avventura della teologia progressista*, pp. 288–9.
[110] Enrico Zoffoli C.P., *Chiesa ed uomini di Chiesa*, (Udine, Il Segno, 1994), pp. 46–8, 35.

On the eve of his death, in 1975, Mgr Josemaría Escrivá de Balaguer, beatified by John Paul II, stated:

"When I became a priest, the Church of God seemed as strong as a rock, without a crack. It offered an external aspect that immediately expressed unity: it was a marvellously solid block. Now, to look at it with human eyes, it seems like a building in ruins, a mound of sand that is crumbling, is trodden upon, scattered, destroyed.... The Pope has sometimes said that the Church is destroying itself. Hard words, tremendous! But this cannot happen because Jesus promised that the Holy Spirit will always assist it, until the end of time. And what will we do? Pray, pray...."[111]

John Paul II, who had succeeded Paul VI after the very short pontificate of John Paul I,[112] from the very beginning admitted the existence of the crisis in unequivocal terms:

"One must be realistic and acknowledge with a deep and pained sentiment that a great part of today's Christians feel lost, confused, perplexed, and even disillusioned: ideas contradicting the revealed and unchanging Truth have been spread far and wide; outright heresies in the dogmatic and moral fields have been disseminated, creating doubt, confusion, and rebellion; even the liturgy has been altered. Immersed in intellectual and moral 'relativism' and therefore in permissiveness, Christians are tempted by atheism, agnosticism, a vaguely moralistic illuminism, a sociological Christianity, without defined dogmas and without objective morality."[113]

However the document which caused the most commotion was the now famous *Rapporto sulla Fede* by Cardinal Joseph Ratzinger, Prefect of the Congregation for the Doctrine of the Faith:

"It is incontestable that the last ten years have been decidedly unfavourable for the Catholic church. Developments since the Council seem to be in striking contrast to the expectations of all, beginning with those of John XXIII and Paul VI. Christians are

---

[111] Cit. in Pilar Urbano, *Josemaría Escrivá, romano*, (Milan, Leonardo, 1996), pp. 442-3.

[112] During the conclave of August 1978, in describing the legend of Wyszynski the *Cunctator* who, "playing for time" with Communism, would have saved the cause of the Church, Plinio Corrêa de Oliveira foretold the possibility of an election of the Primate of Poland to the throne of Peter (P. Corrêa de Oliveira, "O Cunctator, um maximalista?", Folha de S. Paulo, 24 August 1978). The conclave chose Cardinal Albino Luciani, Patriarch of Venice, but after a month it had to meet again and elected to the Pontifical throne the Archbishop of Cracow, Karol Wojtila, with the name of John Paul II.

[113] John Paul II, Speech of 6 February 1981, L'Osservatore Romano of 7 February 1981.

once again a minority, more than they have ever been since the end of antiquity. (...) What the Popes and the Council Fathers were expecting was a new Catholic unity, and instead one has encountered a dissension which – to use the words of Paul VI – seems to have passed over from self-criticism to self-destruction. There had been the expectation of a new enthusiasm, and instead too often it has ended in boredom and discouragement. There had been the expectation of a step forward, and instead one found oneself facing a progressive process of decadence that to a large measure has been unfolding under the sign of a summons to a presumed 'spirit of the Council' and by so doing has actually and increasingly discredited it. (...) the Church of the post-conciliar period is a huge construction site. But a critical spirit later added that it was a construction site where the blueprint had been lost and everyone continues to build according to his taste."[114] "My diagnosis is that we are dealing with an authentic crisis and that it must be treated and cured."[115]

The description of the crisis outlined by Cardinal Ratzinger soon became a fact. Twenty years after the conclusion of the Council, La Civiltà Cattolica, which, above all through the work of Father Caprile, had enthusiastically followed the event step by step, wrote:

"It is undeniable that in the twenty-year period after the Council there was, first of all, a crisis of faith: all Christian revelation, in its fundamental dogmas – existence and knowability of God, Trinity, Incarnation, Redemption, Resurrection of Jesus, eternal life, Church, Eucharist – was questioned and an attempt was made to reinterpret it according to philosophical and scientific categories that empty it of its authentic supernatural content. (...) Unlike those of the past, the current crisis is a radical and global one: radical because it attacks the very roots of the faith and of Christian life; global, because it attacks Christianity in all its aspects."[116]

---

[114] Cardinal J. Ratzinger, *The Ratzinger Report*, pp. 29–30. "It appears to me that, by now, something in this last decade has become quite clear: an interpretation of the Council that understands its dogmatic texts as only being the prelude to a Conciliar spirit yet to reach maturity; which considers them all only as an introduction to *Gaudium et Spes*, and this text, in turn, is regarded as the point of departure of a long straight line towards an ever greater future with what is called progress. Such an interpretation is not only in contradiction with the intention and desires of the Council Fathers themselves, but the course of events has brought it to the absurd. The spirit of the council has turned against its letter and has been reduced to a vague distillate, the product of an evolution supposedly coming from the pastoral Constitution. It has become a spectre and leads to emptiness. The devastation caused by such a mentality is so evident as not to be seriously contestable." Cardinal J. Ratzinger, *Les principes de la Théologie catholique*, p. 436.
[115] Cardinal J. Ratzinger, *The Ratzinger Report*, p. 34.

Plinio Corrêa de Oliveira, from his first work to the last, *Nobility and Analogous Traditional Elites*,[117] did not ignore this crisis, positioning it in the wide historical view of *Revolution and Counter-Revolution*. Its point of view is not that of the theologian, but of the lay person, the philosopher, the historian and the man of action. It is not on the theological merit of the Conciliar documents, but on the reality of the facts and their historical consequences that he bases the denunciation of "the Second Vatican Council's enigmatic, disconcerting, incredible, and apocalyptically tragic silence about communism".[118]

"It was the desire of this Council – he wrote – to be pastoral and not dogmatic. And, in fact, it did not have a dogmatic scope. But its omission regarding communism might make it go down in history as the a-pastoral Council. (...) The work of this Council cannot be inscribed as effectively pastoral either in history or in the Book of Life.

"It is painful to say this. But, in this sense, the evidence singles out the Second Vatican Council as one of the greatest calamities, if not the greatest, in the history of the Church.[119] From the Council on, the '*smoke of Satan*' penetrated the Church in unbelievable proportions.[120] And this smoke is spreading day by day, with the terrible force of gases in expansion. To the scandal of uncountable souls, the Mystical Body of Christ entered a sinister process of self-destruction, as it were.

"History narrates the innumerable dramas the Church has suffered in the twenty centuries of her existence: oppositions that germinated outside her and tried to destroy her from outside; malignancies that formed within her, were cut off by her, and thereafter ferociously tried to destroy her from outside.

"When, however, has history witnessed an attempted demolition

---

[116] "Il Concilio causa della crisi nella Chiesa?", La Civiltà Cattolica, no. 3247, 5 October 1985. For *Civiltà Cattolica*, as for many authors, the crisis of the Church is simply the reflection of the even greater crisis that struck Western society in the 60s and 70s. "This crisis is due to the wave of secularism, permissiveness and hedonism that in those years struck the Western world with such violence as to upset all the moral and social defences built for so many centuries of "Christianity" (even if more in name than in fact)" (ibid).

[117] In this work, the Brazilian thinker speaks of a "crisis of totally unprecedented magnitude that afflicts the Catholic Church, the pillar and foundation of morality and the good order of society". P. Corrêa de Oliveira, *Nobility and Analogous Traditional Elites*, p. 128.

[118] This judgement is expressed in the Appendix of 1977 to P. Corrêa de Oliveira, *Revolution and Counter-Revolution*, p. 144.

[119] On the calamities of the Postconciliar phase of the Church, of fundamental importance is the historical declaration of Paul VI of 29 June 1972, pp. 707–08.

[120] Ibid, p. 707.

of the Church like the present one? No longer undertaken by an adversary, it was termed a *'self-destruction'*[121] in a most lofty pronouncement having world-wide repercussion?"[122]

The term "self-destruction", used by Plinio Corrêa de Oliveira to describe the crisis of the Church, recalls that used by Paul VI, to whom, in the same book in which he expresses his reserves about the Council, the Brazilian thinker addresses "a tribute of filial devotion and unrestricted obedience", in the conviction that "ubi Ecclesia ibi Christus, ubi Petrus ibi Ecclesia".[123] Every theory, even the severe one just expressed on the Council, is subjected "unrestrictedly to the judgement of the Vicar of Jesus Christ and we are disposed to renounce immediately any one of them if it depart even slightly from the teaching of the Holy Church, our Mother, the Ark of Salvation, and the Gate of Heaven".[124]

The historical judgement of the Brazilian thinker about Vatican Council II coincides, as we have seen, with that of many religious figures of our day. Through the intellectual categories of *Revolution and Counter-Revolution*, however, he proposes a key to interpreting the crisis of the Church within the revolutionary process that he had studied and described. This judgement is born from a deep love for the Papacy and the Church and because of its consistency it appears quite different from the sometimes contradictory or eccentric positions of many "traditionalist" exponents or groups. The Pontifical Magisterium, the Canon Law of the Church and the perennial norms of the Catholic religion were the unchangeable points of reference of Plinio Corrêa de Oliveira and of all those who took their reference from him.[125]

---

[121] Paul VI, Speech of 7 December 1968, p. 1188.

[122] P. Corrêa de Oliveira, *Revolution and Counter-Revolution*, pp. 144–8.

[123] Ibid, pp. 167–8.

[124] Ibid, p. 168.

[125] Faced with the situation of confusion and bewilderment in which the Church is at this time, the American TFP has thus summarized its position: "1. They declare their perplexity at certain reforms and events that have occurred in the Church beginning with the pontificate of John XXIII; 2. This perplexity is characterized by incomprehension and puzzlement; 3. This perplexity is not an affirmation that there was error in those events and reforms; nor is it an affirmation that there was no error. Those who make up the TFPs are knowledgeable and cultured Catholics, but they are not specialists and do not have the conditions to resolve all the extremely complex theological, moral, canonical and liturgical questions which are at the root of this perplexity", *Let the other side also be heard: the TFPs' defense against* Fidelity*'s onslaught* (Pleasantville (NY), edited by the American Society for the Defense of Tradition, Family and Property, 1989), p. 78.

13. Old and new Ordo Missae

In the apostolic letter *Ecclesia Dei* of 2 July 1988, John Paul II decrees that

"there must be respect everywhere for the spirit of those who feel tied to the traditional Latin liturgy, through an ample and generous application of the directives which were already emanated by the Apostolic See some time ago, for the use of the Roman Missal according to the typical edition of 1962".[126]

He also asks the bishops and all those who carry out pastoral ministry in the Church to "guarantee respect for the just aspirations" of all the Catholic faithful "who feel they are tied to some previous liturgical and disciplinary forms of the Latin tradition".

This important document considers what happened in the Church after Vatican Council II: the "Lefèbvre case", which reached its climax with the unlawful Episcopal consecrations of 30 June 1988, is only the worrisome symptom of a widespread uneasiness that followed the liturgical reform that culminated in the *Novus Ordo Missae* of 1969.[127] "The theological attraction of the Tridentine Mass" stated Cardinal Alfons Stickler "compares with the theological deficiencies of the Mass that emerged from Vatican II."[128] The result of the liturgical reform, according to Cardinal Ratzinger himself, "in its concrete realization (...) was not a reanimation but a devastation".[129]

When, in 1969, the new *Ordo Missae* came into effect, some important members of the hierarchy and indeed many theologians and lay

---

[126] Cf. the text of the *Apostolic Letter* by John Paul II in AAS, vol. 80, 1988, pp. 1495-7. Many religious institutes recognized by the Holy See have obtained permission to celebrate Holy Mass according to the traditional Roman Missal. Among these, the Society of St Peter, the Fraternity of St Vincent Ferrer, Opus Sacerdotale, the Benedictine monks of the Monastery of Sainte Madeleine du Barroux, the Institute of Christ the King Sovereign Priest of Gricigliano.

[127] On 3 April 1969 the apostolic Constitution *Missale Romanum* appeared. It was made up of two documents: the *Institutio generalis missalis Romani* and the new *Ordo Missae* in the strict sense of the word, that is the new text of the Mass and of the rubrics that accompany it. One of its main authors, Mgr Annibale Bugnini, secretary of the *Consilium ad exsequendam Constitutionem de Sacra Liturgia*, in his book *La riforma liturgica (1948-1975)* (Roma, Edizioni Liturgiche, 1983), reiterates the role played by Paul VI, who he indicates as "the real achiever of the liturgical reform." "The Pope had seen everything, had followed everything, had examined everything, had approved everything" (p. 13).

[128] Cardinal Alfons M. Stickler, *L'attrattiva teologica della Messa Tridentina*, Conference held in New York at the *Christi fideles* association in May 1995.

[129] Cardinal J. Ratzinger, *Klaus Gamber. L'intrépidité d'un vrai témoin*, preface to Mgr Klaus Gamber, *La réforme liturgique en question*, (Le Barroux, Editions Sainte-Madeleine, 1992), p. 6.

persons made a close criticism of the new liturgy of the Mass.[130] Since October of that year, Cardinals Ottaviani and Bacci had presented Paul VI with a *Brief critical examen of the Novus Ordo Missae,* edited by a select group of theologians of different nationalities. In the letter they addressed to the Pontiff, it was stated that

"the Novus Ordo Missae (...) represents both as a whole and in its particularities a remarkable departure from the Catholic theology of the Holy Mass, as formulated in the twenty-second session of the Tridentine Council which, by definitely fixing the 'canons' of the rite, erected an insuperable barrier against any heresy that should attack the integrity of the mystery".[131]

From that date on the appeals of faithful of every nationality began to multiply: they asked for the re-establishment, or at least the *"par condicio"* for the traditional Mass.[132] We should also mention a *"memorandum"* in 1971 in which over one hundred important personages from the whole world asked the Holy See "to consider with the greatest seriousness the great responsibility that it would have in the history of the human spirit if it should not allow the traditional Mass to continue to exist".[133]

Plinio Corrêa de Oliveira carefully followed the phases of the controversy that developed in the press and specialized magazines and kept his fellow countrymen abreast of the matter.[134] The problem

---

[130] Among the numerous critical studies on the "New Mass" and Liturgical Reform, for the most part composed of lay studies, we mention: A. Vidigal Xavier da Silveira, *La nouvelle Messe de Paul VI qu'en penser?*; Jean Vaquié, *La Révolution liturgique*, Chiré-en-Montreuil, Diffusion de la Pensée Française, 1971; Louis Salleron, *La Nouvelle Messe*, Paris, Nouvelles Editions Latines, 1976 (1971); Wolfgang Waldstein, *Hirtensorge und Liturgiereform*, Schaan (Fl), Lumen Gentium, 1977; Mgr K. Gamber, *Die Reform der Römischen Liturgie*, Regensburg, F. Pustet, 1979 (this work in the French version (cit.) contains prefaces by Cardinals Silvio Oddi, Joseph Ratzinger and Alfons M. Stickler); Michael Davies, *Pope Paul's New Mass*, Dickinson (Texas), The Angelus Press, 1980.

[131] The study, promoted by Una Voce-Italia, was republished by the same association together with a *New Critical Examen of the "Novus Ordo Missae"* the work of a French liturgicist and theologian (*Il Novus Ordo Missae: due esami critici*, Una Voce, suppl. to nos. 48-9 of the January-July 1979 bulletin).

[132] Three international pilgrimages of Catholics took place in Rome to reconfirm loyalty to the traditional Mass and to the catechism of St Pius X (Cf. Guglielmo Rospigliosi, "La manifestazione dei cattolici tradizionalisti riconfermano la fedeltà al messale e al catechismo", Il Tempo, 19 June 1970). A collection of the appeals up to 1980 in ... *Et pulsanti aperietur* (Luke 11:10), Clarens, FI-Una Voce, 1980.

[133] Among those who signed were: Romano Amerio, Augusto Del Noce, Marius Schneider, Marcel Brion, Julien Green, Henri de Montherlant, Jorge Luis Borges, the English writers Agatha Christie, Robert Graves, Graham Green, Malcolm Muggeridge, Bernard Wall, the violinist Yehudi Menuhin. Cf. the text and the list of those who signed, Una Voce, no. 7, July 1971.

concerned every Catholic and, as such, the Brazilian thinker could not be indifferent since he was so attentive and sensitive to every matter that concerned the Church in any way. He studied the matter and had it studied, and sympathized with the study of Arnaldo V. Xavier da Silveira.[135] However, at the request of a very highly placed ecclesiastical authority, he abstained from going public with the subject matter of the book.[136] The conclusions of the book were the object of a solid and profound consensus among the members of the several TFPs without, however, becoming an official position of the associations.[137]

We may perhaps notice an analogy between the position that he assumed with regard to the *Ostpolitik* and that towards the *Novus Ordo* of Paul VI: in both cases, he demonstrated a "resistance" to

---

[134] Cf., for example, "O direito de saber", Folha de S. Paulo, 25 January 1970 and, Catolicismo, no. 230, February 1970, in which he informed the Brazilian public of the first demonstrations of resistance to the *Novus Ordo*. Bishop de Castro Mayer published on his part a *Carta Pastoral sôbre o Santo Sacríficio da Missa*, in no. 227 (November 1969) of *Catolicismo*. In 1971, a large and documented article appeared edited by Gregorio Vivanco Lopes, "Sôbre a nova missa: repercussões que o público brasileiro ainda não conhece", Catolicismo, no. 242, February 1971.

[135] The already referred to study by Arnaldo Xavier da Silveira profoundly analyzes the *Novus Ordo* taking into consideration complex theological, canonical and moral problems of authority. The book was launched in São Paulo in 1970 and was privately circulated before being published in French in 1975 under the title *La Nouvelle Messe de Paul VI: qu'en penser?*. The work merged three studies that had already been published in portuguese: *Considerações sobre o Ordo Missae de Paulo VI* (São Paulo, June 1970), *Modificações introduzidas no Ordo de 1969* (São Paulo, August 1970), *A infalibilidade das leis eclesiásticas* (São Paulo, January 1971). "In his book, Mr. Arnaldo V. Xavier da Silveira expressly affirms his unshakeable fidelity to the doctrine and discipline of the Church. And if he raises certain delicate problems of Theology or Canon Law, he does so by first stating that he obeys, to the fullest extent perscribed by Canon Law, what the Church herself decides. This is precisely the TFP's position. Therefore, our consciences are entirely tranquil as regards our entire union with the Holy Roman Catholic and Apostolic Church" (P. Corrêa de Oliveira, *Sobre o decreto antiTFP de D. Isnard*, Folha de S. Paulo, 27 May 1973; P. Corrêa de Oliveira, "The Vatican policy of distension").

[136] Cf., *Sobre o decreto antiTFP de D. Isnard*.

[137] "Once the position of the TFPs as associations has been defined, it should be observed that their members and volunteers, as Catholics, personally feel the repercussions of the specifically religious problems that have convulsed the Church ever since the Second Vatican Council. It is inevitable that, simply in their capacity as Catholics, they should exchange their opinions abut these matters. In fact, this exchange of opinions has never given rise to dissensions. On the contrary, a firm and well matured consensus has arisen regarding the principal themes concerning the mysterious process of self-destruction the Church is in and about the smoke of Satan that has penetrated Her. (...) The entirely personal consensus of the members and volunteers of the TFP in certain matters foreign to the civic sphere does not consitute the official thinking of the TFP. But it gives rise to an extra-official consensus in the TFP. Cf. *Imbroglio, Detraction, Delirium. Remarks on a report about the TFPs*, (Pleasntville (NY), The American Society for the Defense of Tradition, Family and Property, 1983), pp. 113-14.

what he felt was damaging to the faith and an imposition on his conscience.[138] But whereas the position he assumed towards *Ostpolitik* was public, because it concerned that social order that is the responsibility of the laity to establish according to the doctrine of the Church, his attitude towards the new Mass remained extra-official and personal. Encouraged by the opinions of numerous distinguished bishops and theologians, Plinio Corrêa de Oliveira wished to remain faithful to the liturgical tradition in which he had been educated, convinced that the problem, in any case, lay within the more extensive crisis of the post-Conciliar Church, and that only in this light could the problem be one day resolved.

14. Passion of Christ, Passion of the Church

"Rome" one of the leaders of modernism had written at the beginning of the century "cannot be destroyed in a day, but it should be allowed to fall into dust and ashes gradually and inoffensively; then we would have a new religion and a new Decalogue."[139] How can we fail to see in what subsequently happened an attempt to fulfil this sinister "prophecy"?

Plinio Corrêa de Oliveira sensed this process of dissolution within the Church, he suffered from it deeply and used all his energy to oppose it, convinced as he was that there was no salvation outside union with the Papacy.

"It is a sign and condition of spiritual health that the faithful, in everything pertaining to the safety, glory and tranquillity of the Roman Pontificate, be extremely sensitive and have a most delicate and lively sensibility. After love of God, this is one of the highest loves that Religion teaches us. (...) *Ubi Petrus, ibi Ecclesia* – where St Peter is, there is the Church. The Catholic Church is so linked with the Chair of St Peter that where no Papal approval exists, Catholicism does not exist. The true faithful knows that the Pope synthesizes and contains in himself the whole Catholic Church. And this is so real and indissoluble that, if by some absur-

---

[138] The Dominican, Father Roger Thomas Calmel, in an article that appeared in the number of November 1971 of *Itinéraires*, dealing with the problem of assistance at the New Mass, affirmed that "the conditions of legal obligation have been annulled", while there remained the serious obligation to openly confess one's faith in the Catholic Mass ("L'assistance à la Messe suivie de l'apologie pour le Canon Romain", Itinéraires, no. 157, November 1971, p. 6). Cf. also *A Missa Nova: um caso de consciência, compilado sob a responsabilidade dos padres tradicionalistas da Diocese de Campos*, São Paulo, Artpress, 1982.

[139] George Tyrrell, *Lettres a Henri Brémond*, (Paris, Aubier, 1971), p. 287.

dity all the Bishops of the world, all the priests, all the faithful abandoned the Supreme Pontiff, the true Catholics would gather around him. Because all holiness, all authority, all supernatural virtue, absolutely everything the Church has, without exception without conditions or restrictions, is subordinated, conditioned, dependent on union with the Chair of St Peter. The most sacred institutions, the most venerable works, the holiest traditions, the most conspicuous people, everything that can genuinely and loftily express Catholicism and adorn the Church of God, all this would become null, cursed, sterile, worthy of eternal fire and the wrath of God if it be separated from the Roman Pontiff."[140]

Plinio Corrêa de Oliveira constantly, to the very end, reaffirmed this love for the Papacy:

"Today I do not stand before the Holy See with the enthusiasm of my youth, but with an even greater, a much greater enthusiasm. In fact, to the extent that I live, think and gain experience, I increasingly understand and love the Pope and the Papacy."[141]

The history of the twentieth century is that of the progressive revelation of a tragedy. At the centre of the drama, is the Holy Catholic Church, apparently submerged by the waves of a terrible storm miraculously sustained by the infallible promise of its Divine Founder. Plinio Corrêa de Oliveira saw in this tragedy the Passion of the Church, reflected in the history of the Passion of Our Lord Jesus Christ. "How many are they who live in union with the Church during this moment that is tragic as the Passion was tragic, this crucial moment of history when all mankind is choosing to be for Christ or against Christ?"[142] He had dedicated his life to the Church,[143] and to it he gave himself with all the generosity of Veronica.

"The representation of the Divine Face" he wrote "was made on the veil as in a painting. In the Holy Roman Catholic and Apostolic Church, His Face is reflected as in a mirror.

---

[140] P. Corrêa de Oliveira, "A guerra e o Corpo Místico", O Legionário, no. 610, 16 April 1944.
[141] P. Corrêa de Oliveira, *Il crepuscolo artificiale del Cile cattolico*, (Piacenza, Cristianità, 1973), p. 21.
[142] P. Corrêa de Oliveira, "Via Sacra, VIII estação", Catolicismo, no. 3, March 1981, En. tr. *The Way of the Cross*, (York, The American Society for the Defense of Tradition, Family and Property, 1990), eighth station, p. 37.
[143] On the night of 1 February 1975, in a meeting with members of the TFP, Plinio Corrêa de Oliveira heroically offered himself to Our Lady to suffer for the TFP in the interests of Holy Mother Church. Just 36 hours later, he was seriously injured in a road accident, near Jundiaí. The serious consequences of this accident lasted until the end of his life: they consisted of twenty years of crosses borne with a resolute and manly soul.

"In her institutions, in her doctrine, in her laws, in her unity, in her universality, in her unsurpassable catholicity, the Church is a true mirror in which our Divine Saviour is reflected.

"And we, all of us, have the grace of belonging to the Church, of being living stones of the Church!

"How we ought to give thanks for this favour! Let us not forget, however, that noblesse oblige. Belonging to the Church is a very great and very demanding thing. We must think as the Church thinks, have the Mind of the Church, proceed as the Church wishes in all the circumstances of our lives. This supposes a real Catholic sense, an authentic and complete purity of customs, and a profound and sincere piety. In other words it supposes the sacrifice of an entire lifetime.

"And what is the reward? '*Christianus alter Christus.*' I will be in an eminent way a reproduction of Christ Himself. The likeness of Christ, vivid and sacred, will be imprinted on my own soul."[144]

---

[144] P. Corrêa de Oliveira, *The Way of the Cross*, sixth station, pp. 28-9.

Chapter VII

Towards the Reign of Mary

"Beyond the highly probable
sadness and punishments
towards which we advance,
we have the sacred lights
of the dawn of the Reign of Mary."

1. The chaos of the end of the millennium

Having begun in a climate of optimistic hope in the future, the twentieth century ends in an atmosphere of uncertainty and confusion. The word "chaos", often used by Plinio Corrêa de Oliveira to indicate the anarchic goal of the Revolution, has entered into general use, in the Nineties, by the media and even in the simple conversations of the man on the street, to indicate a total lack of clarity and of points of reference. The euphoria with which the West had welcomed the end of the cold war, the liberation of the East European countries from Communism, the reunification of Germany, was succeeded by an increasingly widespread feeling of anxiety and worry.[1]

The "crisis" described forty years in advance by Plinio Corrêa de Oliveira in *Revolution and Counter-Revolution* seems to have arrived at its final maturation. Never before in its history has mankind seemed

---

[1] Nowadays, according to Ignacio Ramonet, "one can actually talk of the 'geo-politics of chaos' to describe the epoch the world is presently experiencing" ("La planète des désordres", in an issue dedicated to the "geopolitics of chaos", Manière de Voir 33 – Le Monde Diplomatique, February 1997). Already in 1991 the *Corriere della Sera* carried an editorial significantly headlined "The world disorder", its editor Ugo Stille stated: "The year 1990 began under the sign of hope and optimism, 1991 appears as a rather difficult year, full of unknowns and dangers, against a background of turbulence and confusion" (U. Stille, "Il disordine mondiale", Corriere della Sera, 2 January 1991). Among the new literature on the subject, cf. Pierre Lellouche, *Le nouveau monde. De l'ordre de Yalta au désordre des nations*, Paris, Grasset, 1992; Gianni Statera, Roberto Gritti, *Il nuovo disordine mondiale*, Milan, Franco Angeli, 1994; Alberto Cavallari, *L'Atlante del disordine. La crisi geopolitica di fine secolo*, Milan, Garzanti, 1994. "The most superficial examination of the situation — wrote Plinio Corrêa de Oliveira in 1992 — shows that the word 'chaos', which until a short time ago was thought to be a scarecrow by people considered sensible, has become a fashionable word." P. Corrêa de Oliveira, "Os dedos do caos e os dedos de Deus", Catolicismo, no. 499, July 1992.

so far from the ideal model of Christian civilization as indicated by the Pontifical Magisterium.

The century coming to an end, declared John Paul II at the beginning of his Pontificate, "has so far been one of great calamities for man, of great devastations, not only material ones, but also moral ones, indeed perhaps above all moral ones".[2] In his encyclical *Evangelium Vitae*, the Pope confirmed this evaluation of our time: "The twentieth century will have been an era of massive attacks on life, an endless series of wars and a continual taking of innocent life."[3] This judgement reverses the optimistic one that had greeted the dawn of the century, to the rhythm of the Excelsior Ballet. The nineteen hundreds will not be remembered as the triumphant era of Progress, but as the age of mass human sacrifices and of technological barbarism. The globalization of wars, the birth of the concentration camp universe, abortion on a world-wide scale, are different but coinciding expressions of the great holocaust offered in this century to the myth of Modernity.[4]

The "dream of construction" of a new world is today fading and is being succeeded by the "dream of destruction" that attacks the building of modernity, knocking it down from its foundations.[5] With the failure of the pseudo "new order" advocated by totalitarian regimes, the world sinks into a "new world disorder" in which the self-destructive march of the Revolution seems to find its definite conclusion. "Chaos and post-modernity are concepts that are growing ever closer together, up to the point that they tend to melt into one another."[6]

The great philosophies of history that were born with the French Revolution – Hegelianism, Positivism, Marxism – show that they are incapable of understanding the meaning of the events and forecasting their direction. The crisis of the idea of Progress unmasks the deception of a profane philosophy of history that is opposed to Christian philosophy. The Christian theology of history, which is the basis of Counter-Revolutionary thinking, re-emerges vigorously in all its up-to-dateness.

---

[2] John Paul II, Encyclical *Redemptor Hominis* of 4 March 1979, no. 17.

[3] John Paul II, Encyclical *Evangelium Vitae* of 25 March 1995, no. 17. This judgement reiterates that already pronounced by the Pontiff on 14 August 1993 in Denver, on the occasion of the VIII World Youth Day, AAS, vol. 86, 1994, p. 419.

[4] The first to demolish this myth are today its authors themselves. Cf. for example the volume of the famous English Marxist historian Eric Hobsbawm, *The Age of Extremes. The Short Twentieth Century, 1914–1991,* London, Penguin Group, 1994.

[5] R. de Mattei, *1900–2000. Due sogni si succedono*, p. 11–28. On the new theory of chaos, cf. also James Gleick, *Chaos*, London, Heineman, 1989.

[6] P. Corrêa de Oliveira, *Os dedos do caos e os dedos de Deus*.

2. The theology of history of Plinio Corrêa de Oliveira

If it is true, as Cardinal Ratzinger affirms, that "a theology and philosophy of history are born above all during periods of crisis of the history of man",[7] it can be understood how Plinio Corrêa de Oliveira's uninterrupted reflection on his own era is in proportion to the size and depth of the contemporary crisis.

This reflection, like every Christian theology of history, takes shape according to two historical dimensions: one natural, founded on the freedom of man; the other supernatural, based on the intervention of Providence in human facts. "In truth, from the Catholic point of view" observes Donoso Cortés "there is only one general reason for all human facts, and this is Divine Providence."[8]

For Christianity, history is not only *magistra vitae*, but *historia salutis*, sacred, universal history, that embraces the future of all mankind.[9] It is "sacred", because its author is God himself and its centre is Jesus Christ and His Mystical Body, the Holy Catholic Church, in a course of events that begins with Creation and concludes with the Judgement at the end of time.

The first great Christian theology of history was, as Leo XIII affirms, the Augustinian theology:

"First of all Augustine, the great doctor of the Church, conceived and perfected the philosophy of history. Those who came after him, worthy of being remembered in this branch of studies, took Augustine as their author and their teacher."[10]

In this perspective, the history of mankind appears as a struggle between the City of Satan and the City of God, described in the *De Civitate Dei*: "two societies have issued from two kinds of love. Worldly society has flowered from a selfish love which dares to despise even God, whereas the communion of saints is rooted in a

---

[7] J. Ratzinger, *La théologie de l'histoire de saint Bonaventure*, Fr. tr. (Paris, Presses Universitaires de France, 1988), p. 1.

[8] J. Donoso Cortés, *Estudios sobre la Historia*, in *Obras*, vol. II, p. 234. "*Prorsus divina Providentia regna* - St Augustine had written - *constituuntur humana*", St Augustine *De Civitate Dei*, book V, chap. 1, no. 1.

[9] On Christian theology of history, always authoritative is the great sketch by Bishop Jacques-Bénigne Bossuet, *Discours sur l'histoire universelle*, Paris, Flammarion, 1966 (1681); cf. also C. Fabro C.P.S., *La storiografia nel pensiero cristiano*, in GAF, vol. V, 1954, pp. 311-40; R.-T. Calmel O.P., *Théologie de l'histoire*, Paris, Dominique Martin Morin, 1984 (1966).

[10] Leo XIII, Letter *Saepenumero considerantes* of 18 August 1883.

love of God that is ready to trample on self."[11] The love of God and the love of oneself are also for Plinio Corrêa de Oliveira the poles that offer the ultimate cue for reading historical events.

"In other words, either the world converts and faithfully reproduces the Augustinian vision of the *'civitas Dei'*, where each nation takes the love of God to the point of renouncing everything that harms other nations; or otherwise the world will be that city of the devil where everyone takes love of self to the point of forgetting about God."[12]

The theology of history of Plinio Corrêa de Oliveira, before having its ideal reference point in the Augustinian vision of the two cities, was however concretely experienced in the practice of the Ignatian meditation on the two standards, "one of Christ, our supreme leader and lord, the other of Lucifer, the deadly enemy of our human nature".[13]

"St Ignatius was right" he wrote "to expect great fruit from his meditation on the two standards. Since the panorama of the world was crystal clear, it was as good as a page of apologetics."[14]

This theological vision of Dr Plinio is born of and can especially be related to the famous and not less profound work *Treatise on the true devotion to the Blessed Virgin* written by a great saint of the eighteenth century St Louis Marie Grignion de Montfort.[15]

Commenting on the words of *Genesis* quoted in the *Treatise*:

"I will put enmities between you and the woman, and thy seed and her seed: she shall crush your head, and you will lie in wait for her heel", St Louis Marie de Montfort teaches: "God only

---

[11] St Augustine *De Civitate Dei*, book XIV, chap. 28. On the Augustinian concept of the two cities, cf. Mgr Antonino Romeo, *L'antitesi delle due Città spirituali di sant'Agostino*, in *Sanctus Augustinus Vitae Spiritualis Magister*, (Rome, Analecta Augustiniana, 1959), vol. I, pp. 113–46; Michele F. Sciacca, *Interpretazione del concetto di storia in S. Agostino*, Tolentino, Edizioni Agostiniane, 1960.

[12] P. Corrêa de Oliveira, "Um remédio que agravará o mal", O Legionário, no. 491, 8 February 1942.

[13] St Ignatius of Loyola, *Spiritual Exercises*, nos. 136–8.

[14] P. Corrêa de Oliveira, "3ᵃ Acto? ", O Legionário, no. 419, 22 September 1940.

[15] St Louis Marie Grignion de Montfort, *A treatise on the true devotion to the Blessed Virgin* (1712), London, Burns Oates & Washbourne, 1937. This work, composed in 1712, remained hand-written and buried "in the darkness and silence of a trunk" for over a century, as its author had foreseen. Found in 1842, it had a widespread distribution, with over 300 editions in about thirty languages. In England it was translated and spread by Fr Frederick William Faber of the Oratory in 1862.

ever made or formed one enmity, but one that is irreconcilable, and that will last, indeed will increase until the end of time: that between Mary, his worthy Mother and the devil; between the children and servants of the Holy Virgin, and the children and followers of Lucifer."[16]

For Plinio Corrêa de Oliveira, as for St Louis Marie de Montfort the antithesis between these two spiritual families is destined to unrelentlessly divide mankind until the end of history. This war is none other than the historical extension of the opposition between the Virgin and the serpent, between the spiritual descendants of Mary and the spiritual descendants of the devil.

"The suppression of this struggle for an ecumenical reconciliation between the Virgin and the serpent, between the race of the Virgin and the race of the serpent" comments Plinio Corrêa de Oliveira "leads to the regression (or rather the retrogression) to the proud tower of Babel, that Neo-Paganism tries in every way to rebuild."[17]

For St Louis de Montfort, as for St Ignatius and St Augustine, it is a case of moral and not ontological dualism, according to which history cannot be explained without the action of evil, which with "infernal strategy, uses every means and commits all its forces to destroying the faith, morals, the Kingdom of God".[18] God in fact "judged it better and more in accord with His power to bring some greater good even out of evil than to permit no evil whatsoever".[19] It is against this background, according to Plinio Corrêa de Oliveira, that "the struggle between the Church and the Revolution, a struggle that would be mortal if one of the contenders were not immortal",[20] is situated.

3. St Louis Marie Grignion de Montfort and the *Treatise on the true devotion to the Blessed Virgin*

St Louis Marie Grignion de Montfort was born in Brittany on 31 January 1673 and died in Saint-Laurent-sur-Sèvre, in the Vendée,

---

[16] St Louis Marie Grignion de Montfort, *A treatise on the true devotion*, no. 52.
[17] P. Corrêa de Oliveira, "Volta à Torre de Babel? ", Folha de S. Paulo, 12 August 1980.
[18] Pius XII, Radiomessage *Bendito seja o Senhor*, of 13 May 1946, in DR, vol. VIII, p. 89.
[19] St Augustine *De Civitate Dei*, book XXII, chap. 1, no. 2.
[20] P. Corrêa de Oliveira, *Revolution and Counter-Revolution*, p. 167.

worn out by his apostolic labours on 28 April 1716.[21] His life, as has already been observed,[22] coincides almost perfectly within the chronological limits (1680–1715) of the period covered by Paul Hazard in his work, by now rightly a classic, on the crisis of the European conscience.[23] De Montfort was beatified by Leo XIII on 22 January 1888 and proclaimed a saint by Pius XII on 20 July 1947.[24] He, declared Pius XII, was "the apostle, par excellence, of Poitou, of Brittany and of Vendée". The Vendeans who took up arms against the revolutionary impiety were descendants of the country people whom the great saint, with his popular missions, had preserved from the germs of the revolution, so much so that, as the same Pontiff affirms, it was written without exaggeration "that the Vendée of 1793 was the work of his hands".[25]

"The great incentive for his whole apostolic ministry, his great secret for attracting and giving souls to Jesus, is his devotion to Mary."[26] Our Lady, in her role of Mediatrix between Jesus Christ and men, was the object of the ardent meditation of de Montfort. Around the universal Mediation of Mary, the French saint, according to Plinio Corrêa de Oliveira, "built a whole Mariology that is the greatest monument of all times to the Virgin Mother of God".[27]

Plinio Corrêa de Oliveira and St Louis Marie de Montfort, in a certain sense, necessarily had to find one another. Devotion to Our Lady was in fact the foundation of the spirituality of Doctor Plinio who learnt it as a child through his mother's example, especially one

---

[21] Among the numerous biographies of St Louis Marie Grignion de Montfort, the best remain the oldest. Cf. especially P.-J. Picot de Clorivière, *La vie de M. Louis-Marie Grignion de Montfort*, Paris-St. Malo-Rennes 1785. The main works of the Saint are: *The Love of Eternal Wisdom* (1703–04), *Letters* (1694–1716), *Hymns* (1700–16), *True Devotion to the Blessed Virgin* and *The Secret of Mary* (1712), *The Secret of the Rosary* (1712), *Prayer for Missionaries* (1713), *Letter to the Friends of the Cross* (1714), *Original Rule of the Daughters of Wisdom* (1715), now collected in *God alone. The Collected Writings of St. Louis Marie de Montfort*, New York, Montfort Publications, 1987. The Daughters of Hope, the Missionaries of the Company of Mary, the Brothers of Christian Education of St Gabriel refer to de Montfort as their founder or spiritual inspirer. On 8 June 1981 the superiors general of these religious families addressed an appeal to John Paul II that St Louis Marie de Montfort be declared a 'Doctor of the Church' "considering his great holiness, the importance of his doctrine, the remarkable influence that he continues to exercise over the universal Church" (Personal letter to the Holy Father).

[22] Marco Tangheroni, Introduction to St Louis Marie Grignion de Montfort, *Il segreto ammirabile del Santo Rosario*, It. tr. (Siena, Edizioni Cantagalli, 1975), pp. 7–8.

[23] P. Hazard, *The European mind*.

[24] Pius XII, Homily for the canonization of St Louis Marie Grignion de Montfort of 21 July 1947, in DR, vol. IX, pp. 177–83.

[25] Ibid, p. 178.

[26] Ibid, p. 182.

[27] P. Corrêa de Oliveira, Prologue to the Argentine edition of *Revolución y Contra-Revolución*, (Buenos Aires, Tradición, Familia, Propriedad, 1970), p. 16.

aspect of it: that of the divine maternity.[28] The most holy Virgin – wrote the Brazilian thinker – is

> "the incomparable quintessence, the most extensive synthesis of all the mothers that have ever existed, that exist and that will exist; of all the maternal virtues that the intelligence and heart of man can know. Even more, of those great degrees of virtue that only the saints can find, and to which only they are able to approach, flying on the wings of grace and heroism. She is the mother of all children and of all mothers. She is the mother of all men. She is the mother of the Man. Yes, of the God-Man, of God who was made man in the virginal womb of this Mother, to redeem all men. She is a Mother who can be defined with just one word – the sea (*mare*) – which in its turn gives origin to a name. A name that is a heaven: it is Mary."[29]

Plinio Corrêa de Oliveira, who had been a member of the Marian congregation and a Carmelite tertiary throughout his whole life, knew, practised and spread the main devotions to Our Lady: he recited the Holy Rosary daily, as well as the Angelus and the Little Office of the Immaculate Conception; he wore the scapular of Our Lady of Mount Carmel and always carried the Miraculous Medal revealed to St Catherine Labouré. But among all the devotions he found the most perfect to be the de Montfort consecration to the Most Holy Virgin known as "slavery of love".

Father Antonio Royo Marín affirms that no Marian devotion can be compared to that promoted by St Louis de Montfort in the *Treatise on the true devotion to the Blessed Virgin*.[30] It is "the book" par excellence, that contains a "sublime doctrine".[31] "This little treatise" writes Father Garrigou-Lagrange in his turn "is a treasure for the Church, as is its summary that the Blessed made for a religious sister under the title *The Secret of Mary*."[32] "It may be said" according to Father de Finance "that with him consecration reached its perfect expression."[33]

---

[28] On the divine maternity of Mary, solemnly proclaimed in Ephesus in 431, cf. J. Collantes S.J., *La fede nella Chiesa cattolica*, pp. 298–301.

[29] P. Corrêa de Oliveira, "O serviço uma alegria", Folha de S. Paulo, 13 September 1980, It. tr. Cristianità, no. 85, May 1982, p. 14.

[30] Antonio Royo Marín O.P., *La Virgen Maria*, (Madrid, BAC, 1968), p. 367.

[31] Ibid, p. 393.

[32] R. Garrigou-Lagrange O.P., *Vita spirituale*, (Rome, Città Nuova, 1965), p. 254.

[33] Joseph de Finance S.J., *Consécration*, in DSp, vol. II,2 (1953), col. 1583 (coll. 1576–83); Jean Weeger, André Derville, *Esclave (spiritualité de l')*, in DSp, vol. IV,1 (1960), coll. 1067–80; H. M. Gebhard, *La devotion du Saint Esclavage du point de vue dogmatique*, Lyon, J. Poncet, 1967.

Among the numerous testimonies, that of John Paul II himself is significant: he thus described the role of the *Treatise* in his spiritual formation:

> "Reading this book marked a decisive turning-point in my life. I say a turning-point, because it was the time of a long interior journey that coincided with my clandestine preparation for the priesthood. It was then that I happened on this unique *Treatise*, one of those books that it is not sufficient to 'have read'. I remember that I carried it with me for a long time, even in the soda factory, so much so that its lovely cover was stained with lime. Time and again, I read certain passages over and over. I soon realized that beyond the Baroque form of the book, there was something fundamental. The result was that, the devotion of my infancy and even of my youth towards the Mother of Christ was replaced by a new attitude, a devotion that came from the most profound depth of my faith, as if from the very heart of the Trintarian and Christological reality."[34]

Plinio Corrêa de Oliveira "discovered" the *Treatise* and consecrated himself to Our Lady at the age of twenty-two, after having made a novena to St Thérèse of Lisieux to ask for progress in his spiritual life. His life and work may be considered a continuous meditation on the work of St Louis Marie Grignion de Montfort.

> "If a work exists in which one can understand that 'intellectual light' full of love, of which Dante speaks, that work is the one of Grignion de Montfort."[35]
>
> "I believe I err not by affirming that, in essence, the *Treatise* is but an exposé of two great truths taught by the Church. Truths from which she extracts all the necessary consequences and under whose light is examined every spiritual life. These two truths are the spiritual maternity of Our Lady in relation to the human race and the universal mediation of Mary Most Holy."[36]

From the *Treatise on the true devotion to the Blessed Virgin* originates *Revolution and Counter-Revolution*, of which the author himself illustrated the main points of connection with the de Montfort masterpiece.[37]

---

[34] John Paul II, *N'ayez pas peur*, edited by André Frossard, (Paris, Editions Robert Laffont, 1982), p. 184. Father Ernesto Mura, in *Il corpo mistico di Cristo* (Alba, Paoline, 1949), vol. II, pp. 131–3, 167–73, recalls the influence of the *Treatise* on St Pius X and on his Encyclical *Ad diem illum*, of 2 February 1904.

[35] P. Corrêa de Oliveira, "Grignion de Montfort", O Legionário, no. 376, 26 November 1939.

[36] P. Corrêa de Oliveira, "Grignion de Montfort", O Legionário", no. 378, 10 December 1939.

[37] P. Corrêa de Oliveira, "Grignion de Montfort", articles cit.; ID., "Pro Maria fiant maxima", O Legionário, no. 379, 17 December 1939; ID., Prologue to the Argentine edition of *Revolution and Counter-Revolution*.

With the approach of the canonization of de Montfort, while the nuclear flame was consuming Nagasaki and Hiroshima, Plinio Corrêa de Oliveira pointed out the deep connection of this episode with the distribution of the "True Devotion" in the world.

"The atomic bomb of Catholicism has been ready for two centuries. When it finally explodes, one will understand the full meaning of the words of Scripture: *'non est qui se abscondat a calore ejus'* (Ps. 18:7). This bomb has a sweet name, because the bombs of the Church are those of a Mother. It is called *Treatise on the true devotion to the Blessed Virgin*. A book just over one hundred pages long. In it, each word, each letter is a treasure. This is the book of the new times to come. (...) And, we repeat, this 'True devotion', is the atomic bomb, not to kill but to resurrect, that God placed in the hands of the Church forseeing the grief of this century."[38]

The Brazilian thinker always stressed the prophetic nature of St Louis Marie Grignion de Montfort and his relevance for the twentieth century: "If someone asked me to indicate the type of apostle for our times, I would unhesitatingly answer by mentioning the name of a missionary ... who died precisely 239 years ago!"[39]

St Louis de Montfort is still modern, just as the prophet Elias would be very modern today in the sense of being the most adapted and adequate person for our time.

"'Adapted', in the sense of being apt to do good. 'Adequate', also, in the sense of having the adequate means of correcting our time. And for these very reasons most modern. Because to be modern is not necessarily to be like the times. Frequently it could be just the opposite. But, for an apostle, to be modern is to be in condition to do good to the century in which he lives...."[40]

4. Marian devotion and Counter-Revolutionary apostolate

"The struggle between the Revolution and the Counter-Revolution" writes Plinio Corrêa de Oliveira "is a struggle that is religious in its

---

[38] P. Corrêa de Oliveira, "Grignion de Montfort", O Legionário, no. 689, 21 October 1945.
[39] P. Corrêa de Oliveira, "Doutor, Profeta e Apóstolo na crise contemporánea", Catolicismo, no. 53, May 1955, p. 1. Cf. also ID., "O Reino de Maria, Realização do mundo melhor", Catolicismo, no. 55, July 1955; ID., "Exsurge Domine! Quare obdormis?", Catolicismo, no. 56, August 1955, and the article by Cunha Alvarenga (= José de Azeredo Santos), "Servo de Maria, Amigo da Cruz e apóstolo da Contra-Revolução", Catolicismo, no. 64, April 1956.
[40] P. Corrêa de Oliveira, *Doutor, Profeta e Apóstolo na crise contemporánea*.

essence. "[41] Just like every religious problem, it cannot be separated from the role of Grace, on which every moral regeneration depends.

> "Grace depends on God, but undoubtedly God, with a free act of His will, wished for the distribution of graces to depend on Our Lady. Mary is the Universal Mediatrix, she is the channel through which all graces pass. Therefore, her assistance is necessary so that there not be a Revolution or that it be defeated by the Counter-Revolution. (...) Therefore devotion to Our Lady is the *sine qua non* condition for the Revolution to be crushed, so that the Counter-Revolution wins."[42]

The problem of the contribution of Our Lady to the Counter-Revolutionary apostolate is not however limited to that of grace. We should not in fact forget the devil's part in the explosion and progresses of the Revolution. "It is only logical to think that an explosion of the disordered passions, so deep and so general as that which gave rise to the Revolution, could not have occurred without a preternatural action."[43] Therefore, this driving factor of the Revolution also depends on the command and power of Our Lady, to whom God reserved the right to crush the head of the devil.

The ascertainment of this sovereign power of Our Lady introduces the idea of the royalty of Mary in which, according to Plinio Corrêa de Oliveira, we should not see a purely decorative title, but "a personal, absolutely authentic power of government".[44]

"The faith of Catholics in the royalty of Mary" writes a famous Mariologist "can be said to be as old as the Catholic Church is old."[45]

---

[41] P. Corrêa de Oliveira, Prologue to the Argentine edition of *Revolution and Counter-Revolution*, pp. 22-3.

[42] Ibid. The universal mediation of Mary, not yet officially defined as dogma, was confirmed in the encyclicals of Leo XIII *Octobri Mense* (1891), of St Pius X *Ad diem illum* (1904), of Pius XII *Mystici Corporis* (1943). Cf. J. Collantes S.J., *La fede nella Chiesa cattolica*, pp. 327-32.

[43] P. Corrêa de Oliveira, Prologue to the Argentine edition of *Revolution and Counter-Revolution*, pp. 26-7.

[44] Ibid., p. 28.

[45] P. G. M. Roschini O.S.M., *Maria Santissima nella storia della salvezza*, (Isola del Liri, Tipografia Editrice Pisani, 1969), vol. II, p. 486. According to another famous Mariologist "the empire of Mary is extending, even if it is of a subordinated order, as much as the kingdom of Christ himself is extending, of which St Paul says, that before him all things must bend their knee in reverence: in heaven and on earth and under the earth (Phil. 2:10). Thus it is for Mary: because she is queen of the world, she is queen of heaven, of earth, of purgatory, and she also makes her royal power felt by those confined in Avernus", Don Emilio Campana, *Maria nel dogma cattolico*, (Turin, Marietti, 1936), p. 937. On the royalty of Mary cf. Théodore Köhler, *Royauté de Marie*, in DSp, vol. XIII, 1988, coll. 1098-103; G. M. Roschini O.S.M., *Maria Santissima*, vol. II, pp. 345-516; Tommaso M. Bartolomei O.S.M., "Giustificazione dei titoli o fondamenti dommatici della Regalità di Maria", Ephemerides Mariologicae, vol. XV, 1965, pp. 49-82.

This truth of faith was admirably summarized in the Encyclical *Ad Caeli Reginam* of Pius XII,[46] promulgated on the occasion of the institution of the liturgical feast of Mary, the Most Holy Queen, at the conclusion of the Marian Year of 1954.

"Jesus is the King of the eternal centuries by nature and by conquest; for him, with him, subject to him, Mary is Queen by grace, by divine relationship, by conquest, by special election. And her Kingdom is as vast as that of her Divine Son, because nothing has been subtracted from her dominion."[47]

Our Lord – writes Plinio Corrêa de Oliveira – wished to make Our Lady "a royal instrument of his love",[48] establishing her as queen of the universe so that she may govern it, and, above all, govern the poor decayed and sinning human race. "There is therefore, in the government of the universe, an authentically Marian regime."[49]

"Obviously Our Lady is infinitely inferior to God, but he wished to attribute this to her as an act of liberality. And by distributing graces at times with greater or lesser abundance, by blocking the action of the devil sometimes less, sometimes more, Our Lady exercises her royalty during the course of earthly events. In this sense the duration of the Revolution and the victory of the Counter-Revolution depend on her."[50]

5. The Reign of Mary in the de Montfort perspective

"It was through the Most Holy Virgin Mary that Jesus Christ came into the world; again it is through her that he must reign in the world."[51] The opening words of the *Treatise* constitute its wonderful summary. It immediately clears the field of any ambiguity by defining perfectly the distinction of nature and roles between Most Holy Mary and Jesus Christ: Mary is the means, Jesus Christ is the only end. The author furthermore establishes a relationship between two different but closely connected events: the first constituted by the Incarnation of the Word and the Nativity; the second, surrounded by

---

[46] Pius XII, Encyclical *Ad Caeli Reginam* of 11 October 1954, in AAS, vol. 46, 1954, pp. 625–40.
[47] Pius XII, Radiomessage *Bendito seja o Senhor*, pp. 87–8.
[48] P. Corrêa de Oliveira, Prologue to the Argentine edition of *Revolution and Counter-Revolution*, p. 29.
[49] Ibid.
[50] Ibid.
[51] St L. M. Grignion de Montfort, *A treatise on the true devotion*, no. 1.

mystery, because as yet unrealized, is the Kingdom of God in the world. It is a kingdom in history that, as will appear clearly from the development of the *Treatise*, should not be understood as Parousia, but as the triumph of his Mystical Body, the Church. This will be the result of the marvels produced once again, after the Incarnation, by the union between the Holy Spirit and the Virgin Mary.[52] This Reign is defined by the saint as the Reign of Mary.

> "The reign especially attributed to God the Father lasted until the Flood" writes St Louis de Montfort in the *Prayer for Missionaries* "and ended in a deluge of water. The reign of Jesus Christ ended in a deluge of blood, but your reign, Spirit of the Father and the Son, is still unended and will come to a close with a deluge of fire, love and justice."[53]

St Louis de Montfort is a prophet who announces the coming of the Reign of Mary, asking the Lord for a flood of fire of pure love that will purify mankind and that will burn "gently yet so forcefully, that all nations, Moslems, idolaters and even Jews, will be caught up in its flames and be converted".[54]

When will this fortunate time come "when God's Mother is enthroned in men's hearts as Queen, subjecting them to the dominion of her great and princely Son? (...) That day – writes de Montfort – will dawn only when the devotion I teach is understood and put into practice: '*Ut adveniat regnum tuum, adveniat regnum Mariae*': Lord, that your kingdom may come, may the reign of Mary come".[55]

St Louis de Montfort affirms that the Reign of Mary will be a time of flourishing of the Church such as never has been known in history. He even states that, to establish this period, "the Almighty God and His Holy Mother are to raise up great saints who will surpass in holiness most other saints as much as the cedars of Lebanon tower above little shrubs."[56]

The way in which this special union of Mary with the souls of her apostles will be realized will in practice be the "True devotion" of which he, in the *Treatise*, reveals and deepens the secret. The royalty of Our Lady must be achieved in the first place inside souls; from

---

[52] "The union between the Immaculate and the Holy Spirit is so inexpressible and perfect – writes St Maximilian Maria Kolbe – that the Holy Spirit acts solely through the Immaculate, his Spouse. As a result, she is the mediatrix of all the graces of the Holy Spirit" (Letter to Fra Salesio Mikolajczyk of 28 July 1935). The Polish saint goes so far as declaring that the Immaculate "is in a certain way the incarnation of the Holy Spirit". Cf. H. M. Manteau-Bonamy, O.P., *Lo Spirito Santo e l'Immacolata*, (It. tr., Rome, LEMI, 1977), p. 61.
[53] St L. M. Grignion de Montfort, *Prayer for Missionaries*, no. 16.
[54] Ibid, no. 17.
[55] St L. M. Grignion de Montfort, *A treatise on true devotion*, no. 217.

here it will reflect on the religious and civil life of the people as a whole.

"The Reign of Mary" concludes Plinio Corrêa de Oliveira "will therefore be a time when the union of souls with Our Lady will reach an intensity that is unprecedented in history, except – obviously – for individual cases. What form does this, in a certain sense, supreme union have? I do not know a more perfect means of expressing and achieving this union than the holy slavery to Our Lady, as taught by St Louis Marie Grignion de Montfort in the *Treatise on the true devotion to the Blessed Virgin*."[57]

6. Servitudo ex caritate: obey to be free

Consecration to Mary, under various forms, is considered an essential part of the charism, not only of the Montfortans, but also of the Marianists, of the Claretians and of various other religious institutes.[58] It is also used in many associations such as the Legion of Mary, the Militia of the Immaculate, the World Apostolate of Fatima, the Mary Queen of Hearts Association and in the Marian Congregations themselves.

"With the election of John Paul II to the Pontificate and his renewed acts of consecration of individual churches and nations, of the universal Church and of the whole world (1981, 1982, 1984)" observes the Montfortan Father Stefano De Fiores "consecration/entrusting to Mary becomes a theological theme without frontiers."[59]

Although it has always been part of the tradition of the Church, conse-

---

[56] Ibid, no. 47. On the "apostles of the latter days", cf. A. Lhouneau, *La Vierge Marie et les apôtres des derniers temps d'après le B. Louis-Marie de Montfort*, Tours, Mame, 1919; H. Frehen, "Le second avènement de Jésus-Christ et la 'méthode' de saint Louis-Marie de Montfort", Documentation Montfortaine, vol. 7, 1962, no. 3; Stefano De Fiores S.M.M., *La 'missione' nell'itinerario spirituale e apostolico di S. Luigi Maria di Montfort*, in various authors, *La missione monfortana ieri ed oggi*, Acts of the 2nd Intermontfortan Convention (1984), Rome, Centro intermonfortano di Documentazione, 1985.

[57] P. Corrêa de Oliveira, Prologue to the Argentine edition of *Revolution and Counter-Revolution*, p. 33.

[58] On the relationship of the consecration to Mary of St Louis Marie Grignion de Montfort and that of St Maximilian Kolbe, cf. Father Antonio M. Di Monda O.F.M. CONV., *La consacrazione a Maria*, Naples, Milizia dell'Immacolata, 1968.

[59] Stefano De Fiores S.M.M., *Maria nella teologia contemporanea*, (Rome, Centro "Madre della Chiesa", 1987), p. 314–15. Cf. also A. Rivera, "Boletín bibliográfico de la consagración a la Virgen", Ephemerides Mariologicae, vol. 34, 1984, pp. 125–33.

cration to Mary has however suffered misunderstandings of various kinds. Two types of criticism converge in the opposition to this consecration: the first regards its very object, the most Holy Virgin, to whom an improper cult of "latria" would be rendered[60]; the second criticism regards the method of consecration, understood, according to the Montfortan perspective, as "slavery" to Our Lady.

The first point is clearly refuted by St Louis Marie de Montfort himself: all devotions must be directed towards Christ as the end and centre of all things, "otherwise they would be false and misleading".[61] It is obvious, he explains, that consecration to Mary also can have no other end than Christ. "If then" says de Montfort "we are establishing sound devotion to Our Blessed Lady, it is only in order to establish devotion to Our Lord more perfectly."[62] It is not therefore a question of a cult of "latria", but of a legitimate cult of "hyperdulia". "Theology" in fact "tells us that we must have for Mary not only a dulia cult, such as that owed to the saints, but a hyperdulia cult, which comes immediately after the latria cult, reserved for God and the divine Humanity of the Saviour."[63]

It is above all the second point, regarding the idea of "slavery",[64] that does however offend modern sensitivity, because it expresses a relation of dependency and antithetical subjection to that idea of "liberation" and self-determination, the *leitmotiv* of the progressivist mentality.[65] Modern man cannot imagine that there is anyone who wishes to find his freedom in the dependence on another. "Nobody wishes to be a slave anymore, not even a slave of love",[66] objects a famous progressivist theologian.

And yet the saints and the Popes, from the ninth century to present,

---

[60] "A consecration in the real sense of the word – objects for example the progressivist theologian Juan Alfaro – is only made to a divine Person because consecration is an act of latria, whose final end can only be God" (J. Alfaro, *Il cristocentrismo della consacrazione a Maria nella congregazione mariana*, (Rome, Stella Matutina, 1962), p. 21.

[61] St L. M. Grignion de Montfort, *A treatise on true devotion*, no. 61.

[62] Ibid, no. 62.

[63] R. Garrigou-Lagrange O.P., *Vita spirituale*, p. 254.

[64] The doctrine of the Church on slavery is expressed in the phrase of St Paul: "There is neither Jew nor Greek; there is neither bond nor free; there is neither male nor female. For you are all one in Christ Jesus", (Gal. 3:28). "The house of every man is a city – adds St John Chrysostom – and, in it there is a hierarchy: the husband has power over the wife, the wife over the slaves, the slaves over their wives, the men and women over their children" in *Epistula ad Ephesios*, cit. in Paul Allard, *Les esclaves chrétiens depuis les premiers temps de l'Eglise jusqu'à la fin de la domination romaine en Occident*, (Paris, Didier et C., 1876), p. 279.

[65] On slavery and Christian morals: Pietro Palazzini, entry *Schiavitù*, in EC, vol. XI (1953), col. 58; Viktor Cathrein, S.J., *Filosofia morale*, It. tr. (Florence, Libreria Editrice Fiorentina, 1920), vol. II, pp. 475–90.

[66] Edward H. Schillebeeckx, *Maria Madre della Redenzione*, It. tr. (Catania, Edizioni Paoline, 1965), p. 142.

took on the title of *Servus servorum Dei* in official acts,[67] who were honoured to consecrate themselves as slaves to Jesus Christ, to the Most Holy Virgin and to their neighbour.[68] "The Lord has made me a slave of the people of Hippo", wrote St Augustine;[69] while St John Chrysostom affirmed: "If he who was in the image of God, humbled himself, taking the image of a slave to save slaves, what is there to wonder at if I, who am only a slave, make myself a slave of my companions of slavery?"[70]

Plinio Corrêa de Oliveira, in a series of articles that appeared in *Folha de S. Paulo* formulated the problem with the usual clarity, bringing the terms of "slavery" and "freedom" back to their authentic meaning[71]:

"One used to say of a man who fulfilled his duties that he was a 'slave of duty'. Actually he was a man at the climax of his freedom, who understood with a completely personal act the roads that he should follow; decided with manly force to follow them; and conquered the assault of the disordered passions that tried to blind him, to soften his resolve and to block the way he had freely chosen. The man who, having obtained this supreme victory, continued with a strong step in the right way, was free.

"'Slave', on the contrary, was he who allowed himself be drawn along by the disordered passions, towards that which his reason did not approve of, nor his will had chosen. These authentic losers were called 'slaves of vice'. They had, through slavery to vice, 'freed' themselves from the healthy dominion of reason. (...) Today everything has been reversed. As the model of a 'free' man we take the hippie with a flower in his hand, who wanders without a fixed abode and without a goal, or else the hippie who, with a

---

[67] A. Pietro Frutaz, *Servus Servorum Dei*, in EC, vol. XI (1953), coll. 420-2. St Gregory the Great was the first pope to make widespread use of this title. Cf. Paolo Diacono, *Vita S. Gregorii*, in PL, vol. 75, p. 87.

[68] S. L. M. Grignion de Montfort, *A treatise on true devotion*, no. 135, but also *Imitation of Christ*, book III, chap. X.

[69] P. Allard, *Les esclaves chrétiens*, p. 242.

[70] St John Chrysostom, *De mutatione nominum*, Homilia II, 1, 1 cit. in P. Allard, *Les esclaves chrétiens*, pp. 242-3. According to Father Garrigou-Lagrange, "if in the world there are slaves of human respect, of ambition, of money and of other more shameful passions, fortunately there are also slaves of a promise made, of conscience and of duty. Holy slavery belongs to this last class. We have here a living metaphor that is the opposite to the slavery of sin" (R. Garrigou-Lagrange O.P., *La Mère du Sauveur et notre vie intérieure*, (Paris, Editions du Cerf, 1975), appendix IV.

[71] The teaching of Plinio Corrêa de Oliveira here reflects that of Leo XIII, in the encyclical *Libertas* of 20 June 1888 (in IP, vol. VI, *La pace interna delle nazioni*, pp. 143-76) and anticipates that of John Paul II, in his encyclical *Veritatis Splendor* of 6 August 1993.

bomb in hand, sows terror as he pleases. Contrarily, we consider a person to be bound or not free if he obeys the laws of God and of men.

"In the current situation, 'free' is the man whom the law authorizes to buy the drugs he wants, to use them as he pleases, and finally ... to become their slave. And the law that forbids man to become a slave of drugs is tyrannical, enslaving.

"Again in this cross-eyed perspective, made of inversions of values, enslaving is the religious vow, through which, in full consciousness and freedom, the monk devotes himself, renouncing any step back, to the service, full of self-sacrifice, of the highest Christian ideals. To defend this free decision from the tyranny of one's weakness, the monk, in this act, subjects himself to the authority of the watchful superiors. One who thus binds himself, to preserve himself free from evil passions, is today likely to be described as a cowardly slave. It is as if the superior put a yoke on him that would limit his will ... when, on the contrary, the superior serves as a guide for the elevated souls who aspire, freely and courageously – without giving in to the dangerous vertigo of the heights – to climb up to the top of the ladder of supreme ideals.

"So, for some, 'free' is he who, with clouded reason and broken will, driven by the madness of his senses, has the chance to voluptuously slip on the slide of bad habits. And 'slave' is he who bends to his reason, conquers his passions with the strength of his will, obeys divine and human laws, and puts order into practice.

"Above all, 'slave' in this erroneous perspective is he who, to guarantee his freedom more completely, freely chooses to subject himself to authorities who may guide him towards the goal that he wants to reach. It is to this point that today's opinion, filled with Freudism, brings us!"[72]

In what sense can we conjugate the word "love" to that slavery which seems to contradict the former in as much as it is a hateful imposition of one will over another?

"In good philosophy" explains Plinio Corrêa de Oliviera again "'love' is the act with which the will freely wants something. Thus, even in current language, 'will' and 'love' are words that can be used in the same sense. 'Slavery of love' is the noble climax of the act with which someone gives himself freely to an ideal, a cause. Or, sometimes, he binds himself to another.

"Sacred affection and the duties of marriage have something that

---

[72] P. Corrêa de Oliveira, "Obedecer para ser livre", Folha de S. Paulo, 20 September 1980.

binds, that links, that ennobles. In Spanish, handcuffs are called *esposas*, 'spouses'. The metaphor makes us smile, and it may make supporters of divorce shiver. It in fact alludes to the indissolubility. In Portuguese and in Italian, we speak of the marriage 'bond'. More binding than the marriage state is that of the priesthood. And, in a certain sense, the religious state is even more so. The higher the state freely chosen, the stronger the bond and the more authentic the freedom."[73]

Plinio Corrêa de Oliveira recalls how the consecration of St Louis Marie Grignion de Montfort is of a wonderful radicality. It not only sacrifices the material goods of man, but even the merit of his good works and prayers, his life, his body and his soul. It has no limits, because the slave, by definition, has nothing of his own, he belongs wholly to his master. Our Lady obtains in exchange for her "slave of love" special divine graces that enlighten his intelligence and strengthen his will.

"In exchange for this consecration, Our Lady acts in the innermost being of her slave in a marvellous way, establishing an incomparable union with him.

"The fruits of this union will be seen in the Apostles of the Latter Days, whose moral profile is outlined by the saint with lines of fire in his famous *Prayer for Missionaries*. To this end he uses a language of apocalyptic greatness, in which all the fire of a John the Baptist, all the preaching power of a John the Evangelist and all the zeal of a Paul of Tarsus seem to live again.

"The extraordinary men who will fight against the devil, for the Reign of Mary, by gloriously leading until the end of time the struggle against the devil, the world and the flesh, are described by St Louis as magnificent models who invite to the perfect slavery to Our Lady all those who, in the current dark days, fight in the ranks of the Counter-Revolution."[74]

---

[73] P. Corrêa de Oliveira, ibid, "By calling all men to the summits of freedom of the 'slavery of love', St Louis de Montfort does so in such prudent terms as to leave the field free for important nuances. His 'slavery of love', so full of particular significance for the people bound by a vow to the religious state, can be equally practised by secular priests and the laity. In fact, contrary to religious vows that are binding for a certain period or for one's whole life, the 'slave of love' can leave this very elevated position at any time, without *ipso facto* committing a sin. And, whereas the religious who disobeys commits a sin, the lay 'slave of love' commits no sin by the simple fact of contradicting in some way the total generosity of the gift that he has made. Having said this, the lay person maintains this position of slave with a free act, implicitly or explicitly repeated every day, or better at every instant" (ibid).

[74] P. Corrêa de Oliveira, Prologue to the Argentine edition of *Revolution and Counter-Revolution*, pp. 33-4.

7. The fruits of consecration: a new Middle Ages?

In what sense and in what way does consecration to Mary have Christian civilization as its fruit? To consecrate is, by definition, to subordinate man and society to God.[75] The term "Reign of Mary" expresses that ideal of the sacralization of the temporal order through the intercession of Mary, which is none other than the Christian civilization always indicated by the Pontiffs as a goal. Christian civilization, which subjects itself completely to God and recognizes the supreme royalty of Jesus Christ and of Mary, is in this sense "sacral" and hierarchically ordered.

The Reign of Mary will be a sacral civilization because it is fundamentally ordered in God. The law that governs relations with God and among men will be that of dependence, that will find its highest expression in "slavery of love" to the Most Holy Virgin.

The human mediation of Marian slavery shows analogies with the Medieval feudal relationship: this in fact expressed a Christian concept of dependence that did not exclude, but rather enhanced, the freedom and responsibility of the subjects. Feudal society was a society of freemen, founded on a bilateral relation of mutual loyalty.[76] Slavery is certainly immoral if it is considered as total subjection of one man to another, in the sense of denying him his natural inalienable rights. Dependence on another man is not however immoral if these rights are acknowledged, and if it is freely chosen, as happens in the religious orders and as happened in Medieval Christendom.[77]

> "What the Middle Ages felt and expressed was that every man had a superior. This superior was his lord, his king, who, in turn, had a lord, a king. This society offered a view of what Augustin Thierry magnificently defined as 'a great chain of duties'."[78]

In this sense the Reign of Mary will be similar to the Middle Ages, the sacral and Christian age *par excellence*, but it will bear in mind the errors that led to its decadence:

---

[75] St Augustine, *De Civitate Dei*, lib. 10, c. 6; cf. the entry *Consacrare* of S. de Fiores S.M.M., in *Nuovo Dizionario di Mariologia*, edited by S. De Fiores e Salvatore Meo, (Milan, Paoline, 1985), pp. 394–417 and that of J. de Finance, *Consécration*.

[76] Cf. François-Louis Ganshof, *Qu'est-ce que la féodalité*, Paris, Tallandier, 1982; Robert Boutruche, *Seigneurie et féodalité*, Paris, Aubier, 1968 (1959); Joseph Calmette, *La société feudale*, 6th edn., Paris, Colin, 1947; Marc Bloch, *La société féodale*, Paris, Albin Michel, 1989.

[77] Cf. P. Allard, *Les origines du servage en France*, 2nd edn., Paris, J. Gabalda, 1913; Charles Verlinden, *L'esclavage dans l'Europe médiévale*, 2 vols., Brugge, De Tempel, 1955 – Gent 1977; Francesco Michelini, *Schiavitù, religioni antiche e cristianesimo primitivo*, Manduria, Lacaita, 1963.

[78] Bertrand de Jouvenel, *De la souveraineté*, (Paris, Genin, 1955), p. 218.

"The order born of the Counter-Revolution will have to shine even more than that of the Middle Ages in the three principal points in which the latter was wounded by the Revolution:

"1) A profound respect for the rights of the Church and of the Papacy, and a sacralization, to the utmost possible extent, of the values of temporal life, all of this out of opposition to secularism, interconfessionalism, atheism, and pantheism, as well as their respective consequences.

"2) A spirit of hierarchy marking all aspects of society and State, of culture and life, out of opposition to the egalitarian metaphysics of the Revolution.

"3) A diligence in detecting and combating evil in its embryonic or veiled forms, in fulminating it with execration and a note of infamy, and in punishing it with unbreakable firmness in all its manifestations, particularly in those that offend against orthodoxy and purity of customs, in opposition to the liberal metaphysics of the Revolution and its tendency to give free rein and protection to evil."[79]

Will the Reign of Mary be a return to the past, or will it open a new and unforeseeable future?

"To both questions" according to Plinio Corrêa de Oliveira "the answer should be in the affirmative. Human nature has its constants, which are invariable for all times and for all places. The basic principles of Christian civilization are also unchangeable. Therefore, certainly, this new order of things, this new Christian civilization will be profoundly similar, or better identical, to the old one in its essential lines. And it will be, please God, in the twenty-first century the same as that of the thirteenth century. But on the other hand the technical and material conditions of life have undergone profound transformations, and there would be nothing more inorganic than to disregard these modifications. On this specific point it is necessary not to make many plans. The founders of the Christian civilization in the Late Middle Ages did not have in mind the thirteenth century as it was. They simply had the general intention to make a Catholic world. Therefore every generation solved with a depth of views and Catholic sense the problems within its reach. And as regards the others, they did not waste time in conjectures.

"Let us do likewise. Generally speaking, we know all the formulas from history and from the Magisterium of the Church. As for

---

[79] P. Corrêa de Oliveira, *Revolution and Counter-Revolution*, p. 76.

the particulars, we will advance step by step, without purely theoretical plans, elaborated at the table: '*sufficit diei malitia sua*'."[80]

"The admirers of the Middle Ages" he wrote again "express
themselves poorly when they uphold that the world attained its
greatest development at that time. There was still further to go
along the lines medieval civilization was following. The grandiose
and delicate charm of the Middle Ages does not come so much
from what it accomplished, but from the sparkling truth and
profound harmony of the principles upon which it was built. No
other possessed such a profound knowledge of the natural order of
things; no other had the lively sense of the insufficiency of the
natural – even when developed to the plenitude of its own order –
and the necessity of the supernatural; no other shone under the sun
of supernatural influence with such purity and in the candour of an
even greater sincerity."[81]

In the family of souls that acknowledges the spiritual paternity of
Plinio Corrêa de Oliveira, trust in the Reign of Mary is not a
secondary and accessory element.

Scepticism toward this perspective is typical of those who wish to
deny every true progress in the spiritual and civil life of individuals
and of peoples. During the nineteenth century, a suspicion of this kind
grew up around the concept of the Kingship of Christ and the great
devotion that was intimately linked to it, that of the Sacred Heart. A
similarly profound connection today unites the concept of the Reign
of Mary to the devotion to the Immaculate Heart of the Virgin which
was confirmed in the apparitions of 1917 in Fatima.[82] But the concept
of the Royalty of Christ is in its turn bound to that of the Royalty of
Mary, just as the devotions to the Sacred Hearts of Jesus and Mary
are closely linked one to the other. The Kingdom of Christ in souls
and in society is not different from the Reign of Mary, and the devotion to the two Sacred Hearts prepares for the coming of the same
triumph.

"For all the faithful, the 'slavery of love' is therefore the angelic
and supreme freedom with which Our Lady awaits them on the

---

[80] P. Corrêa de Oliveira, "A sociedade cristã e organica e a sociedade mecanica e pagã",
Catolicismo, no. 11, November 1951. On this point cf. also ID., *A réplica da autenticidade*,
pp. 233–7.
[81] P. Corrêa de Oliveira, *A grande experiença de 10 anos de luta*.
[82] Péricles Capanema, "Fátima e Paray-le-Monial: uma visão de conjunto", Catolicismo, no.
522, June 1994. It was St John Eudes, in 1643, who began among his religious the liturgical
feast of the Heart of Mary that Pius XII, in 1944, extended to the whole Church. Pius XII
himself on 31 October 1942, in reply to the entreaties of the Portuguese Episcopate, solemnly
consecrated the Church and all mankind to the Immaculate Heart of Mary.

threshold of the twenty-first century: smiling and attractive, she invites them into her Kingdom, according to her promise in Fatima: '*In the end, my Immaculate Heart will triumph*'."[83]

8. "De Fatima numquam satis"

In 1917, in Fatima, Our Lady entrusted three Portuguese children with a message that opened horizons of tragedy but also of a sweet hope contained in the promise of the triumph of her Immaculate Heart.[84] Plinio Corrêa de Oliveira discovered the message of Fatima only many years later, finding in it the echo of the profound desire that had come to his heart from afar: the aspiration of St Louis Marie Grignion de Montfort and of all the souls who for centuries had desired and prophesied the "Reign of Mary".

In the first days of April 1945, while the Second World War was reaching its tragic epilogue, Dr Plinio, in *Legionário*, raised his eyes to Mary seeing in the apparitions of Fatima the most important and significant event of the century.

"'*De Maria numquam satis*' ('Of Mary, one cannot have enough'). '*De Fatima numquam satis*' one could say. Fatima is not only an event that happened in Portugal, and is not only of interest in our days. Fatima is a new mark in the very History of the Church. Fatima is, whether they like it or not, the real dawn of the new era, whose early lights broke over the battlefields...."[85]

"When the earth was in confusion" he wrote in Catolicismo in 1952 "the heavens opened and the Virgin appeared at Fatima to tell men the truth. An austere truth, one of reprimand and penance, but one rich in promises of salvation. The miracle of Fatima almost repeated itself at the close of this sad and shameful year of confusion, in the eyes of the Vicar of Christ, to bear witness to the fact that the threats of God continue to hover over men, but that the protection of the Virgin will never abandon the Church and her true children."[86]

"The Triumph of the Immaculate Heart of Mary" again he wrote

---

[83] P. Corrêa de Oliveira, *Obedecer para ser livre*, p. 16.

[84] The six apparitions of Our Lady to Lucia dos Santos, a ten-year-old, and her little cousins, Francisco and Jacinta Marto, nine and seven years old respectively, took place between 3 May and 13 October 1917. In 1930, the Bishop of Leiria, José Alves Correia authorized the cult of Our Lady of Fatima. In 1946 Cardinal Aloisi Masella solemnly crowned the statue of Our Lady of Fatima in the presence of 600,000 pilgrims.

[85] P. Corrêa de Oliveira, "Livros versus canhões", O Legionário, no. 661, 8 April 1945. On Fatima cf. also O Legionário no. 597, 16 January 1944, no. 598, 23 January 1944 and no. 614, 14 May 1944.

[86] P. Corrêa de Oliveira, "Nolite timere pusillus grex", Catolicismo, no. 13, January 1952.

in Catolicismo in 1957 "what can it be other than the Reign of the Most Holy Virgin as foreseen by St Louis Marie Grignion de Montfort? And what can this Reign be other than that era of virtue when humanity, reconciled with God, in the bosom of the Church, will live on earth according to the Law, preparing itself for the glories of Heaven?"[87]

The Message of Fatima consists, as Sister Lucia affirms, in a single secret divided into three different parts.[88] Two of the three parts were revealed by Sister Lucia herself in 1941. The first is the terrible vision of the hell into which the souls of sinners fall; this is contrasted to the mercy of the Immaculate Heart of Mary, the supreme remedy offered by God to mankind for the salvation of souls. The second part of the secret regards the dramatic historical alternative of our time: peace, fruit of the conversion of the world and the fulfilment of the requests of Our Lady, or a terrible punishment that would be brought on mankind if it persevered in the ways of sin. Essential conditions requested by Our Lady to avoid the punishment are the consecration of Russia to her Immaculate Heart and the practice of reparatory Communion on the first Saturday of the month. Implicit in this appeal is the necessity of a conversion, understood above all as a re-christianization of society and a re-moralization of its habits.

"If they will listen to my requests, Russia will be converted and there will be peace; otherwise it will spread its errors throughout the world, causing wars and persecutions of the Church; the good will be martyred, the Holy Father will have to suffer, several nations will be destroyed; in the end my Immaculate Heart will triumph. The Holy Father will consecrate Russia to me and the world will be granted a period of peace."[89]

The reference to Fatima characterized almost every public intervention of Plinio Corrêa de Oliveira. In the introduction to the little volume by Dr Antônio Augusto Borelli Machado, he thus presented Fatima in an overall view:

"The Roman Empire of the West closed with a catastrophe illuminated and analysed by the genius of a great doctor, Saint Augustine. The waning of the Middle Ages was foreseen by the great prophet Saint Vincent Ferrer. The French Revolution was foreseen by

---

[87] P. Corrêa de Oliveira, "Hodie in terra canunt angeli, laetantur archangeli, hodie exsultant justi", Catolicismo, no. 84, December 1957.
[88] *Memorias e Cartas da Irmã Lucia*, with Introduction and notes by Father Antonio Maria Martins S.J., (Oporto, Guimarães, 1976), pp. 218–19.
[89] Ibid.

another great prophet and teacher, Saint Louis de Montfort. But our times, which seem about to close with a new catastrophe, have an even greater priviliege: Our Lady herself came to speak to us.

"Saint Augustine could only explain for posterity what caused the tragedy he witnessed. Saint Vincent Ferrer and Saint Louis de Montfort laboured in vain to turn aside the tempests – men would not listen to them. Our Lady explained the reasons for the crisis and pointed out the remedy, predicting catastrophes if she were not heeded.

"From every viewpoint, by the nature of their content as well as the dignity of her who brought them, the revelations of Fatima surpass all other times when Providence has revealed to man the imminence of the great tempests of history.

"Therefore it can be categorically affirmed, without any fear of being contradicted, that the apparitions of Our Lady and of the Angel of Peace in Fatima constitute the most important and exciting event of the twentieth century."[90]

9. The "third secret" of Fatima

The "third part" of the secret of Fatima, according to the indications of Our Lady to Sister Lucia, should have been made known at the latest in 1960.

John XXIII, the first pontiff who read Sister Lucia's text refused to reveal it however. On 8 February 1960, with a terse press release, the Vatican made it known that the secret of Fatima would not be revealed.

Paul VI, elected on 23 June 1963, also read the message, but maintained in its regard the same position as his predecessor.[91]

---

[90] P. Corrêa de Oliveira, Preface to Antônio Augusto Borelli Machado, *As aparições e a mensagem de Fátima conforme os manuscritos da Irmã Lucia*, It. tr. *Le apparizioni e il messaggio di Fatima*, (Piacenza, Cristianità, 1977), p. 6. The first version of this study was published, Catolicismo, no. 197, May 1967, on the occasion of the fiftieth anniversary of the apparitions. The work was completely revised and enlarged on the base of the manuscripts of Sister Lucia, published in 1973, and reprinted, Catolicismo, no. 295, July 1975. The work has since then been widely distributed in hundreds of thousands of copies in the main languages. En. tr. *Our Lady at Fátima: Prophesies of Tragedy or Hope?*, 6th edn., York (PA), The American Society for the Defense of Tradition, Family and Property, 1996.

[91] Not even John Paul II believed it opportune to reveal the last part of the message of Fatima, which thus appears, in the age of the "transparent society", the most jealously guarded secret of our time. "A secret is a secret. And to be logical, no one can draw conclusions from its content, until he knows it. However, it is not out of place at this point to make a conjecture. The part of the secret that has still not been divulged probably contains terrifying particulars on the way in which the punishments announced at Fatima will be carried out. This is in fact the only reason that explains why it may seem hard to make it publicly known. If it contained conciliatory prospects, everything leads to believe that it would have already been made public." P. Corrêa de Oliveira, Preface to A. A. Borelli Machado, *Le apparizioni e il messaggio di Fatima*, p. 16.

On 13 May 1973, the members and volunteers of the TFP welcomed to their headquarters in São Paulo the pilgrim statue of Our Lady of Fatima, which had miraculously wept in New Orleans in 1972, with a vigil of prayers, during which they renewed their consecration to Our Lady according to the de Montfort method. Convinced that the "third secret" must contain decisive words of warning, of guidance and of comfort for mankind at this decisive time, Plinio Corrêa de Oliveira formulated, on that occasion, a message to Sister Lucia, the surviving seer, that she should break her silence and reveal the unknown part of the heavenly message of which she was the trustee, in order to "open the eyes of those who are sleeping as the apostles slept in the Garden of Olives". The message was signed with particular solemnity by 735 members of the TFPs of Brazil and of other nations present that evening in the São Paulo headquarters of the association.[92] That August saw the beginning of the distribution of the updated version of the leaflet of Dr Antônio Augusto Borelli Machado: *As aparições e a Mensagem de Fatima conforme os manuscritos da Irmã Lucia*.[93]

The persistent silence maintained by the ecclesiastical authorities regarding the "third secret" has surrounded it with a halo of mystery of apocalyptic proportions. Public opinion generally believes that the third secret regards a nuclear war, accompanied by natural catastrophes. The majority of scholars of the message of Fatima do not agree with this.

Fatimologists, such as the Spanish Claretian Joaquín María Alonso,[94] the French Michel de la Sainte Trinité[95] and Dr Antônio Augusto Borelli Machado himself[96] believe that the essential part of the third secret regards not so much a material catastrophe, as a spiritual one constituted of the internal crisis of the Church. "Before this crisis became well-known" writes Antônio Borelli "it is clear that a compassionate spirit would have been horrified in face of such an

---

[92] Cf. the text in *Um homem, uma obra, uma gesta*, pp. 201–02.

[93] The work has letters of approval from about forty bishops, among whom The Most Rev Philip M. Hannan, archbishop of New Orleans, Cardinal Bernardino Echeverría Ruiz O.F.M., archbishop of Guayaquil, Cardinal Silvio Oddi, the archbishop of Braga Eurico Dias Nogueira, Primate of Portugal, The Most Rev German Villa Gaviria, archbishop of Barranquilla in Colombia.

[94] Among the various works of Father Alonso, who died in 1981, cf. Joaquín M. Alonso C.M.F., *La verdad sobre el Secreto de Fatima*, Madrid, Centro Mariano, 1976.

[95] Brother Michel de la Sainte Trinité, *Toute la Vérité sur Fatima*, Saint Parres-les-Vaudes, Editions Renaissance Catholique – Contre-Réforme Catholique, 1984-5, 3 vv., summaries by Brother François de Marie des Anges, *Fatima. Joie intime événement mondial*, Saint Parres-les-Vaudes, Editions la Contre-Réforme Catholique, 1991. Cf. especially the III volume, *Le Troisième Secret* (1985).

[96] A. A. Borelli Machado, *Le apparizioni e il messaggio di Fatima*, pp. 71-7.

hypothesis. But, from the time when the crisis became public, there is no reason to draw back from this prediction."[97]

Among those who support this hypothesis is Cardinal Silvio Oddi, former Prefect of the Congregation for the Clergy, who remarked:

"I would not be surprised if the third secret referred to dark times for the Church: serious confusion, disturbing apostasies which would take place within Catholicism. If we look at the serious crisis experienced since the time of the Council, the signs of the realization of this prophecy do not seem to be lacking."[98]

The reason for the decision not to publish the third secret, according to words which Cardinal Oddi attributes to Sister Lucia, is that

"they might be mistakenly interpreted". "I think" the Cardinal added "that the secret of Fatima contains a sad prophecy for the Church, and it is for this reason that Pope John did not divulge it, and Paul VI and John Paul II did likewise. In my opinion, the secret more or less says that in 1960 the Pope would convene a Council which would indirectly bring about, contrary to expectations, many difficulties for the Church."[99] "At this point" comments the cardinal "I dare to advance an hypothesis: that the third secret of Fatima foretold something serious that the Church would have done, of course unintentionally. Because of bad interpretations, acts of disobedience or something of this nature, the Church would go through a rather difficult period. (...) But if this is really the case, the secret is already known because the crisis of the Church is there for all to see. And all the wisest minds have been aware of it for years."[100]

10. Apocalyptics and millenarianism

The prospect of Fatima centred on the idea of a punishment for mankind, and that of de Montfort of the Reign of Mary based on the idea of an age of triumph of the Church, are at times erroneously defined as "apocalyptic" and "millenarianist".

Today with the term "apocalyptic" there is a tendency to define every eschatological prospect that foretells a more or less imminent

---

[97] Ibid, p. 76.
[98] Cardinal Silvio Oddi, Interview to Il Sabato of 17 March 1990, p. 9.
[99] Cardinal S. Oddi, Interview to 30 Giorni, no. 11, November 1990, p. 69.
[100] 30 Giorni, no. 4, April 1991, p. 57; "Fatima, una profezia ancora incompiuta", Lepanto, nos. 108–10, March–April–May 1991.

catastrophe in history; whereas the word "millenarianism" refers, in a generic manner, to the forecast of a "golden period" in the future of mankind. With such a broad meaning, the two terms end up by including every prospect relative to the end of an era of mankind and the establishment of a new *civilization*, to generally indicate a psychological attitude to the radical change and the expectation of a "new age".[101]

These accusations are extended by some people to the theology of history of Plinio Corrêa de Oliveira, which in the school of Fatima and of St Louis de Montfort foresees a great triumph of the Church and of Christian civilization, after a crisis that was metaphorically defined in the daily language of the TFP as a "bagarre" (confusion). The terms of apocalyptics and millenarianism, so inexpertly used, should be therefore clarified in their authentic meaning in the light of Catholic doctrine.

Millenarianism,[102] or chiliasm, is, in fact, the eschatological doctrine according to which Jesus Christ will visibly reign on earth with his chosen people for a period of a thousand years, between a first resurrection of the Saints and the second, universal, resurrection, at the end of the world. This theory, based on the literal interpretation of a passage of the Book of the Apocalypse,[103] was upheld during the early centuries of the Church by such Greek and Latin Fathers as St Ireneus,[104] St Justin,[105] Tertullian,[106] Lactantius.[107]

St Augustine, who confesses to have been fascinated by the attraction of Millenarianism, decidedly rejects its system in *De Civitate Dei*,[108] just as St Thomas does in *Summa Theologica*.[109] "Although chiliasm was not catalogued as a heresy" affirms Father Allo "the

---

[101] Cf. for example Jean Séguy, "Millénarisme", in Catholicisme, vol. IX, 1982, coll. 158–65; ID., "Sur l'apocalyptique catholique", Archives de Sciences Sociales des Religions, no. 41, 1978, pp. 165–72.

[102] On millenarianism: cf. the entries by H. Lesêtre, in DB, vol. IV, 1908, coll. 1090–7; Gustave Bardy, in DTC, vol. X, 1929, coll. 1700–63; Antonio Piolanti, in EC, vol. VIII, 1952, coll. 1008–11; Maurilio Adriani, in ER, vol. IV, 1972, coll. 383–7. Cf. also Ted Daniels, *Millennialism: An International Bibliography*, New-York-London, Garland, 1992; *Il Millenarismo. Testi dei secoli I–II*, edited by Carlo Nardi, Fiesole, Nardini Editore, 1995.

[103] "And I saw an angel coming down from heaven, having the key of the bottomless pit, and a great chain in his hand. And he laid hold on the dragon the old serpent, which is the devil and Satan, and bound him for a thousand years. And he cast him into the bottomless pit, and shut him up, and set a seal upon him, that he should no more seduce the nations, till the thousand years be finished. And after that, he must be loosed a little time (...)" (Apoc. 20:1–4).

[104] St Ireneus *Adversus Haereses*, V, 32–5, in PG, vol. VII, coll. 1210–21.

[105] St Justin, *Dialoghi con Trifone*, 80–1, in PG, vol. VI, coll. 664–9.

[106] Tertullian, *Adversus haereses*, 5, 32, 1.

[107] Lactantius, *De Divinis Institutionibus*, VII, 24, in PL, vol. VI, col. 808.

[108] St Augustine, *De Civitate Dei*, book XX, chap. 7, in PL, vol. XLI, coll. 667–8.

[109] St Thomas Aquinas, *Summa Theologica*, III, q. 77, art. 1, ad. 4.

common feeling of theologians of all schools is to see it as an 'erroneous' doctrine to which some early Fathers had been drawn because of certain conditions of the early ages."[110]

The Holy Office, with the decree of 19–21 July 1944, affirmed that millenarianism, even if moderated, understood as the system according to which "Christ the Lord, before the universal judgement, whether it precedes or not the resurrection of the majority of the just, will come visibly, to reign over this earth, (...) cannot be taught without danger ('tuto doceri non posset')."[111]

Any Catholic who is minimally familiar with the history of the doctrine of the Church can easily understand how millenarianism constitutes an unmistakable and well defined doctrine, very different from the message of Fatima and from the theory of St Louis Marie Grignion de Montfort and of Plinio Corrêa de Oliveira.

We can however legitimately speak of Catholic apocalyptics, if by this term we mean theological speculation on the Book of the Apocalypse which is, for every Christian, the prophetic and inspired book that closes the New Testament.[112] It describes, in connection with the present, the history of the future, embracing the conflict of every age between Jesus Christ and his eternal adversary, until the "last persecution, occurring while the final judgement is imminent, which shall be endured by the Holy Church throughout the world, the whole city of Christ being assailed by the whole city of the devil".[113]

"For there shall be then great tribulation, such as has not been from the beginning of the world until now, neither shall be. And unless those days had been shortened, no flesh should be saved: but for the sake of the elect those days shall be shortened."[114]

The history of mankind will not end with an apotheosis following an irreversible historical ascent, but with a catastrophe, a universal tyranny of evil. "In the tradition of the philosophy of the history of the West" observes a famous contemporary Catholic philosopher "even the end of time itself bears the name: reign of the

---

[110] E. B. Allo O.P., *Saint Jean, L'apocalypse*, 3rd edn., (Paris, J. Gabalda et C., 1933), p. 323.
[111] AAS, vol. 36, 1944, p. 212; Denz-H, no. 3839. "The decree affirms therefore that millenarianism (or chiliasm), even if mitigated or spiritual, according to which Christ would return visibly on earth to reign there, before the final judgement, preceded or not by the resurrection of a certain number of just people, this doctrine cannot be taught without imprudence with regard to the faith." G. Gilleman, S.J., "Condamnation du millénarisme mitigé", Nouvelle Revue Théologique, t. 67, May–June 1945, p. 240.
[112] Mgr A. Romeo, *Apocalisse*, in EC, vol. I, 1948, coll. 1600–14.
[113] St Augustine *De civitate Dei*, book XX, chap. 11.
[114] Mt. 24:21–22.

Antichrist".[115] The Antichrist, comments Mgr Antonino Romeo, "is the capital enemy of Christ" who at the end of time "will seduce many Christians with satanic marvels and cunning" before being destroyed by Christ in his Parousia.[116]

Christian life is, in this dimension, an invocation and "expectation" of the Parousia,[117] described in the Book of the Apocalypse: the second coming "with much power and majesty"[118] of the Lord to fulfil his Messianic Kingdom, with the defeat of the Antichrist and the establishment of the heavenly Jerusalem. The liturgy of Advent, like that of Easter, expresses the pleading expectation of this coming that urges Christians to "be always ready".[119]

> "Actually," comments Cardinal Billot "it is sufficient to barely open the Gospel to acknowledge that the Parousia is truly the alpha and omega, the beginning and the end, the first and last word of the preaching of Jesus, who is its key, its solution, its explanation, its reason for existence, its confirmation: indeed that it is the supreme event to which all the rest refers and without which all the rest collapses and disappears."[120]

This Catholic apocalyptics, always preached by the Church, has nothing in common with ancient millenarianism, neither with the modern version whose origins according to certain scholars may be found in the thinking of Joachim of Fiore, nor in its distortion.

Much has been said about the figure, still surrounded by a veil of mystery, of the abbot from Calabria.[121] He elaborated a theology of history in which, by following the Trinitarian plan, he distinguishes between an age of the Father, begun with Adam, an age of the Son, which has its fulfilment in Christ, and a third age of the Holy Spirit, announced by St Benedict. What is heterodox, in him or in his

---

[115] Josef Pieper, *Über das Ende der Zeit*, München, Hochland-Bücherei, *Sulla fine del tempo*, It. tr. (Brescia, Morcelliana, 1959), p. 113. At the end of history, according to Pieper, looms the image of a "pseudo-order maintaned by the use of force" (ibid, p. 121). The world state of the Antichrist will be a totalitarian state in the extreme sense. Ibid, p. 123.

[116] A. Romeo, *Anticristo*, in EC, vol. I, 1948, col. 1433, coll. 1433–41. Cf. also A. Arrighini, *L'anticristo, la venuta e il regno del vicario di Satana*, Milan, Fratelli Melita, 1988. For a recent meditation on the subject, cf. Cardinal Giacomo Biffi, *Attenti all'Anticristo! L'ammonimento profetico di V. S. Solovèv*, Casale Monferrato, Piemme, 1991.

[117] J. Chaine, *Parousie*, in DTC, vol. XI (1932), coll. 2043–54; A. Romeo, *Parusia*, in EC, vol. IX, 1952, coll. 875–82.

[118] Mt. 24:30.

[119] St Bernard of Clairvaux, *In adventu Domini sermones VII*, in PL, vol. 183, coll. 35–56.

[120] Cardinal Louis Billot S.J., *La Parousie*, (Paris, Beauchesne, 1920), p. 10.

"posterity",[122] was not however the Trinitarian division of history, nor the expectation of a "new age", but the denial, if there was one, of the divine unity of the Persons, of the perennity of the Gospel of Christ and of the saving mission of the Church in the "third age". According to some scholars, Joachim would have given birth to a process of "immanentizing" escathology destined to animate the modern utopia of a self-redemption of man.[123]

What is certain is that the fourteenth century sees the beginning of an apocalyptics that is the antithesis of the theology of Christian history. Modern millenarianism develops with the left wing of the Protestant Revolution, starting from Thomas Müntzer and from the Anabaptists, and proposes an earthly revolution aimed at establishing the Kingdom of God in the purely temporal order. The humanist idea of Rebirth,[124] such as the Protestant one of *Reformatio*,[125] express the eschatological expectation of a new age characterized by the end of the Catholic Church and of the Papacy, often identified with the

---

[121] On Joachim of Fiore (1130–1202) and Gioachimism the bibliography is vast. Cf. the numerous studies dedicated by Mgr Giovanni Di Napoli to the abbot from Calabria: "La teologia trinitaria di Gioacchino da Fiore", Divinitas, no. 3, October 1976; ID., "L'ecclesiologia di Gioacchino da Fiore", Doctor communis, no. 3, September-December 1979; ID., "Teologia e storia in Gioacchino", in *Storia e messaggio in Gioacchino da Fiore*, Acts of the International Congress of Gioachimite Studies (19–23 September 1979), (S. Giovanni in Fiore, Centro di Studi Gioachimiti, 1980), pp. 71–150. Cf. also Marjorie Reeves, Beatrice Hirsch-Reich, *The Figure of Joachim of Fiore*, Oxford, Clarendon Press, 1972; Delno C. West and Sandra Zimdars-Swartz, *Joachim of Fiore: a Study in Perception and History*, Bloomigton, Indiana University Press, 1983; Bernard McGinn, *L'abate calabrese. Gioacchino da Fiore nella storia del pensiero occidentale*, Genoa, It. tr., Marietti, 1990.

[122] It is necessary to distinguish between the abbot from Calabria and his "posterity", whose philosophical and literary itineraries have been traced to our days. Father de Lubac who tried to follow the traces of Gioachimism through the centuries, states that "the story of the spiritual posterity of Joachim is also, and for the greater part, the story of betrayals of his thinking" (Henri de Lubac S.J., *La postérité spirituelle de Joachim de Flore*, (Paris, Dessain et Tobra, 1979), vol. I, p. 67). Cf. also Marjorie Reeves-Warwick Gould, *Joachim of Fiore and the Myth of Eternal Evangel in the Nineteenth Century*, Oxford, Clarendon Press, 1987.

[123] Thus for example Eric Voegelin, *The New Science of Politics. An Introduction*, Chicago, The University of Chicago Press, 1974 (1952); ID., *Il Mito del mondo nuovo. Saggio sui movimenti rivoluzionari del nostro tempo*, Milan, It. tr., Rusconi, 1970.

[124] Cf. Harry Levin, *The Myth of the Golden Age in the Renaissance*, London, Faber & Faber, 1969; Gustavo Costa, *La leggenda dei secoli d'oro nella letteratura italiana*, Bari, Laterza, 1972.

[125] On Protestant apocalyptics, especially among the English sects of the seventeenth century, cf. Bernard S. Capp, *Fifth Monarchy Men: a Study in Seventeenth Century English Millenialism*, Totowa, Bowman and Littlefield, 1972; Eric Russel Chamberlin, *Anti-Christ and the Millennium*, New York, Saturday Review Press, 1975; William B. Ball, *A Great Expectation: Eschatological Thought in English Protestantism*, Leiden, E. J. Brill, 1975; Paul Christianson, *Reformers in Babylon: English Apocalyptic Visions from the Reformation to the Eve of the Civil War*, Toronto, University of Toronto Press, 1978; Catherine Firth, *The Apocalyptic Tradition in Reformation Britain 1530-1645*, New York, Oxford University Press, 1979; Robin Bruce Barnes, *Prophecy and Gnosis: Apocalypticism in the wake of the Lutheran Reformation*, Stanford, Stanford University Press, 1988.

Antichrist. Rather than of millenarianism, it is a question of Messianism that characterizes the sects of the Anglo-Saxon and Germanic environment, permeates the origins of modern philosophy, and results in the French Revolution.[126] The nineteenth-century myth of progress, that of the Marxist society without classes, the National Socialist society of the Third Reich and the ecological society of the Greens,[127] can be traced to this line of lay Messianism: it presupposes the denial of Original Sin and of the mission of the Church and the self-redemption of mankind in history and through history.[128]

The contrast could not be more clear: Christian eschatology wants to sacralize society and history by ordering it for God; lay Messianism wants an implicit deification of man and social structures to achieve the "Kingdom of God" on earth, in its absolute perfection.[129]

The idea of an historical age when Catholicism reaches its fullness, bringing about the motto and hope of St Paul and of the great pontiffs of this century: "*Instaurare omnia in Christo*"[130] has nothing in common with millenarianism.

11. Visions of Popes and of saints of the future

The idea of an historical age of triumph of the Church and of Christian civilization dates, prior to St Louis Marie Grignion de Montfort and to Plinio Corrêa de Oliveira, to saints like St Bonaventure, and in our century it was made his own by another great Marian apostle like St Maximilian Kolbe.

---

[126] Cf. Renzo De Felice, *Note e ricerche sugli "Illuminati" e il misticismo rivoluzionario (1789-1800)*, Rome, Storia e Letteratura, 1960; Clarke Garrett, *Respectable Folly Millenarians and the French Revolution in France and England*, London, John Hopkins University Press, 1975, on which D. Menozzi, "Millenarismo e rivoluzione francese", Critica Storica, vol. 14, 1977, pp. 70–82.

[127] Cf. Romolo Gobbi, *Figli dell'Apocalisse*, (Milan, Rizzoli, 1993), pp. 264–81.

[128] On the modern utopia cf. Walter Nigg, *Das ewige Reich*, Zürich, Artemis, 1954; E. Gilson, *Les métamorphoses de la cité de Dieu*, Paris, Vrin, 1952; T. Molnar, *Utopia. The perennial heresy*; Bronislaw Baczko, *L'utopia*, Turin, It. tr. Einaudi, 1979; Cf. also Alexander Cioranescu, *L'avenir du passé. Utopie et littérature*, Paris, Gallimard, 1972; Massimo Baldini, *La storia delle utopie*, Rome, Armando, 1994.

[129] Cf. Father Reginald Grégoire, *Rapporti tra apocalittica medievale e messianismi laici odierni*, in *Storia e messaggio in Gioacchino da Fiore*, pp. 225–44. Lay Messianism, observes Father Grégoire, "creates a sentiment of satisfaction, of admiration for the man capable of creating his own happiness in the innermost part of that same humanity. Absolute no longer possesses any meaning. It is the apogee of naturalism" (ibid, p. 237). This naturalism is destined to find its expression not only in Marxist and Nazi political atheism, but also in some forms of "liberation theology" which seek the purely historical realization of the Kingdom of God. On postmedieval millenariarism, cf. also the entry, *Chiliasmus IV* of Richard Bauckham in TRE, vol. 7, 1981, pp. 737–45.

[130] Eph. 1:10.

This prospect of triumph of the Church is absolutely foreign to every form of millenarianism condemned by the Church. In fact it is an historical period that precedes not only the Parousia, but the actual dominion of the Antichrist and does not propose any "visible Kingdom" of Jesus Christ on earth. The visible presence of Jesus Christ would render the mission of the Church useless, while the theory of Plinio Corrêa de Oliveira is that the Reign of Mary is an age in which the Church, the Mystical body of Christ, has an influence and plays a role as has never before happened in history. Even if we apply the enigmatic passage of the Book of the Apocalypse to it, the social Reign of Jesus Christ and of Mary hoped for by Plinio Corrêa de Oliveira does not exclude the presence of original sin and the action of the devil.

> "As much as the earthly reality of the Kingdom of Christ is concrete, evident and tangible – as for example in the thirteenth century – it is necessary not to forget" writes Plinio Corrêa de Oliveira "that this kingdom is only a preparation and an introduction. In its fullness the kingdom of God will be realized in heaven: '*My kingdom is not of this world*' (John 18:36)."[131]
>
> "In fact the Church teaches us that this world is a place of exile, a vale of tears, a field of battle, and not a place of delight. (...) Therefore, to imagine a world without struggles and adversity is like imagining a world without Jesus Christ."[132]

While waiting for this blessed age, the Brazilian thinker finds himself in the company of numerous saints and both old and modern theologians. Cardinal Ratzinger made a parallel between the *City of God* of St Augustine, born during the crisis of the Roman Empire and that "moment of climax in the Christian way of thinking history"[133] represented by the *Collationes in Hexaèmeron* by St Bonaventure.[134]

In this work, St Bonaventure tries to do something similar to what

---

[131] P. Corrêa de Oliveira, *A cruzada do século XX*.

[132] P. Corrêa de Oliveira, "A utopia e a mensagem", Folha de S. Paulo, 19 July 1980.

[133] J. Ratzinger, *La théologie de l'histoire de saint Bonaventure*, p. 25.

[134] St Bonaventure, *Collationes in Hexaèmeron, seu Illuminationes Ecclesiae*, in *S. Bonaventurae opera omnia*, (Quaracchi, Collegium S. Bonaventurae, 1883–1902), vol. V, pp. 372–454, Span. tr. *Hexameron*, Madrid, BAC, 1972. These conferences were given in Paris in front of a large audience of Brothers, between Easter and Pentecost of 1273. Alois Dempf saw in it "the greatest and last philosophy of the history of the Middle Ages" (A. Dempf, *Sacrum Imperium*, p. 311). Cardinal Ratzinger sees a strong influence of Joachim of Fiore on St Bonaventure (*La théologie de l'histoire de saint Bonaventure*, pp. 120–1) in which he sees "the precursor of a new concept of history that today appears to us as being so obviously Christian that it is hard for us to believe that at one time it was different". Ibid, p. 122.

St Augustine had done in the *City of God*: "make the present and the future of the Church comprehensible by starting from its past".[135]

The glory of the "seventh age", of which the Seraphic Doctor speaks in the *Hexaèmeron*, refers to a temporal triumph of the Church in the world and in history.[136]

"The theology of history of Bonaventure culminates in the hope of an age, within history, of sabbatical calm donated by God. (...) It is not that peace in the eternity of God that will never end and that will follow the ruin of this world; it is a peace that God will establish on this earth, the witness of so much blood and tears, as if he still wanted to show in the last moment how the reality according to His plan could and should have been."[137]

The affirmations of Cardinal Ratzinger, regarding the theology of history of St Bonaventure, can also be well understood in the light of the thinking of St Thomas. If in fact as the Angelic Doctor teaches, man is by nature a social being,[138] he is obviously called not only to his personal sanctification, but to the sanctification of society, and if human history should not reach this summit of social perfection, that glory of God which is the ultimate goal of creation would be compromised.

This theological and philosophical foundation is implicit in the eschatological perspective of many saints of the twentieth century.

"A great age is approaching!" announces Blessed Luigi Orione: "We will have *novos coelos et novam terram*. Society restored in Christ will reappear younger, more brilliant, it will reappear reanimated, renewed and guided by the Church. Catholicism, full of divine truth, of love, of youth, of supernatural strength, will stand up in the world, and will put itself at the head of the century being born, to lead it to honesty, faith, happiness and salvation."[139]

"We live in an age" writes St Maximilian Kolbe in his turn "that

---

[135] J. Ratzinger, *La théologie de l'histoire de saint Bonaventure*, p. 13.

[136] Ibid, pp. 24–34. Cf. also Miguel Beccar Varela, "São Bonaventura, Doutor para o Reino de Maria", Catolicismo, no. 536, August 1995.

[137] J. Ratzinger, *La théologie de l'histoire de saint Bonaventure*, pp. 63, 182.

[138] St Thomas Aquinas, *De Regimine Principum*, I, 1. The theory of St Thomas is taken up by Leo XIII in the encyclical *Libertas* and by Pius XI in the *Quadragesimo Anno*. Cf. Josephus Goenaga, S.J., *Philosophia socialis*, (Rome, C.I.S.I.C., 1964), pp. 39–40.

[139] Blessed Luigi Orione, Letter of 3 July 1936, in *Lettere*, 3rd edn. enlarged, (Rome, Postulazione, 1969), vol. II, pp. 369–70. On Blessed Luigi Orione (1872–1940), founder of the "Piccola opera" of Divine Providence, cf. Carlo Sterpi, *Lo spirito di don Orione*, Venice, Libreria Emiliana Editrice, 1941; Giorgio Papasogli, *Vita di don Orione*, with a preface by His Eminence Cardinal Giuseppe Siri, Turin, Gribaudi, 1974.

could be called the beginning of the age of the Immaculate."[140] "...Under her standard a great battle will be fought and we will raise her flags on the fortresses of the king of darkness. And the Immaculate will become the Queen of the whole world and of every single soul, as Blessed Catherine Labouré foresaw."[141] "Class struggles will then disappear and mankind will come close, in as much as it is possible on this earth, to happiness, a sort of anticipation of that happiness towards which each one of us already naturally tends, that is to say to the happiness without limits, in God, in paradise."[142] "In fact, when that happens the earth will become a paradise. True peace and happiness will enter the families, the cities, the villages and the nations of all human society, because where she will reign, the graces of conversion and of sanctification and happiness will make their appearance."[143]

Pius XII himself, in establishing the feast of Mary the Queen and in ordering that each year the consecration of mankind to the Immaculate Heart of Mary be renewed on that day, placed in this gesture "the hope that a new era may begin, joyous in Christian peace and in the triumph of religion"[144] and he stated that "the invocation of the reign of Mary is (...) the voice of Christian faith and hope",[145] while confirming in one of his last speeches the "certainty that the restoration of the Kingdom of Christ through Mary cannot fail to be realized."[146]

12. Towards the century of the immense triumph

The theology of history of Plinio Corrêa de Oliveira lies therefore within the realm of the most orthodox doctrine of the Church, with an

---

[140] St Maximilian Kolbe O.F.M. CONV. (1894–1941), "La difesa della Chiesa sotto il vessillo dell'Immacolata: la fondazione della Milizia dell'Immacolata e i suoi primi sviluppi", Miles Immaculatae, July-September 1939, now in *Gli Scritti di Massimiliano Kolbe*, It. tr. (Florence, Edizioni Città di Vita, 1975–78), vol. III, p. 555. On the Polish saint, cf. also Antonio Ricciardi O.F.M. CONV., *Padre Massimiliano Kolbe*, Rome, Postulatione Generale, 1960; Maria Winowska, *Le secret de Maximilien Kolbe*, Paris-Fribourg, Ed. Saint Paul, 1971; *La mariologia di S. Massimiliano Kolbe*, Acts of the International Congress of Rome (8–12 October 1984), edited by F. S. Pancheri, Rome, Miscellanea Francescana, 1985.

[141] St M. Kolbe O.F.M. CONV., Letter to Father Floriano Koziura of 30 May 1931, now in *Gli Scritti*, vol. I, p. 550.

[142] St M. Kolbe O.F.M. CONV., "La Regina della Polonia", Rycerz, May 1925, now in *Gli Scritti*, vol. III, p. 209.

[143] St M. Kolbe O.F.M. CONV., Calendar of "Rycerz" for the year 1925, now in *Gli Scritti*, vol. III, p. 189.

[144] Pius XII, Encyclical *Ad Caeli Reginam*.

[145] Pius XII, Speech of 1 November 1954, in DR, vol. XVI, p. 238.

[146] Pius XII, Radiomessage of 17 September 1958 to the Marian Congress of Lourdes, in DR, vol. XX, p. 365.

eminently Monfortan emphasis. It gushes forth from a deep theological meditation and from an even deeper Marian piety that led him to desire ardently, but also to sense prophetically, the Reign of Mary invoked by de Montfort and foretold by the Most Holy Virgin herself in Fatima. It is understood as "an historical age of faith and virtue, that will be inaugurated by a spectacular victory of Our Lady over the Revolution", an age when "the devil will be driven away and will return to the hellish dens and Our Lady will reign over mankind through the institutions that she will have chosen for this purpose".[147]

Up to the last day of his life Dr Plinio wished to inspire his disciples with ardent love for Our Lady and confidence in her triumph. On the eve of the twenty-first century, the first century of the Third Millennium, the ruins of Christendom to which he had dedicated his life appeared resplendent and transfigured to him.

> "Beyond the highly probable sadness and punishments towards which we advance, we have the sacred lights of the dawn of the Reign of Mary: 'In the end, my Immaculate Heart will triumph'. It is a mighty prospect of universal victory of the royal and maternal Heart of the most holy Virgin. It is a pacifying, attractive and, above all, majestic and exciting promise."[148]

To the Brazilian thinker and man of action we can well apply the words written by a contemporary Mariologist with regard to de Montfort: "If the surest criterion for verifying if he is a prophet is 'the realization of his prophecy', in other words 'the verdict of history' (W. Vogels), we must say that today history advances in the direction foreseen by de Montfort".[149]

As the twentieth century draws to its end, the words with which Plinio Corrêa de Oliveira, in one of his most famous articles, summarized his vision of the future, illuminate the historical turning-point of the Third Millennium with a tragic light, but with one that is dense in supernatural hope:

---

[147] P. Corrêa de Oliveira, Prologue to the Argentine edition of *Revolution and Counter-Revolution*, p. 31.

[148] P. Corrêa de Oliveira, *Fatima in una visione d'insieme*, preface to A. A. Borelli Machado, op. cit., p. 16.

[149] S. de Fiores S.M.M., "Le Saint-Esprit et Marie dans les derniers temps selon Grignion de Montfort", Etudes Mariales, 1986, monographic issue dedicated to "Marie et la fin des temps", vol. III, *Approche historico-théologique*, p. 156 (pp. 133–71). "Montfort appears as a man who is open to the great horizons of the history of Salvation and projected towards the future. On the basis – not all being equally sure – of private revelations, of the Bible and of his personal theological-prophetic charism, he sees the recent times as 'the kingdom of the Father and of the Son' and – the first in Catholic tradition – he places Marian devotion in the perspective of the second coming of Jesus Christ'. Ibid, p. 160.

"War, death and sin are preparing once again to destroy the world, this time in greater proportions than ever. In 1513 the incomparable talent of Dürer represented them in the form of a knight that is leaving for war, fully dressed in his armour, and accompanied by death and sin, this last portrayed by a unicorn. Europe, which was even then immersed in the disturbances that preceded the Pseudo-Reform, was heading for the tragic age of the religious, political and social wars that Protestantism triggered off.

"The next war, without being explicitly and directly a war of religion, will so affect the sacred interests of the Church that a true Catholic cannot fail to see in it mainly the religious aspect. And the devastation that will be unleashed will certainly be incomparably more destructive than those of the past centuries.

"Who will win? The Church?

"The clouds we have before us are not rosy. But they animate us with an unconquerable certainty and that is that not only the Church – which is obvious, given the divine promise – will not disappear, but in our days it will obtain an even greater triumph than that of Lepanto.

"How? When? The future belongs to God. Many reasons for sadness and anxiety appear before us, even when we look at some of our brothers in faith. In the heat of the struggle it is possible and even probable that there are terrible defections. But it is absolutely certain that the Holy Spirit continues to inspire in the Church admirable and indomitable spiritual energies of faith, purity, obedience and dedication, which at the opportune moment will once more cover the Christian name with glory.

"The twentieth century will not only be the century of the great struggle, but above all the century of the immense triumph."[150]

---

[150] P. Corrêa de Oliveira, "O século da guerra, da morte e do peccado", Catolicismo, no. 2, February 1951.

Conclusion

*"I am certain that the principles to which I dedicated my life
are as relevant today as ever and that they indicate
the path the world will follow in the coming centuries.
The sceptics will smile, but the smiles of sceptics were never
able to hinder the victorious march of those who have Faith."*

Plinio Corrêa de Oliveira died aged almost 87 in São Paulo, Brazil, on 3 October 1995, the feast, according to the old calendar, of a saint who was particularly dear to him: St Thérèse of Lisieux.

"The life of the Church and the spiritual life of each faithful Catholic" wrote Plinio Corrêa de Oliveira, referring to St Thérèse "is a ceaseless struggle. Sometimes God gives souls admirable moments of interior or exterior consolation, and sometimes He gives His Church days of splendid, visible and palpable grandeur. However, the true glory of the Church and of the faithful comes from suffering and from fighting. It is an arid fight, with neither palpable beauty nor defined poetry. In this fight, one sometimes advances in the night of anonymity, in the mud of indifference or incomprehension, under the storms and the bombardment unleashed by the conjugated forces of the world, the flesh and the devil. But this fight fills the angels of heaven with admiration and attracts the blessings of God."[1]

This corresponds to what St Louis Marie Grignion de Montfort asks of Our Lady in the page that concludes *The Secret of Mary*:

"As for my portion here on earth, I wish only to have a share in yours, that is, to have simple faith without seeing or tasting, to suffer joyfully without the consolations of men, to die daily to myself without flinching, to work gallantly for you even until death without any self-interest, as the most worthless of your slaves."[2]

---

[1] P. Corrêa de Oliveira, "A verdadeira gloria só nasce da dor", Catolicismo, no. 78 (June 1957).
[2] St Louis Marie Grignion de Montfort, *The Secret of Mary*, no. 69.

The spiritual life of Plinio Corrêa de Oliveira was not the main object of this study, which desired, above all, to bring into focus the public aspect of his thinking and his work. It is however clear that it is only in the depths of his inner life that we can understand the mystery of a limitless love for Christian civilization and an implacable hatred of the Revolution which was attacking it. Of this love and of this hatred he made the axis around which his ideals and activities revolved,[3] in this way offering himself as a paradigm and as a stone of contradiction of his time.

His life, wrote Cardinal Bernardino Echeverría Ruiz, "has moved us to reflect that the more intense the evils of an epoch, the more exceptional are the figures Divine Providence calls to face them. It is a reflection on His design to fight crises, calling souls of fire".[4]

Plinio Corrêa de Oliveira was a crusader of the twentieth century: he squarely faced the destructive march of the anti-Christian Revolution, fighting each time, and often contemporaneously, the National Socialist pseudo-mysticism, the hedonistic American way of life, the Socialist and Communist egalitarian utopia, Catholic progressivism that tried to demolish the Church from within.

> "Christian combativity" he wrote "can only mean legitimate defence. There is no other way for combativity to be legitimate. A Christian is always moved to fight out of love for something that has been offended. The greater the love with which one fights, the more vigorous the fight will be. This is why a Catholic's greatest combativity is in defence of Holy Mother Church when she has been outraged, denied and trodden under foot."[5]

During his struggles and difficulties, next to the virtue of strength, Plinio Corrêa de Oliveira exercised above all that of hope, convinced as he was, as he wrote to his mother in 1930, that: "from him to whom God gives Faith, He demands Hope".[6] The supreme synthesis of these two Christian virtues is confidence, which St Thomas profoundly defines "*spes roborata*", "a hope strengthened by a sound conviction".[7]

The difference between hope and confidence, comments Father Thomas de Saint-Laurent in his turn, is not in the nature, but only in the degree and intensity. "The faint glimmer of the dawn and the

---

[3] Cf. P. Corrêa de Oliveira, *Revolution and Counter-Revolution* p. 81.
[4] Cardinal Bernardino Echeverría Ruiz, O.F.M., "Plinio Corrêa de Oliveira: distinguished apostle, ardent and intrepid polemist", Crusade, January–February 1996.
[5] P. Corrêa de Oliveira, "Passio Christi, conforta me", O Legionário, no. 637, 22 October 1944.
[6] J. S. Clá Dias, *Dona Lucilia*, vol. I, p. 107.
[7] St Thomas Aquinas, *Summa Theologica*, II–IIae, q. 129, art. 6 ad 3

dazzling light of the sun at its zenith form part of the same day. So hope and confidence pertain to the same virtue; one is the complete blossoming of the other".[8]

His confidence in the final victory of the Catholic Counter-Revolution and in the coming of the Reign of the Immaculate Heart of Mary was the virtue that Plinio Corrêa de Oliveira inspired most deeply into his numerous disciples spread throughout the world, even outside the ranks of the TFP. He nourished this confidence, not only at the spring of Fatima, but with a Marian devotion that was especially dear to him: that of Our Lady of Good Counsel of Genazzano, from whom in 1967, on the occasion of a serious illness and of a distressing spiritual trial, he had received a great interior grace: the supernatural certainty that he would not have died before fulfilling the mission entrusted to him by Divine Providence.[9] He fulfilled this mission and fully realized his vocation.

At the end of this study, as an historian and as a Catholic, I feel that I can affirm with tranquil certainty that the words of St Paul so often applied to the great defenders of the faith suit few men in the history of the Church as well as they do Plinio Corrêa de Oliveira: *"Bonum certamen certavi"*, "I have fought the good fight, I have finished the race, I have kept the faith".[10]

The procession that, with the great standards of the TFP raised high, on 5 October 1995 accompanied Plinio Corrêa de Oliveira with purposeful solemnity to his final resting place, wound its way through a São Paulo that was very different from that in which he had been born. Perhaps no city in the world underwent, during this period, the urban and architectural devastation of São Paulo and none, in this radical transformation, better reflects the nihilistic itinerary of the twentieth century, from the Belle Epoque to the turbulent chaos that precedes the turning point of the millennium.

During an age when, like in his native city, everything was dizzily changed, overwhelming values and institutions, Plinio Corrêa de Oliveira remained steadfast in the principles he believed in. He was consistently faithful to that ideal of Christian civilization in which he had seen not only the past, but also the irreversible future of history if men should respond to the divine Grace.

---

[8] Raymond de Thomas de Saint Laurent, *The Book of Confidence*, 3rd edn., (Pleasantville (NY), The American Society for the Defense of Tradition, Family and Property 1989), pp. 19–20. This inspired work was particularly loved and spread by Plinio Corrêa de Oliveira.

[9] Cf. the statement of Plinio Corrêa de Oliveira himself, published in the bulletin *Madre del Buon Consiglio* (July–August 1985) and quoted as a document in J. S. Clá Dias, *The Mother of Good Counsel of Genazzano. With a foreword by Plinio Corrêa de Oliveira*, (Sunbury (PA), Western Hemisphere Cultural Society 1992), pp. 225–6.

[10] 2 Tim. 4:7.

"I am certain" he wrote "that the principles to which I consecrated my life are as relevant today as ever and that they indicate the path the world will follow in the coming centuries. The sceptics will smile, but the smiles of sceptics were never able to hinder the victorious march of those with Faith."[11]

In this simple and absolute consistency lies all the heroism and greatness of Plinio Corrêa de Oliveira. His spiritual testimony which we quote in conclusion of our work explains, better than any other words, the secret of this greatness.

"In the name of the Most Holy and Undivided Trinity, Father, Son, and Holy Spirit, and of the Blessed Virgin Mary, my Mother and Lady, I, Plinio Corrêa de Oliveira, declare: that I have lived and hope to die in the Holy, Roman Catholic and Apostolic Faith, which I hold with all the strength of my soul.

"I cannot find sufficient words to thank Our Lady for the privilege of having lived since my very first days and of dying, as I hope, in the Holy Church. To it I have always devoted, currently devote, and hope to devote until my last breath absolutely all my love. All the persons, institutions, and doctrines I have loved in the course of my life and currently love, I have loved and love solely because they were or are in accord with the Holy Church, and in the measure to which they were or are in accord with the Holy Church. Likewise, I never opposed institutions, persons, or doctrines except insofar as they were opposed to the Holy Catholic Church.

"In the same manner, I thank Our Lady – without being able to find adequate words – for the grace of having read and disseminated the *Treatise on the true devotion to the Blessed Virgin*, by St Louis Marie Grignion de Montfort, and of having consecrated myself to Her as Her perpetual slave. Our Lady was always the Light of my life and from Her clemency I hope she will continue to be my Light and my Help until the last moment of my existence.

"Again I thank Our Lady – and with what emotion – for having granted me to be born of Dona Lucilia. I revered and loved her to the utmost of my capacity and, after her death, not a single day passed without my remembering her with unspeakable longings. Of her soul I also ask that she assist me until my last moment with her ineffable goodness. I hope to meet her in Heaven amidst the luminous cohort of souls who most specially loved Our Lady.

"I am fully conscious of having fulfilled my duty by having

---

[11] P. Corrêa de Oliveira, *Philosophical self-portrait*.

founded and directed my glorious and dear TFP. In spirit, I kiss its standards. The spiritual link that unites me to each member of the Brazilian TFP, as well as to those of the other TFPs, is such that it is impossible to mention any one in particular to express to him my affection.

"After death, I hope to be near Her, praying for all of them, thus helping them more efficaciously than in this earthly life. I forgive with my whole soul those who have given me cause for complaint. I express my wishes that my death may be a reason for great graces for everyone. I have no instructions to give for the eventuality of my death; Our Lady will provide better than I. In any event, from the depth of my soul and on my knees, I beseech each and every one to be completely devoted to Our Lady all the days of their lives."

Index